WRITTEN on OUR HEARTS

Mary Reed Newland committed much of her life to the needy. For this reason, her family wishes to dedicate this, her final project, in her honor to those who suffer for lack of shelter, nourishment, and dignity.

 Genuine recycled paper with 10 percent post-consumer waste. Printed with soy-based ink.

The Ad Hoc Committee to Oversee the Use of the Catechism, United States Conference of Catholic Bishops, has found this catechetical text, copyright 2002, to be in conformity with the *Catechism of the Catholic Church.*

Imprimatur: †Most Rev. Bernard J. Harrington, DD
                      Bishop of Winona
                      7 March 2002

Written on Our Hearts: The Old Testament Story of God's Love is the revised edition of *The Hebrew Scriptures: The Biblical Story of God's Promise to Israel and Us* (1990), by Mary Reed Newland.

The publishing team included John Ferrie and Stephan Nagel, consulting editors; Shirley Kelter, activities writer and consulting editor; Jerry Windley-Daoust, development editor; Mary Duerson and Brooke E. Saron, copy editors; Gary J. Boisvert and Barbara Bartelson, production editors and typesetters; Gary J. Boisvert, page designer; Andy Palmer, cover designer; Alan S. Hanson, pre-press specialist; Maurine R. Twait, art director; Penny Koehler and Genevieve Nagel, photo researchers; Deborah Huelsbergen, artist of paper artworks; Evy Abrahamson, illustrator; Patricia Deminna, indexer.

The acknowledgments continue on page 302.

Printed in the United States of America

Printing: 9 8 7 6 5 4

Year: 2010 09 08 07 06 05

ISBN 0-88489-776-1

Library of Congress Cataloging-in-Publication Data

Newland, Mary Reed.
      Written on our hearts : the Old Testament story of God's love / Mary Reed Newland ; revised by Barbara Allaire.—[Rev. ed.].
      p. cm.
Includes index.
ISBN 0-88489-776-1 (pbk.)
      1. Bible. O.T.—Textbooks. I. Allaire, Barbara. II. Title.
BS1194 .N49 2002
221.6'1—dc21

2002003425

Saint Mary's Press™

Written on Our Hearts

The Old Testament Story of God's Love

Mary Reed Newland

Second Edition
Revised by Barbara Allaire

Contents

Objects First with Java

A Companion Website accompanies *Objects First with Java,*
second edition by David Barnes and Michael Kölling

Visit the *Objects First with Java* Companion Website at
www.booksites.net/barnes to find valuable learning materials including:

For students:
- Program style guide for all examples in the book
- Links to further material of interest

PEARSON
Education

We work with leading authors to develop the
strongest educational materials in computing,
bringing cutting-edge thinking and best
learning practice to a global market.

Under a range of well-known imprints, including
Prentice Hall, we craft high quality print and
electronic publications which help readers to understand
and apply their content, whether studying or at work.

To find out more about the complete range of our
publishing, please visit us on the World Wide Web at:
www.pearsoned.co.uk

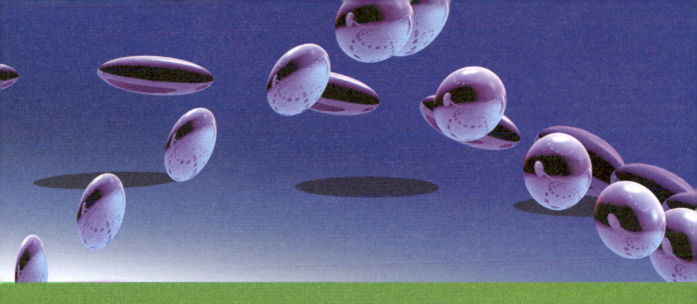

Objects First with Java

A Practical Introduction using BlueJ

David J. Barnes and Michael Kölling

Second edition

PEARSON
Prentice
Hall

Harlow, England • London • New York • Boston • San Francisco • Toronto
Sydney • Tokyo • Singapore • Hong Kong • Seoul • Taipei • New Delhi
Cape Town • Madrid • Mexico City • Amsterdam • Munich • Paris • Milan

Pearson Education Limited
Edinburgh Gate
Harlow
Essex CM20 2JE
England

and Associated Companies throughout the world

Visit us on the World Wide Web at:
www.pearsoned.co.uk

First published 2003
Second edition published 2005

ISBN 0131 24933 9

British Library Cataloguing-in-Publication Data
A catalogue record for this book is available from the British Library

Library of Congress Cataloging-in-Publication Data
Barnes, David J. (David John), 1959 June 7th-
    Objects first with Java : a practical introduction using Blue J / David J. Barnes and Michael Kölling.-- 2nd ed.
        p. cm.
    ISBN 0-13-124933-9
    1. Object-oriented programming (Computer science) 2. Java (Computer program language) 3. Computer science--Study and teaching. I. Kölling, Michael, II. Title.

    QA76.64.B385 2005
    005.1'17--dc22

                                                    2004040129

10 9 8 7 6 5 4 3 2
08 07 06 05 04

Typeset in 10/12pt TimesNewRomanPS by 30
Printed by Ashford Colour Press Ltd, Gosport

The publisher's policy is to use paper manufactured from sustainable forests.

Contents

Appendices

Index

Website resources

For Students:
- Program style guide for all examples in the book
- Links to further material of interest

For Lecturers:
- Powerpoint slides that can be downloaded and used as OHTs
- Solutions to exercises
- Additional activities, exercises and projects for use in teaching

Foreword
by James Gosling, Sun Microsystems

Watching my daughter Kate, and her middle school classmates, struggle through a Java course using a commercial IDE was a painful experience. The sophistication of the tool added significant complexity to the task of learning. I wish that I had understood earlier what was happening. As it was, I wasn't able to talk to the instructor about the problem until it was too late. This is exactly the sort of situation for which BlueJ is a perfect fit.

BlueJ is an interactive development environment with a mission: it is designed to be used by students who are learning how to program. It was designed by instructors who have been in the classroom facing this problem every day. It's been refreshing to talk to the folks who developed BlueJ: they have a very clear idea of what their target is. Discussions tended to focus more on what to leave out, than what to throw in. BlueJ is very clean and very targeting.

None the less, this book isn't about BlueJ. It is about programming.

In Java.

Over the past several years Java has become widely used in the teaching of programming. This is for a number of reasons. One is that Java has many characteristics that make it easy to teach: it has a relatively clean definition; extensive static analysis by the compiler informs students of problems early on; and it has a very robust memory model that eliminates most 'mysterious' errors that arise when object boundaries or the type system are compromised. Another is that Java has become commercially very important.

This book confronts head-on the hardest concept to teach: objects. It takes students from their very first steps all the way through to some very sophisticated concepts.

It manages to solve one of the stickiest questions in writing a book about programming: how to deal with the mechanics of actually typing in and running a progam. Most books silently skip over the issue, or touch it lightly, leaving it up to the instructor to figure out how to solve the problem. And leaving the instructor with the burden of relating the material being taught to the steps that students have to go through to work on the exercises. Instead, it assumes the use of BlueJ and is able to integrate the tasks of understanding the concepts with the mechanics of how students can explore them.

I wish it had been around for my daughter last year. Maybe next year . . .

Preface to the instructor

This book is an introduction to object-oriented programming for beginners. The main focus of the book is general object-oriented and programming concepts from a software engineering perspective.

While the first chapters are written for students with no programming experience, later chapters are suitable for more advanced or professional programmers as well. In particular, programmers with experience in a non-object-oriented language who wish to migrate their skills into object orientation should also be able to benefit from the book.

We use two tools throughout the book to enable the concepts introduced to be put into practice: the Java programming language and the Java development environment BlueJ.

Java

Java was chosen because of a combination of two aspects: the language design and its popularity. The Java programming language itself provides a very clean implementation of most of the important object-oriented concepts, and serves well as an introductory teaching language. Its popularity ensures an immense pool of support resources.

In any subject area, having a variety of sources of information available is very helpful, for teachers and students alike. For Java in particular, countless books, tutorials, exercises, compilers, environments, and quizzes already exist, in many different kinds and styles. Many of them are online and many are available free of charge. The large amount and good quality of support material makes Java an excellent choice as an introduction to object-oriented programming.

With so much Java material already available, is there still room for more to be said about it? We think there is, and the second tool we use is one of the reasons . . .

BlueJ

The second tool, BlueJ, deserves more comment. This book is unique in its completely integrated use of the BlueJ environment.

BlueJ is a Java development environment that is being developed and maintained at the University of Southern Denmark, Deakin University, Australia, and the University of Kent in Canterbury, UK, explicitly as an environment for teaching introductory object-oriented programming. It is better suited to introductory teaching than other environments for a variety of reasons:

- The user interface is much simpler. Beginning students can typically use the BlueJ environment in a competent manner after 20 minutes of introduction. From then on, instruction can concentrate on the important concepts at hand – object orientation and Java – and no time needs to be wasted talking about environments, file systems, class paths, DOS commands, or DLL conflicts.

- The environment supports important teaching tools not available in other environments. One of them is visualization of class structure. BlueJ automatically displays a UML-like diagram representing the classes and relationships in a project. Visualizing these important concepts is a great help to both teachers and students. It is hard to grasp the concept of an object when all you ever see on the screen is lines of code! The diagram notation is a simple subset of UML, again tailored to the needs of beginning students. This makes it easy to understand, but also allows migration to full UML in later courses.

- One of the most important strengths of the BlueJ environment is the user's ability to directly create objects of any class, and then to interact with their methods. This creates the opportunity for direct experimentation with objects, for little overhead in the environment. Students can almost 'feel' what it means to create an object, call a method, pass a parameter, or receive a return value. They can try out a method immediately after it has been written, without the need to write test drivers. This facility is an invaluable aid in understanding the underlying concepts and language details.

BlueJ is a full Java environment. It is not a cut-down, simplified version of Java for teaching. It runs on top of Sun Microsystems' Java Development Kit, and makes use of the standard compiler and virtual machine. This ensures that it always conforms to the official and most up-to-date Java specification.

The authors of this book have several years of teaching experience with the BlueJ environment (and many more years without it before that). We both have experienced how the use of BlueJ has increased the involvement, understanding, and activity of students in our courses. One of the authors is also a developer of the BlueJ system.

Real objects first

One of the reasons for choosing BlueJ was that it allows an approach where teachers truly deal with the important concepts first. 'Objects first' has been a battle cry for many textbook authors and teachers for some time. Unfortunately, the Java language does not make this noble goal very easy. Numerous hurdles of syntax and detail have to be overcome before the first experience with a living object arises. The minimal Java program to create and call an object typically includes:

- writing a class;
- writing a main method, including concepts such as static methods, parameters, and arrays in the signature;
- a statement to create the object ('new');
- an assignment to a variable;
- the variable declaration, including variable type;
- a method call, using dot notation;

- possibly a parameter list.

As a result, textbooks typically either

- have to work their way through this forbidding list, and only reach objects somewhere around Chapter 4; or

- use a 'Hello, world'-style program with a single static main method as the first example, thus not creating any objects at all.

With BlueJ, this is not a problem. A student can create an object and call its methods as the very first activity! Because users can create and interact with objects directly, concepts such as classes, objects, methods, and parameters can easily be discussed in a concrete manner before looking at the first line of Java syntax. Instead of explaining more about this here, we suggest that the curious reader dip into Chapter 1 – things will quickly become clear then.

An iterative approach

Another important aspect of this book is that it follows an iterative style. In the computing education community, a well-known educational design pattern exists that states that important concepts should be taught early and often.[1] It is very tempting for textbook authors to try and say everything about a topic at the point where it is introduced. For example, it is common, when introducing types, to give a full list of built-in data types, or to discuss all available kinds of loop when introducing the concept of a loop.

These two approaches conflict: we cannot concentrate on discussing important concepts first, and at the same time provide complete coverage of all topics encountered. Our experience with textbooks is that much of the detail is initially distracting, and has the effect of drowning the important points, thus making them harder to grasp.

In this book we touch on all of the important topics several times, both within the same chapter and across different chapters. Concepts are usually introduced at a level of detail necessary for understanding and applying the task at hand. They are revisited later in a different context, and understanding deepens as the reader continues through the chapters. This approach also helps to deal with the frequent occurrence of mutual dependences between concepts.

Some teachers may not be familiar with an iterative approach. Looking at the first few chapters, teachers used to a more sequential introduction will be surprised about the number of concepts touched on this early. It may seem like a steep learning curve.

It is important to understand that this is not the end of the story. Students are not expected to understand everything about these concepts immediately. Instead, these fundamental concepts will be revisited again and again throughout the book, allowing students to get a deeper and deeper understanding over time. Since their knowledge level changes as they work their way forward, revisiting important topics later allows them to gain a deeper understanding overall.

---

[1] The 'Early Bird' pattern, in J. Bergin: 'Fourteen pedagogical patterns for teaching computer science', *Proceedings of the Fifth European Conference on Pattern Languages of Programs* (EuroPLop 2000), Irsee, Germany, July 2000.

We have tried this approach with students many times. It seems that students have fewer problems dealing with it than some long-time teachers. And remember: a steep learning curve is not a problem as long as you ensure that your students can climb it!

No complete language coverage

Related to our iterative approach is the decision not to try to provide complete coverage of the Java language within the book.

The main focus of this book is to convey object-oriented programming principles in general, not Java language details in particular. Students studying with this book may be working as software professionals for the next 30 or 40 years of their life – it is a fairly safe bet that the majority of their work will not be in Java. Every serious textbook must of course attempt to prepare them for something more fundamental than the language flavor of the day.

On the other hand, many Java details are important for actually doing the practical work. In this book we cover Java constructs in as much detail as is necessary to illustrate the concepts at hand and implement the practical work. Some constructs specific to Java have been deliberately left out of the discussion.

We are aware that some instructors will choose to cover some topics that we do not discuss in detail. That is expected and necessary. However, instead of trying to cover every possible topic ourselves (and thus blowing the size of this book out to 1500 pages), we deal with it using *hooks*. Hooks are pointers, often in the form of questions that raise the topic and give references to an appendix or outside material. These hooks ensure that a relevant topic is brought up at an appropriate time, and leave it up to the reader or the teacher to decide to what level of detail that topic should be covered. Thus hooks serve as a reminder of the existence of the topic, and as a placeholder indicating a point in the sequence where discussion can be inserted.

Individual teachers can decide to use the book as it is, following our suggested sequence, or to branch out into sidetracks suggested by the hooks in the text.

Chapters also often include several questions suggesting discussion material related to the topic, but not discussed in this book. We fully expect teachers to discuss some of these questions in class, or students to research the answers as homework exercises.

Project-driven approach

The introduction of material in the book is project driven. The book discusses numerous programming projects and provides many exercises. Instead of introducing a new construct and then providing an exercise to apply this construct to solve a task, we first provide a goal and a problem. Analyzing the problem at hand determines what kinds of solutions we need. As a consequence, language constructs are introduced as they are needed to solve the problems before us.

Early chapters provide at least two discussion examples. These are projects that are discussed in detail to illustrate the important concepts of each chapter. Using two very different examples supports the iterative approach: each concept is revisited in a different context after it is introduced.

In designing this book we have tried to use a large number and wide variety of different example projects. This will hopefully serve to capture the reader's interest, but it also helps to illustrate the variety of different contexts in which the concepts can be applied. Finding good example projects is hard. We hope that our projects serve to give teachers good starting points and many ideas for a wide variety of interesting assignments.

The implementation for all our projects is written very carefully, so that many peripheral issues may be studied by reading the projects' source code. We are strong believers in the benefit of learning by reading and imitating good examples. For this to work, however, one must make sure that the examples students read are well written and worth imitating. We have tried to do this.

All projects are designed as open-ended problems. While one or more versions of each problem are discussed in detail in the book, the projects are designed so that further extensions and improvements can be done as student projects. Complete source code for all projects is included. A list of projects discussed in this book is provided on page xxvi.

Concept sequence rather than language constructs

One other aspect that distinguishes this book from many others is that it is structured along fundamental software development tasks and not necessarily according to the particular Java language constructs. One indicator of this is the chapter headings. In this book you will not find many of the traditional chapter titles, such as 'Primitive data types' or 'Control structures'. Structuring by fundamental development tasks allows us to give a much more general introduction that is not driven by intricacies of the particular programming language utilized. We also believe that it is easier for students to follow the motivation of the introduction, and that it makes much more interesting reading.

As a result of this approach, it is less straightforward to use the book as a reference book. Introductory textbooks and reference books have different, partly competing, goals. To a certain extent a book can try to be both, but compromises have to be made at certain points. Our book is clearly designed as a textbook, and wherever a conflict occurred, the textbook style took precedence over its use as a reference book.

We have, however, provided support for use as a reference book by listing the Java constructs introduced in each chapter in the chapter introduction.

Chapter sequence

Chapter 1 deals with the most fundamental concepts of object orientation: objects, classes, and methods. It gives a solid, hands-on introduction to these concepts without going into the details of Java syntax. It also gives a first look at some source code. We do this by using an example of graphical shapes that can be interactively drawn, and a second example of a simple laboratory class enrollment system.

Chapter 2 opens up class definitions and investigates how Java source code is written to create behavior of objects. We discuss how to define fields and implement methods. Here, we also introduce the first types of statement. The main example is an implementation of a ticket machine. We also look back to the laboratory class example from Chapter 1 to investigate that a bit further.

Chapter 3 then enlarges the picture to discuss interaction of multiple objects. We see how objects can collaborate by invoking each other's methods to perform a common task. We also discuss how one object can create other objects. A digital alarm clock display is discussed that uses two number display objects to show hours and minutes. As a second major example, we examine a simulation of an email system in which messages can be sent between mail clients.

In Chapter 4 we continue by building more extensive structures of objects. Most importantly, we start using collections of objects. We implement an electronic notebook and an auction system to introduce collections. At the same time, we discuss iteration over collections, and have a first look at loops. The first collection being used is an `ArrayList`. In the second half of the chapter we introduce arrays as a special form of a collection, and the for loop as another form of a loop. We discuss an implementation of a web-log analyzer as an example for array use.

Chapter 5 deals with libraries and interfaces. We introduce the Java standard library and discuss some important library classes. More importantly, we explain how to read and understand the library documentation. The importance of writing documentation in software development projects is discussed, and we end by practicing how to write suitable documentation for our own classes. `Random`, `Set`, and `Map` are examples of classes that we encounter in this chapter. We implement an *Eliza*-like dialog system and a graphical simulation of a bouncing ball to apply these classes.

Chapter 6, titled *Well-behaved objects*, deals with a whole group of issues connected to producing correct, understandable, and maintainable classes. It covers issues ranging from writing clear, understandable code – including style and commenting – to testing and debugging. Test strategies are introduced, and a number of debugging methods are discussed in detail. We use an example of a diary for appointment scheduling and an implementation of an electronic calculator to discuss these topics.

In Chapter 7 we discuss more formally the issues of dividing a problem domain into classes for implementation. We introduce issues of designing classes well, including concepts such as responsibility-driven design, coupling, cohesion, and refactoring. An interactive, text-based adventure game (*World of Zuul*) is used for this discussion. We go through several iterations of improving the internal class structure of the game and extending its functionality, and end with a long list of proposals for extensions that may be done as student projects.

Chapters 8 and 9 introduce inheritance and polymorphism with many of the related detailed issues. We discuss a simple database of CDs and videos to illustrate the concepts. Issues of code inheritance, subtyping, polymorphic method calls, and overriding are discussed in detail.

In Chapter 10 we implement a predator/prey simulation. This serves to discuss additional abstraction mechanisms based on inheritance, namely interfaces and abstract classes.

Chapter 11 introduces two new examples: an image viewer and a sound player. Both examples serve to discuss how to build graphical user interfaces (GUIs).

Chapter 12 then picks up the difficult issue of how to deal with errors. Several possible problems and solutions are discussed, and Java's exception-handling mechanism is discussed in detail. We extend and improve an address book application to illustrate the concepts. Input/output is used as an error-prone case study.

Chapter 13 steps back to discuss in more detail the next level of abstraction: How to structure a vaguely described problem into classes and methods. In previous chapters we have assumed that large parts of the application structure already exist, and we have made improvements. Now it is time to discuss how we can get started from a clean slate. This involves detailed discussion of what the classes should be that implement our application, how they interact, and how responsibilities should be distributed. We use class–responsibilities–collaborators (CRC) cards to approach this problem, while designing a cinema booking system.

In Chapter 14 we try to bring everything together and integrate many topics from the previous chapters of the book. It is a complete case study, starting with the application design, through design of the class interfaces, down to discussing many important functional and non-functional characteristics and implementation details. Topics discussed in earlier chapters (such as reliability, data structures, class design, testing, and extendibility) are applied again in a new context.

Second edition

This is the second edition of this book. Several things have been changed since the first edition: most important are the addition of a new chapter (Chapter 11: Building graphical user interfaces), the use of JUnit in Chapter 6, and the addition of more exercises. Overall, however, the concept and style of this book remain unchanged.

Feedback we received from readers of the first edition was overwhelmingly positive, and many people have helped in making this book better by sending in comments and suggestions, finding errors and telling us about them, contributing material to the book's web site, contributing to the discussions on the mailing list, or translating the book into foreign languages.

Overall, however, the book seems to be 'working.' So this second edition is an attempt at improvements in the same style, rather than a radical change.

Additional material

This book includes all projects used as discussion examples and exercises on a CD. The CD also includes the Java development environment (JDK) and BlueJ for various operating systems.

There is a support web site for this book at

    http://www.bluej.org/objects-first

On this web site, updates to the examples can be found, and additional material is provided. For instance, the style guide used for all examples in this book is available on the web site in electronic form, so that instructors can modify it to meet their own requirements.

The web site also includes a password-protected, teacher-only section that provides additional material.

A set of slides to teach a course with this book is also provided.

Discussion groups

The authors maintain two email discussion groups for the purpose of facilitating exchange of ideas and mutual support for and by readers of this book and other BlueJ users.

The first list, **bluej-discuss**, is public (anyone can subscribe) and has a public archive. To join, or to read the archives, go to

```
http://lists.bluej.org/mailman/listinfo/bluej-discuss
```

The second list, **objects-first**, is a closed list for teachers only. It can be used to discuss solutions, teaching tips, exams, and other teaching-related issues. For instructions to join, please look at the book web site (see above).

Guided Tour

Exercises
With hundreds of these provided throughout the text, at the end of every section, students are able to practice with the concepts until they understand them.

Concept reviews
These boxes summarize along the way, the concepts students have just read about – an ideal revision tool!

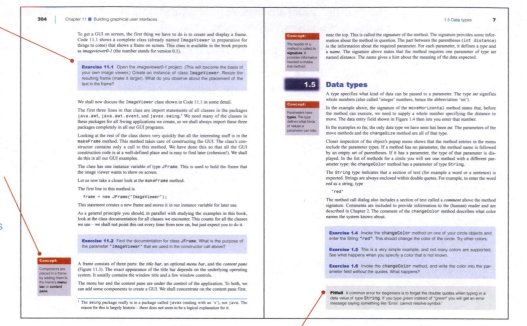

Pitfalls
Highlight common errors made by programmers when writing programs.

Integration of BlueJ throughout
Exercises and activities throughout the text make students use the BlueJ software to practice and visualize the concepts being learnt.

Code examples
Example code from carefully constructed projects is included and discussed in the text, with full versions of all projects on the accompanying CD.

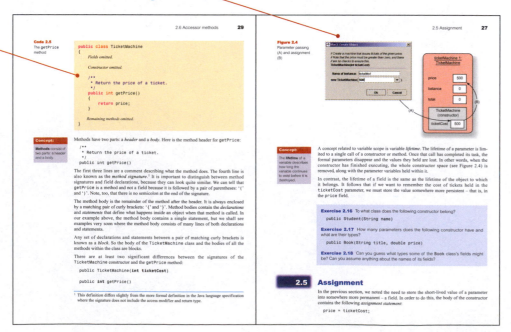

Objects First Approach

BlueJ supports teaching tools that are not available in other environments, including the visualization of class structure. This means that the student can interact with objects even before looking at the first line of Java syntax!

End of chapter summaries and concept summaries

These succinct summaries have a descriptive element and a list element. The lists of concept summaries tie in with the concept summaries at the start of the chapter and act as a great checklist and revision tool.

Project driven approach to problem solving

Each chapter contains problems which are analysed before the language constructs are introduced to solve them. What is more, the book is structured along the lines of fundamental development tasks, giving clear coverage of the principles of object-oriented programming. The preface lists the projects discussed in the book.

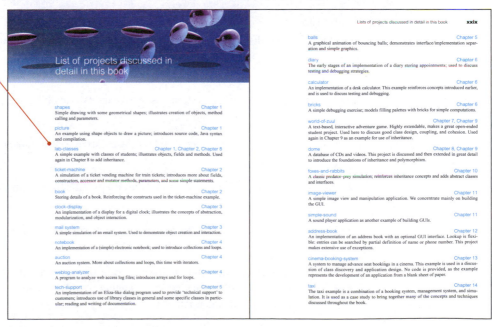

List of projects discussed in detail in this book

balls   Chapter 5

A graphical animation of bouncing balls; demonstrates interface/implementation separation and simple graphics.

diary   Chapter 6

The early stages of an implementation of a diary storing appointments; used to discuss testing and debugging strategies.

calculator   Chapter 6

An implementation of a desk calculator. This example reinforces concepts introduced earlier, and is used to discuss testing and debugging.

bricks   Chapter 6

A simple debugging exercise; models filling palettes with bricks for simple computations.

world-of-zuul   Chapter 7, Chapter 9

A text-based, interactive adventure game. Highly extendable, makes a great open-ended student project. Used here to discuss good class design, coupling, and cohesion. Used again in Chapter 9 as an example for use of inheritance.

dome   Chapter 8, Chapter 9

A database of CDs and videos. This project is discussed and then extended in great detail to introduce the foundations of inheritance and polymorphism.

foxes-and-rabbits   Chapter 10

A classic predator–prey simulation; reinforces inheritance concepts and adds abstract classes and interfaces.

image-viewer   Chapter 11

A simple image view and manipulation application. We concentrate mainly on building the GUI.

simple-sound   Chapter 11

A sound player application as another example of building GUIs.

address-book   Chapter 12

An implementation of an address book with an optional GUI interface. Lookup is flexible: entries can be searched by partial definition of name or phone number. This project makes extensive use of exceptions.

cinema-booking-system   Chapter 13

A system to manage advance seat bookings in a cinema. This example is used in a discussion of class discovery and application design. No code is provided, as the example represents the development of an application from a blank sheet of paper.

taxi   Chapter 14

The taxi example is a combination of a booking system, management system, and simulation. It is used as a case study to bring together many of the concepts and techniques discussed throughout the book.

Acknowledgements

Many people have contributed in many different ways to this book and made its creation possible.

First, and most importantly, John Rosenberg must be mentioned. John is now a Deputy Vice-Chancellor at Deakin University, Australia. It is by mere coincidence of circumstance that John is not one of the authors of this book. He was one of the driving forces in the development of BlueJ and the ideas and pedagogy behind it from the very beginning, and we talked about the writing of this book for several years. Much of the material in this book was developed in discussions with John. Simply the fact that there are only twenty-four hours in a day, too many of which were already taken up with too much other work, prevented him from actually writing this book. John has contributed to this text continuously while it was being written and helped improve it in many ways. We have appreciated his friendship and collaboration immensely.

Two other people who helped make BlueJ what it is are Bruce Quig and Andrew Patterson. Both have worked on BlueJ for many years, improving and extending the design and implementation while trying to write their PhDs at the same time. Without their work, BlueJ would never have reached the quality and popularity it has today, and this book might never have been written.

On the other side of the globe, two more people work on maintaining and improving BlueJ: Ian Utting and Damiano Bolla, who have contributed a great deal to the system.

Another important contribution that made the creation of BlueJ and this book possible was very generous support from Sun Microsystems. Emil Sarpa, working for Sun in Palo Alto, CA, has believed in the BlueJ project from the very beginning. His support and amazingly unbureaucratic way of cooperation has helped us immensely along the way.

Everyone at Pearson Education worked really hard to fit the production of this book into a very tight schedule, and accommodated many of our idiosyncratic ways. Thanks to Kate Brewin for her determined support for this project, and to the rest of the team, including Bridget Allen, Kevin Ancient, Tina Cadle-Bowman, Tim Parker, Veronique Seguin, Fiona Sharples, and Owen Knight.

The Pearson sales team also have done a terrific job in making the first edition of this book visible, managing to avert every author's worst fear – that his book might go unnoticed. Special mention here must go to Sami Taalas, who drives faster than anyone.

Our reviewers also worked very hard on the manuscript, often at busy times of the year for them, and we would like to express our appreciation to Michael Caspersen, Devdatt Dubhashi, Khalid Mughal, and Richard Snow for their encouragement and constructive input.

Axel Schmolitzky, who produced the excellent German translation of this book, must have been our most careful and scrupulous reader; he suggested a good number of possible improvements on sometimes very subtle points.

David would like to add his personal thanks to both staff and students of the Computer Science Department at the University of Kent. The students who have taken the introductory OO course have always been a privilege to teach. They also provide the essential stimulus and motivation that makes teaching so much fun. Without the valuable assistance of colleagues and postgraduate supervisors, running classes would be impossible, and Simon Thompson provides outstanding support in his role as Head of Department. Outside University life, various people have supplied a wonderful recreational and social outlet to prevent writing from taking over completely: thanks to my climbing friends, Chris Phillips and Martin Stevens, who help keep me up in the air, Joe Rotchell, who helps keep my feet on the ground, and Dave and Stella Byrne, who help in many other ways.

Finally, I would like to thank my wife Helen, whose love is so special; and my children, whose lives are so precious.

Michael would like to thank Andrew and Bruce for many hours of intense discussion. Apart from the technical work that got done as a result of these, I enjoyed them immensely. I like a good argument. John Rosenberg has been a mentor to me for many years since the start of my academic career. Without his hospitality and support I would have never made it to Australia, and without him as a PhD supervisor and colleague I would never have achieved as much as I did in my work. It is a pleasure working with him, and I owe him a lot. Thanks to Michael Caspersen, who is not only a good friend, but has influenced my way of thinking about teaching during various workshops we have given together. My colleagues in the software engineering group at the Mærsk Institute in Denmark – Bent Bruun Kristensen, Palle Nowack, Bo Nørregaard Jørgensen, Kasper Hallenborg Pedersen, and Daniel May – have patiently put up with my missing every deadline for every delivery possible while I was writing this book, and introduced me to life in Denmark at the same time.

Finally, I would like to thank my wife Leah and my two little girls, Sophie and Feena. Many times they had to put up with my long working hours at all times of day while I was writing for this book. Their love gives me the strength to continue, and makes it all worthwhile.

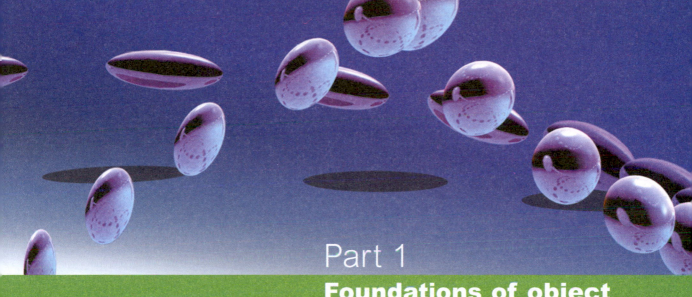

Part 1

Foundations of object orientation

Main concepts discussed in this chapter:

- objects
- classes
- methods
- parameters

This chapter is the start of our journey into the world of object-oriented programming. Here we introduce the most important concepts you will learn about: *objects* and *classes*. By the end of the chapter you should have an understanding of what objects and classes are, what they are used for, and how to interact with them. This chapter forms the basis of all other explorations in the book.

1.1 Objects and classes

Concept:

Java **objects** model objects from a problem domain.

If you write a computer program in an object-oriented language, you are creating, in your computer, a model of some part of the world. The parts that the model is built up from are the objects that appear in the problem domain. These objects must be represented in the computer model being created.

Objects may be categorized, and a class describes – in an abstract way – all objects of a particular kind.

We can make these abstract notions clearer by looking at an example. Assume you want to model a traffic simulation. One kind of entity you then have to deal with is cars. What is a car in our context: is it a class or an object? A few questions may help us to make a decision.

What color is a car? How fast can it go? Where is it right now?

You will notice that we cannot answer these questions until we talk about one specific car. The reason is that the word 'car' in this context refers to the *class* car – we are talking about cars in general, not about one particular car.

Concept:

Objects are created from **classes**. The class describes the kind of object; the objects represent individual instantiations of the class.

If I say, 'My old car that is parked at home in my garage,' we can answer the questions above. That car is red, it doesn't go very fast, and it is in my garage. Now I am talking about an object – about one particular example of a car.

We usually refer to a particular object as an *instance*. We shall use the term 'instance' quite regularly from now on. Instance is roughly synonymous with object – we refer to objects as instances when we want to emphasize that they are of a particular class (such as, 'this object is an instance of class car').

Before we continue this rather theoretical discussion, let us look at an example.

1.2 Creating objects

Start BlueJ and open the example named *shapes*.[1] You should see a window similar to that shown in Figure 1.1.

Figure 1.1

The *shapes* project in BlueJ

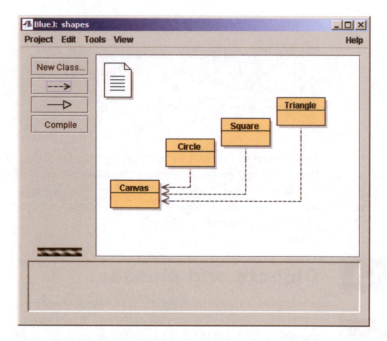

In this window, a diagram should become visible. Every one of the colored rectangles in the diagram represents a class in our project. In this project we have classes named `Circle`, `Square`, `Triangle`, and `Canvas`.

Right-click on the `Circle` class and choose

```
new Circle()
```

from the popup menu. The system asks you for a 'name of the instance' – click Ok, the default name supplied is good enough for now. You will see a red rectangle towards the bottom of the screen labeled 'circle1' (Figure 1.2).

You have just created your first object! 'Circle,' the rectangular icon in Figure 1.1, represents the class `Circle`; `circle1` is an object created from this class. The area at the bottom of the screen where the object is shown is called the *object bench*.

---

[1] We regularly expect you to undertake some activities and exercises while reading this book. At this point we assume that you already know how to start BlueJ and open the example projects. If not, read Appendix A first.

Figure 1.2
An object on the
object bench

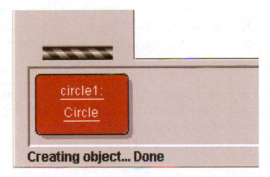

Convention We start names of classes with capital letters (such as `Circle`) and names of objects with lowercase letters (such as `circle1`). This helps to distinguish what we are talking about.

Exercise 1.1 Create another circle. Then create a square.

1.3 Calling methods

Right-click on one of the circle objects (not the class!) and you will see a popup menu with several operations. Choose `makeVisible` from the menu – this will draw a representation of this circle in a separate window (Figure 1.3).

You will notice several other operations in the circle's menu. Try invoking `moveRight` and `moveDown` a few times to move the circle closer to the center of the screen. You may also like to try `makeInvisible` and `makeVisible` to hide and show the circle.

Figure 1.3
A drawing of a circle

Concept:

We can communicate with objects by invoking **methods** on them. Objects usually do something if we invoke a method.

Exercise 1.2 What happens if you call `moveDown` twice? Or three times? What happens if you call `makeInvisible` twice?

The entries in the circle's menu represent operations that you can use to manipulate the circle. These are called *methods* in Java. Using common terminology, we say that these methods are *called* or *invoked*. We shall use this proper terminology from now on. We might ask you to 'invoke the `moveRight` method of `circle1`.'

1.4 Parameters

Concept:

Methods can have **parameters** to provide additional information for a task.

Now invoke the `moveHorizontal` method. You will see a dialog appear that prompts you for some input (Figure 1.4). Type in 50 and click Ok. You will see the circle move 50 pixels to the right.[2]

The `moveHorizontal` method that was just called is written in such a way that it requires some more information to execute. In this case, the information required is the distance – how far the circle should be moved. Thus the `moveHorizontal` method is more flexible than the `moveRight` or `moveLeft` methods. The latter always move the circle a fixed distance, whereas `moveHorizontal` lets you specify how far you want to move the circle.

Figure 1.4

A method call dialog

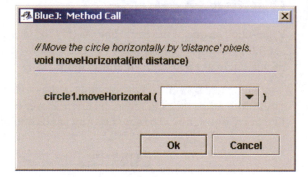

Exercise 1.3 Try invoking the `moveVertical`, `slowMoveVertical`, and `changeSize` methods before you read on. Find out how you can use `moveHorizontal` to move the circle 70 pixels to the left.

The additional values that some methods require are called *parameters*. A method indicates what kinds of parameters it requires. When calling, for example, the `moveHorizontal` method as shown in Figure 1.4, the dialog displays the line

```
void moveHorizontal(int distance)
```

---

[2] A pixel is a single dot on your screen. Your whole screen is made up of a grid of single pixels.

near the top. This is called the *signature* of the method. The signature provides some information about the method in question. The part between the parentheses (`int distance`) is the information about the required parameter. For each parameter, it defines a *type* and a *name*. The signature above states that the method requires one parameter of type *int* named *distance*. The name gives a hint about the meaning of the data expected.

1.5 Data types

A type specifies what kind of data can be passed to a parameter. The type *int* signifies whole numbers (also called 'integer' numbers, hence the abbreviation 'int').

In the example above, the signature of the `moveHorizontal` method states that, before the method can execute, we need to supply a whole number specifying the distance to move. The data entry field shown in Figure 1.4 then lets you enter that number.

In the examples so far, the only data type we have seen has been *int*. The parameters of the move methods and the `changeSize` method are all of that type.

Closer inspection of the object's popup menu shows that the method entries in the menu include the parameter types. If a method has no parameter, the method name is followed by an empty set of parentheses. If it has a parameter, the type of that parameter is displayed. In the list of methods for a circle you will see one method with a different parameter type: the `changeColor` method has a parameter of type `String`.

The `String` type indicates that a section of text (for example a word or a sentence) is expected. Strings are always enclosed within double quotes. For example, to enter the word *red* as a string, type

```
"red"
```

The method call dialog also includes a section of text called a *comment* above the method signature. Comments are included to provide information to the (human) reader and are described in Chapter 2. The comment of the `changeColor` method describes what color names the system knows about.

Exercise 1.4 Invoke the `changeColor` method on one of your circle objects and enter the String **"red"**. This should change the color of the circle. Try other colors.

Exercise 1.5 This is a very simple example, and not many colors are supported. See what happens when you specify a color that is not known.

Exercise 1.6 Invoke the `changeColor` method, and write the color into the parameter field *without* the quotes. What happens?

Pitfall A common error for beginners is to forget the double quotes when typing in a data value of type `String`. If you type *green* instead of *"green"* you will get an error message saying something like 'Error: cannot resolve symbol.'

Java supports several other data types including, for example, decimal numbers and characters. We shall not discuss all of them right now, but rather come back to this issue later. If you want to find out about them now, look at Appendix B.

1.6 Multiple instances

> **Exercise 1.7** Create several circle objects on the object bench. You can do so by selecting `new Circle()` from the popup menu of the Circle class. Make them visible, then move them around on the screen using the 'move' methods. Make one big and yellow, make another one small and green. Try the other shapes too: create a few triangles and squares. Change their positions, sizes, and colors.

Concept:

Multiple instances. Many similar objects can be created from a single class.

Once you have a class, you can create as many objects (or instances) of that class as you like. From the class `Circle`, you can create many circles. From `Square`, you can create many squares.

Every one of those objects has its own position, color, and size. You change an attribute of an object (such as its size) by calling a method on that object. This will affect this particular object, but not others.

You may also notice an additional detail about parameters. Have a look at the `changeSize` method of the triangle. Its signature is

```
void changeSize(int newHeight, int newWidth)
```

Here is an example of a method with more than one parameter. This method has two, and a comma separates them in the signature. Methods can, in fact, have any number of parameters.

1.7 State

The set of values of all attributes defining an object (such as *x*-position, *y*-position, color, diameter, and visibility status for a circle) is also referred to as the object's *state*. This is another example of common terminology that we shall use from now on.

Concept:

Objects have **state**. The state is represented by storing values in fields.

In BlueJ, the state of an object can be inspected by selecting the *Inspect* function from the object's popup menu. When an object is inspected, a window similar to that shown in Figure 1.5 is displayed. This window is called the *object inspector*.

> **Exercise 1.8** Make sure you have several objects on the object bench and then inspect each of them in turn. Try changing the state of an object (for example by calling the `moveLeft` method) while the object inspector is open. You should see the values in the object inspector change.

Figure 1.5
An object inspection
dialog

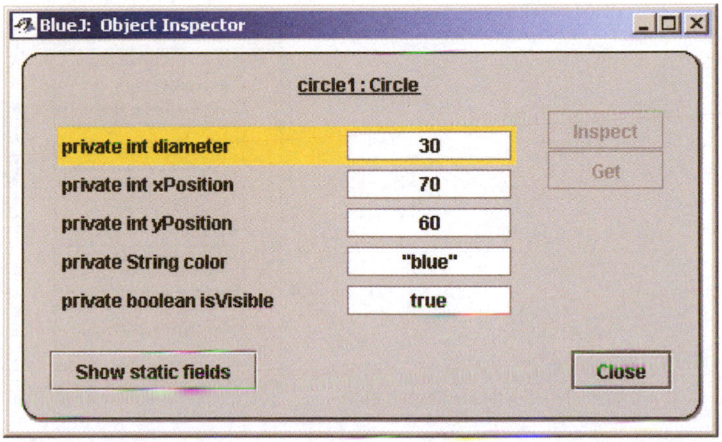

Some methods, when called, change the state of an object. For example, `moveLeft`
changes the `xPosition` attribute. Java refers to these object attributes as *fields*.

1.8 What is in an object?

On inspecting different objects you will notice that objects of the *same* class all have the
same fields. That is, the number, type, and names of the fields are the same, while the actual value of a particular field in each object may be different. In contrast, objects of a *different* class may have different fields. A circle, for example, has a field 'diameter,' while a
triangle has fields for 'width' and 'height.'

The reason is that the number, types, and names of fields are defined in a class, not in an
object. So the class `Circle` defines that each circle object will have five fields, named
`diameter`, `xPosition`, `yPosition`, `color`, and `isVisible`. It also defines the types
for these fields. That is, it specifies that the first three are of type `int`, while the color is
of type `String` and the `isVisible` flag is of type `boolean`. (Boolean is a type that can
represent two values: `true` and `false`. We shall discuss it in more detail later.)

When an object of class `Circle` is created, the object will automatically have these fields.
The values of these fields are stored in the object. That ensures that each circle has a color,
for instance, and each can have a different color (Figure 1.6).

The story is similar for methods. Methods are defined in the class of the object. As a result,
all objects of a given class have the same methods. However, the methods are invoked on
objects. This makes it clear which object to change when, for example, a `moveRight`
method is invoked.

Exercise 1.9 Use the shapes from the *shapes* project to create an image of a
house and a sun, similar to that shown in Figure 1.7. While you are doing this, write
down what you have to do to achieve this. Could it be done in different ways?

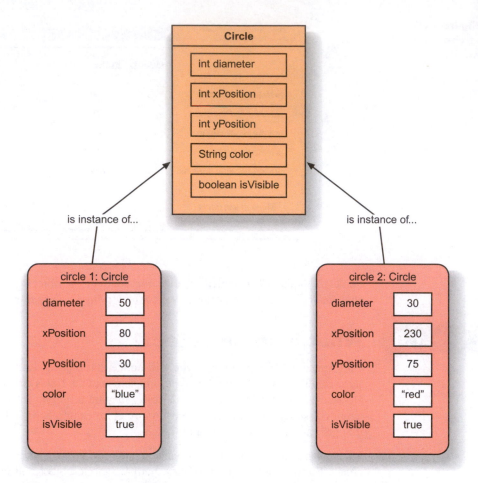

1.9 Object interaction

For the next section we shall work with a different example project. Close the *shapes* project if you still have it open, and open the project called *picture*.

> **Exercise 1.10** Open the *picture* project. Create an instance of class `Picture` and invoke its `draw` method. Also, try out the `setBlackAndWhite` and `setColor` methods.
>
> **Exercise 1.11** How do you think the `Picture` class draws the picture?

Four of the classes in the project are identical to the classes in the *shapes* project. But we now have an additional class: `Picture`. This class is programmed to do exactly what we have done by hand in Exercise 1.9.

In reality, if we want a sequence of tasks done in Java, we would not normally do it by hand as in Exercise 1.9. Instead, we create a class that does it for us. This is the `Picture` class.

The `Picture` class is written so that, when you create an instance, that instance creates two square objects (one for the wall, one for the window), a triangle and a circle, moves them around, and changes their color and size, until it looks like the picture we see in Figure 1.7.

Figure 1.7
An image created from a set of shape objects

Concept:

Method-calling. Objects can communicate by **calling** each other's **methods**.

The important point here is: objects can create other objects and they can call each other's methods. In a normal Java program you may well have hundreds or thousands of objects. The user of a program just starts the program (which typically creates a first object), and all other objects are created – directly or indirectly – by that object.

The big question now is: How do we write the class for such an object?

1.10 Source code

Concept:

The **source code** of a class determines the structure and the behavior (the fields and methods) of each of the objects in that class.

Each class has some *source code* associated with it. The source code is text that defines the details of the class. In BlueJ, the source code of a class can be viewed by selecting the *Open Editor* function from the class's popup menu, or by double-clicking the class icon.

> **Exercise 1.12** Look at the popup menu of class `Picture` again. You will see an option labeled *Open Editor*. Select it. This will open a text editor displaying the source code of the class.

The source code is text written in the Java programming language. It defines what fields and methods a class has, and precisely what happens when a method is invoked. In the next chapter we shall discuss exactly what the source code of a class contains and how it is structured.

A large part of learning the art of programming is learning how to write these class definitions. To do this, we shall learn to use the Java language (although there are many other programming languages that could be used to write code).

When you make a change to the source code and close the editor,[3] the icon for that class appears striped in the diagram. The stripes indicate that the source has been changed. The

---

[3] In BlueJ, there is no need to save the text in the editor explicitly before closing. If you close the editor, the source code will automatically be saved.

class now needs to be compiled by clicking the *Compile* button. (You may like to read the 'About compilation' note for more information about what is happening when you compile a class.) Once a class has been compiled, objects can be created again and you can try out your change.

About compilation

When people write computer programs, they typically use a 'higher level' programming language, such as Java. A problem with that is that a computer cannot execute Java source code directly. Java was designed to be reasonably easy to read for humans, not for computers. Computers, internally, work with a binary representation of a machine code, which looks quite different from Java. The problem for us is: it looks so complex that we do not want to write it directly. We prefer to write Java. What can we do about this?

The solution is a program called the *compiler*. The compiler translates the Java code into machine code. We can write Java, run the compiler – which generates the machine code – and the computer can then read the machine code. As a result, every time we change the source code we must first run the compiler before we can use the class again to create an object. Otherwise the machine code version that the computer needs does not exist.

Exercise 1.13 In the source code of class `Picture`, find the part that actually draws the picture. Change it so that the sun will be blue rather than yellow.

Exercise 1.14 Add a second sun to the picture. To do this, pay attention to the field definitions close to the top of the class. You will find this code:

```
private Square wall;
private Square window;
private Triangle roof;
private Circle sun;
```

You need to add a line here for the second sun. For example:

```
private Circle sun2;
```

Then write the appropriate code for creating the second sun.

Exercise 1.15 *Challenge exercise* (This means that this exercise might not be solved quickly. We do not expect everyone to be able to solve this at the moment. If you do – great. If you don't, then don't worry. Things will become clearer as you read on. Come back to this exercise later.) Add a sunset to the single-sun version of `Picture`. That is: make the sun go down slowly. Remember: The circle has a method `slowMoveVertical` that you can use to do this.

Exercise 1.16 *Challenge exercise* If you added your sunset to the end of the `draw` method (so that the sun goes down automatically when the picture is drawn), change this now. We now want the sunset in a separate method, so that we can call `draw` and see the picture with the sun up, and then call `sunset` (a separate method!) to make the sun go down.

1.11 Another example

In this chapter, we have already discussed a large number of new concepts. To help in understanding these concepts, we shall now revisit them in a different context. For this, we use a different example. Close the *picture* project if you still have it open, and open the *lab-classes* project.

This project is a simplified part of a student database designed to keep track of students in laboratory classes and to print class lists.

Exercise 1.17 Create an object of class `Student`. You will notice that this time you are prompted not only for a name of the instance, but also for some other parameters. Fill them in before clicking Ok. (Remember that parameters of type `String` must be written in double quotes.)

1.12 Return values

As before, you can create multiple objects. And again, as before, the objects have methods that you can call from their popup menu.

Concept:

Results. Methods may return information about an object via a **return value**.

Exercise 1.18 Create some student objects. Call the `getName` method on each object. Explain what is happening.

When calling the `getName` method of the `Student` class, we notice something new: methods may return a result value. In fact, the signature of each method tells us whether or not it returns a result, and what the type of the result is. The signature of `getName` (as shown in the object's popup menu) is defined as

```
String getName()
```

The word `String` before the method name specifies the return type. In this case it states that calling this method will return a result of type `String`. The signature of `changeName` states:

```
void changeName(String)
```

The word `void` indicates that this method does not return any result.

Methods with return values enable us to get information from an object via a method call. This means that we can use methods either to change an object's state or to find out about its state.

1.13 Objects as parameters

Exercise 1.19 Create an object of class `LabClass`. As the signature indicates, you need to specify the maximum number of students in that class (an integer).

Exercise 1.20 Call the `numberOfStudents` method of that class. What does it do?

Exercise 1.21 Look at the signature of the `enrollStudent` method. You will notice that the type of the expected parameter is `Student`. Make sure you have two or three students and a `LabClass` object on the object bench, then call the `enrollStudent` method of the `LabClass` object. With the input cursor in the dialog entry field, click on one of the student objects – this enters the name of the student object into the parameter field of the `enrollStudent` method (Figure 1.8). Click Ok, and you have added the student to the `LabClass`. Add one or more other students as well.

Exercise 1.22 Call the `printList` method of the `LabClass` object. You will see a list of all the students in that class printed to the BlueJ terminal window (Figure 1.9).

Figure 1.8
Adding a student to
a `LabClass`

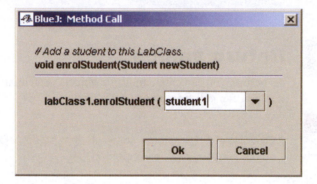

Figure 1.9
Output of the
`LabClass` class
listing

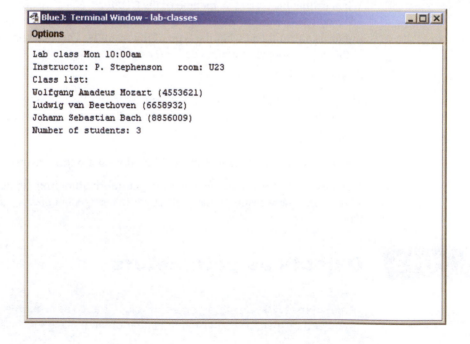

As the exercises show, objects can be passed as parameters to methods of other objects. In the case where a method expects an object as a parameter, the expected object's class name is specified as the parameter type in the method signature.

Explore this project a bit more. Try to identify the concepts discussed in the *shapes* example in this context.

> **Exercise 1.23** Create three students with the following details:
>
> *Snow White*, student ID: *100234*, credits: *24*
> *Lisa Simpson*, student ID: *122044*, credits: *56*
> *Charlie Brown*, student ID: *12003P*, credits: *6*
>
> Then enter all three into a lab and print a list to the screen.
>
> **Exercise 1.24** Use the inspector on a `LabClass` object to discover what fields it has.
>
> **Exercise 1.25** Set the instructor, room, and time for a lab, and print the list to the terminal window to check that these new details appear.

1.14 Summary

In this chapter we have explored the basics of classes and objects. We have discussed the fact that objects are specified by classes. Classes represent the general concept of a thing, while objects represent concrete instances of a class. We can have many objects of any class.

Objects have methods that we use to communicate with them. We can use a method to make a change to the object or to get information from the object. Methods can have parameters, and parameters have types. Methods have return types, which specify what type of data they return. If the return type is void, they do not return anything.

Objects store data in fields (which also have types). All the data values of an object together are referred to as the object's state.

Objects are created from class definitions that have been written in a particular programming language. Much of programming in Java is about learning to write class definitions. A large Java program will have many classes, each with many methods that call each other in many different ways.

To learn to develop Java programs, we need to learn how to write class definitions, including fields and methods, and how to put these classes together well. The rest of this book deals with these issues.

Terms introduced in this chapter

object, class, instance, method, signature, parameter, type, state, source code, return value, compiler.

Concept summary

- **object** Java objects model objects from a problem domain.

- **class** Objects are created from classes. The class describes the kind of object; the objects represent individual instantiations of the class.

- **method** We can communicate with objects by invoking methods on them. Objects usually do something if we invoke a method.

- **parameter** Methods can have parameters to provide additional information for a task.

- **signature** The header of a method is called its signature. It provides information needed to invoke that method.

- **type** Parameters have types. The type defines what kinds of values a parameter can take.

- **multiple instances** Many similar objects can be created from a single class.

- **state** Objects have state. The state is represented by storing values in fields.

- **method-calling** Objects can communicate by calling each other's methods.

- **source code** The source code of a class determines the structure and the behavior (the fields and methods) of each of the objects in that class.

- **result** Methods may return information about an object via a return value.

Exercise 1.26 In this chapter we have mentioned the data types `int` and `String`. Java has more predefined data types. Find out what they are and what they are used for. To do this, you can check Appendix B, or look it up in another Java book or in an online Java language manual. One such manual is at

```
http://java.sun.com/docs/books/tutorial/java/nutsandbolts/
datatypes.html
```

Exercise 1.27 What are the types of the following values?

```
0
"hello"
101
−1
true
"33"
3.1415
```

Exercise 1.28 What would you have to do to add a new field, for example one called `name`, to a circle object?

Exercise 1.29 Write the signature for a method named **send** that has one parameter of type `String`, and does not return a value.

Exercise 1.30 Write the signature for a method named **average** that has two parameters, both of type `int`, and returns an `int` value.

Exercise 1.31 Look at the book you are reading right now. Is it an object or a class? If it is a class, name some objects. If it is an object, name its class.

Exercise 1.32 Can an object have several different classes? Discuss.

Understanding class definitions

Main concepts discussed in this chapter:

- fields
- constructors
- parameters

- methods (accessor, mutator)
- assignment and conditional statement

Java constructs discussed in this chapter:

field, constructor, comment, parameter, assignment (=), block, return statement, `void`, compound assignment operators (+=, –=), if

In this chapter we take our first proper look at the source code of a class. We will discuss the basic elements of class definitions: *fields*, *constructors*, and *methods*. Methods contain statements, and initially we look at methods containing only simple arithmetic and printing statements. Later we introduce *conditional statements* that allow choices between different actions to be made within methods.

We shall start by examining a new project in a fair amount of detail. This project represents a naïve implementation of an automated ticket machine. As we start by introducing the most basic features of classes, we shall quickly find that this implementation is deficient in a number of ways. So we shall then proceed to describe a more sophisticated version of the ticket machine that represents a significant improvement. Finally, in order to reinforce the concepts introduced in this chapter, we take a look at the internals of the *lab-classes* example encountered in Chapter 1.

2.1 Ticket machines

Train stations often provide ticket machines that print a ticket when a customer inserts the correct money for their fare. In this chapter we shall define a class that models something like these ticket machines. As we shall be looking inside our first Java example classes, we shall keep our simulation fairly simple to start with. That will give us the opportunity to ask some questions about how these models differ from the real-world versions, and how we might change our classes to make the objects they create more like the real thing.

Our ticket machines work by customers 'inserting' money into them, and then requesting a ticket to be printed. A machine keeps a running total of the amount of money it has collected throughout its operation. In real life, it is often the case that a ticket machine offers a selection of different types of ticket from which customers choose the one they want. Our simplified machines only print tickets of a single price. It turns out to be significantly more complicated to program a class to be able to issue tickets of different values than it does to have a single price. On the other hand, with object-oriented programming it is very easy to create multiple instances of the class, each with its own price setting, to fulfill a need for different types of ticket.

2.1.1 Exploring the behavior of a naïve ticket machine

Open the *naive-ticket-machine* project in BlueJ. This project contains only one class – `TicketMachine` – which you will be able to explore in a similar way to the examples we discussed in Chapter 1. When you create a `TicketMachine` instance, you will be asked to supply a number that corresponds to the price of tickets that will be issued by that particular machine. The price is taken to be a number of cents, so a positive whole number such as 500 would be appropriate as a value to work with.

Exercise 2.1 Create a `TicketMachine` object on the object bench and take a look at its methods. You should see the following: `getBalance`, `getPrice`, `insertMoney`, and `printTicket`. Try out the `getPrice` method. You should see a return value containing the price of the tickets that was set when this object was created. Use the `insertMoney` method to simulate inserting an amount of money into the machine and then use `getBalance` to check that the machine has a record of the amount inserted. You can insert several separate amounts of money into the machine, just like you might insert multiple coins or notes into a real machine. Try inserting the exact amount required for a ticket. As this is a simple machine, a ticket will not be issued automatically, so once you have inserted enough money, call the `printTicket` method. A facsimile ticket should be printed in the BlueJ terminal window.

Exercise 2.2 What value is returned if you check the machine's balance after it has printed a ticket?

Exercise 2.3 Experiment with inserting different amounts of money before printing tickets. Do you notice anything strange about the machine's behavior? What happens if you insert too much money into the machine – do you receive any refund? What happens if you do not insert enough and then try to print a ticket?

Exercise 2.4 Try to obtain a good understanding of a ticket machine's behavior by interacting with it on the object bench before we start looking at how the `TicketMachine` class is implemented in the next section.

Exercise 2.5 Create another ticket machine for tickets of a different price. Buy a ticket from that machine. Does the printed ticket look different?

2.2 Examining a class definition

Examination of the behavior of `TicketMachine` objects within BlueJ reveals that they only really behave in the way we might expect them to if we insert exactly the correct amount of money to match the price of a ticket. As we explore the internal details of the class in this section, we shall begin to see why this is so.

Take a look at the source code of the `TicketMachine` class by double-clicking its icon in the class diagram. It should look something like Figure 2.1.

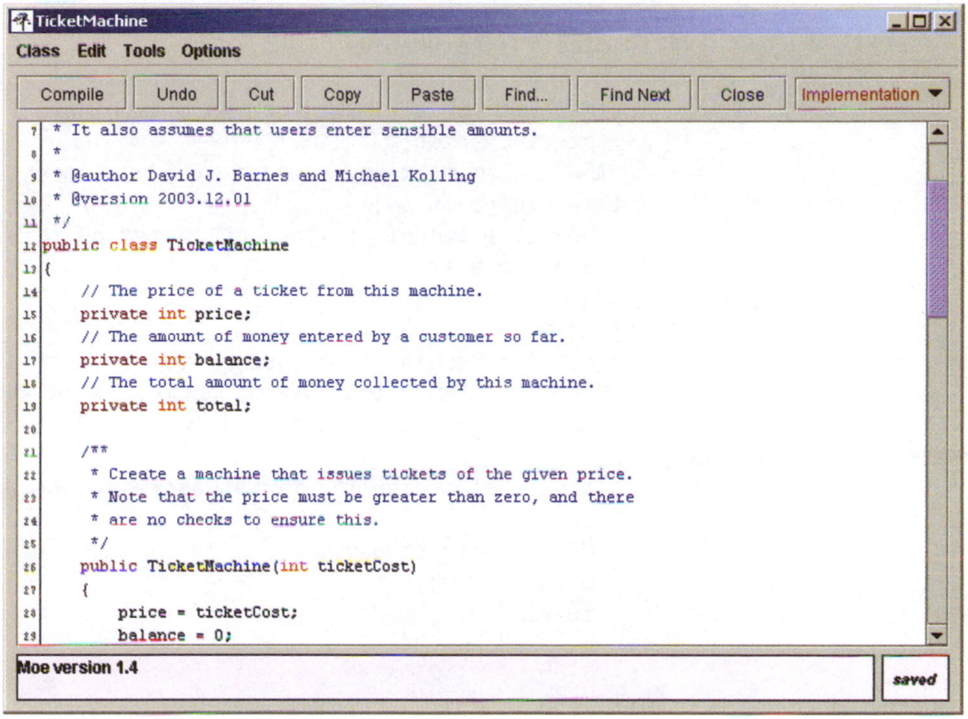

Figure 2.1
The BlueJ editor window

```
 7  * It also assumes that users enter sensible amounts.
 8  *
 9  * @author David J. Barnes and Michael Kolling
10  * @version 2003.12.01
11  */
12 public class TicketMachine
13 {
14     // The price of a ticket from this machine.
15     private int price;
16     // The amount of money entered by a customer so far.
17     private int balance;
18     // The total amount of money collected by this machine.
19     private int total;
20
21     /**
22      * Create a machine that issues tickets of the given price.
23      * Note that the price must be greater than zero, and there
24      * are no checks to ensure this.
25      */
26     public TicketMachine(int ticketCost)
27     {
28         price = ticketCost;
29         balance = 0;
```

The complete text of the class is shown in Code 2.1. By looking at the text of the class definition piece by piece we can flesh out some of the object-oriented concepts that we talked about in Chapter 1.

Code 2.1

The
`TicketMachine`
class

```java
/**
 * TicketMachine models a naive ticket machine that issues
 * flat-fare tickets.
 * The price of a ticket is specified via the constructor.
 * It is a naive machine in the sense that it trusts its users
 * to insert enough money before trying to print a ticket.
 * It also assumes that users enter sensible amounts.
 *
 * @author David J. Barnes and Michael Kölling
 * @version 2003.12.01
 */
public class TicketMachine
{
    // The price of a ticket from this machine.
    private int price;
    // The amount of money entered by a customer so far.
    private int balance;
    // The total amount of money collected by this machine.
    private int total;

    /**
     * Create a machine that issues tickets of the given price.
     * Note that the price must be greater than zero, and there
     * are no checks to ensure this.
     */
    public TicketMachine(int ticketCost)
    {
        price = ticketCost;
        balance = 0;
        total = 0;
    }

    /**
     * Return the price of a ticket.
     */
    public int getPrice()
    {
        return price;
    }

    /**
     * Return the amount of money already inserted for the
     * next ticket.
     */
    public int getBalance()
    {
        return balance;
    }
```

**Code 2.1
continued**
The
`TicketMachine`
class

```
/**
 * Receive an amount of money in cents from a customer.
 */
public void insertMoney(int amount)
{
    balance = balance + amount;
}


/**
 * Print a ticket.
 * Update the total collected and
 * reduce the balance to zero.
 */
public void printTicket()
{
    // Simulate the printing of a ticket.
    System.out.println("##################");
    System.out.println("# The BlueJ Line");
    System.out.println("# Ticket");
    System.out.println("# " + price + " cents.");
    System.out.println("##################");
    System.out.println();

    // Update the total collected with the balance.
    total = total + balance;
    // Clear the balance.
    balance = 0;
}
}
```

2.3 Fields, constructors, and methods

The source of most classes can be broken down into two main parts: a small outer wrapping that simply names the class, and a much larger inner part that does all the work. In this case, the outer wrapping appears as follows:

```
public class TicketMachine
{
    Inner part of the class omitted.
}
```

The outer wrappings of different classes all look pretty much the same; their main purpose is to provide a name for the class.

Exercise 2.6 Write out what you think the outer layers of the **Student** and **LabClass** classes might look like – do not worry about the inner part.

Exercise 2.7 Does it matter whether we write

```
public class TicketMachine
```

or

```
class public TicketMachine
```

in the outer wrapper of a class? Edit the source of the `TicketMachine` class to make the change and then close the editor window. Do you notice a change in the class diagram?

What error message do you get when you now press the *Compile* button? Do you think this message clearly explains what is wrong?

Exercise 2.8 Check whether or not it is possible to leave out the word `public` from the outer wrapper of the `TicketMachine` class.

The inner part of the class is where we define the *fields*, *constructors,* and *methods* that give the objects of that class their own particular characteristics and behavior. We can summarize the essential features of those three components of a class as follows:

- The fields store data for each object to use.
- The constructors allow each object to be set up properly when it is first created.
- The methods implement the behavior of the objects.

In Java there are very few rules about the order in which you choose to define the fields, constructors, and methods within a class. In the `TicketMachine` class we have chosen to list the fields first, the constructors second, and finally the methods (Code 2.2). This is the order that we shall follow in all of our examples. Other authors choose to adopt different styles, and this is mostly a question of preference. Our style is not necessarily better than all others. However, it is important to choose one style and then to use it consistently, because then your classes will be easier to read and understand.

Code 2.2
Our ordering of fields, constructors, and methods

```
public class ClassName
{
    Fields
    Constructors
    Methods
}
```

Exercise 2.9 From your earlier experimentation with the ticket machine objects within BlueJ you can probably remember the names of some of the methods – `printTicket`, for instance. Look at the class definition in Code 2.1 and use this knowledge, along with the additional information about ordering we have given you, to try to make a list of the names of the fields, constructors, and methods in the `TicketMachine` class. *Hint:* There is only one constructor in the class.

Exercise 2.10 Do you notice any features of the constructor that make it significantly different from the other methods of the class?

2.3.1   Fields

The TicketMachine class has three fields: price, balance, and total. Fields are also known as *instance variables*. We have defined these right at the start of the class definition (Code 2.3). All of the fields are associated with monetary items that a ticket machine object has to deal with:

- The price field stores the fixed price of a ticket.

- The balance field stores the amount of money inserted into the machine by a user prior to asking for a ticket to be printed.

- The total field stores a record of the total amount of money inserted into the machine by all users since the machine object was constructed.

Code 2.3

The fields of the TicketMachine class

```
public class TicketMachine
{
    private int price;
    private int balance;
    private int total;

    Constructor and methods omitted.

}
```

Fields are small amounts of space inside an object that can be used to store values. Every object, once created, will have some space for every field declared in its class. Figure 2.2 shows a diagrammatic representation of a ticket machine object with its three fields. The fields have not yet been assigned any values; once they have, we can write each value into the box representing the field. The notation is similar to that used in BlueJ to show objects on the object bench, except that we show a bit more detail here. In BlueJ, for space reasons, the fields are not displayed on the object icon. We can, however, see them by opening an inspector window.

Figure 2.2

An object of class TicketMachine

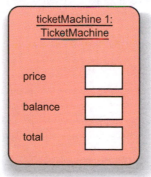

Each field has its own declaration in the source code. On the line above each, in the full class definition, we have added a single line of text – a *comment* – for the benefit of human readers of the class definition:

```
// The price of a ticket from this machine.
private int price;
```

A single-line comment is introduced by the two characters '//', which are written with no spaces between them. More detailed comments, often spanning several lines, are usually written in the form of multi-line comments. These start with the character pair '/*' and end with the pair '*/'. There is a good example preceding the header of the class in Code 2.1.

The definitions of the three fields are quite similar:

■ All definitions indicate that they are *private* fields of the object; we shall have more to say about what this means in Chapter 5, but for the time being we will simply say that we always define fields to be private.

■ All three fields are of type `int`. This indicates that each can store a single whole-number value, which is reasonable given that we wish them to store numbers that represent amounts of money in cents.

Because fields can store values that can vary over time, they are also known as *variables*. The value stored in a field can be changed if we wish to. For instance, as more money is inserted into a ticket machine we shall want to change the value stored in the balance field. In the following sections we shall also meet other kinds of variables in addition to fields.

The `price`, `balance`, and `total` fields are all the data items that a ticket machine object needs to fulfill its role of receiving money from a customer, printing tickets, and keeping a running total of all the money that has been put into it. In the following sections we shall see how the constructor and methods use those fields to implement the behavior of naïve ticket machines.

Exercise 2.11 What do you think is the *type* of each of the following fields?

```
private int count;
private Student representative;
private Server host;
```

Exercise 2.12 What are the *names* of the following fields?

```
private boolean alive;
private Person tutor;
private Game game;
```

Exercise 2.13 In the following field declaration from the `TicketMachine` class

```
private int price;
```

does it matter which order the three words appear in? Edit the `TicketMachine` class to try different orderings. After each change, close the editor. Does the appearance of the class diagram after each change give you a clue as to whether or not other orderings are possible? Check by pressing the *Compile* button to see if there is an error message.

Make sure that you reinstate the original version after your experiments!

Exercise 2.14 Is it always necessary to have a semicolon at the end of a field declaration? Once again, experiment via the editor. The rule you will learn here is an important one, so be sure to remember it.

Exercise 2.15 Write in full the declaration for a field of type `int` whose name is `status`.

2.3.2 Constructors

The constructors of a class have a special role to fulfill. It is their responsibility to put each object of that class into a fit state to be used once it has been created. This is also called *initialization*. The constructor initializes the object to a reasonable state. Code 2.4 shows the constructor of the `TicketMachine` class.

One of the distinguishing features of constructors is that they have the same name as the class in which they are defined – `TicketMachine` in this case.

Code 2.4

The constructor of the `TicketMachine` class

```java
public class TicketMachine
{
    Fields omitted.

    /**
     * Create a machine that issues tickets of the given price.
     * Note that the price must be greater than zero, and there
     * are no checks to ensure this.
     */
    public TicketMachine(int ticketCost)
    {
        price = ticketCost;
        balance = 0;
        total = 0;
    }

    Methods omitted.

}
```

The fields of the object are initialized in the constructor. Some fields, such as `balance` and `total`, can be set to sensible initial values by assigning a constant number, zero in this case. With others, such as the ticket price, it is not that simple as we do not know the price that tickets from a particular machine will have until that machine is constructed: recall that we might wish to create multiple machine objects to sell tickets with different prices, so no one initial price will always be right. You will recall from experimenting with creating `TicketMachine` objects within BlueJ that you had to supply the cost of the tickets whenever you created a new ticket machine. An important point to note here is that the price of a ticket is initially determined *outside* the ticket machine, and then has to be *passed into* a ticket machine object. Within BlueJ you decide the value and enter it into a dialog box. One task of the constructor is to receive that value and store it in the `price` field of the newly created ticket machine so that the machine can remember what that value was without you having to keep reminding it. We can see from this that one of the most important roles of a field is to remember information, so that it is available to an object throughout that object's lifetime.

Figure 2.3 shows a ticket machine object after the constructor has executed. Values have now been assigned to the fields. From this diagram we can tell that the ticket machine was created by passing in 500 as the value for the ticket price.

In the next section we discuss how values are received by an object from outside.

Figure 2.3
A `TicketMachine`
object after
initialization
(created for 500
cent tickets)

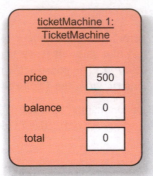

Note In Java, all fields are automatically initialized to a default value if they are not explicitly initialized. For integer fields this default value is 0. So, strictly speaking, we could have done without setting `balance` and `total` to 0, relying on the default value to give us the same result. However, we prefer to write the explicit assignments anyway. There is no disadvantage to it, and it serves well to document what is actually happening. We do not rely on a reader of the class knowing what the default value is, and we document that we really want this value to be zero, and have not just forgotten to initialize it.

2.4 Passing data via parameters

The way in which both constructors and methods receive values is via their *parameters*. You may recall that we briefly encountered parameters in Chapter 1. Parameters are defined in the header of the constructor or method:

```
public TicketMachine(int ticketCost)
```

This constructor has a single parameter, `ticketCost`, which is of type `int` – the same type as the `price` field it will be used to set. Figure 2.4 illustrates how values are passed via parameters. In this case, a BlueJ user enters a value into the dialog box when creating a new ticket machine (shown on the left), and that value is then copied into the `ticket-Cost` parameter of the new machine's constructor. This is illustrated with the arrow labeled (A). The box in the ticket machine object in Figure 2.4, labeled 'TicketMachine (constructor),' is additional space for the object that is created only when the constructor executes. We shall call it the *constructor space* of the object (or *method space* when we talk about methods instead of constructors, as the situation there is the same). The constructor space is used to provide space to store the values for the constructor's parameters (and other variables that we will come across later).

We distinguish between parameter names inside a constructor or method, and parameter values outside, by referring to the names as *formal parameters* and the values as *actual parameters*. So `ticketCost` is a formal parameter, and a user-supplied value, such as 500, is an actual parameter. Because they are able to store values, formal parameters are another sort of variable. In our diagrams, all variables are represented by white boxes.

Concept:

The **scope** of a variable defines the section of source code from where the variable can be accessed.

A formal parameter is available to an object only within the body of a constructor or method that declares it. We say that the *scope* of a parameter is restricted to the body of the constructor or method in which it is declared. In contrast, the scope of a field is the whole of the class definition – it can be accessed from anywhere in the same class.

Figure 2.4
Parameter passing
(A) and assignment
(B)

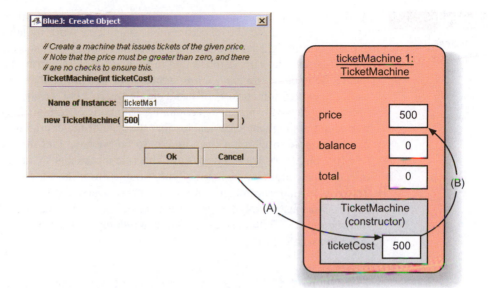

A concept related to variable scope is variable *lifetime*. The lifetime of a parameter is limited to a single call of a constructor or method. Once that call has completed its task, the formal parameters disappear and the values they held are lost. In other words, when the constructor has finished executing, the whole constructor space (see Figure 2.4) is removed, along with the parameter variables held within it.

In contrast, the lifetime of a field is the same as the lifetime of the object to which it belongs. It follows that if we want to remember the cost of tickets held in the `ticketCost` parameter, we must store the value somewhere more persistent – that is, in the `price` field.

Exercise 2.16 To what class does the following constructor belong?

```
public Student(String name)
```

Exercise 2.17 How many parameters does the following constructor have and what are their types?

```
public Book(String title, double price)
```

Exercise 2.18 Can you guess what types some of the **Book** class's fields might be? Can you assume anything about the names of its fields?

2.5 Assignment

In the previous section, we noted the need to store the short-lived value of a parameter into somewhere more permanent – a field. In order to do this, the body of the constructor contains the following *assignment statement*:

```
price = ticketCost;
```

Assignment statements are recognized by the presence of an assignment operator, such as '=' in the example above. Assignment statements work by taking the value of what appears on the right-hand side of the operator and copying that value into a variable on the left-hand side. This is illustrated in Figure 2.4 by the arrow labeled (B). The right-hand side is called an *expression*: expressions are things that compute values. In this case, the expression consists of just a single variable but we shall see some examples of more complicated expressions containing arithmetic operations later in this chapter. One rule about assignment statements is that the type of the expression must match the type of the variable to which it is assigned. So far we have met three different types: `int`, `String`, and (very briefly) `boolean`. This rule means that we are not allowed to store an integer-type expression in a string-type variable, for instance. This same rule also applies between formal parameters and actual parameters: the type of an actual-parameter expression must match the type of the formal-parameter variable. For now, we can say that the types of both must be the same, although we shall see in later chapters that this is not the whole truth.

Exercise 2.19 Suppose that the class `Pet` has a field called `name` that is of type `String`. Write an assignment statement in the body of the following constructor so that the `name` field will be initialized with the value of the constructor's parameter.

```
public Pet(String petsName)
{
    ...
}
```

Exercise 2.20 *Challenge exercise* What is wrong with the following version of the constructor of `TicketMachine`?

```
public TicketMachine(int ticketCost)
{
    int price = ticketCost;
    balance = 0;
    total = 0;
}
```

Once you have spotted the problem, try out this version in the *naive-ticket-machine* project. Does this version compile? Create an object and then inspect its fields. Do you notice something wrong about the value of the `price` field in the inspector with this version? Can you explain why this is?

2.6 Accessor methods

The `TicketMachine` class has four methods: `getPrice`, `getBalance`, `insertMoney`, and `printTicket`. We shall start our look at the source code of methods by considering `getPrice` (Code 2.5).

Code 2.5

The `getPrice` method

```java
public class TicketMachine
{
    Fields omitted.

    Constructor omitted.

    /**
     * Return the price of a ticket.
     */
    public int getPrice()
    {
        return price;
    }

    Remaining methods omitted.
}
```

Methods have two parts: a *header* and a *body*. Here is the method header for `getPrice`:

```java
/**
 * Return the price of a ticket.
 */
public int getPrice()
```

The first three lines are a comment describing what the method does. The fourth line is also known as the *method signature*.[1] It is important to distinguish between method signatures and field declarations, because they can look quite similar. We can tell that `getPrice` is a method and not a field because it is followed by a pair of parentheses: '(' and ')'. Note, too, that there is no semicolon at the end of the signature.

The method body is the remainder of the method after the header. It is always enclosed by a matching pair of curly brackets: '{' and '}'. Method bodies contain the *declarations* and *statements* that define what happens inside an object when that method is called. In our example above, the method body contains a single statement, but we shall see examples very soon where the method body consists of many lines of both declarations and statements.

Any set of declarations and statements between a pair of matching curly brackets is known as a *block*. So the body of the `TicketMachine` class and the bodies of all the methods within the class are blocks.

There are at least two significant differences between the signatures of the `TicketMachine` constructor and the `getPrice` method:

```java
public TicketMachine(int ticketCost)
```

```java
public int getPrice()
```

---

[1] This definition differs slightly from the more formal definition in the Java language specification where the signature does not include the access modifier and return type.

- The method has a *return type* of `int`, but the constructor has no return type. A return type is written just before the method name.

- The constructor has a single formal parameter, `ticketCost`, but the method has none – just a pair of empty parentheses.

It is an absolute rule in Java that a constructor may not have a return type. On the other hand, both constructors and methods may have any number of formal parameters, including none.

Within the body of `getPrice` there is a single statement:

```
return price;
```

This is a *return statement*. It is responsible for returning an integer value to match the `int` return type in the method's signature. Where a method contains a return statement, it is always the final statement of that method, because no further statements in the method will be executed once the return statement is executed.

The `int` return type of `getPrice` is a form of promise that the body of the method will do something that ultimately results in an integer value being calculated and returned as the method's result. You might like to think of a method call as being a form of question to an object, and the return value from the method being the object's answer to that question. In this case, when the `getPrice` method is called on a ticket machine, the question is, 'What do tickets cost?' A ticket machine does not need to perform any calculations to be able to answer that, because it keeps the answer in its `price` field. So the method answers by just returning the value of that variable. As we gradually develop more complex classes, we shall inevitably encounter more complex questions that require more work to supply their answers.

We often describe methods such as the two `get` methods of `TicketMachine` (`getPrice` and `getBalance`) as *accessor methods* (or just *accessors*). This is because they return information to the caller about the state of an object – they provide access to that state. An accessor usually contains a return statement in order to pass back that information as a particular value, but this is not exclusively the case. A method that prints information about an object's state may also be classified as an accessor.

Exercise 2.21 Compare the `getBalance` method with the `getPrice` method. What are the differences between them?

Exercise 2.22 If a call to `getPrice` can be characterized as 'What do tickets cost?', how would you characterize a call to `getBalance`?

Exercise 2.23 If the name of `getBalance` is changed to `getAmount`, does the return statement in the body of the method need to be changed, too? Try it out within BlueJ.

Exercise 2.24 Define an accessor method, `getTotal`, that returns the value of the `total` field.

Exercise 2.25 Try removing the return statement from the body of `getPrice`. What error message do you see now when you try compiling the class?

Exercise 2.26 Compare the method signatures of `getPrice` and `printTicket` in Code 2.1. Apart from their names, what is the main difference between them?

2.7   Mutator methods

Concept:

Mutator methods change the state of an object.

The `get` methods of a ticket machine perform similar tasks – returning the value of one of their object's fields. The remaining methods – `insertMoney` and `printTicket` – have a much more significant role, primarily because they *change* the value of one or more fields of a ticket machine object each time they are called. We call methods that change the state of their object *mutator methods* (or just *mutators*).

In the same way as we think of accessors as requests for information (questions), we can think of mutators as requests for an object to change its state.

One distinguishing effect of a mutator is that an object will often exhibit slightly different behavior before and after it is called. We can illustrate this with the following exercise.

The signature of `insertMoney` has a `void` return type and a single formal parameter, `amount`, of type `int`. A `void` return type means that the method does not return any value to its caller. This is significantly different from all other return types. Within BlueJ the difference is most noticeable in that no return-value dialog is shown following a call to a `void` method. Within the body of a `void` method, this difference is reflected in the fact that there is no return statement.[2]

Code 2.6

The `insertMoney` method

```
/**
 * Receive an amount of money in cents from a customer.
 */
public void insertMoney(int amount)
{
    balance = balance + amount;
}
```

---

[2] In fact, Java does allow `void` methods to contain a special form of return statement in which there is no return value. This takes the form

`return;`

and simply causes the method to exit without executing any further code.

In the body of `insertMoney` there is a single statement that is another form of assignment statement. We always consider assignment statements by first examining the calculation on the right-hand side of the assignment symbol. Here, its effect is to calculate a value that is the sum of the number in the `amount` parameter and the number in the `balance` field. This combined value is then assigned to the `balance` field. So the effect is to increase the value in `balance` by the value in `amount`.[3]

Exercise 2.29 How can we tell from just its header that `setPrice` is a method and not a constructor?

```
public void setPrice(int ticketCost)
```

Exercise 2.30 Complete the body of the `setPrice` method so that it assigns the value of its parameter to the `price` field.

Exercise 2.31 Complete the body of the following method, whose purpose is to add the value of its parameter to a field named `score`.

```
/**
 * Increase score by the given number of points.
 */
public void increase(int points)
{
    ...
}
```

Exercise 2.32 Can you complete the following method, whose purpose is to subtract the value of its parameter from a field named `price`?

```
/**
 * Reduce price by the given amount.
 */
public void discount(int amount)
{
    ...
}
```

2.8 Printing from methods

Code 2.7 shows the most complex method of the class: `printTicket`. To help your understanding of the following discussion, make sure that you have called this method on

---

[3] Adding an amount to the value in a variable is so common that there is a special **compound assignment operator** to do this: +=. For instance:

```
balance += amount;
```

Code 2.7

The `printTicket` method

```java
/**
 * Print a ticket and reduce the
 * current balance to zero.
 */
public void printTicket()
{
    // Simulate the printing of a ticket.
    System.out.println("##################");
    System.out.println("# The BlueJ Line");
    System.out.println("# Ticket");
    System.out.println("# " + price + " cents.");
    System.out.println("##################");
    System.out.println();

    // Update the total collected with the balance.
    total = total + balance;
    // Clear the balance.
    balance = 0;
}
```

a ticket machine. You should have seen something like the following printed in the BlueJ terminal window:

```
##################
# The BlueJ Line
# Ticket
# 500 cents.
##################
```

This is the longest method we have seen so far, so we shall break it down into more manageable pieces:

- The signature indicates that the method has a void return type and that it takes no parameters.

- The body comprises eight statements plus associated comments.

- The first six statements are responsible for printing what you see in the BlueJ terminal window.

- The seventh statement adds the balance inserted by the customer (through previous calls to `insertMoney`) to the running total of all money collected so far by the machine.

- The eighth statement resets the balance to zero with a basic assignment statement, ready for the next customer to insert some money.

By comparing the output that appears with the statements that produced it, it is easy to see that a statement such as

```java
System.out.println("# The BlueJ Line");
```

Concept:

The method **System.out. println** prints its parameter to the text terminal.

literally prints the string that appears between the matching pair of double quote characters. All of these printing statements are calls to the `println` method of the `System.out` object that is built into the Java language. In the fourth statement the actual parameter to `println` is a little more complicated:

```
System.out.println("# " + price + " cents.");
```

The two '+' operators are being used to construct a single string parameter from three components:

- the string literal: `"# "` (note the space character after the hash);
- the value of the `price` field (note there are no quotes around the field name);
- the string literal: `" cents."` (note the space character before the word cents).

When used between a string and anything else, '+' is a string-concatenation operator (i.e. it concatenates or joins strings together to create a new string) rather than an arithmetic-addition operator.

Note that the final call to `println` contains no string parameter. This is allowed, and the result of calling it will be to leave a blank line between this output and any that follows after. You will easily see the blank line if you print a second ticket.

Exercise 2.33 Add a method called **prompt** to the **TicketMachine** class. This should have a **void** return type and take no parameters. The body of the method should print something like:

```
Please insert the correct amount of money.
```

Exercise 2.34 Add a **showPrice** method to the **TicketMachine** class. This should have a **void** return type and take no parameters. The body of the method should print something like:

```
The price of a ticket is xyz cents.
```

where **xyz** should be replaced by the value held in the **price** field when the method is called.

Exercise 2.35 Create two ticket machines with differently priced tickets. Do calls to their **showPrice** methods show the same output, or different? How do you explain this effect?

Exercise 2.36 What do you think would be printed if you altered the fourth statement of **printTicket** so that **price** also has quotes around it, as follows?

```
System.out.println("# " + "price" + " cents.");
```

Exercise 2.37 What about the following version?

```
System.out.println("# price cents.");
```

Exercise 2.38 Could either of the previous two versions be used to show the price of tickets in different ticket machines? Explain your answer.

2.9 Summary of the naïve ticket machine

We have now examined the internal structure of the naïve ticket machine class in some detail. We have seen that the class has a small outer layer that gives a name to the class, and a more substantial inner body containing fields, a constructor, and several methods. Fields are used to store data that enable objects to maintain a state. Constructors are used to set up an initial state when an object is created. Having a proper initial state will enable an object to respond appropriately to method calls immediately following its creation. Methods implement the defined behavior of the class's objects. Accessors provide information about an object's state, and mutators change an object's state.

We have seen that constructors are distinguished from methods by having the same name as the class in which they are defined. Both constructors and methods may take parameters, but only methods may have a return type. Non-void return types allow us to pass a result out of a method. A method with a non-void return type will have a return statement as the final statement of its body. Return statements are only applicable to methods, because constructors never have a return type of any sort – not even `void`.

Before attempting these exercises, be sure that you have a good understanding of how ticket machines behave, and how that behavior is implemented through the fields, constructor, and methods of the class.

Exercise 2.39 Modify the constructor of `TicketMachine` so that it no longer has a parameter. Instead, the price of tickets should be fixed at 1000 cents. What effect does this have when you construct ticket machine objects within BlueJ?

Exercise 2.40 Implement a method, `empty`, that simulates the effect of removing all money from the machine. This method should have a `void` return type, and its body should simply set the `total` field to zero. Does this method need to take any parameters? Test your method by creating a machine, inserting some money, printing some tickets, checking the total, and then emptying the machine. Is this method a mutator or an accessor?

Exercise 2.41 Implement a method, `setPrice`, that is able to set the price of tickets to a new value. The new price is passed in as a parameter value to the method. Test your method by creating a machine, showing the price of tickets, changing the price, and then showing the new price. Is this method a mutator?

Exercise 2.42 Give the class two constructors. One should take a single parameter that specifies the price, and the other should take no parameter and set the price to be a default value of your choosing. Test your implementation by creating machines via the two different constructors.

2.10 Reflecting on the design of the ticket machine

In the next few sections we shall examine the implementation of an improved ticket machine class that attempts to deal with some of the inadequacies of the naïve implementation.

From our study of the internals of the `TicketMachine` class you should have come to appreciate how inadequate it would be in the real world. It is deficient in several ways:

- It contains no check that the customer has entered enough money to pay for a ticket.

- It does not refund any money if the customer pays too much for a ticket.

- It does not check to ensure that the customer inserts sensible amounts of money: experiment with what happens if a negative amount is entered, for instance.

- It does not check that the ticket price passed to its constructor is sensible.

If we could remedy these problems, then we would have a much more functional piece of software that might serve as the basis for operating a real-world ticket machine. In order to see that we can improve the existing version, open the *better-ticket-machine* project. As before, this project contains a single class – TicketMachine. Before looking at the internal details of the class, experiment with it by creating some instances and see whether you notice any differences in behavior between this version and the previous naïve version. One specific difference is that the new version has one additional method, refundBalance. Later in this chapter we shall use this method to introduce an additional feature of Java, so take a look at what happens when you call it.

2.11 Making choices: the conditional statement

Code 2.8 shows the internal details of the better ticket machine's class definition. Much of this definition will already be familiar to you from our discussion of the naïve ticket machine. For instance, the outer wrapping that names the class is the same because we have chosen to give this class the same name. In addition, it contains the same three fields to maintain object state, and these have been declared in the same way. The constructor and the two get methods are also the same as before.

Code 2.8
A more sophisticated ticket machine

```java
/**
 * TicketMachine models a ticket machine that issues
 * flat-fare tickets.
 * The price of a ticket is specified via the constructor.
 * Instances will check to ensure that a user only enters
 * sensible amounts of money, and will only print a ticket
 * if enough money has been input.
 * @author David J. Barnes and Michael Kölling
 * @version 2003.12.01
 */
public class TicketMachine
{
    // The price of a ticket from this machine.
    private int price;
    // The amount of money entered by a customer so far.
    private int balance;
    // The total amount of money collected by this machine.
    private int total;
```

**Code 2.8
continued**

A more
sophisticated ticket
machine

```java
/**
 * Create a machine that issues tickets of the given price.
 */
public TicketMachine(int ticketCost)
{
    price = ticketCost;
    balance = 0;
    total = 0;
}

/**
 * Return the price of a ticket.
 */
public int getPrice()
{
    return price;
}

/**
 * Return the amount of money already inserted for the
 * next ticket.
 */
public int getBalance()
{
    return balance;
}

/**
 * Receive an amount of money in cents from a customer.
 * Check that the amount is sensible.
 */
public void insertMoney(int amount)
{
    if(amount > 0) {
        balance = balance + amount;
    }
    else {
        System.out.println("Use a positive amount: " +
                                amount);
    }
}

/**
 * Print a ticket if enough money has been inserted, and
 * reduce the current balance by the ticket price. Print
 * an error message if more money is required.
 */
public void printTicket()
{
```

**Code 2.8
continued**

A more
sophisticated ticket
machine

```
        if(balance >= price) {
            // Simulate the printing of a ticket.
            System.out.println("##################");
            System.out.println("# The BlueJ Line");
            System.out.println("# Ticket");
            System.out.println("# " + price + " cents.");
            System.out.println("##################");
            System.out.println();

            // Update the total collected with the price.
            total = total + price;
            // Reduce the balance by the price.
            balance = balance - price;
        }
        else {
            System.out.println("You must insert at least: " +
                                (price - balance) + " cents.");
        }
    }

    /**
     * Return the money in the balance.
     * The balance is cleared.
     */
    public int refundBalance()
    {
        int amountToRefund;
        amountToRefund = balance;
        balance = 0;
        return amountToRefund;
    }
}
```

The first significant change can be seen in the `insertMoney` method. We recognized
that the main problem with the naïve ticket machine was its failure to check certain conditions. One of those missing checks was on the amount of money inserted by a
customer, as it was possible for a negative amount of money to be inserted. We have
remedied that failing by making use of a *conditional statement* to check that the amount
inserted has a value greater than zero:

```
if(amount > 0) {
    balance = balance + amount;
}
else {
    System.out.println("Use a positive amount: " + amount);
}
```

Conditional statements are also known as *if statements*, from the word used in most programming languages to introduce them. A conditional statement allows us to take one of
two possible actions based upon the result of a check or test. If the test is true, then we do

one thing, otherwise we do something different. A conditional statement has the general form described in the following *pseudo-code*:

```
if(perform some test that gives a true or false result) {
    Do the statements here if the test gave a true result
}
else {
    Do the statements here if the test gave a false result
}
```

It is important to appreciate that only one of the sets of statements following the test will ever be performed following the evaluation of the test. So, in the example from the `insertMoney` method, following the test of an inserted amount we shall only either add the amount to the balance, or print the error message. The test uses the *greater-than operator*, '>', to compare the value in `amount` against zero. If the value is greater than zero then it is added to the balance. If it is not greater than zero, then an error message is printed. By using a conditional statement we have, in effect, protected the change to `balance` in the case where the parameter does not represent a valid amount.

The test used in a conditional statement is an example of a *boolean expression*. Earlier in this chapter we introduced arithmetic expressions that produced numerical results. A boolean expression has only two possible values, `true` or `false`: either the value of `amount` is greater than zero (`true`) or it is not greater (`false`). A conditional statement makes use of those two possible values to choose between two different actions.

Concept:

Boolean expressions have only two possible values: true and false. They are commonly found controlling the choice between the two paths through a conditional statement.

Exercise 2.43 Check that the behavior we have discussed here is accurate by creating a `TicketMachine` instance and calling `insertMoney` with various actual parameter values. Check the balance both before and after calling `insertMoney`. Does the balance ever change in the cases when an error message is printed? Try to predict what will happen if you enter the value zero as the parameter, and then see if you are right.

Exercise 2.44 Predict what you think will happen if you change the test in `insertMoney` to use the *greater-than or equal-to operator*:

```
if(amount >= 0)
```

Check your predictions by running some tests. What difference does it make to the behavior of the method?

Exercise 2.45 In the *shapes* project we looked at in Chapter 1 we used a `boolean` field to control a feature of the circle objects. What was that feature? Was it well suited to being controlled by a type with only two different values?

2.12 A further conditional-statement example

The `printTicket` method contains a further example of a conditional statement. Here it is in outline:

```
    if(balance >= price) {

        Printing details omitted.

        // Update the total collected with the price.
        total = total + price;
        // Reduce the balance by the price.
        balance = balance − price;
    }
    else {
        System.out.println("You must insert at least: " +
                            (price − balance) + " more cents.");
    }
```

We wish to remedy the fact that the naïve version makes no check that a customer has inserted enough money to be issued with a ticket. This version checks that the value in the `balance` field is at least as large as the value in the `price` field. If it is, then it is okay to print a ticket. If it is not, then we print an error message instead.

> **Exercise 2.46** In this version of `printTicket` we also do something slightly different with the `total` and `balance` fields. Compare the implementation of the method in Code 2.1 with that in Code 2.8 to see whether you can tell what those differences are. Then check your understanding by experimenting within BlueJ.

The `printTicket` method reduces the value of `balance` by the value of `price`. As a consequence, if a customer inserts more money than the price of the ticket, then some money will be left in the balance that could be used towards the price of a second ticket. Alternatively, the customer could ask to be refunded the remaining balance, and that is what the `refundBalance` method does, as we shall see in the next section.

> **Exercise 2.47** After a ticket has been printed, could the value in the `balance` field ever be set to a negative value by subtracting `price` from it? Justify your answer.
>
> **Exercise 2.48** So far we have introduced you to two arithmetic operators, + and −, that can be used in **arithmetic expressions** in Java. Take a look at Appendix D to find out what other operators are available.
>
> **Exercise 2.49** Write an assignment statement that will store the result of multiplying two variables, `price` and `discount`, into a third variable, `saving`.
>
> **Exercise 2.50** Write an assignment statement that will divide the value in `total` by the value in `count` and store the result in `mean`.
>
> **Exercise 2.51** Write an if statement that will compare the value in `price` against the value in `budget`. If `price` is greater than `budget` then print the message 'Too expensive', otherwise print the message 'Just right'.
>
> **Exercise 2.52** Modify your answer to the previous exercise so that the message if the price is too high includes the value of your budget.

2.13 Local variables

The refundBalance method contains three statements and a declaration. The declaration illustrates a new sort of variable:

```
public int refundBalance()
{
    int amountToRefund;
    amountToRefund = balance;
    balance = 0;
    return amountToRefund;
}
```

What sort of variable is amountToRefund? We know that it is not a field, because fields are defined outside methods. It is also not a parameter, as those are always defined in the method header. The amountToRefund variable is what is known as a *local variable* because it is defined *inside* a method. It is quite common to initialize local variables within their declaration. So we could abbreviate the first two statements of refundBalance as

```
int amountToRefund = balance;
```

Local variable declarations look similar to field declarations, but they never have private or public as part of them. Like formal parameters, local variables have a scope that is limited to the statements of the method to which they belong. Their lifetime is the time of the method execution: they are created when a method is called and destroyed when a method finishes. Constructors can also have local variables.

Local variables are often used as temporary storage locations to help a method complete its task. In this method amountToRefund is used to hold the value of the balance immediately prior to the latter being set to zero. The method then returns the old value of the balance. The following exercises will help to illustrate why a local variable is needed here, as we try to write the refundBalance method without one.

Exercise 2.53 Why does the following version of refundBalance not give the same results as the original?

```
public int refundBalance()
{
    balance = 0;
    return balance;
}
```

What tests can you run to demonstrate that it does not?

Exercise 2.54 What happens if you try to compile the TicketMachine class with the following version of refundBalance?

```
public int refundBalance()
{
    return balance;
    balance = 0;
}
```

What do you know about return statements that helps to explain why this version does not compile?

2.14 Fields, parameters, and local variables

With the introduction of `amountToRefund` in the `refundBalance` method we have now seen three different kinds of variable: fields, formal parameters, and local variables. It is important to understand the similarities and differences between these three kinds. Here is a summary of their features:

- All three kinds of variable are able to store a value that is appropriate to their defined type. For instance, a defined type of `int` allows a variable to store an integer value.

- Fields are defined outside constructors and methods.

- Fields are used to store data that persists throughout the life of an object. As such, they maintain the current state of an object. They have a lifetime that lasts as long as their object lasts.

- Fields have class scope: their accessibility extends throughout the whole class, and so they can be used within any of the constructors or methods of the class in which they are defined.

- As long as they are defined as `private`, fields cannot be accessed from anywhere outside their defining class.

- Formal parameters and local variables persist only for the period that a constructor or method executes. Their lifetime is only as long as a single call, so their values are lost between calls. As such, they act as temporary rather than permanent storage locations.

- Formal parameters are defined in the header of a constructor or method. They receive their values from outside, being initialized by the actual parameter values that form part of the constructor or method call.

- Formal parameters have a scope that is limited to their defining constructor or method.

- Local variables are defined inside the body of a constructor or method. They can be initialized and used only within the body of their defining constructor or method. Local variables must be initialized before they are used in an expression – they are not given a default value.

- Local variables have a scope that is limited to the block in which they are defined. They are not accessible from anywhere outside that block.

Exercise 2.55 Add a new method, `emptyMachine`, that is designed to simulate emptying the machine of money. It should both return the value in **total** and reset **total** to be zero.

Exercise 2.56 Is `emptyMachine` an accessor, a mutator, or both?

Exercise 2.57 Rewrite the **printTicket** method so that it declares a local variable, **amountLeftToPay**. This should then be initialized to contain the difference between **price** and **balance**. Rewrite the test in the conditional statement to check the value of **amountLeftToPay**. If its value is less than or equal to zero, a ticket should be printed, otherwise an error message should be printed stating the amount still required. Test your version to ensure that it behaves in exactly the same way as the original version.

Exercise 2.58 *Challenge exercise* Suppose we wished a single `TicketMachine` object to be able to issue tickets with different prices. For instance, users might press a button on the physical machine to select a particular ticket price. What further methods and/or fields would need to be added to `TicketMachine` to allow this kind of functionality? Do you think that many of the existing methods would need to be changed as well?

Save the *better-ticket-machine* project under a new name and implement your changes to the new project.

2.15 Summary of the better ticket machine

In developing a more sophisticated version of the `TicketMachine` class, we have been able to address the major inadequacies of the naïve version. In doing so, we have introduced two new language constructs: the conditional statement, and local variables.

- A conditional statement gives us a means to perform a test and then, on the basis of the result of that test, perform one or other of two distinct actions.

- Local variables allow us to calculate and store temporary values within a constructor or method. They contribute to the behavior that their defining method implements, but their values are lost once that constructor or method finishes its execution.

You can find more details of conditional statements and the form that their tests can take in Appendix C.

2.16 Reviewing a familiar example

By this point in the chapter you have met a lot of new concepts. To help reinforce those concepts, we shall now revisit them in a different but familiar context. Open the *lab-classes* project that we introduced in Chapter 1 and then examine the `Student` class in the editor (Code 2.9).

Code 2.9

The `Student` class

```java
/**
 * The Student class represents a student in a
 * student administration system.
 * It holds the student details relevant in our context.
 *
 * @author Michael Kölling and David Barnes
 * @version 2001.05.24
 */
public class Student
{
    // the student's full name
    private String name;
    // the student ID
    private String id;
    // the amount of credits for study taken so far
    private int credits;
```

**Code 2.9
continued**

The Student class

```java
/**
 * Create a new student with a given name and ID number.
 */
public Student(String fullName, String studentID)
{
    name = fullName;
    id = studentID;
    credits = 0;
}

/**
 * Return the full name of this student.
 */
public String getName()
{
    return name;
}

/**
 * Set a new name for this student.
 */
public void changeName(String newName)
{
    name = newName;
}

/**
 * Return the student ID of this student.
 */
public String getStudentID()
{
    return id;
}

/**
 * Add some credit points to the student's
 * accumulated credits.
 */
public void addCredits(int newCreditPoints)
{
    credits += newCreditPoints;
}

/**
 * Return the number of credit points this student
 * has accumulated.
 */
public int getCredits()
{
    return credits;
}
```

**Code 2.9
continued**

The **Student** class

```java
/**
 * Return the login name of this student.
 * The login name is a combination
 * of the first four characters of the
 * student's name and the first three
 * characters of the student's ID number.
 */
public String getLoginName()
{
    return name.substring(0,4) +
            id.substring(0,3);
}

/**
 * Print the student's name and ID number
 * to the output terminal.
 */
public void print()
{
    System.out.println(name + " (" + id + ")");
}
}
```

The class contains three fields: name, id, and credits. Each of these is initialized in the single constructor. The initial values of the first two are set from parameter values passed into the constructor. Each of the fields has an associated get- accessor method, but only name and credits have associated mutator methods. This means that the value of an id field remains fixed once the object has been constructed.

The getLoginName method illustrates a new feature that is worth exploring:

```java
public String getLoginName()
{
    return name.substring(0,4) +
            id.substring(0,3);
}
```

Both name and id are strings, and the String class has an accessor method, substring, with the following signature:

```java
/**
 * Return a new string containing the characters from
 * beginIndex to (endIndex-1) from this string.
 */
public String substring(int beginIndex, int endIndex)
```

An index value of zero represents the first character of a string, so getLoginName takes the first four characters of the name string, the first three characters of the id string, and concatenates them together to form a new string. This new string is returned as the method's result. For instance, if name is the string "Leonardo da Vinci" and id is the string "468366", then the string "Leon468" would be returned by this method.

Exercise 2.59 Draw a picture of the form shown in Figure 2.3 representing the initial state of a **Student** object following its construction with the following actual parameter values:

```
new Student("Benjamin Jonson", "738321")
```

Exercise 2.60 What would be returned by **getLoginName** for a student with the name "Henry Moore" and the id "557214"?

Exercise 2.61 Create a **Student** with **name** "djb" and **id** "859012". What happens when **getLoginName** is called on this student? Why do you think this is?

Exercise 2.62 The **String** class defines a **length** accessor method with the following signature:

```
/**
 * Return the number of characters in this string.
 */
public int length()
```

Add conditional statements to the constructor of **Student** to print an error message if either the length of the **fullName** parameter is less than four characters or the length of the **studentId** parameter is less than three characters. However, the constructor should still use those parameters to set the **name** and **id** fields, even if the error message is printed. *Hint:* Use if statements of the following form (that is, having no **else** part) to print the error messages.

```
if(perform a test on one of the parameters) {
    Print an error message if the test gave a true result
}
```

See Appendix C for further details of the different types of **if** statement, if necessary.

Exercise 2.63 *Challenge exercise* Modify the **getLoginName** method of **Student** so that it always generates a login name, even if either of the **name** and **id** fields is not strictly long enough. For strings shorter than the required length, use the whole string.

2.17 Summary

In this chapter we have covered the basics of how to create a class definition. Classes contain fields, constructors, and methods that define the state and behavior of objects. Within constructors and methods a sequence of statements defines how an object accomplishes its designated tasks. We have covered assignment statements and conditional statements, and will be adding further types of statement in later chapters.

Terms introduced in this chapter

field, instance variable, constructor, method, method signature, method body, parameter, accessor, mutator, declaration, initialization, block, statement, assignment statement, conditional statement, return statement, return type, comment, expression, operator, variable, local variable, scope, lifetime.

Concept summary

- **field** Fields store data for an object to use. Fields are also known as instance variables.
- **comment** Comments are inserted into the source code of a class to provide explanations to human readers. They have no effect on the functionality of the class.
- **constructor** Constructors allow each object to be set up properly when it is first created.
- **scope** The scope of a variable defines the section of source code from where the variable can be accessed.
- **lifetime** The lifetime of a variable describes how long the variable continues to exist before it is destroyed.
- **assignment** Assignment statements store the value represented by the right-hand side of the statement in the variable named on the left.
- **method** Methods consist of two parts: a header and a body.
- **accessor method** Accessor methods return information about the state of an object.
- **mutator method** Mutator methods change the state of an object.
- **println** The method `System.out.println` prints its parameter to the text terminal.
- **conditional** A conditional statement takes one of two possible actions based upon the result of a test.
- **boolean expression** Boolean expressions have only two possible values: true and false. They are commonly found controlling the choice between the two paths through a conditional statement.
- **local variable** A local variable is a variable declared and used within a single method. Its scope and lifetime are limited to that of the method.

The following exercises are designed to help you experiment with the concepts of Java that we have discussed in this chapter. You will create your own classes that contain elements such as fields, constructors, methods, assignment statements, and conditional statements.

Exercise 2.64 Below is the outline for a **Book** class, which can be found in the *book-exercise* project. The outline already defines two fields and a constructor to initialize the fields. In this exercise and the next few, you will add further features to the class outline.

Add two accessor methods to the class – `getAuthor` and `getTitle` – that return the **author** and **title** fields as their respective results. Test your class by creating some instances and calling the methods.

```
/**
 * A class that maintains information on a book.
 * This might form part of a larger application such
 * as a library system, for instance.
 *
 * @author (Insert your name here.)
 * @version (Insert today's date here.)
 */
```

```
public class Book
{
    // The fields.
    private String author;
    private String title;

    /**
     * Set the author and title fields when this object
     * is constructed.
     */
    public Book(String bookAuthor, String bookTitle)
    {
        author = bookAuthor;
        title = bookTitle;
    }

    // Add the methods here ...
}
```

Exercise 2.65 Add two methods, `printAuthor` and `printTitle`, to the outline `Book` class. These should print the author and title fields, respectively, to the terminal window.

Exercise 2.66 Add a further field, `pages`, to the `Book` class to store the number of pages. This should be of type `int`, and its initial value should be passed to the single constructor, along with the `author` and `title` strings. Include an appropriate `getPages` accessor method for this field.

Exercise 2.67 Add a method, `printDetails`, to the `Book` class. This should print details of the author, title, and pages to the terminal window. It is your choice how the details are formatted. For instance, all three items could be printed on a single line, or each could be printed on a separate line. You might also choose to include some explanatory text to help a user work out which is the author and which is the title, for example

```
Title: Robinson Crusoe, Author: Daniel Defoe, Pages: 232
```

Exercise 2.68 Add a further field, `refNumber`, to the `Book` class. This field can store a reference number for a library, for example. It should be of type `String` and initialized to the zero length string (`""`) in the constructor as its initial value is not passed in a parameter to the constructor. Instead, define a mutator for it with the following signature:

```
public void setRefNumber(String ref)
```

The body of this method should assign the value of the parameter to the `refNumber` field. Add a corresponding `getRefNumber` accessor to help you check that the mutator works correctly.

Exercise 2.69 Modify your `printDetails` method to include printing the reference number. However, the method should print the reference number only if it has been set – that is, the `refNumber` string has a non-zero length. If it has not been set, then print the string `"ZZZ"` instead. *Hint:* Use a conditional statement whose test calls the `length` method on the `refNumber` string.

Exercise 2.70 Modify your `setRefNumber` mutator so that it sets the `refNumber` field only if the parameter is a string of at least three characters. If it is less than three, then print an error message and leave the field unchanged.

Exercise 2.71 Add a further integer field, `borrowed`, to the `Book` class. This keeps a count of the number of times a book has been borrowed. Add a mutator, `borrow`, to the class. This should update the field by 1 each time it is called. Include an accessor, `getBorrowed`, that returns the value of this new field as its result. Modify `printDetails` so that it includes the value of this field with an explanatory piece of text.

Exercise 2.72 *Challenge exercise* Create a new project, *heater exercise*, within BlueJ. Edit the details in the project description – the text note you see in the diagram. Create a class, `Heater`, that contains a single integer field, `temperature`. Define a constructor that takes no parameters. The `temperature` field should be set to the value 15 in the constructor. Define the mutators `warmer` and `cooler`, whose effect is to increase or decrease the value of temperature by 5° respectively. Define an accessor method to return the value of `temperature`.

Exercise 2.73 *Challenge exercise* Modify your `Heater` class to define three new integer fields: `min`, `max`, and `increment`. The values of `min` and `max` should be set by parameters passed to the constructor. The value of `increment` should be set to 5 in the constructor. Modify the definitions of `warmer` and `cooler` so that they use the value of increment rather than an explicit value of 5. Before proceeding further with this exercise, check that everything works as before. Now modify the `warmer` method so that it will not allow the temperature to be set to a value greater than `max`. Similarly modify `cooler` so that it will not allow `temperature` to be set to a value less than `min`. Check that the class works properly. Now add a method, `setIncrement`, that takes a single integer parameter and uses it to set the value of `increment`. Once again, test that the class works as you would expect it to by creating some Heater objects within BlueJ. Do things still work as expected if a negative value is passed to the `setIncrement` method? Add a check to this method to prevent a negative value from being assigned to `increment`.

Object interaction

Main concepts discussed in this chapter:

- abstraction
- modularization
- object creation
- object diagrams
- method calls
- debuggers

Java constructs discussed in this chapter:

class types, logic operators (**&&**, **||**), string concatenation, modulo operator (**%**), object construction (new), method calls (dot notation), *this*

In the previous chapters we have examined what objects are, and how they are implemented. In particular, we discussed fields, constructors, and methods when we looked at class definitions.

We shall now go one step further. To construct interesting applications it is not enough to build individual working objects. Instead, objects must be combined so that they cooperate to perform a common task. In this chapter we shall build a small application from three objects, and arrange for methods to call other methods to achieve their goal.

3.1 The clock example

The project we shall use to discuss interaction of objects is a display for a digital clock. The display shows hours and minutes, separated by a colon (Figure 3.1). For this exercise we shall first build a clock with a European-style 24-hour display. Thus the display shows the time from 00:00 (midnight) to 23:59 (one minute before midnight). It turns out on closer inspection that building a 12-hour clock is slightly more difficult – we shall leave this to the end of this chapter.

Figure 3.1
A display of a
digital clock

11:03

3.2 Abstraction and modularization

A first idea might be to implement the whole clock display in a single class. That is, after all, what we have seen so far: how to build classes to do a job.

However, here we shall approach this problem slightly differently. We will see whether we can identify subcomponents in the problem that we could turn into separate classes. The reason is *complexity*. As we progress in this book, the examples we use and the programs we build will get more and more complex. Trivial tasks like the ticket machine can be solved as a single problem. You can look at the complete task and devise a solution using a single class. For more complex problems that is too simplistic. As a problem grows larger, it becomes increasingly difficult to keep track of all details at the same time.

The solution we use to deal with the complexity problem is *abstraction*. We divide the problem into sub-problems, then again into sub-sub-problems, and so on, until the individual problems are small enough to be easy to deal with. Once we solve one of the sub-problems, we do not think about the details of that part any more, but treat the solution as a single building block for our next problem. This technique is sometimes referred to as *divide-and-conquer*.

> **Concept:**
>
> **Abstraction** is the ability to ignore details of parts to focus attention on a higher level of a problem.

Let us discuss this with an example. Imagine engineers in a car company designing a new car. They may think about the parts of the car, such as the shape of the outer body, the size and location of the engine, the number and size of the seats in the passenger area, the exact spacing of the wheels, and so on. Another engineer, on the other hand, whose job it is to design the engine (well, that's a whole team of engineers in reality, but we can simplify a bit here for the sake of the example), thinks of the many parts of an engine: the cylinders, the injection mechanism, the carburetor, the electronics, etc. She will think of the engine not as a single entity, but as a complex work of many parts. One of these parts may be a spark plug.

Then there is an engineer (maybe in a different company) who designs the spark plugs. He will think of the spark plug as a complex artifact of many parts. He might have done complex studies to determine exactly what kind of metal to use for the contacts, or what kind of material and production process to use for the insulation.

The same is true for many other parts. A designer at the highest level will regard a wheel as a single part. Another engineer much further down the chain may spend her days thinking about the chemical composition to produce the right materials to make the tires. For the tire engineer the tire is a complex thing. The car company will just buy the tire from the tire company, and then view it as a single entity. This is abstraction.

The engineer in the car company *abstracts from* the details of the tire manufacture to be able to concentrate on the details of the construction of, say, the wheel. The designer designing the body shape of the car abstracts from the technical details of the wheels and the engine to concentrate on the design of the body (he will just be interested in the size of the engine and the wheels).

The same is true for every other component. While someone might be concerned with designing the interior passenger space, someone else may work on developing the fabric that will eventually be used to cover the seats.

The point is: if viewed in enough detail, a car consists of so many parts that it is impossible for a single person to know every detail about every part at the same time. If that were necessary, no car could ever be built.

Concept:

Modularization is the process of dividing a whole into well-defined parts, which can be built and examined separately, and which interact in well-defined ways.

The reason why cars are built successfully is that the engineers use *modularization* and abstraction. They divide the car into independent modules (wheel, engine, gear box, seat, steering wheel, etc.) and get separate people to work on separate modules independently. When a module is built, they use abstraction. They view that module as a single component that is used to build more complex components.

Modularization and abstraction thus complement each other. Modularization is the process of dividing large things (problems) into smaller parts, while abstraction is the ability to ignore details to focus on the bigger picture.

3.3 Abstraction in software

The same principles of modularization and abstraction discussed in the previous section are used in software development. To help us maintain an overview in complex programs, we try to identify subcomponents that we can program as independent entities. Then we try to use those subcomponents as if they were simple parts without being concerned about their inner complexities.

In object-oriented programming these components and subcomponents are objects. If we were trying to construct a car in software, using an object-oriented language, we would try to do what the car engineers do. Instead of implementing the car in a single, monolithic object, we would first construct separate objects for an engine, gearbox, wheel, seat, and so on, and then assemble the car object from those smaller objects.

Identifying what kinds of objects (and with these, classes) you should have in a software system for any given problem is not always easy, and we shall have a lot more to say about that later in this book. For now, we shall start with a relatively simple example. Now, back to our digital clock.

3.4 Modularization in the clock example

Let us have a closer look at the clock-display example. Using the abstraction concepts we have just described we want to try to find the best way to view this example so that we can write some classes to implement it. One way to look at it is to consider it as consisting of a single display with four digits (two digits for the hours, two for the minutes). If we now abstract away from that very low-level view, we can see that it could also be viewed as two separate two-digit displays (one pair for the hours and one pair for the minutes). One pair starts at zero, increases by one each hour and rolls back to zero after reaching its limit of 23. The other rolls back to zero after reaching its limit of 59. The similarity in behavior of these two displays might then lead us to abstract away even further from viewing the hours display and minutes display distinctly. Instead we might think of them as being objects that can display values from 0 up to a given limit. The value can be incremented, but, if the value reaches the limit, it rolls over back to zero. Now we seem to have reached an appropriate level of abstraction that we can represent as a class: a two-digit display class.

For our clock display we shall first program a class for a two-digit number display (Figure 3.2), and give it an accessor method to get its value and two mutator methods to set the value and to increment it. Once we have defined this class, we can just create two objects of this class with different limits to construct the whole clock display.

Figure 3.2
A two-digit number
display

```
03
```

3.5 Implementing the clock display

As discussed above, in order to build the clock display we will first build a two-digit number display. This display needs to store two values. One is the limit to which it can count before rolling over to zero. The other is the current value. We shall represent both of these as integer fields in our class (Code 3.1).

Code 3.1
Class for a two-digit
number display

```
public class NumberDisplay
{
    private int limit;
    private int value;

    Constructor and methods omitted.

}
```

Concept:

**Classes define
types.** A class
name can be used
as the type for a
variable. Variables
that have a class as
their type can store
objects of that
class.

We shall look at the remaining details of this class later. First, let us assume that we can build the class `NumberDisplay`, and think a bit more about the complete clock display. We would build a complete clock display by having an object that has, internally, two number displays (one for the hours and one for the minutes). Each of the number displays would be a field in the clock display (Code 3.2). Here, we make use of a detail that we have not mentioned before: *classes define types*.

Code 3.2
The `ClockDisplay`
class containing two
`NumberDisplays`

```
public class ClockDisplay
{
    private NumberDisplay hours;
    private NumberDisplay minutes;

    Constructor and methods omitted.

}
```

When we discussed fields in Chapter 2, we said that the word 'private' in the field declaration is followed by a type and a name for the field. Here we use the class `NumberDisplay` as the type for the fields named `hours` and `minutes`. This shows that class names can be used as types.

The type of a field specifies what kind of values can be stored in the field. If the type is a class, the field can hold objects of that class.

3.6 Class diagrams versus object diagrams

The structure described in the previous section (one `ClockDisplay` object holding two `NumberDisplay` objects) can be visualized in an *object diagram* as shown in Figure 3.3a. In this diagram, you see that we are dealing with three objects. Figure 3.3b shows the *class diagram* for the same situation.

Figure 3.3 Object diagram and class diagram for the `ClockDisplay`

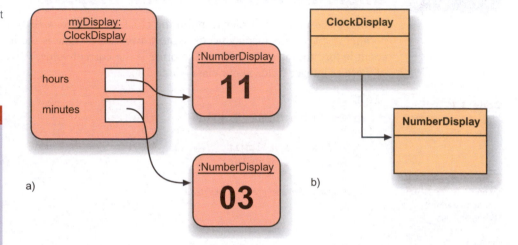

a)

b)

Note that the class diagram shows only two classes, whereas the object diagram shows three objects. This has to do with the fact that we can create multiple objects from the same class. Here, we create two `NumberDisplay` objects from the `NumberDisplay` class (Code 3.3).

These two diagrams offer different views of the same application. The class diagram shows the *static* view. It depicts what we have at the time of writing the program. We have two classes, and the arrow indicates that the class `ClockDisplay` makes use of the class `NumberDisplay` (that is, `NumberDisplay` is mentioned in the source code of `ClockDisplay`). We also say that `ClockDisplay` *depends on* `NumberDisplay`.

To start the program, we will create an object of class `ClockDisplay`. We will program the clock display so that it automatically creates two `NumberDisplay` objects for itself. Thus the object diagram shows the situation at *runtime* (when the application is running). This is also called the *dynamic view*.

The object diagram also shows another important detail: when a variable stores an object, the object is not stored in the variable directly, but rather an *object reference* is stored in the variable. In the diagram, the variable is shown as a white box, and the object reference is shown as an arrow. The object referred to is stored outside the referring object, and the object reference links the two.

It is very important to understand these two different diagrams and different views. BlueJ displays only the static view. You see the class diagram in its main window. In order to plan and understand Java programs you need to be able to construct object diagrams on paper or in your head. When we think about what our program will do, we will think

Code 3.3

Implementation of the `NumberDisplay` class

```java
/**
 * The NumberDisplay class represents a digital number
 * display that can hold values from zero to a given limit.
 * The limit can be specified when creating the display. The
 * values range from zero (inclusive) to limit-1. If used, for
 * example, for the seconds on a digital clock, the limit
 * would be 60, resulting in display values from 0 to 59.
 * When incremented, the display automatically rolls over to
 * zero when reaching the limit.
 *
 * @author Michael Kölling and David J. Barnes
 * @version 2001.05.26
 */
public class NumberDisplay
{
    private int limit;
    private int value;

    /**
     * Constructor for objects of class Display
     */
    public NumberDisplay(int rollOverLimit)
    {
        limit = rollOverLimit;
        value = 0;
    }

    /**
     * Return the current value.
     */
    public int getValue()
    {
        return value;
    }

    /**
     * Set the value of the display to the new specified
     * value. If the new value is less than zero or over the
     * limit, do nothing.
     */
    public void setValue(int replacementValue)
    {
        if((replacementValue >= 0) &&
        (replacementValue < limit))
            value = replacementValue;
    }

    /**
     * Return the display value (that is, the current value
     * as a two-digit String. If the value is less than ten,
     * it will be padded with a leading zero).
```

Code 3.3 continued

Implementation of the `NumberDisplay` class

```java
        */
    public String getDisplayValue()
    {
        if(value < 10)
            return "0" + value;
        else
            return "" + value;
    }

    /**
     * Increment the display value by one, rolling over to zero if
     * the limit is reached.
     */
    public void increment()
    {
        value = (value + 1) % limit;
    }
}
```

about the object structures it creates, and how these objects interact. Being able to visualize the object structures is essential.

Exercise 3.1 Think again about the *lab-classes* project that we discussed in Chapter 1 and Chapter 2. Imagine we create a `LabClass` object and three `Student` objects. We then enroll all three students in that lab. Try to draw a class diagram and an object diagram for that situation. Identify and explain the differences between them.

Exercise 3.2 At what time(s) can a class diagram change? How is it changed?

Exercise 3.3 At what time(s) can an object diagram change? How is it changed?

Exercise 3.4 Write a definition of a field named `tutor` that can hold references to objects of type `Instructor`.

3.7 Primitive types and object types

Concept:

The **primitive types** in Java are the non-object types. Types such as `int`, `boolean`, `char`, `double` and `long` are the most common primitive types. Primitive types have no methods.

Java knows two very different kinds of type: *primitive types* and *object types*. Primitive types are all predefined in the Java language. They include `int` and `boolean`. A complete list of primitive types is given in Appendix B. Object types are those defined by classes. Some classes are defined by the standard Java system (such as `String`); others are those classes we write ourselves. Both primitive types and object types can be used as types, but there are situations in which they behave differently. One difference is how values are stored. As we could see from our diagrams, primitive values are stored directly in a variable (we have written the value directly into the variable box, for example in Chapter 2, Figure 2.3). Objects, on the other hand, are not stored directly in the variable, but instead a reference to the object is stored (drawn as an arrow in our diagrams, Figure 3.3a).

We will see other differences between primitive types and object types later.

3.8 The `ClockDisplay` source code

Before we start to analyze the source code, it will help if you have a look at the example yourself.

> **Exercise 3.5** Start BlueJ, open the *clock-display* example and experiment with it. To use it, create a `ClockDisplay` object, then open an inspector window for this object. With the inspector open, call the object's methods. Watch the `displayString` field in the inspector. Read the project comment (by double-clicking the text note icon on the main screen) to get more information.

3.8.1 Class `NumberDisplay`

We shall now analyze a complete implementation of this task. The project *clock-display* in the examples attached to this book contains the solution. First, we shall look at the implementation of the class `NumberDisplay`. Code 3.3 shows the complete source code. Overall, this class is fairly straightforward. It has the two fields discussed above (section 3.5), one constructor, and four methods (`getValue`, `setValue`, `getDisplayValue`, and `increment`).

The constructor receives the roll-over limit as a parameter. If, for example, 24 is passed in as the roll-over limit, the display will roll over to zero at that value. Thus the range for the display value would be zero to 23. This allows us to use this class for both hour and minute displays. For the hour display we will create a `NumberDisplay` with limit 24; for the minute display we will create one with limit 60.

The constructor then stores the roll-over limit in a field and sets the current value of the display to zero.

Next follows a simple accessor method for the current display value (`getValue`). This allows other objects to read the current value of the display.

The following mutator method `setValue` is more interesting. It reads:

```java
public void setValue(int replacementValue)
{
    if((replacementValue >= 0) && (replacementValue < limit))
        value = replacementValue;
}
```

Here, we pass the new value for the display as a parameter into the method. However, before we assign the value, we have to check whether the value is legal. The legal range for the value, as discussed above, is zero to one below the limit. We use an if statement to check that the value is legal before we assign it. The symbol '&&' is a logical 'and' operator. It causes the condition in the if statement to be true if both the conditions on either side of the '&&' symbol are true. See the 'Logic operators' note that follows for details. Appendix D shows a complete table of logic operators in Java.

Logic operators Logic operators operate on boolean values (true or false) and produce a new boolean value as a result. The three most important logical operators are **and**, **or** and **not**. They are written in Java as:

&& (and)
|| (or)
! (not)

The expression

  a && b

is true if **a** and **b** both are true, and false in all other cases. The expression

  a || b

is true if either **a** or **b** or both are true, and false if they are both false. The expression

  !a

is true if **a** is false, and false if **a** is true.

Exercise 3.6 What happens when the `setValue` method is called with an illegal value? Is this a good solution? Can you think of a better solution?

Exercise 3.7 What would happen if you replaced the '>=' operator in the test with '>', so that it read

```
if((replacementValue > 0) && (replacementValue < limit))
```

Exercise 3.8 What would happen if you replaced the '&&' operator in the test with '||', so that it read

```
if((replacementValue >= 0) || (replacementValue < limit))
```

Exercise 3.9 Which of the following expressions return *true*?

```
! (4 < 5)
! false
(2 > 2) || ((4 == 4) && (1 < 0))
(2 > 2) || (4 == 4) && (1 < 0)
(34 != 33) && ! false
```

Exercise 3.10 Write an expression using boolean variables **a** and **b** that evaluates to *true* when either **a** and **b** are both *true* or both *false*.

Exercise 3.11 Write an expression using boolean variables **a** and **b** that evaluates to *true* when only one of **a** and **b** is *true*, and which is *false* if **a** and **b** are both *false* or both *true*. (This is also called an *exclusive or*.)

Exercise 3.12 Consider the expression (a && b). Write an equivalent expression (one that evaluates to *true* at exactly the same values for **a** and **b**) without using the && operator.

The next method, getDisplayValue, also returns the display's value, but in a different format. The reason is that we want to display the value as a two-digit string. That is, if the current time is 3:05 a.m., we want the display to read 03:05, and not 3:5. To enable us to do this easily, we have implemented the getDisplayValue method. This method returns the current value as a string, and it adds a leading zero if the value is less than 10. Here is the relevant section of the code:

```
if(value < 10)
    return "0" + value;
else
    return "" + value;
```

Note that the zero ("0") is written in double quotes. Thus we have written the *string* 0, not the *integer number* 0. Then the expression

```
"0" + value
```

'adds' a string and an integer (since the type of value is integer). Thus the plus operator represents string concatenation again, as seen in section 2.8. Before continuing, we will now look at string concatenation a little more closely.

3.8.2 String concatenation

The plus operator (+) has different meanings, depending on the type of its operands. If both operands are numbers, it represents addition, as we would expect. Thus:

```
42 + 12
```

adds those two numbers, and the result is 54. However, if the operands are strings, then the meaning of the plus sign is string concatenation, and the result is a single string that consists of both operands stuck together. For example, the result of the expression

```
"Java" + "with BlueJ"
```

is the single string

```
"Javawith BlueJ"
```

Note that the system does not automatically add a space between the strings. If you want a space, you have to include it yourself within one of the strings.

If one of the operands of a plus operation is a string, and the other is not, then the other operator is automatically converted to a string, and then a string concatenation is performed. Thus

```
"answer: " + 42
```

results in the string

```
"answer: 42"
```

This works for all types. Whatever type is 'added' to a string is automatically converted to a string and then concatenated.

Back to our code in the getDisplayValue method. If value contains 3, for example, then the statement

```
return "0" + value;
```

will return the string `"03"`. In the case where the value is greater than 9, we have used a little trick:

```
return "" + value;
```

Here, we concatenate `value` with an empty string. The result is that the value will be converted to a string, and no other characters will be prefixed to it. We are using the plus operator for the sole purpose of forcing a conversion of the integer value to a value of type `String`.

> **Exercise 3.13** Does the `getDisplayValue` method work correctly in all circumstances? What assumptions are made within it? What happens if you create a number display with limit 800, for instance?
>
> **Exercise 3.14** Is there any difference in the result of writing
>
> ```
> return value + "";
> ```
>
> rather than
>
> ```
> return "" + value;
> ```
>
> in the `getDisplayValue` method?

3.8.3 The modulo operator

The last method in the `NumberDisplay` class increments the display value by 1. It takes care that the value resets to zero when the limit is reached:

```
public void increment()
{
    value = (value + 1) % limit;
}
```

This method uses the *modulo* operator (`%`). The modulo operator calculates the remainder of an integer division. For example, the result of the division

```
27 / 4
```

can be expressed in integer numbers as

```
result = 6, remainder = 3
```

The modulo operator returns just the remainder of such a division. Thus the result of the expression (`27 % 4`) would be 3.

> **Exercise 3.15** Explain the modulo operator. You may need to consult more resources (online Java language resources, other Java books, etc.) to find out the details.
>
> **Exercise 3.16** What is the result of the expression (`8 % 3`)?
>
> **Exercise 3.17** What are all possible results of the expression (`n % 5`), where `n` is an integer variable?

Exercise 3.18 What are all possible results of the expression (n % m), where n and m are integer variables?

Exercise 3.19 Explain in detail how the increment method works.

Exercise 3.20 Rewrite the increment method without the modulo operator, using an if statement. Which solution is better?

Exercise 3.21 Using the *clock-display* project in BlueJ, test the `NumberDisplay` class by creating a few `NumberDisplay` objects and calling their methods.

3.8.4 Class `ClockDisplay`

Now that we have seen how we can build a class that defines a two-digit number display, we shall look in more detail at the `ClockDisplay` class – the class that will create two number displays to create a full time display. Code 3.4 shows the complete source code of the `ClockDisplay` class.

As with the `NumberDisplay` class, we shall briefly discuss all fields, constructors, and methods.

Code 3.4

Implementation of the `ClockDisplay` class

```java
/**
 * The ClockDisplay class implements a digital clock display
 * for a European-style 24 hour clock. The clock shows hours
 * and minutes.
 * The range of the clock is 00:00 (midnight) to 23:59 (one
 * minute before midnight).
 *
 * The clock display receives "ticks" (via the timeTick
 * method) every minute and reacts by incrementing the
 * display. This is done in the usual clock fashion: the hour
 * increments when the minutes roll over to zero.
 *
 * @author Michael Kölling and David J. Barnes
 * @version 2001.05.26
 */
public class ClockDisplay
{
    private NumberDisplay hours;
    private NumberDisplay minutes;
    private String displayString; // simulates the actual display

    /**
     * Constructor for ClockDisplay objects. This constructor
     * creates a new clock set at 00:00.
     */
```

**Code 3.4
continued**
Implementation of
the `ClockDisplay`
class

```java
public ClockDisplay()
{
    hours = new NumberDisplay(24);
    minutes = new NumberDisplay(60);
    updateDisplay();
}

/**
 * Constructor for ClockDisplay objects. This constructor
 * creates a new clock set at the time specified by the
 * parameters.
 */
public ClockDisplay(int hour, int minute)
{
    hours = new NumberDisplay(24);
    minutes = new NumberDisplay(60);
    setTime(hour, minute);
}

/**
 * This method should get called once every minute - it
 * makes the clock display go one minute forward.
 */
public void timeTick()
{
    minutes.increment();
    if(minutes.getValue() == 0) { // it just rolled over!
        hours.increment();
    }
    updateDisplay();
}

/**
 * Set the time of the display to the specified hour and
 * minute.
 */
public void setTime(int hour, int minute)
{
    hours.setValue(hour);
    minutes.setValue(minute);
    updateDisplay();
}

/**
 * Return the current time of this display in the format
 * HH:MM.
 */
```

**Code 3.4
continued**

Implementation of
the `ClockDisplay`
class

```java
    public String getTime()
    {
        return displayString;
    }


    /**
     * Update the internal string that represents the
     * display.
     */
    private void updateDisplay()
    {
        displayString = hours.getDisplayValue() + ":" +
                        minutes.getDisplayValue();

    }
}
```

In this project, we use the field `displayString` to simulate the actual display device of the clock (as you could see in exercise 3.5). Were this software to run in a real clock, we would present the output on the real clock display instead. So this string serves as our software simulation for the clock's output device.

To achieve this, we use one string field and a method:

```java
public class ClockDisplay
{
    private String displayString;

    Other fields and methods omitted.

    /**
     * Update the internal string that represents the display.
     */
    private void updateDisplay()
    {
        Method implementation omitted.
    }
}
```

Whenever we want the display of the clock to change, we shall call the internal method `updateDisplay`. In our simulation, this method will change the display string (we will examine the source code to do this below). In a real clock, this method would also exist – there it would change the real clock display.

Apart from the display string, the `ClockDisplay` class has only two more fields: `hours` and `minutes`. Each of these fields can hold an object of type `NumberDisplay`. The logical value of the clock's display (the current time) is stored in these `NumberDisplay` objects. Figure 3.4 shows an object diagram of this application when the current time is 15:23.

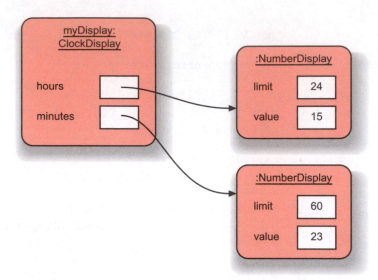

3.9 Objects creating objects

The first question we have to ask ourselves is: Where do these three objects come from? When we want to use a clock display, we might create a `ClockDisplay` object. We then assume that our clock display has hours and minutes. So by simply creating a clock display, we expect that we have implicitly created two number displays for the hours and minutes.

As writers of the `ClockDisplay` class, we have to make this happen. We simply write code in the constructor of the `ClockDisplay` that creates and stores two `NumberDisplay` objects. Since the constructor is automatically executed when a `ClockDisplay` object is created, the `NumberDisplay` objects will automatically be created at the same time. Here is the code of the `ClockDisplay` constructor that makes this work:

```
public class ClockDisplay
{
    private NumberDisplay hours;
    private NumberDisplay minutes;

    Remaining fields omitted.

    public ClockDisplay()
    {
        hours = new NumberDisplay(24);
        minutes = new NumberDisplay(60);
        updateDisplay();
    }

    Methods omitted.
}
```

Each of the first two lines in the constructor creates a new `NumberDisplay` object and assigns it to a variable. The syntax of an operation to create a new object is

```
new ClassName ( parameter-list )
```

The new operation does two things:

1. It creates a new object of the named class (here: `NumberDisplay`).
2. It executes the constructor of that class.

If the constructor of the class is defined to have parameters, then the actual parameters must be supplied in the `new` statement. For instance, the constructor of class `NumberDisplay` was defined to expect one integer parameter:

formal parameter

```
public NumberDisplay (int rollOverLimit)
```

Thus the new operation for the `NumberDisplay` class, which calls this constructor, must provide one actual parameter of type `int` to match the defined constructor header:

actual parameter

```
new NumberDisplay (24);
```

This is the same as for methods discussed in section 2.4. With this constructor, we have achieved what we wanted: if someone now creates a `ClockDisplay` object, the `ClockDisplay` constructor will automatically execute and create two `NumberDisplay` objects. Then the clock display is ready to go.

Exercise 3.22 Create a `ClockDisplay` object by selecting the following constructor:

```
new ClockDisplay()
```

Call its `getTime` method to find out the initial time the clock has been set to. Can you work out why it starts at that particular time?

Exercise 3.23 How many times would you need to call the `tick` method on a newly created `ClockDisplay` object to make its time reach 01:00? How else could you make it display that time?

Exercise 3.24 Write the signature of a constructor that matches the following object creation instruction:

```
new Editor("readme.txt", −1)
```

Exercise 3.25 Write Java statements that define a variable named `window` of type `Rectangle`, and then create a rectangle object and assign it to that variable. The rectangle constructor has two `int` parameters.

3.10 Multiple constructors

You might have noticed when you created a `ClockDisplay` object that the popup menu offered you two ways to do that:

```
new ClockDisplay()
new ClockDisplay(hour, minute)
```

This is because the `ClockDisplay` class contains two constructors. What they provide are alternative ways of initializing a `ClockDisplay` object. If the constructor with no parameters is used, then the starting time displayed on the clock will be 00:00. If, on the other hand, you want to have a different starting time, you can set that up by using the second constructor. It is common for class definitions to contain alternative versions of constructors or methods that provide various ways of achieving a particular task via their distinctive sets of parameters. This is known as *overloading* a constructor or method.

> **Exercise 3.26** Look at the second constructor in `ClockDisplay`'s source code. Explain what it does and how it does it.
>
> **Exercise 3.27** Identify the similarities and differences between the two constructors. Why is there no call to `updateDisplay` in the second constructor, for instance?

3.11 Method calls

3.11.1 Internal method calls

The last line of the first `ClockDisplay` constructor consists of the statement

```
updateDisplay();
```

This statement is a *method call*. As we have seen above, the `ClockDisplay` class has a method with the following signature:

```
private void updateDisplay()
```

The method call above invokes this method. Since this method is in the same class as the call of the method, we also call it an *internal method call*. Internal method calls have the syntax

```
methodName ( parameter-list )
```

In our example, the method does not have any parameters, so the parameter list is empty. This is signified by the set of parentheses with nothing between them.

When a method call is encountered, the matching method is executed, and then execution returns to the method call and continues at the next statement after the call. For a method signature to match the method call, both the name and the parameter list of the method must match. Here, both parameter lists are empty, so they match. This need to match against both method name and parameter lists is important because there may be more than one method of the same name in a class – if that method is overloaded.

In our example, the purpose of this method call is to update the display string. After the two number displays have been created, the display string is set to show the time indicated by the number display objects. The implementation of the `updateDisplay` method will be discussed below.

3.11.2 External method calls

Now let us examine the next method: `timeTick`. The definition is:

```
public void timeTick()
{
    minutes.increment();
    if(minutes.getValue() == 0) {  // it just rolled over!
        hours.increment();
    }
    updateDisplay();
}
```

Concept:

Methods can call methods of other objects using dot notation. This is called an **external method call**.

Were this display connected to a real clock, this method would be called once every 60 seconds by the electronic timer of the clock. For now, we just call it ourselves to test the display.

When the `timeTick` method is called, it first executes the statement

```
minutes.increment();
```

This statement calls the `increment` method of the `minutes` object. Thus, when one of the methods of the `ClockDisplay` object is called, it in turn calls a method of another object to do part of the task. A method call to a method of another object is referred to as an *external method call*. The syntax of an external method call is

```
object . methodName ( parameter-list )
```

This syntax is known as *dot notation*. It consists of an object name, a dot, the method name, and parameters for the call. It is particularly important to appreciate that we use the name of an *object* here and not the name of a class. We use the name `minutes` rather than `NumberDisplay`.

The `timeTick` method then has an if statement to check whether the hours should also be incremented. As part of the condition in the if statement, it calls another method of the minutes object: `getValue`. This method returns the current value of the minutes. If that value is zero, then we know that the display just rolled over, and we should increment the hours. That is exactly what the code does.

If the value of the minutes is not zero, then we're done. We don't have to change the hours in that case. Thus the if statement does not need an *else* part.

We should now also be able to understand the remaining three methods of the `ClockDisplay` class (see Code 3.4). The method `setTime` takes two parameters – the hour and the minute – and sets the clock to the specified time. Looking at the method body, we can see that it does so by calling the `setValue` methods of both number displays, the one for the hours and the one for the minutes. Then it calls `updateDisplay` to update the display string accordingly, just as the constructor does.

The `getTime` method is trivial – it just returns the current display string. Since we always keep the display string up to date, this is all there is to do.

Finally, the `updateDisplay` method is responsible for updating the display string so that the string correctly reflects the time as represented by the two number display objects. It is called every time the time of the clock changes. It works by calling the `getDisplayValue` methods of each of the `NumberDisplay` objects. These methods return the value of each separate number display. It then uses string concatenation to concatenate these two values with a colon in the middle to a single string.

Exercise 3.28 Given a variable

```
Printer p1;
```

which currently holds a printer object, and two methods inside the `Printer` class with the headers

```
public void print(String filename, boolean doubeSided)
public int getStatus(int delay)
```

write two possible calls to each of these methods.

3.11.3 Summary of the clock display

It is worth looking for a minute at the way this example uses abstraction to divide the problem into smaller parts. Looking at the source code of the class `ClockDisplay`, you will notice that we just create a `NumberDisplay` object without being particularly interested in what that object looks like internally. We can then just call methods (`increment`, `getValue`) of that object to make it work for us. At this level, we just assume that `increment` will correctly increment the display's value, without being concerned with how it does it.

In real-world projects, these different classes are often written by different people. You might already have noticed that all these two people have to agree on is what method signatures the class should have and what they should do. Then one person can concentrate on implementing the methods, while the other person can just use them.

The set of methods an object makes available to other objects is called its *interface*. We shall discuss interfaces in much more detail later in this book.

Exercise 3.29 *Challenge exercise* Change the clock from a 24-hour clock to a 12-hour clock. Be careful: this is not as easy as it might at first seem. In a 12-hour clock the hours after midnight and after noon are not shown as 00:30, but as 12:30. Thus the minute display shows values from 0 to 59, while the hour display shows values from 1 to 12!

Exercise 3.30 There are (at least) two ways in which you can make a 12-hour clock. One possibility is to just store hour values from 1 to 12. On the other hand, you can just leave the clock to work internally as a 24-hour clock, but change the display string of the clock display to show **4:23** or **4.23pm** when the internal value is **16:23**. Implement both versions. Which option is easier? Which is better? Why?

3.12 Another example of object interaction

We shall now examine the same concepts with a different example, using different tools. We are still concerned with understanding how objects create other objects, and how objects call each other's methods. In the first half of this chapter we have used the most fundamental technique to analyze a given program: code reading. The ability to read and understand source code is one of the most essential skills for a software developer, and

Concept:

A **debugger** is a software tool that helps in examining how an application executes. It can be used to find bugs.

we will need to apply it in every project we work on. However, sometimes it is beneficial to use additional tools in order to help us gain a deeper understanding about how a program executes. One tool we will now look at is a **debugger**.

A debugger is a program that lets programmers execute an application one step at a time. It typically provides functions to stop and start a program at selected points in the source code, and to examine the values of variables.

The name 'debugger' Errors in computer programs are commonly known as 'bugs.' Thus programs that help in the removal of errors are known as 'debuggers.'

It is not entirely clear where the term 'bug' comes from. There is a famous case of what is known as 'The first computer bug' – a real bug (a moth, in fact) that was found inside the Mark II computer by Grace Murray Hopper, an early computing pioneer, in 1945. A logbook still exists in the National Museum of American History of the Smithsonian Institute that shows an entry with this moth taped into the book and the remark 'first actual case of a bug being found.' The wording, however, suggests that the term 'bug' had been in use before this real one caused trouble in the Mark II.

To find out more, do a web search for 'first computer bug' – you will even find pictures of the moth!

Debuggers vary widely in complexity. Those for professional developers have a large number of functions useful for sophisticated examination of many facets of an application. BlueJ has a built-in debugger that is much simpler. We can use it to stop our program, step through it one line of code at a time, and examine the values of our variables. Despite the debugger's apparent lack of sophistication, this is enough to give us a great deal of information.

Before we start experimenting with the debugger we will take a look at the example we will use for debugging: a simulation of an email system.

3.12.1 The mail system example

We start by investigating the functionality of the *mail-system* project. At this stage it is not important to read the source, but mainly to execute the existing project to get an understanding of what it does.

Exercise 3.31 Open the *mail-system* project, which you can find in the book's support material. Create a `MailServer` object. Create two `MailClient` objects. When doing this, you need to supply the `MailServer` instance, which you just created, as a parameter. You also need to specify a username for the mail client. (A mail client is a program to read and write email. Every instance you create represents an email program for a different user.)

Experiment with the `MailClient` objects. They can be used to send messages from one mail client to another (using the `sendMessage` method) and to receive messages (using the `getNextMailItem` or `printNextMailItem` methods).

Examining the mail system project we see that:

- It has three classes: `MailServer`, `MailClient`, and `MailItem`.

- One mail server object must be created that is used by all mail clients. It handles the exchange of messages.

- Several mail client objects can be created. Every mail client has an associated user name.

- Messages can be sent from one mail client to another via a method in the mail client class.

- Messages can be received by a mail client from the server one at a time, using a method in the mail client.

- The `MailItem` class is never instantiated explicitly by the user. It is used internally in the mail clients and server to store and exchange messages.

> **Exercise 3.32** Draw an object diagram of the situation you have after creating a mail server and three mail clients. Object diagrams were discussed in section 3.6.

The three classes have different degrees of complexity. `MailItem` is fairly trivial. We shall discuss only one small detail, and leave the rest up to the reader to investigate. `MailServer` is quite complex at this stage – it makes use of concepts discussed only much later in this book. We shall not investigate that class in detail here. Instead, we just trust that it does its job – another example of the way abstraction is used to hide detail that we do not need to be aware of.

The `MailClient` class is the most interesting, and we shall examine it in some detail.

3.12.2   The `this` key word

The only section we will discuss from the `MailItem` class is the constructor. It uses a Java construct that we have not encountered before. The source code is shown in Code 3.5.

Code 3.5
Fields and constructor of the `MailItem` class

```java
public class MailItem
{
    // The sender of the item.
    private String from;
    // The intended recipient.
    private String to;
    // The text of the message.
    private String message;

    /**
     * Create a mail item from sender to the given recipient,
     * containing the given message.
     * @param from    The sender of this item.
     * @param to      The intended recipient of this item.
```

**Code 3.5
continued**

Fields and
constructor of the
MailItem class

```
     * @param message The text of the message to be sent.
     */
    public MailItem(String from, String to, String message)
    {
        this.from = from;
        this.to = to;
        this.message = message;
    }


    Methods omitted.

}
```

The new Java feature in this code fragment is the use of the this key word:

```
    this.from = from;
```

The whole line is an assignment statement. It assigns the value from the right-hand side (from) to the variable on the left (this.from).

The reason for using this construct is that we have a situation that is known as *name overloading* – the same name being used for two different entities. The class contains three fields, named from, to, and message. The constructor has three parameters, also named from, to, and message!

So while we are executing the constructor, how many variables exist? The answer is six – three fields and three parameters. It is important to understand that the fields and the parameters are separate variables that exist independently of each other, even though they share similar names. A parameter and a field sharing a name is not really a problem in Java.

The problem we do have, though, is how to reference the six variables so as to be able to distinguish between the two sets. If we simply use the variable name 'from' in the constructor (for example in a statement System.out.println(from)), which variable will be used – the parameter or the field?

The Java specification answers this question. It specifies that the definition from the closest enclosing block will always be used. Since the from parameter is defined in the constructor, and the from field is defined in the class, the parameter will be used. Its definition is 'closer' to the statement that uses it.

Now all we need is a mechanism to access a field when there is a more closely defined variable with the same name. That is what the this key word is used for. The expression this refers to the current object. Writing this.from refers to the from field in the current object. Thus this construct gives us a means to refer to the field instead of the parameter with the same name. Now we can read the assignment statement again:

```
    this.from = from;
```

This statement, as we can see now, has the following effect:

field named "from" = *parameter named* "from";

In other words, it assigns the value from the parameter to the field with the same name. This is, of course, exactly what we need to do to initialize the object properly.

One last question remains: why are we doing this at all? The whole problem could easily be avoided just by giving the fields and the parameters different names. The reason is readability of source code.

Sometimes there is one name that perfectly describes the use of a variable. It fits so well that we do not want to invent a different name for it. We want to use it for the parameter, where it serves as a hint to the caller indicating what needs to be passed, and we want to use it for the field, where it is useful as a reminder for the implementer of the class, indicating what the field is used for. If one name perfectly describes the use, it is reasonable to use it for both and to go through the trouble of using the `this` key word in the assignment to resolve the name conflict.

3.13 Using a debugger

The most interesting class in the mail system example is the mail client. We shall now investigate it in more detail by using a debugger. The mail client has three methods: `getNextMailItem`, `printNextMailItem`, and `sendMessage`. We will first investigate the `printNextMailItem` method.

Before we start with the debugger, set up a scenario we can use to investigate (exercise 3.33).

> **Exercise 3.33** Set up a scenario for investigation: Create a mail server, then create two mail clients for the users 'Sophie' and 'Juan' (you should name the instances 'sophie' and 'juan' as well, so that you can better distinguish them on the object bench). Then use Sophie's `sendMessage` method to send a message to Juan. Do not yet read the message.

After the setup in exercise 3.33, we have a situation where one mail item is stored on the server for Juan, waiting to be picked up. We have seen that the `printNextMailItem` method picks up this mail item and prints it to the terminal. Now we want to investigate exactly how this works.

3.13.1 Setting breakpoints

To start our investigation, we set a breakpoint (exercise 3.34). A breakpoint is a flag attached to a line of source code that will stop the execution of a method at that point when it is reached. It is represented in the BlueJ editor as a small stop sign (Figure 3.5).

You can set a breakpoint by opening the BlueJ editor, selecting the appropriate line (in our case the first line of the `printNextMailItem` method), and selecting 'Set Breakpoint' from the Tools menu. You can also just click into the area next to the line of code where the breakpoint symbol appears to set or remove breakpoints. Note that the class has to be compiled to do this, and that recompiling will remove all breakpoints.

> **Exercise 3.34** Open the editor for the `MailClient` class and set a breakpoint at the first line of the `printNextMailItem` method, as shown in Figure 3.5.

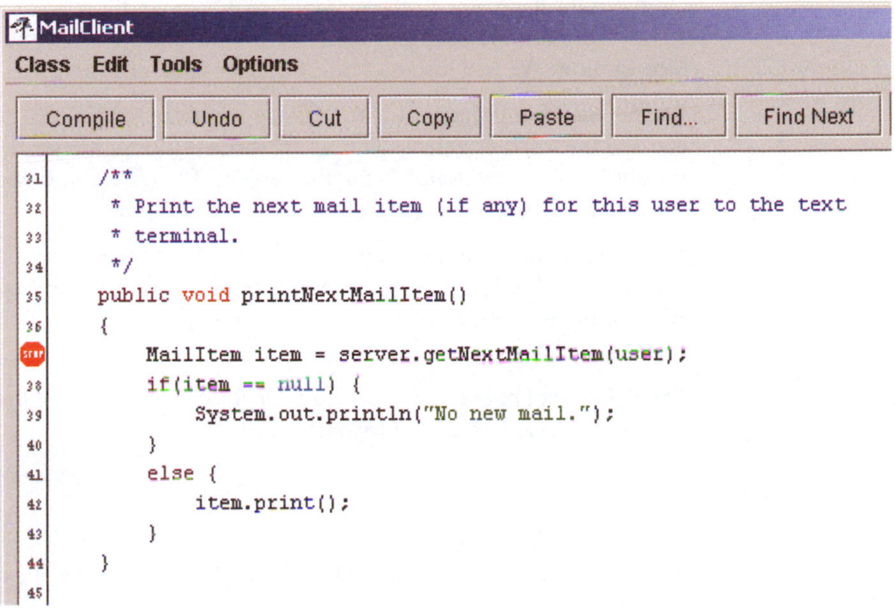

Figure 3.5

A breakpoint in the BlueJ editor

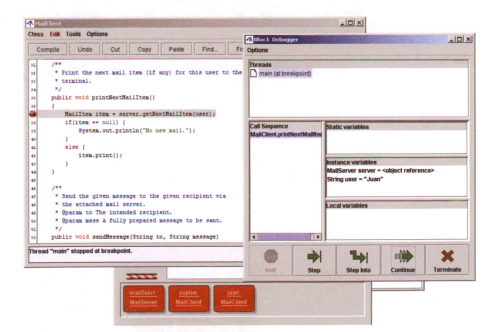

Once you have set the breakpoint, invoke the `printNextMailItem` method on Juan's mail client. The editor window for the `MailClient` class and a debugger window will pop up (Figure 3.6).

Along the bottom of the debugger window are some control buttons. They can be used to continue or interrupt the execution of the program. (For a more detailed explanation of the debugger controls, see Appendix G.)

Figure 3.6

The debugger window, execution stopped at a breakpoint

On the right-hand side of the debugger window are three areas for variable display, titled *static variables*, *instance variables*, and *local variables*. We will ignore the static variable area for now. We will discuss static variables later, and this class does not have any.

We see that this object has two instance variables (or fields), `server` and `user`, and we can see the current values. The `user` variable stores the string `"Juan"`, and the server variable stores a reference to another object. The object reference is what we have drawn as an arrow in the object diagrams.

Note that there is no local variable yet. This is because execution stops *before* the line with the breakpoint is executed. Since the line with the breakpoint contains the declaration of the only local variable, and that line has not yet been executed, no local variable exists at the moment.

The debugger not only allows us to interrupt the execution of the program and inspect the variables, it also lets us step forward slowly.

3.13.2 Single stepping

When stopped at a breakpoint, clicking the *Step* button executes a single line of code and then stops again.

> **Exercise 3.35** Step one line forward in the execution of the `printNextMailItem` method by clicking the *Step* button.

The result of executing the first line of the `printNextMailItem` method is shown in Figure 3.7. We can see that execution has moved on by one line (a small black arrow next to the line of source code indicates the current position), and the local variable list in the debugger window indicates that a local variable item has been created, and an object has been assigned to it.

Figure 3.7
Stopped again after a single step

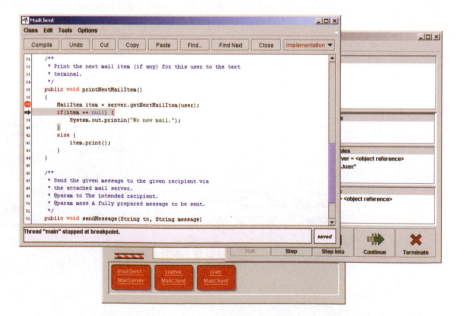

We can now repeatedly use the *Step* button to step to the end of the method. This allows us to see the path the execution takes. This is especially interesting in conditional statements: we can clearly see which branch of an if statement is executed, and use this to see whether it matches our expectations.

3.13.3 Stepping into methods

When stepping through the `printNextMailItem` method, we have seen two method calls to objects of our own classes. The line

```
MailItem item = server.getNextMailItem(user);
```

includes a call to the `getNextMailItem` method of the `server` object. Checking the instance variable declarations, we can see that the `server` object is declared of class `MailServer`.

The line

```
item.print();
```

calls the `print` method of the `item` object. We can see in the first line of the `printNextMailItem` method that `item` is declared to be of class `MailItem`.

Using the step command in the debugger we have used abstraction: we have viewed the `print` method of the `item` class as a single instruction, and we could observe that its effect is to print out the details (sender, addressee, and message) of the mail item.

If we are interested in more detail, we can look further into the process, and see the print method itself execute step by step. This is done by using the *Step Into* command in the debugger, instead of the *Step* command. *Step Into* will step into the method being called, and stop at the first line inside that method.

3.14 Method calling revisited

In the experiments in section 3.13 we have seen another example of object interaction similar to one we had seen before: objects calling methods of other objects. In the printNextMailItem method the MailClient object made a call to a MailServer object to retrieve the next mail item. This method (getNextMailItem) returned a value – an object of type MailItem. Then there was a call to the print method of the mail item. Using abstraction, we can view the print method as a single command. Or, if we are interested in more detail, we can go to a lower level of abstraction and look inside the print method.

In a similar style, we can use the debugger to observe one object creating another one. The sendMessage method in the MailClient class shows a good example. In this method, a MailItem object is created in the first line of code:

```
MailItem mess = new MailItem(user, to, message);
```

The idea here is that the mail item is used to encapsulate a mail message. The mail item contains information about the sender, the addressee, and the message itself. When sending a message, a mail client creates a mail item with all this information, and then stores this mail item on the mail server. There it can later be picked up by the mail client of the addressee.

In the line of code above we see the new key word being used to create the new object, and we see the parameters being passed to the constructor. (Remember: Constructing an object does two things – the object is being created and the constructor is executed.) Calling the constructor works in a very similar fashion to calling methods. This can be observed by using the *Step Into* command at the line where the object is being constructed.

Exercise 3.39 Set a breakpoint in the first line of the **sendMessage** method in the **MailClient** class. Then invoke this method. Use the *Step Into* function to step into the constructor of the mail item. In the debugger display for the **MailItem** object, you can see the instance variables and local variables that have the same names, as discussed in section 3.12.2. Step further to see the instance variables get initialized.

Exercise 3.40 Use a combination of code reading, execution of methods, breakpoints, and single stepping to familiarize yourself with the **MailItem** and **MailClient** classes. Note that we have not discussed enough for you to understand the implementation of the **MailServer** class yet, so you can ignore this for now. (You can, of course, look at it if you feel adventurous, but don't be surprised if you find it slightly baffling …) Explain in writing how the **MailClient** and **MailItem** classes interact. Draw object diagrams as part of your explanations.

3.15 Summary

In this chapter we have discussed how a problem can be divided into sub-problems. We can try to identify subcomponents in those objects that we want to model, and we can implement subcomponents as independent classes. Doing so helps in reducing the complexity of implementing larger applications, since it enables us to implement, test, and maintain individual classes separately.

We have seen how this results in structures of objects working together to solve a common task. Objects can create other objects, and they can invoke each other's methods. Understanding these object interactions is essential in planning, implementing, and debugging applications.

We can use pen-and-paper diagrams, code reading and debuggers to investigate how an application executes or to track down bugs.

Terms introduced in this chapter

abstraction, modularization, divide and conquer, class diagram, object diagram, object reference, overloading, internal method call, external method call, dot notation, debugger, breakpoint.

Concept summary

- **abstraction** Abstraction is the ability to ignore details of parts to focus attention on a higher level of a problem.

- **modularization** Modularization is the process of dividing a whole into well-defined parts, which can be built and examined separately, and which interact in well-defined ways.

- **classes define types** A class name can be used as the type for a variable. Variables that have a class as their type can store objects of that class.

- **class diagram** The class diagram shows the classes of an application and the relationships between them. It gives information about the source code. It presents the static view of a program.

- **object diagram** The object diagram shows the objects and their relationships at one moment in time during the execution of an application. It gives information about objects at runtime. It presents the dynamic view of a program.

- **object references** Variables of object types store references to objects.

- **primitive type** The primitive types in Java are the non-object types. Types such as `int`, `boolean`, `char`, `double` and `long` are the most common primitive types. Primitive types have no methods.

- **object creation** Objects can create other objects using the `new` operator.

- **overloading** A class may contain more than one constructor, or more than one method of the same name, as long as each has a distinctive set of parameter types.

- **internal method call** Methods can call other methods of the same class as part of their implementation. This is called an internal method call.

- **external method call** Methods can call methods of other objects using dot notation. This is called an external method call.

- **debugger** A debugger is a software tool that helps in examining how an application executes. It can be used to find bugs.

Exercise 3.41 Use the debugger to investigate the *clock-display* project. Set breakpoints in the `ClockDisplay` constructor and each of the methods, and then single-step through them. Does it behave as you expected? Did this give you new insights? If so, what were they?

Exercise 3.42 Use the debugger to investigate the `insertMoney` method of the *better-ticket-machine* project from Chapter 2. Conduct tests that cause both branches of the if statement to be executed.

Exercise 3.43 Add a subject line for an email to mail items in the *mail-system* project. Make sure printing messages also prints the subject line. Modify the mail client accordingly.

Exercise 3.44 Given the following class (only shown in fragments here):

```java
public class Screen
{
    public Screen(int xRes, int yRes)
    { ... }

    public int numberOfPixels()
    { ... }

    public void clear(boolean invert)
    { ... }
}
```

Write some lines of Java code that create a `Screen` object, and then call its `clear` method if (and only if) its number of pixels is greater than 2 million. (Don't worry about things being logical here – the goal is only to write something that is syntactically correct, i.e. that would compile if we typed it in.)

4

Grouping objects

Main concepts discussed in this chapter:

- collections
- loops

- iterators
- arrays

Java constructs discussed in this chapter:

`ArrayList`, `Iterator`, while loop, `null`, cast, anonymous objects, array, for loop

The main focus of this chapter is to introduce some of the ways in which objects may be grouped together into collections. In particular, we discuss the `ArrayList` class as an example of flexible-size collections, and the use of array objects for fixed-size collections. Closely associated with collections is the need to iterate over the elements they contain. For this purpose, we introduce two new control structures: the while loop, and the for loop.

4.1 Grouping objects in flexible-size collections

When writing programs, we often need to be able to group objects into collections. For instance:

- Personal electronic organizer devices store notes about appointments, meetings, birthdays, and so on.

- Libraries record details about the books and journals they own.

- Universities maintain records of past and present students.

It is typical that in such situations the number of items stored in the collection will vary from time to time. For instance, in an electronic organizer, new notes are added as future events are arranged, and old notes are deleted as details of past events are no longer needed. In a library, the stock changes as new books are bought and old ones are put into storage or discarded.

So far, we have not met any feature of Java that would allow us to group together arbitrary numbers of items. We could define a class with a lot of individual fields to cover a fixed but very large number of items, but programs typically have a need for a more general solution than this provides. A proper solution would not require us either to know in advance how many items we wish to group together, or to fix an upper limit to that number.

In the next few sections, we shall use the example of a personal notebook to illustrate one of the ways in which Java allows us to group together an arbitrary number of objects in a single container object.

4.2   A personal notebook

We shall model a personal notebook application that has the following basic features:

■ It allows notes to be stored.

■ It has no limit on the number of notes it can store.

■ It will show individual notes.

■ It will tell us how many notes it is currently storing.

We shall find that we can support all of these features very easily if we have a class that is able to store an arbitrary number of objects (the notes). Such a class is readily available in one of the *libraries* that comes as a standard part of a Java environment.

Before we analyze the source code needed to make use of such a class, it is helpful to explore the behavior of the notebook example.

Exercise 4.1   Open the *notebook1* project in BlueJ and create a `Notebook` object. Store a few notes into it – they are simply strings – then check that the number of notes returned by `numberOfNotes` matches the number that you stored. When you use the `showNote` method, you will need to use a parameter value of `0` (zero) to print the first note, `1` (one) to print the second note, and so on. We shall explain the reason for this numbering in due course.

4.3   A first look at library classes

One of the features of object-oriented languages that makes them powerful is that they are often accompanied by *class libraries*. These libraries typically contain many hundreds or thousands of different classes that have proved useful to developers on a wide range of different projects. Java has many such libraries, and we shall be selecting classes from several of them throughout the course of this book. Java calls its libraries *packages,* and we shall deal with packages in more detail in later chapters. We can use library classes in exactly the same way as we would use our own classes. Instances are constructed using `new`, and the classes have fields, constructors, and methods. For the `Notebook` class, we shall be making use of the `ArrayList` class that is defined in the `java.util` package. We shall show how to do this in the next section. `ArrayList` is an example of a *collection* class. Collections can store an arbitrary number of elements, with each element being another object.

Concept:

Collection objects are objects that can store an arbitrary number of other objects.

4.3.1 An example of using a library

Code 4.1 shows the full definition of our `Notebook` class, which makes use of the library class `ArrayList`.

Code 4.1

The `Notebook` class

```java
import java.util.ArrayList;

/**
 * A class to maintain an arbitrarily long list of notes.
 * Notes are numbered for external reference by a human user.
 * In this version, note numbers start at 0.
 *
 * @author David J. Barnes and Michael Kölling.
 * @version 2001.06.08
 */
public class Notebook
{
    // Storage for an arbitrary number of notes.
    private ArrayList notes;

    /**
     * Perform any initialization that is required for the
     * notebook.
     */
    public Notebook()
    {
        notes = new ArrayList();
    }

    /**
     * Store a new note into the notebook.
     * @param note The note to be stored.
     */
    public void storeNote(String note)
    {
        notes.add(note);
    }

    /**
     * @return The number of notes currently in the notebook.
     */
    public int numberOfNotes()
    {
        return notes.size();
    }

    /**
     * Show a note.
     * @param noteNumber The number of the note to be shown.
     */
    public void showNote(int noteNumber)
    {
```

Code 4.1
continued
The Notebook
class

```
        if(noteNumber < 0) {
            // This is not a valid note number, so do nothing.
        }
        else if(noteNumber < numberOfNotes()) {
            // This is a valid note number, so we can print it.
            System.out.println(notes.get(noteNumber));
        }
        else {
            // This is not a valid note number, so do nothing.
        }
    }
}
```

The very first line of the class file illustrates the way in which we gain access to a library class in Java, via an *import statement*:

```
import java.util.ArrayList;
```

This makes the ArrayList class from the java.util package available to our class definition. Import statements must always be placed before class definitions in a file. Once a class name has been imported from a package in this way, we can use that class just as if it were one of our own classes. So we use ArrayList at the head of the Notebook class to define a notes field:

```
private ArrayList notes;
```

This is what we shall use to store the notes. In the constructor of the notebook, we create an ArrayList object and store it into our notes field:

```
notes = new ArrayList();
```

The ArrayList class defines quite a lot of methods, but we shall make use of only three at this stage to support the functionality we require: add, size, and get.

The first two are illustrated in the relatively straightforward storeNote and number-OfNotes methods respectively. The add method of an ArrayList stores an object into the list, and the size method returns how many items are currently stored in it.

4.4 Object structures with collections

To understand how a collection object such as an ArrayList operates, it is helpful to examine an object diagram. Figure 4.1 illustrates how a Notebook object might look with two notes stored in it. Compare Figure 4.1 with Figure 4.2, where a third note has been stored.

There are at least three important features of the ArrayList class that you should observe:

■ It is able to increase its internal capacity as required: as more items are added, it simply makes enough room for them.

■ It keeps its own private count of how many items it is currently storing. Its size method returns the number of objects currently stored in it.

■ It maintains the order of items you insert into it. You can later retrieve them in the same order.

Figure 4.1
A `Notebook` containing two notes

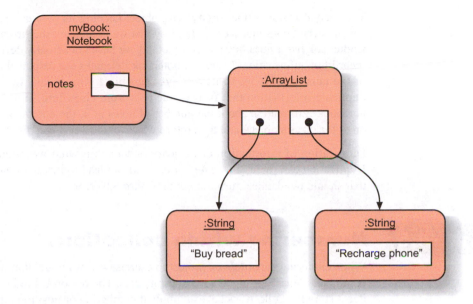

Figure 4.2
A `Notebook` containing three notes

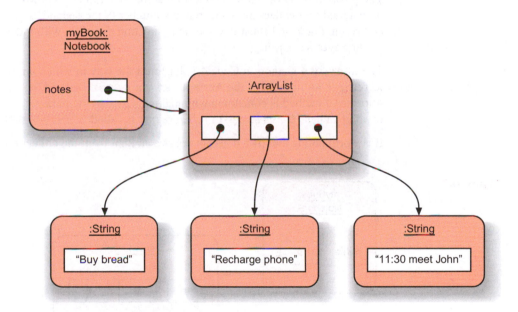

We notice that the Notebook object looks quite simple – it has only a single field that stores an `ArrayList` object. All the difficult work seems to be done in the `ArrayList` object. This is one of the great advantages of using library classes: someone has invested time and effort to implement something useful, and we are getting access to this functionality almost for free by using this class.

At this stage, we do not need to worry about *how* an `ArrayList` is able to support these features. It is sufficient to appreciate just how useful this ability is. It means that we can utilize it to write any number of different classes that require storage of an arbitrary number of objects.

The second feature – the `ArrayList` object keeping its own count of inserted objects – has important consequences for the way that we implement the `Notebook` class. Although a notebook has a `numberOfNotes` method, we have not actually defined a specific field to record this information. Instead, a notebook delegates the responsibility for keeping track of the number of items to its `ArrayList` object. This means that a notebook does not duplicate information that is available to it from elsewhere. If a user requests from the notebook information about the number of notes in it, the notebook will pass the question on to the `notes` object, and then return whatever answer it gets from there.

Duplication of information or behavior is something that we often work hard to avoid. Duplication can represent wasted effort, and can lead to inconsistencies where two things that should be identical turn out not to be through error.

4.5 Numbering within collections

When exploring the *notebook* project in exercise 4.1, we noted that it was necessary to use parameter values starting at zero to print notes. The reason behind this requirement is that items stored in collections have an implicit numbering or positioning that starts from zero. The position of an object in a collection is more commonly known as its *index*. The first item added to a collection is given index number 0, the second is given index number 1, and so on. Figure 4.3 illustrates the same situation as above, with index numbers shown in the `ArrayList` object.

The `showNote` method in Code 4.1 illustrates the way in which an index number is used to retrieve an item from the `ArrayList` via its `get` method. Most of the code in the `showNote` method is concerned with making sure that the parameter value is in the range of valid values `[0 ... (size−1)]` before `get` is called.

It is worth noting that `get` does not remove an item from the collection.

Figure 4.3

Index numbers of elements in a collection

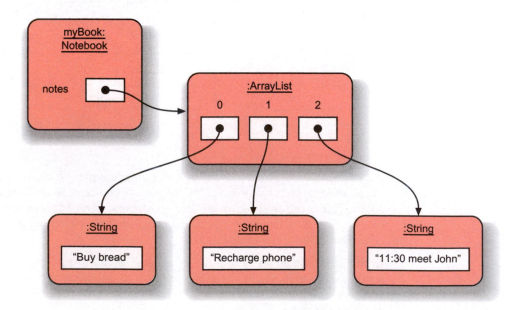

Pitfall: If you are not careful, you may try to access a collection element that is outside the valid indices of the **ArrayList**. When you do this, you will get an error message. Such an error is called an *index-out-of-bounds* error. In Java, you will see a message about an *IndexOutOfBoundsException*.

Exercise 4.2 If a collection stores 10 objects, what value would be returned from a call to its **size** method?

Exercise 4.3 Write a method call using **get** to return the fifth object stored in a collection called **items**.

Exercise 4.4 What is the index of the last item stored in a collection of 15 objects?

Exercise 4.5 Write a method call to add the object held in the variable **meeting** to a collection called **notes**.

4.6 Removing an item from a collection

It would be useful to be able to remove old notes from the Notebook when they are no longer of interest. In principle, this is easy because the ArrayList class has a remove method that takes the index of the note to be removed. When a user wants to remove a note from the notebook, we can just invoke the remove method of the notes object. Code 4.2 illustrates a removeNote method that we might add to the Notebook class.

Code 4.2

Removing a note from a notebook

```java
public void removeNote(int noteNumber)
{
    if(noteNumber < 0) {
        // This is not a valid note number, so do nothing.
    }
    else if(noteNumber < numberOfNotes()) {
        // This is a valid note number, so we can remove it.
        notes.remove(noteNumber);
    }
    else {
        // This is not a valid note number, so do nothing.
    }
}
```

One complication of the removal process is that it can change the index values at which other notes in the collection are stored. If an item with a low index number is removed, then the collection moves all following items along by one position to fill in the gap. As a consequence, their index numbers will be decreased by 1.

Figure 4.4 illustrates the way in which some of the index values of items in an `Array-List` are changed by the removal of an item from the middle of the list. Starting with the situation depicted in Figure 4.3, note number 1 ("Recharge phone") has been removed. As a result, the index of the note originally at index number 2 ("11:30 meet John") has changed to be 1, whereas the note at index number 0 remains unchanged.

Figure 4.4
Index number
changes following
removal of an item

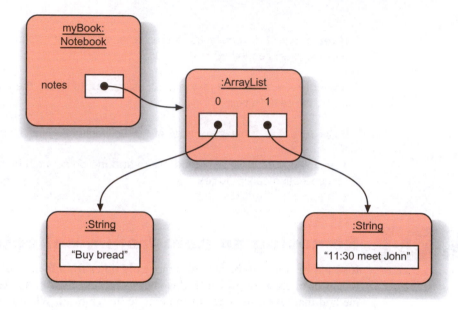

Furthermore, we shall see later that it is also possible to insert items into an `ArrayList` other than right at the end of it. This means that items already in the list may have their index numbers increased when a new item is added. Users have to be aware of this possible change of indices when adding or removing notes.

> **Exercise 4.6** Write a method call to remove the third object stored in a collection called `dates`.
>
> **Exercise 4.7** Suppose that an object is stored at index 6 in a collection. What will be its index immediately after the objects at index 0 and index 9 are removed?
>
> **Exercise 4.8** Implement a `removeNote` method in your notebook.

4.7 Processing a whole collection

If adding and removing notes means that index numbers could change from time to time, it would be useful to have a method in the `Notebook` class that will list all of the notes, along with their current index numbers. We can state what the method would do in another way by saying that we should like to take each valid index number and show the note that is at that number. Before reading further, try the following exercises to see whether we can easily write such a method with the Java that we already know.

Exercise 4.9 What might the header of a `listAllNotes` method look like? What sort of return type should it have? Does it need to take any parameters?

Exercise 4.10 We know that the first note is stored at index zero in the `Array-List`, so could we write the body of `listAllNotes` along the following lines?

```
System.out.println(notes.get(0));
System.out.println(notes.get(1));
System.out.println(notes.get(2));
```

etc.

How many `println` statements would be required to complete the version of `list-Notes` described in exercise 4.10?

You have probably appreciated that it is not really possible to answer that question, because it depends on how many notes are in the notebook at the time they are printed. If there are three notes then three `println` statements would be required; if there are four notes then four statements would be needed, and so on. The `showNote` and `removeNote` methods illustrate that the range of valid index numbers at any one time is [0...(size−1)]. So a `listAllNotes` method would also have to take that dynamic size into account in order to do its job.

What we have here is the need to do something several times, but the number of times depends upon circumstances that may vary. We shall meet this sort of problem in many different programs, and most programming languages have several ways to solve such problems. The solution we shall choose to use at this point is to introduce one of Java's *loop statements*: the *while loop*.

4.7.1 The while loop

> **Concept:**
>
> A **loop** can be used to execute a block of statements repeatedly without having to write them multiple times.

A *while loop* is one way to perform a set of actions repeatedly, but without having to write out those actions more than once. We can summarize the actions of a while loop in the following pseudo-code:

```
while(loop condition) {
    loop body
}
```

The main new piece of Java is the word `while`. A while loop has two parts: a parenthesized loop condition following the `while`, and a loop body following the condition. The body contains those statements that we wish to perform over and over again. The condition is a boolean expression used to determine whether the body should be executed at least one more time. If the condition evaluates to `true` then the body is executed. Each time the body has been executed once, we return to check the condition again. This process continues over and over again until the condition evaluates to `false`, at which point the body of the loop is skipped over and execution continues with whatever follows immediately after the body.

A pseudo-code summary of how to list all the notes in the notebook would be:

```
while(there is at least one more note to be printed) {
    show the next note
}
```

Code 4.3 shows an implementation of a `listNotes` method that lists all notes currently in the notebook using such a while loop.

Code 4.3

Using a while loop to list the notes

```java
/**
 * List all notes in the notebook.
 */
public void listNotes()
{
    int index = 0;
    while(index < notes.size()) {
        System.out.println(notes.get(index));
        index++;
    }
}
```

In this while loop, an integer variable `index` is used to iterate through all the notes stored in the notebook. The index is first initialized to zero to ensure that we start with the first note, and then all notes are printed by repeatedly accessing the note at `index`, incrementing `index`, and checking again whether we have reached the end.

The final statement in the body of the while loop illustrates a special operator for incrementing a numerical variable by 1:

```
index++
```

This is equivalent to

```
index = index + 1
```

You should take care not to confuse a while loop with an if statement. Although they look similar at a superficial level, they are very different in how they operate. The biggest difference between the two is that, once the body of the while loop has been executed for the first time, we go back to the test again to see if the body should be executed once more.

Use the following exercises to check that you understand how the various parts of a while loop operate.

Exercise 4.11 Implement the `listNotes` method in your version of the notebook project. (A solution with this method implemented is provided in the *notebook2* version of this project, but to improve your understanding of the subject, we recommend that you write this method yourself.)

Exercise 4.12 Create a `Notebook` and store a few notes into it. Use the `listNotes` method to print them out to check that the method works as it should.

Exercise 4.13 If you wish, you could use the debugger to help yourself understand how the statements in the body of the while loop are repeated. Set a breakpoint just before the loop, and step through the method until the loop's condition evaluates to `false`.

Exercise 4.14 Modify `showNote` and `removeNote` to print out an error message if the note number entered was not valid.

Exercise 4.15 Modify the `listNotes` method so that it prints the value of the `index` local variable in front of each note. For instance:

```
0: Buy some bread.
1: Recharge phone.
2: 11.30: Meeting with John.
```

This makes it much easier to provide the correct index when removing a note.

Exercise 4.16 Within a single execution of the `listNotes` method, the `notes` collection is asked repeatedly how many notes it is currently storing. This is done every time the loop condition is checked. Does the value returned by `size` vary from one check to the next? If you think the answer is 'No,' then rewrite the `listNotes` method so that the size of the `notes` collection is determined only once and stored in a local variable prior to execution of the loop. Then use the local variable in the loop's condition rather than the call to `size`. Check that this version gives the same results. If you have problems completing this exercise, try using the debugger to see where things are going wrong.

Exercise 4.17 Change your notebook so that notes are numbered starting from 1, rather than 0. Remember that the `ArrayList` object will still be using indices starting from zero, but you can present the notes numbered from 1 in your listing. Make sure you modify `showNote` and `removeNote` appropriately.

Exercise 4.18 Some people refer to 'if statements' as 'if loops.' From what we have seen of the operation of a while loop, explain why it is not appropriate to refer to if statements as loops.

4.7.2 Iterating over a collection

Concept:

An **iterator** is an object that provides functionality to iterate over all elements of a collection.

Examining every item in a collection is a very common activity. In fact, it is so common that an `ArrayList` provides a special way to *iterate* over its contents. The `iterator` method of `ArrayList` returns an `Iterator` object.[1] `Iterator` is also defined in the `java.util` package, so we must add a second import statement to the class file to use it:

```
import java.util.ArrayList;
import java.util.Iterator;
```

---

[1] Be careful to distinguish between the different cases of the first letters of the `iterator` method and the `Iterator` class.

An `Iterator` provides two methods to iterate over a collection: `hasNext` and `next`. The way we usually use an `Iterator` can be described in pseudo-code as follows:

```
Iterator it = myCollection.iterator();
while(it.hasNext()) {
    call it.next() to get the next object
    do something with that object
}
```

In this code fragment, we first use the `iterator` method of the `ArrayList` class to obtain an iterator object. Then we use that iterator to repeatedly check whether there are any more objects (`it.hasNext()`) and to get the next object (`it.next()`). One important point to note is that it is the iterator that we ask to return the next item, and not the collection.

Using an iterator, we can write a method to list the notes, as shown in Code 4.4. In effect, the iterator starts at the beginning of the collection and progressively works its way through, one object at a time, each time we call its `next` method.

Code 4.4

Using an
`Iterator` to list
the notes

```java
/**
 * List all notes in the notebook.
 */
public void listNotes()
{
    Iterator it = notes.iterator();
    while(it.hasNext()) {
        System.out.println(it.next());
    }
}
```

Take some time to compare the two versions of `listNotes` shown in Code 4.3 and Code 4.4. A particular point to note about the latest version is that we no longer have a use for the `index` local variable. This is because the `Iterator` keeps track of how far it has got through the collection, so that it knows both whether there are any more items left (`hasNext`) and which one to return (`next`) if there is another.

4.7.3 Index access versus iterators

We have seen in the last two sections that we have at least two different ways in which we can iterate over an `ArrayList`. We can use the `get` method with an index (as seen in section 4.7.1), or we can use an `Iterator` object (seen in section 4.7.2).

From what we know so far, both approaches seem about equal in quality. The first one was maybe slightly easier to understand.

For an `ArrayList`, both methods are in fact equally good. This is not always the case though. Java provides many more collection classes besides the `ArrayList`. We shall see several of them in the following chapters. For some collections, it is either impossible or very inefficient to access individual elements by providing an index. Thus our first version of the loop is a solution particular to the `ArrayList` collection, and may not work for other types of collection.

The second solution, using an iterator, is available for all collections in the Java class library, and thus is an important code pattern that we shall use again in later projects.

4.8 Summary of the notebook example

In the notebook example we have seen how we can use an `ArrayList` object, created from a class out of the class library, to store an arbitrary number of objects in a collection. We do not have to decide in advance how many objects we want to store, and the `ArrayList` object automatically keeps track of the number of elements stored in it.

We have discussed how we can use a loop to iterate over all elements in the collection. Java has several loop constructs – the one we have used here is called a *while loop*.

With an `ArrayList`, we can access elements either by index, or we can iterate over all elements using an `Iterator` object.

Exercise 4.19 Use the *club* project to complete the following exercises. Your task is to complete the **Club** class, an outline of which has been provided in the project. The **Club** class is intended to store **Membership** objects in a collection.

Within **Club**, define a field for an **ArrayList**. Use an appropriate import statement for this field. In the constructor, create the collection object and assign it to the field. Make sure that all the files in the project compile before moving on to the next exercise.

Exercise 4.20 Complete the **numberOfMembers** method to return the current size of the collection. Until you have a method to add objects to the collection this will always return zero, of course, but it will be ready for further testing later.

Exercise 4.21 Membership of a club is represented by an instance of the **Membership** class. A complete version of **Membership** is already provided for you in the *club* project, and it should not need any modification. An instance contains details of a person's name, and the month and year in which they joined the club. All membership details are filled out when an instance is created. A new **Membership** object is added to a **Club** object's collection via the **Club** object's **join** method, which has the following description:

```
/**
 * Add a new member to the club's collection of members.
 * @param member The member object to be added.
 */
public void join(Membership member)
```

Complete the **join** method.

When you wish to add a new **Membership** object to the **Club** object from the object bench, there are two ways you can do this. Either create a new **Membership** object on the object bench, call the `join` method on the `Club` object, and click on the `Membership` object to supply the parameter; or call the `join` method on the `Club` object and type into the constructor's parameter dialogue box:

```
new Membership("member's name ...", month, year)
```

Each time you add one, use the `numberOfMembers` method to check both that the `join` method is adding to the collection, and that the `numberOfMembers` method is giving the correct result.

We shall continue to explore this project with some further exercises later in the chapter.

4.9 Another example: an auction system

In this section, we will follow up some of the new ideas we have introduced in this chapter by looking at them again in a different context.

The *auction* project models part of the operation of an online auction system. The idea is that an auction consists of a set of items offered for sale. These items are called 'lots,' and each is assigned a unique lot number. A person tries to buy a lot they want by bidding an amount of money for it. Our auctions are slightly different from other auctions because ours offer all lots for a limited period.[2] At the end of that period the auction is closed. At the close of the auction, the person who bid the highest amount for a lot is considered to have bought it. Any lots for which there are no bids remain unsold at the close. Unsold lots might be offered in a later auction, for instance.

The *auction* project contains the following classes: `Auction`, `Bid`, `Lot`, and `Person`. Neither the `Person` class nor the `Bid` class initiates any activity within the auction system, so we shall not discuss them here in detail: `Person` simply stores the name of a bidder, and `Bid` stores details of the value of that bid, and of who made the bid. Studying these classes is left as an exercise to the reader. Instead we shall focus on the `Lot` and `Auction` classes.

4.9.1 The `Lot` class

The `Lot` class stores a description of the lot, a lot number, and details of the highest bid received for it so far. The most complex part of the class is the `bidFor` method (Code 4.5). This deals with what happens when a person makes a bid for the lot. When a bid is made, it is necessary to check that the new bid is higher in value than any existing bid on that lot. If it is higher, then the new bid will be stored as the current highest bid within the lot.

Here, we first check whether this bid is the highest bid. This will be the case if there has been no previous bid, or if the current bid is higher than the best bid so far. The first part of the check involves the following test:

```
highestBid == null
```

---

[2] For the sake of simplicity, the time-limit aspects of auctions is not implemented within the classes we are considering here.

Code 4.5
Handle a bid for a lot

```java
public class Lot
{
    // The current highest bid for this lot.
    private Bid highestBid;

    Other fields and constructor omitted.

    /**
     * Attempt to bid for this lot. A successful bid
     * must have a value higher than any existing bid.
     * @param bid A new bid.
     * @return true if successful, false otherwise
     */
    public boolean bidFor(Bid bid)
    {
        if((highestBid == null) ||
                (bid.getValue() > highestBid.getValue())) {
            // This bid is the best so far.
            highestBid = bid;
            return true;
        }
        else {
            return false;
        }
    }

    Other methods omitted.

}
```

Concept:

The Java reserved word **null** is used to mean 'no object' when an object variable is not currently referring to a particular object. A field that has not explicitly been initialized will contain the value **null** by default.

This is actually a test for whether the `highestBid` variable is currently referring to an object or not. The keyword `null` is a special Java value meaning 'no object.' If you check the constructor of the `Lot` class you will see that this field was not assigned an explicit initial value. As a result, it contains the default value for object-reference variables, which is `null`. So until a bid is received for this lot, the `highestBid` field will contain the `null` value.

4.9.2 The Auction class

The Auction class (Code 4.6) provides further illustration of the `ArrayList`, `Iterator`, and while loop concepts we discussed earlier in the chapter.

Code 4.6
The Auction class

```java
import java.util.ArrayList;
import java.util.Iterator;

/**
 * A simple model of an auction.
 * The auction maintains a list of lots of arbitrary length.
```

Code 4.6 continued

The Auction class

```java
 * @author David J. Barnes and Michael Kölling.
 * @version 2003.10.06
 */
public class Auction
{
    // The list of Lots in this auction.
    private ArrayList lots;
    // The number that will be given to the next lot entered
    // into this auction.
    private int nextLotNumber;

    /**
     * Create a new auction.
     */
    public Auction()
    {
        lots = new ArrayList();
        nextLotNumber = 1;
    }

    /**
     * Enter a new lot into the auction.
     * Lots can only be entered into the auction by an
     * Auction object.
     * @param description A description of the lot.
     */
    public void enterLot(String description)
    {
        lots.add(new Lot(nextLotNumber, description));
        nextLotNumber++;
    }

    /**
     * Show the full list of lots in this auction.
     */
    public void showLots()
    {
        Iterator it = lots.iterator();
        while(it.hasNext()) {
            Lot lot = (Lot) it.next();
            System.out.println(lot.toString());
        }
    }

    /**
     * Bid for a lot.
     * A message indicating whether the bid is successful or not
     * is printed.
```

```java
     * @param number The lot number being bid for.
     * @param bidder The person bidding for the lot.
     * @param value  The value of the bid.
     */
    public void bidFor(int lotNumber, Person bidder, long value)
    {
        Lot selectedLot = getLot(lotNumber);
        if(selectedLot != null) {
            if(selectedLot.bidFor(new Bid(bidder, value))) {
                System.out.println(
                        "The bid for lot number " +
                        lotNumber + " was successful.");
            }
            else {
                System.out.println(
                        "Lot number: " + lotNumber +
                        " already has a bid of: "  +
                        selectedLot.getHighestBid().getValue());
            }
        }
    }

    /**
     * Return the lot with the given number. Return null
     * if a lot with this number does not exist.
     * @param lotNumber The number of the lot to return.
     */
    public Lot getLot(int lotNumber)
    {
        if((lotNumber >= 1) && (lotNumber < nextLotNumber)) {
            // The number seems to be reasonable.
            Lot selectedLot = (Lot) lots.get(lotNumber - 1);
            // Include a confidence check to be sure we have the
            // right lot.
            if(selectedLot.getNumber() != lotNumber) {
                System.out.println("Internal error: " +
                                "Wrong lot returned. " +
                                "Number: " + lotNumber);
            }
            return selectedLot;
        }
        else {
            System.out.println("Lot number: " + lotNumber +
                            " does not exist.");
            return null;
        }
    }
}
```

The `lots` field is an `ArrayList`, used to hold the lots offered in this auction. Lots are entered in the auction by passing a simple description to the `enterLot` method. A new lot is created by passing the description and a unique lot number to the constructor of Lot. The new `Lot` object is added to the collection. The following sections discuss some additional features illustrated in the `Auction` class.

4.9.3 Casting

The `showLots` method provides an illustration of how an `Iterator` is used to show the lots in the auction. However, an important new feature – *casting* – is illustrated by the first statement within the body of the while loop:

```
Lot lot = (Lot) it.next();
```

A cast consists of the name of a type written alone between a pair of parentheses:

```
(Lot)
```

Casting is commonly seen when retrieving objects from a collection. It is required because it is possible to store *any* type of object in a collection. Therefore we need to make clear to the compiler what type of object we are retrieving in any particular case. This is the case both when using the `next` method of an iterator, and when using the `get` method of a collection. Using the cast makes it clear that the type of the right-hand side matches the type of the variable in the assignment.

4.9.4 Anonymous objects

The `enterLot` method in `Auction` illustrates a common idiom – anonymous objects. We see this in the following statement:

```
lots.add(new Lot(nextLotNumber, description));
```

Here, we are doing two things:

■ we are creating a new `Lot` object, and

■ we are passing this new object to the `ArrayList`'s `add` method.

We could have written the same in two lines to make the separate steps more explicit:

```
Lot furtherLot = new Lot(nextLotNumber, description);
lots.add(furtherLot);
```

Both versions are equivalent, but if we have no further use for the `furtherLot` variable then the original version avoids defining a variable with such a limited use. In effect we create an anonymous object – an object without a name – by passing it straight to the method that uses it.

Exercise 4.22 Find a further example of casting in the **Auction** class.

Exercise 4.23 What happens if you try to compile the **Auction** class without one of the casts? For instance, edit the **showLots** method so that the first statement in the body of the while loop reads

```
Lot lot = it.next();
```

Exercise 4.24 Add a `close` method to the `Auction` class. This should iterate over the collection of lots and print out details of all the lots. Any lot that has had at least one bid for it is considered to be sold. For lots that have been sold, the details should include the name of the successful bidder, and the value of the winning bid. For lots that have not been sold, print a message that indicates this fact.

Exercise 4.25 Add a `getUnsold` method to the `Auction` class with the following signature:

```
public ArrayList getUnsold()
```

This method should iterate over the `lots` field, storing unsold lots in a new `ArrayList` local variable. At the end of the method, return the list of unsold lots.

Exercise 4.26 Suppose that the `Auction` class includes a method that makes it possible to remove a lot from the auction. Assuming that the remaining lots do not have their `lotNumber` fields changed when a lot is removed, what impact would the ability to remove lots have on the `getLot` method?

Exercise 4.27 Rewrite `getLot` so that it does not rely on a lot with a particular number being stored at index (`number-1`) in the collection. For instance, if lot number 2 has been removed, then lot number 3 will have been moved from index 2 to index 1, and all higher lot numbers will also have been moved by one index position. You may assume that lots are always stored in increasing order of their lot number.

Exercise 4.28 Add a `removeLot` method to the `Auction` class, having the following signature:

```
/**
 * Remove the lot with the given lot number.
 * @param number The number of the lot to be removed.
 * @return The Lot with the given number, or null if
 * there is no such lot.
 */
public Lot removeLot(int number)
```

This method should not assume that a lot with a given number is stored at any particular location within the collection.

Exercise 4.29 The `ArrayList` class is found in the `java.util` package. That package also includes a class called `LinkedList`. Try to find out what you can about the `LinkedList` class, and compare its methods with those of `ArrayList`. Which methods do they have in common and which are different?

4.9.5 Using collections

The `ArrayList` collection class (and others like it) is an important programming tool, because many programming problems involve working with variable-sized collections of objects. Before moving on to the rest of this chapter it is important that you become thoroughly familiar and comfortable with how to work with them. The following exercises will help you to do this.

Exercise 4.30 Continue working with the *club* project from exercise 4.19. Define a method in the **Club** class with the following description:

```
/**
 * Determine the number of members who joined in the
 * given month.
 * @param month The month we are interested in.
 * @return The number of members.
 */
public int joinedInMonth(int month)
```

If the **month** parameter is outside the valid range of 1–12, print an error message and return zero.

Exercise 4.31 Define a method in the **Club** class with the following description:

```
/**
 * Remove from the club's collection all members who
 * joined in the given month, and return them stored
 * in a separate collection object.
 * @param month The month of the Membership.
 * @param year The year of the Membership.
 */
public ArrayList purge(int month, int year)
```

If the **month** parameter is outside the valid range of 1–12, print an error message and return a collection object with no objects stored in it.

Note: The **purge** method is significantly harder to write than any of the others in this class.

Exercise 4.32 Open the *product* project and complete the **StockManager** class through this and the next few exercises. **StockManager** uses an **ArrayList** to store **Product** items. Its **addProduct** method already adds a product to the collection, but the following methods need completing: **delivery**, **findProduct**, **printProductDetails**, and **numberInStock**.

Each product sold by the company is represented by an instance of the **Product** class, which records a product's ID, name, and how many of that product are currently in stock. The **Product** class defines the **increaseQuantity** method to record increases in the stock level of that product. The **sellOne** method records that one item of that product has been sold by reducing the quantity field level by 1. **Product** has been provided for you, and you should not need to make any alterations to it.

Start by implementing the **printProductDetails** method to ensure that you are able to iterate over the collection of products. Just print out the details of each **Product** returned by calling its **toString** method.

Exercise 4.33 Implement the `findProduct` method. This should look through the collection for a product whose ID field matches the ID argument of this method. If a matching product is found it should be returned as the method's result. If no matching product is found, return `null`.

This differs from the `printProductDetails` method in that it will not necessarily have to examine every product in the collection before a match is found. For instance, if the first product in the collection matches the product ID, iteration can finish and that first `Product` can be returned. On the other hand, it is possible that there might be no match in the collection. In that case, the whole collection will be examined, without finding a product to return. In this case the `null` value should be returned.

When looking for a match, you will need to call the `getID` method on a `Product`. This means that you will need to use a cast when you retrieve an item from the list.

Exercise 4.34 Implement the `numberInStock` method. This should locate a product in the collection with a matching ID, and return the current quantity of that product as a method result. If no product with a matching ID is found, return zero. This is relatively simple to implement once the `findProduct` method has been completed. For instance, `numberInStock` can call the `findProduct` method to do the searching, and then call the `getQuantity` method on the result. Take care over products that cannot be found, though.

Exercise 4.35 Implement the `delivery` method using a similar approach to that used in `numberInStock`. It should find the product with the given ID in the list of products and then call its `increaseQuantity` method.

Exercise 4.36 *Challenge exercises* Implement a method in `StockManager` to print details of all products with stock levels below a given value (passed as a parameter to the method).

Modify the `addProduct` method so that a new product cannot be added to the product list with the same ID as an existing one.

Add to `StockManager` a method that finds a product from its name rather than its ID

```
public Product findProduct(String name)
```

In order to do this, you need to know that two `String` objects, `s1` and `s2`, can be tested for equality with the boolean expression

```
s1.equals(s2)
```

More details can be found on this in Chapter 5.

4.10 Flexible collection summary

We have seen that classes such as `ArrayList` conveniently allow us to create collections containing an arbitrary number of objects. The Java library contains more collections like this, and we shall look at some of the others in the next chapter. You will find that being able to use collections confidently is an important skill in writing interesting programs.

There is hardly an application we shall see from now on that does not use collections of some form. However, before we investigate other variants of flexible collections from the library, we first take a look at fixed-size collections.

4.11   Fixed-size collections

Flexible-size collections are powerful both because we do not need to know in advance how many items will be stored in them, and because it is possible to vary the number of items they hold. However, some applications are different in that we *do* know in advance how many items we wish to store in a collection, and that number typically remains fixed for the life of the collection. In such circumstances, we have the option to choose to use a specialized fixed-size collection object to store the items.

A fixed-size collection is called an *array*. Although the fixed-size nature of arrays can be a significant disadvantage in many situations, they do have at least two compensating advantages over the flexible-size collection classes:

■ Access to the items held in an array is often more efficient than access to the items in a comparable flexible-size collection.

■ Arrays are able to store objects or primitive type values. Flexible-size collections can store only objects.

Another distinctive feature of arrays is that they have special syntactic support in Java – accessing them uses a custom syntax different from the usual method calls. The reason for this is mostly historical: arrays are the oldest collection structure in programming languages, and syntax for dealing with arrays has developed over many decades. Java uses the same syntax established in other programming languages to keep things simple for programmers who are used to arrays already, even though it is not consistent with the rest of the language syntax.

In the following sections we shall show how arrays can be used to maintain collections of fixed size. We shall also introduce a new loop structure that is often closely associated with arrays – the *for loop*.

4.11.1   A log-file analyzer

Web servers typically maintain log files of client accesses to the web pages that they store. Given suitable tools, these logs enable web service managers to extract and analyze useful information such as:

■ which are the most popular pages they provide;

■ whether other sites appear to have broken links to this site's pages;

■ how much data is being delivered to clients;

■ the busiest periods over the course of a day, or week, or month.

Such information might help managers to determine, for instance, whether they need to upgrade to more powerful server machines, or when the quietest periods are in order to schedule maintenance activities.

The *weblog-analyzer* project contains an application that performs an analysis of data from such a web server. The server writes a log line to a file each time an access is made.

A sample log file called *weblog.txt* is provided in the project folder. Each line records the date and time of the access in the following format:

```
year month day hour minute
```

For instance, the line below records an access at 03:45am on 7 June 2004:

```
2004 06 07 03 45
```

The project consists of four classes: `LogAnalyzer`, `LogfileReader`, `LogEntry`, and `LoglineTokenizer`. We shall spend most of our time looking at the `LogAnalyzer` class as it contains examples of both creating and using an array (Code 4.7). Later exercises will encourage you to examine and modify `LogEntry` because it also uses an array. The `LogReader` and `LogLineTokenizer` classes use features of the Java language that we have not yet covered, so we shall not explore those in detail.

Code 4.7

The log-file analyzer

```java
/**
 * Read web server data and analyse
 * hourly access patterns.
 *
 * @author David J. Barnes and Michael Kölling.
 * @version 2001.12.31
 */
public class LogAnalyzer
{
    // Array to store the hourly access counts.
    private int[] hourCounts;
    // Use a LogfileReader to access the data.
    private LogfileReader reader;

    /**
     * Create an object to analyze hourly web accesses.
     */
    public LogAnalyzer()
    {
        // Create the array object to hold the hourly
        // access counts.
        hourCounts = new int[24];
        // Create the reader to obtain the data.
        reader = new LogfileReader();
    }

    /**
     * Analyze the hourly access data from the log file.
     */
    public void analyzeHourlyData()
    {
        while(reader.hasMoreEntries()) {
            LogEntry entry = reader.nextEntry();
            int hour = entry.getHour();
            hourCounts[hour]++;
        }
    }
```

```java
/**
 * Print the hourly counts.
 * These should have been set with a prior
 * call to analyzeHourlyData.
 */
public void printHourlyCounts()
{
    System.out.println("Hr: Count");
    for(int hour = 0; hour < hourCounts.length; hour++) {
        System.out.println(hour + ": " + hourCounts[hour]);
    }
}

/**
 * Print the lines of data read by the LogfileReader
 */
public void printData()
{
    reader.printData();
}
}
```

The analyzer currently uses only part of the data stored in a server's log line. It provides information that would allow us to determine which hours of the day, on average, tend to be the busiest or quietest for the server. It does this by counting how many accesses were made in each one-hour period over the duration covered by the log.

Exercise 4.37 Explore the *weblog-analyzer* project by creating a `LogAnalyzer` object and calling its `analyzeHourlyData` method. Follow that with a call to its `printHourlyCounts` method, which will print the results of the analysis. Which are the busiest times of day?

We shall examine how this class uses an array to accomplish this task over the course of the next few sections.

4.11.2 Declaring array variables

The `LogAnalyzer` class contains a field that is of an array type:

```java
private int[] hourCounts;
```

The distinctive feature of an array variable's declaration is a pair of square brackets as part of the type name: `int[]`. This indicates that the `hourCounts` variable is of type *integer array*. We say that `int` is the *base type* of this particular array. It is important to distinguish between an array variable declaration and a similar-looking simple variable declaration:

```java
int hour;
int[] hourCounts;
```

Here, the variable hour is able to store a single integer value, whereas hourCounts will be used to refer to an array object once that object has been created. An array-variable declaration does not itself create the array object. That takes place in a separate stage using the new operator, as with other objects.

The declaration of an array variable illustrates an important distinction between array variables and other collection variables. The declaration of an array variable includes details of the type of item that will be stored in the collection (integers in this case), whereas an ArrayList declaration contains no item-type information.

Exercise 4.38 Write a declaration for an array variable **people** that could be used to refer to an array of **Person** objects.

Exercise 4.39 Write a declaration for an array variable **vacant** that could be used to refer to an array of **boolean** values.

Exercise 4.40 Read through the **LogAnalyzer** class and identify all the places where the **hourCounts** variable is used. At this stage, do not worry about what all the uses mean, as they will be explained in the following sections. Note how often a pair of square brackets is used with the variable.

Exercise 4.41 What is wrong with the following array declarations? Correct them.

```
[]int counts;
boolean[5000] occupied;
```

4.11.3 Creating array objects

The next thing to look at is how an array variable is associated with an array object.

The constructor of the LogAnalyzer class includes a statement to create an array of integers:

```
hourCounts = new int[24];
```

This creates an array object that is able to store 24 separate integer values, and makes the hourCounts array variable refer to that object. Figure 4.5 illustrates the result of this assignment.

Figure 4.5
An array of 24 integers

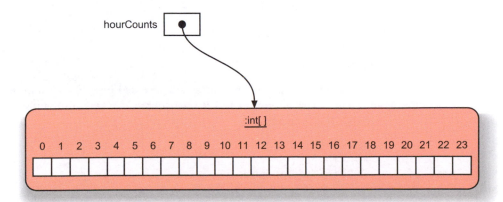

The general form of an array object's construction is

```
new type[integer-expression]
```

The choice of *type* specifies what type of the items are to be stored in the array. The *integer-expression* specifies the size of the array: that is, the fixed number of items that can be stored in it.

When an array object is assigned to an array variable, the type of the array object must match the declared type of the variable. The assignment to `hourCounts` is allowed because the array object is an integer-array, and `hourCounts` is an integer-array variable. The following declares a string-array variable and makes it refer to an array that has a capacity of 10 strings:

```
String[] names = new String[10];
```

It is important to note that the creation of the array assigned to `names` does not actually create 10 strings. Rather, it creates a fixed-size collection that is able to have 10 strings stored within it. Those strings will probably be created in another part of the class to which `names` belongs. Immediately following its creation, an array object can be thought of as empty. In the next section we shall look at the way in which items are stored into (and retrieved from) arrays.

Exercise 4.42 Given the following variable declarations:

```
double[] readings;
String[] urls;
TicketMachine[] machines;
```

write assignments that accomplish the following tasks: (a) Make the `readings` variable refer to an array that is able to hold 60 `double` values; (b) Make the `urls` variable refer to an array that is able to hold 90 `String` objects; (c) Make the `machines` variable refer to an array that is able to hold five `TicketMachine` objects.

Exercise 4.43 How many `String` objects are created by the following declaration?

```
String[] labels = new String[20];
```

Exercise 4.44 What is wrong with the following array creation? Correct it.

```
double[] prices = new double(50);
```

4.11.4 Using array objects

The individual elements of an array are accessed by *indexing* into the array. An index is an integer expression written between square brackets, following the name of an array variable. For instance:

```
labels[6]
machines[0]
people[x + 10 − y]
```

The valid values for an index expression depend upon the length of the array on which they are used. Array indices always start at zero, and go up to one less than the length of the array. So the valid indices for the `hourCounts` array are 0 to 23, inclusive.

> **Pitfall**: Two very common errors are: to think that the valid indices of an array start at 1; and to use the value of the length of the array as an index. Using indices outside the bounds of an array will lead to a runtime error called an `ArrayIndexOutOfBoundsException`.

Expressions that select an element from an array can be used anywhere that a value of the base type of the array could be used. This means that we can use them on both sides of assignments, for instance. Here are some examples that use array expressions in different places:

```
labels[5] = "Quit";
double half = readings[0] / 2;
System.out.println(people[3].getName());
machines[0] = new TicketMachine(500);
```

Using an array index on the left-hand side of an assignment is the array equivalent of a mutator (or *set* method) because the contents of the array will be changed. Using one anywhere else represents the equivalent of an accessor (or *get* method).

4.11.5 Analyzing the log file

The `hourCounts` array created in the constructor of `LogAnalyzer` is used to store an analysis of the access data. The data is stored into it in the `analyzeHourlyData` method and displayed from it in the `printHourlyCounts` methods. As the task of the analyze method is to count how many accesses were made during each hour period, the array needs 24 locations – one for each hour period in a 24-hour day. The analyzer delegates the task of reading its log file to a `LogfileReader`.

The `LogfileReader` class is quite complex, and we suggest that you do not spend too much time investigating its implementation. Its role is to handle the task of breaking up each log line into separate data values, but we can abstract from the implementation details by considering just the headers of two of its methods:

```
public boolean hasMoreEntries()
public LogEntry nextEntry()
```

The `hasMoreEntries` method tells the analyzer whether there is at least one more entry in the log file, and the `nextEntry` method then returns a `LogEntry` object containing the values from the next log line. These two methods mimic the style of the `hasNext` and `next` methods of `Iterator`, as there could be an arbitrary number of entries in any particular log file.

From each `LogEntry`, the `analyzeHourlyData` method of the analyzer obtains the value of the hour field:

```
int hour = entry.getHour();
```

We know that the value stored in the local variable `hour` will always be in the range 0 to 23, which exactly matches the valid range of indices for the `hourCounts` array. Each location in the array is used to represent an access count for the corresponding hour. So each time an hour value is read, we wish to update the count for that hour by 1. We have written this as

```
hourCounts[hour]++;
```

The following alternatives are both equivalent to this, as we can use an array element in exactly the same way as we would an ordinary variable:

```
hourCounts[hour] = hourCounts[hour] + 1;
hourCounts[hour] += 1;
```

By the end of the `analyzeHourlyData` method we have a complete set of cumulative counts for each hour of the log period.

In the next section we look at the `printHourlyCounts` method, as it introduces a new control structure that is well suited to iterating over an array.

4.11.6 The for loop

In section 4.7.1, we introduced the while loop as a convenient means to iterate over a flex-ible-size collection. The *for loop* is an alternative iterative control structure that is particularly appropriate when:

- we wish to execute a set of statements a fixed number of times;
- we need a variable inside the loop whose value changes by a fixed amount – typically increasing by 1 – on each iteration.

For instance, it is common to use a for loop when we wish to do something to every ele-ment in an array, such as printing out the contents of each element. This fits the criteria as the fixed number of times corresponds to the length of the array, and the variable is needed to provide an incrementing index into the array.

A for loop has the following general form:

```
for(initialization; condition; post-body action) {
    statements to be repeated
}
```

The following concrete example is taken from the `printHourlyCounts` method of the log analyzer:

```
for(int hour = 0; hour < hourCounts.length; hour++) {
    System.out.println(hour + ": " + hourCounts[hour]);
}
```

The result of this will be that the value of each element in the array is printed preceded by its corresponding hour number. For instance:

```
0: 149
1: 149
2: 148
...
23: 166
```

We can illustrate the way that a for loop executes by rewriting its general form as an equivalent while loop:

```
initialization;
while(condition) {
    statements to be repeated
    post-body action
}
```

So the alternative form for the body of printHourlyCounts would be

```
int hour = 0;
while(hour < hourCounts.length) {
    System.out.println(hour + ": " + hourCounts[hour]);
    hour++;
}
```

From this rewritten version we can see that the post-body action is not actually executed until after the statements in the loop's body, despite the action's position in the for loop's header. In addition, we can see that the initialization part is executed only once – immediately before the condition is tested for the first time.

In both versions, note in particular the condition

```
hour < hourCounts.length
```

This illustrates two important points:

- All arrays contain a field length that contains the value of the fixed size of that array. The value of this field will always match the value of the integer expression used to create the array object. So the value of length here will be 24.

- The condition uses the less-than operator, '<', to check the value of hour against the length of the array. So in this case, the loop will continue as long as hour is less than 24. In general, when we wish to access every element in an array, a for loop header will have the following general form:

```
for(int index = 0; index < array.length; index++)
```

This is correct, because we do not wish to use an index value that is equal to the array's length – such an element will never exist.

Exercise 4.45 Check to see what happens if the for loop's condition is incorrectly written using the '<=' operator in printHourlyCounts:

```
for(int hour = 0; hour <= hourCounts.length; hour++)
```

Exercise 4.46 Rewrite the body of printHourlyCounts so that the for loop is replaced by an equivalent while loop. Call the rewritten method to check that it prints the same results as before.

Exercise 4.47 Correct all the errors in the following method.

```
/**
 * Print all the values in the marks array that are
 * greater than mean.
 * @param marks An array of mark values.
 * @param mean The mean (average) mark.
 */
public void printGreater(double marks, double mean)
{
    for(index = 0; index <= marks.length; index++) {
        if(marks[index] > mean) {
            System.out.println(marks[index]);
        }
    }
}
```

Exercise 4.48 Rewrite the following method from the **Notebook** class in the *notebook2* project so that it uses a for loop rather than a while loop:

```
/**
 * List all notes in the notebook.
 */
public void listNotes()
{
    int index = 0;
    while(index < notes.size()) {
        System.out.println(notes.get(index));
        index++;
    }
}
```

Exercise 4.49 Complete the **numberOfAccesses** method, below, to count the total number of accesses recorded in the log file. Complete it by using a for loop to iterate over **hourCounts**:

```
/**
 * Return the number of accesses recorded in the log
 * file.
 */
public int numberOfAccesses()
{
    int total = 0;
    // Add the value in each element of hourCounts
    // to total.
    ...
    return total;
}
```

Exercise 4.50 Add your `numberOfAccesses` method to the `LogAnalyzer` class and check that it gives the correct result. *Hint*: You can simplify your checking by having the analyzer read log files containing just a few lines of data. That way you will find it easier to determine whether or not your method gives the correct answer. The `LogfileReader` class has a constructor with the following signature to read from a particular file:

```
/**
 * Create a LogfileReader that will supply data
 * from a particular log file.
 * @param filename The file of log data.
 */
public LogfileReader(String filename)
```

Exercise 4.51 Add a method `busiestHour` to `LogAnalyzer` that returns the busiest hour. You can do this by looking through the `hourCounts` array to find the element with the biggest count. *Hint*: Do you need to check every element to see if you have found the busiest hour? If so, use a for loop.

Exercise 4.52 Add a method `quietestHour` to `LogAnalyzer` that returns the number of the least busy hour. *Note*: This sounds almost identical to the previous exercise, but there is a small trap for the unwary here. Be sure to check your method with some data in which every hour has a non-zero count.

Exercise 4.53 Which hour is returned by your `busiestHour` method if more than one hour has the biggest count?

Exercise 4.54 Add a method to `LogAnalyzer` that finds which two-hour period is the busiest. Return the value of the first hour of this period.

Exercise 4.55 *Challenge exercise* Save the *weblog-analyzer* project under a different name, so that you can develop a new version that performs a more extensive analysis of the available data. For instance, it would be useful to know which days tend to be quieter than others – are there any seven-day cyclical patterns, for instance? In order to perform analysis of daily, monthly, or yearly data, you will need to make some changes to the `LogEntry` class. This already stores all the values from a single log line, but only the hour and minute values are available via accessors. Add further methods that make the remaining fields available in a similar way. Then add a range of additional analysis methods to the analyzer.

Exercise 4.56 *Challenge exercise* If you have completed the previous exercise, you could extend the log file format with additional numerical fields. For instance, servers commonly store a numerical code that indicates whether an access was successful or not. The value 200 stands for a successful access; 403 means that access to the document was forbidden; and 404 means that the document could not be found. Have the analyzer provide information on the number of successful and unsuccessful accesses. This exercise is likely to be very challenging, as it will require you to make changes to every class in the project.

4.12 Summary

In this chapter we have discussed mechanisms to store collections of objects, rather than single objects in separate fields. We have looked at two different collections in detail: the `ArrayList` as an example of a collection with flexible size, and arrays as a fixed-size collection.

Using collections such as these will be very important in all projects from now on. You will see that almost every application has a need somewhere for some form of collection. They are fundamental to writing programs.

When using collections, the need arises to iterate over all elements in a collection to make use of the objects stored in them. For this purpose we have seen the use of loops and iterators.

Loops are also a fundamental concept in computing that you will be using in every project from now on. Make sure you familiarize yourself sufficiently with writing loops – you will not get very far without them.

As an aside we have mentioned the Java class library – a large collection of useful classes that we can use to make our own classes more powerful. We shall need to study the library in some more detail to see what else is in it that we should know about. This will be the topic of the next chapter.

Terms introduced in this chapter

collection, array, iterator, while loop, for loop, index, import statement, library, package, cast, anonymous object

Concept summary

- **collections** Collection objects are objects that can store an arbitrary number of other objects.

- **loop** A loop can be used to execute a block of statements repeatedly without having to write them multiple times.

- **iterator** An iterator is an object that provides functionality to iterate over all elements of a collection.

- **null** The Java reserved word `null` is used to mean 'no object' when an object variable is not currently referring to a particular object. A field that has not explicitly been initialized will contain the value `null` by default.

- **array** An array is a special type of collection that can store a fixed number of elements.

Exercise 4.57 In the *lab-classes* project that we have discussed in previous chapters, the `LabClass` class includes a `students` field to maintain a collection of `Student` objects. Read through the `LabClass` class in order to reinforce some of the concepts we have discussed in this chapter.

Exercise 4.58 The `LabClass` class enforces a limit to the number of students who may be enrolled in a particular tutorial group. In view of this, do you think it would be more appropriate to use a fixed-size array rather than a flexible-size collection for the `students` field? Give reasons both for and against the alternatives.

Exercise 4.59 Java provides another type of loop: the *do-while* loop. Find out how this loop works and describe it. Write an example of a do-while loop that prints out the numbers from 1 to 10. To find out about this loop, find a description of the Java language (for example at

`http://java.sun.com/docs/books/tutorial/java/nutsandbolts/`

in the section *Control Flow Statements*).

Exercise 4.60 Rewrite the notebook's `listNotes` method using a do-while loop.

Exercise 4.61 Find out about Java's *switch-case* statement. What is its purpose? How is it used? Write an example. (This is also a *control flow statement*, so you find information in similar locations as for the *do-while* loop.)

More sophisticated behavior

Main concepts discussed in this chapter:

- using library classes ■ writing documentation ■ reading documentation

Java constructs discussed in this chapter:

`String`, `ArrayList`, `Random`, `HashMap`, `HashSet`, `Iterator`, `Arrays`, `static`, `final`

In Chapter 4 we introduced the class `ArrayList` from the Java class library. We discussed how this enabled us to do something that would otherwise be hard to achieve (in this case storing an arbitrary number of objects).

This was just a single example of a useful class from the Java library. The library consists of thousands of classes, many of which are generally useful for your work (and many of which you will probably never use).

For a good Java programmer it is essential to be able to work with the Java library, and make informed choices about which classes to use. Once you have started work with the library, you will quickly see that it enables you to perform many tasks more easily than you would otherwise have been able to do. Learning to work with library classes is the main topic of this chapter.

Several different library classes will be introduced and discussed. Throughout this chapter, we will work on the construction of a single application (the *TechSupport* system), which makes use of many different library classes. A complete implementation containing all the ideas and source code discussed here, as well as several intermediate versions, is included on the CD and web site for this book. While this enables you to study the complete solution, you are encouraged to follow the path through the exercises in this chapter. These will, after a brief look at the complete program, start with a very simple initial version of the project and then gradually develop and implement the complete solution.

The application makes use of many new library classes and techniques that each requires study on its own, such as random numbers, hash maps, sets, and string tokenization. You should be aware that this is not a chapter to be read and understood in a single day, but that it contains several sections that deserve a few days of study each on their own. Overall, when you finally reach the end and have managed to undertake the implementation suggested in the exercises, you will have learned about a good variety of important topics.

5.1 Documentation for library classes

The Java library is big. It consists of thousands of classes, each of which has many methods, both with and without parameters, and with and without return types. It is impossible to memorize them all, and all of the details that go with them. Instead, a good Java programmer should know:

- some of the most important classes from the library by name (`ArrayList` is one of those important ones); and

- how to find out about other classes and look up the details (such as methods and parameters).

In this chapter we will introduce some of the important classes from the class library, and further library classes will be introduced throughout the book. But, more importantly, we will show you how you can explore and understand the library on your own. This will enable you to write much more interesting programs. Fortunately, the Java library is quite well documented. This documentation is available in HTML format (so that it can be read in a web browser). This is what we shall use to find out about the library classes.

Reading and understanding the documentation is the first part of our introduction to library classes. We will take this approach a step further and also discuss how to prepare our own classes so that other people can use them the same way as they would use standard library classes. This is important for real-world software development, where teams have to deal with large projects and maintenance of software over time.

One thing you may have noted about the `ArrayList` class is that we used it without ever looking at the source code. We did not check how it was implemented. That was not necessary to use its functionality. All we needed to know was the name of the class, the names of the methods, the parameters and return types of those methods, and what exactly these methods do. We did not really care *how* the work was done. This is typical for the use of library classes.

The same is also true for other classes in larger software projects. Typically, several people work together on a project by working on different parts. Each programmer should concentrate on her own area, and not need to understand the details of all the other parts (we discussed this in section 3.2 where we talked about abstraction and modularization). In effect, each programmer should be able to use the classes of other team members as if they were library classes, making informed use of them without the need to know how they work internally.

For this to work, each team member must write documentation about his class similar to the documentation for the Java standard library that enables other people to use the class without the need to read the code. This topic will also be discussed in this chapter.

5.2 The TechSupport system

As always, we shall explore these issues with an example. This time we shall use the *TechSupport* application. You can find it on the CD or web site as a project named *tech-support1*.

TechSupport is a program intended to provide technical support for customers of the fictitious DodgySoft software company. Some time ago, DodgySoft had a technical support department with people sitting at telephones where customers could call to get advice and help with their technical problems with the DodgySoft software products. Recently, though, business has not been going so well, and DodgySoft decided to get rid of the technical support department to save money. They now want to develop the *TechSupport* system to give the impression that support is still provided. The system is supposed to mimic the responses a technical support person might give. Customers can communicate with the technical support system online.

5.2.1 Exploring the TechSupport system

Exercise 5.1 Open and run the project *tech-support-complete*. You run it by creating an object of class `SupportSystem` and calling its `start` method. Enter some problems you might be having with your software to try out the system. See how it behaves. Type 'bye' when you are done. You do not need to examine the source code at this stage. This project is the complete solution that we will have developed by the end of this chapter. The purpose of this exercise is only to give you an idea of what we plan to achieve.

Eliza The idea of the TechSupport project is based on the ground-breaking artificial intelligence program, Eliza, developed by Joseph Weizenbaum at Massachusetts Institute of Technology in the 1960s. You can find out more about the original program by searching the web for 'Eliza' and 'Weizenbaum.'

We will now start our more detailed exploration by using the *tech-support1* project. It is a first, rudimentary, implementation of our system. We will improve it throughout this chapter. This way we should arrive at a better understanding of the whole system than we would by just reading the complete solution.

From exercise 5.1 you will have seen that the program essentially holds a dialog with the user. The user can type in a question, and the system responds. Try the same with our prototype version of the project, *tech-support1*.

In the complete version, the system manages to produce reasonably varied responses. Sometimes they even seem to make sense! In the version we are going to develop, the responses are much more restricted (Figure 5.1). You will notice very quickly that the response is always the same: *"That sounds interesting. Tell me more..."*

This is, in fact, not very interesting at all and not very convincing when trying to pretend that we have a technical support person sitting at the other end of this dialog. We will shortly try to improve this. However, before we do this, we shall explore further what we have so far.

The project diagram shows us three classes: `SupportSystem`, `InputReader`, and `Responder` (Figure 5.2). `SupportSystem` is the main class, which uses the `InputReader` to get some input from the terminal, and the `Responder` to generate a response.

Examine the `InputReader` further by creating an object of this class and then looking at the object's methods. You will see that it has only a single method available, called

Figure 5.1

A first TechSupport dialog

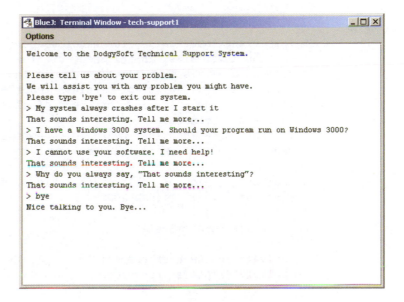

```
Welcome to the DodgySoft Technical Support System.

Please tell us about your problem.
We will assist you with any problem you might have.
Please type 'bye' to exit our system.
> My system always crashes after I start it
That sounds interesting. Tell me more...
> I have a Windows 3000 system. Should your program run on Windows 3000?
That sounds interesting. Tell me more...
> I cannot use your software. I need help!
That sounds interesting. Tell me more...
> Why do you always say, "That sounds interesting"?
That sounds interesting. Tell me more...
> bye
Nice talking to you. Bye...
```

Figure 5.2

TechSupport class diagram

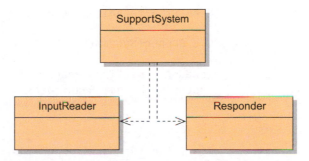

getInput, which returns a string. Try it out. This method lets you type a line of input in the terminal, and then returns whatever you typed as a method result. We will not examine how this works internally at this point, but just note that the InputReader has a getInput method that returns a string.

Do the same with the Responder class. You will find that it has a generateResponse method that always returns the string "That sounds interesting. Tell me more...". This explains what we saw in the dialog earlier.

Now let us look at the SupportSystem class a bit more closely.

5.2.2 Reading the code

The complete source code of the SupportSystem class is shown in Code 5.1. Code 5.2 shows the source code of class Responder.

Looking at Code 5.2, we see that the Responder class is trivial. It has only one method, and that always returns the same string. This is something we shall improve later. For now, we will concentrate on the SupportSystem class.

SupportSystem declares two instance fields to hold an InputReader and a Responder object, and in its constructor creates and assigns those two objects.

Code 5.1
The `SupportSystem`
source code

```java
/**
 * This class implements a technical support system. It is
 * the top level class in this project. The support system
 * communicates via text input/output in the text terminal.
 * This class uses an object of class InputReader to read
 * input from the user, and an object of class Responder to
 * generate responses.
 * It contains a loop that repeatedly reads input and
 * generates output until the user wants to leave.
 *
 * @author    Michael Kölling and David J. Barnes
 * @version   0.1  (1.Feb.2002)
 */
public class SupportSystem
{
    private InputReader reader;
    private Responder responder;

    /**
     * Creates a technical support system.
     */
    public SupportSystem()
    {
        reader = new InputReader();
        responder = new Responder();
    }

    /**
     * Start the technical support system. This will print a
     * welcome message and enter into a dialog with the user,
     * until the user ends the dialog.
     */
    public void start()
    {
        boolean finished = false;

        printWelcome();

        while(!finished) {
            String input = reader.getInput();

            if(input.startsWith("bye")) {
                finished = true;
            }
            else {
                String response = responder.generateResponse();
                System.out.println(response);
```

Code 5.1 continued

The `SupportSystem` source code

```
            }
        }
        printGoodbye();
    }

    /**
     * Print a welcome message to the screen.
     */
    private void printWelcome()
    {
        System.out.println(
            "Welcome to the DodgySoft Technical Support System.");
        System.out.println();
        System.out.println("Please tell us about your problem.");
        System.out.println(
            "We will assist you with any problem you might have.");
        System.out.println(
            "Please type 'bye' to exit our system.");
    }

    /**
     * Print a good-bye message to the screen.
     */
    private void printGoodbye()
    {
        System.out.println("Nice talking to you. Bye...");
    }
}
```

Code 5.2

The `Responder` source code

```
/**
 * The responder class represents a response generator
 * object. It is used to generate an automatic response.
 *
 * @author    Michael Kölling and David J. Barnes
 * @version   0.1  (1.Feb.2002)
 */
public class Responder
{
    /**
     * Construct a Responder - nothing to do
     */
    public Responder()
    {
    }
```

```
/**
 * Generate a response.
 * @return   A string that should be displayed as the
 * response
 */
public String generateResponse()
{
    return "That sounds interesting. Tell me more...";
}
}
```

At the end, it has two methods called `printWelcome` and `printGoodbye`. These simply print out some text – a welcome message and a goodbye message respectively.

The most interesting piece of code is the method in the middle: `start`. We will discuss this method in some more detail.

Toward the top of the method is a call to the `printWelcome` method, and at the end is a call to `printGoodbye`. These two calls take care of printing out these sections of text at the appropriate times. The rest of this method consists of a declaration of a boolean variable and a while loop. The structure is

```
boolean finished = false;

while(!finished) {

    do something

    if(exit condition) {
        finished = true;
    }
    else {
        do something more
    }
}
```

This code pattern is a variation of the while loop idiom discussed in section 4.7. We use `finished` as a flag that becomes true when we want to end the loop (and with it, the whole program). We make sure that it is initially false. (Remember that the exclamation mark is a *not* operator!)

The main part of the loop – the part that is done repeatedly while we are not finished – consists of three statements if we strip it of the check for the exit condition:

```
String input = reader.getInput();
...
String response = responder.generateResponse();
System.out.println(response);
```

Thus the loop repeatedly

■ reads some user input,
■ asks the responder to generate a response, and
■ prints out that response.

(You may have noticed that the response does not depend on the input at all! This is certainly something we shall have to improve later.)

The last part to examine is the check of the exit condition. The intention is that the program should end once a user types the word 'bye.' The relevant section of source code we find in the class reads

```
String input = reader.getInput();

if(input.startsWith("bye")) {
    finished = true;
}
```

If you understand these pieces in isolation, then it is a good idea to look again at the complete start method in Code 5.1 and see whether you can understand everything together.

In the last code fragment examined above a method called startsWith is used. Since that method is called on the input variable, which holds a String object, it must be a method of the String class. But what does this method do? And how do we find out?

We might guess, simply from seeing the name of the method, that it tests whether the input string starts with the word 'bye'. We can verify this by experiment. Run the *TechSupport* system again and type 'bye bye' or 'bye everyone'. You will notice that both versions cause the system to exit. Note, however, that typing 'Bye' or ' bye' – starting with a capital letter or with a space in front of the word – is not recognized as starting with 'bye.' This could be slightly annoying for a user, but it turns out that we can solve these problems if we know a bit more about the String class.

How do we find out more information about the startsWith method or other methods of the String class?

5.3 Reading class documentation

Concept:

The Java **standard library documentation** shows details about all classes in the library. Using this documentation is essential in order to make good use of library classes.

The class String is one of the classes of the Java standard library. We can find out more details about it by reading the library documentation for the String class.

To do this, choose the 'Java Class Libraries' item from the BlueJ Help menu. This will open a web browser displaying the main page of the Java API (Application Programming Interface) documentation.[1]

The web browser will display three frames. In the top left, you see a list of packages. Below that is a list of all classes in the Java library. The large frame on the right is used to display details of selected packages or classes.

In the list of classes on the left, find and select the class String. The frame on the right then displays the documentation of the String class (Figure 5.3).

---

[1] By default, this function accesses the documentation through the Internet. This will not work if your machine does not have network access. BlueJ can be configured to use a local copy of the Java API documentation. This is recommended, since it speeds up access and can work without an Internet connection. For details, see Appendix F.

Figure 5.3

The Java standard
library
documentation

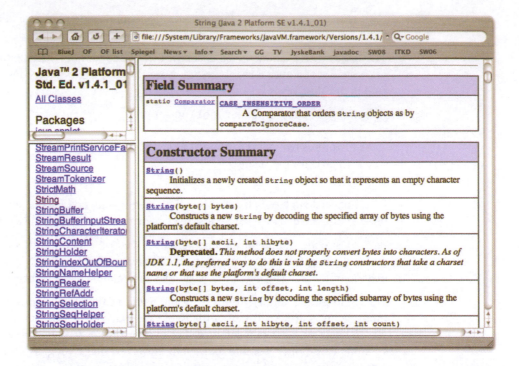

Exercise 5.2 Investigate the **String** documentation. Then look at the documentation for some other classes. What is the structure of class documentation? Which sections are common to all class descriptions? What is their purpose?

Exercise 5.3 Look up the **startsWith** method in the documentation for **String**. Describe in your own words what it does.

Exercise 5.4 Is there a method in the **String** class that tests whether a string ends with a given suffix? If so, what is it called and what are its parameters and return type?

Exercise 5.5 Is there a method in the **String** class that returns the number of characters in the string? If so, what is it called and what are its parameters?

Exercise 5.6 If you found methods for the two tasks above, how did you find them? Is it easy or hard to find methods you are looking for? Why?

5.3.1   Interfaces versus implementation

Concept:

The **interface** of a class describes what a class does and how it can be used without showing the implementation.

You will see that the documentation includes different pieces of information. They are, among other things:

- the name of the class;
- a general description of the purpose of the class;
- a list of the class's constructors and methods;
- the parameters and return types for each constructor and method;
- a description of the purpose of each constructor and method.

This information, taken together, is called the *interface* of a class. Note that the interface does *not* show the source code that implements the class. If a class is well described (that is, if its interface is well written) then a programmer does not need to see the source code to be able to use the class. Seeing the interface provides all the information needed. This is abstraction in action again.

Concept:

The complete source code that defines a class is called the **implementation** of that class.

The source code behind the scene, which makes the class work, is called the *implementation* of the class. Usually a programmer works on the implementation of one class at a time, while making use of several other classes via their interfaces.

This distinction between the interface and the implementation is a very important concept, and it will surface repeatedly in this and later chapters of this book.

> **Note** The word *interface* has several meanings in the context of programming and Java. It is used to describe the publicly visible part of a class (which is how we have just been using it here), but it also has other meanings. The user interface (often a graphical user interface) is sometimes referred to as just *the interface*, but Java also has a language construct called *interface* (discussed in Chapter 10) that is related but distinct from our meaning here.
>
> It is important to be able to distinguish between the different meanings of the word *interface* in a particular context.

The interface terminology is also used for individual methods. For example, the `String` documentation shows us the interface of the `length` method:

```
public int length()
```

> *Returns the length of this string. The length is equal to the number of 16-bit Unicode characters in the string.*

> *Returns:*
>   *the length of the sequence of characters represented by this object.*

The interface of a method consists of the *signature* of the method and a comment (shown here in italics). The signature of a method includes (in this order):

- an access modifier (here `public`) – we shall discuss this below;
- the return type of the method (here `int`);
- the method name;
- a list of parameters (which is empty in this example).

The interface provides everything we need to know to make use of this method.

5.3.2 Using library-class methods

Back to our *TechSupport* system. We now want to improve the processing of input a little. We have seen in the discussion above that our system is not very tolerant: if we type 'Bye' or ' bye' instead of 'bye', for instance. We want to change that by adjusting the text read in from a user. One thing that we have to watch is that a string object cannot actually be changed once it has been created. Instead we have to get the original string to create a new string object.

The documentation of the `String` class tells us that it has a method called `trim` to remove spaces at the beginning and the end of the string. We can use that method to handle the second problem case.

Exercise 5.7 Find the `trim` method in the `String` class's documentation. Write down the signature of that method. Write down an example call to that method on a string variable called `text`. What does the documentation say about control characters at the beginning of the string?

After studying the interface of the `trim` method, we can see that we can remove the spaces from an input string with a line of code similar to this:

```
input = input.trim();
```

This code will request the `String` object stored in the `input` variable to create a new, similar string with the leading and trailing spaces removed. The new string is then stored in the `input` variable because we have no further use for the old one. Thus, after this line of code, `input` refers to a string without spaces at either end.

We can now insert this line into our source code, so that it reads

```
String input = reader.getInput();
input = input.trim();

if(input.startsWith("bye")) {
    finished = true;
}
else {
    ...    Code omitted.
}
```

The first two lines can also be merged into a single line:

```
String input = reader.getInput().trim();
```

The effect of this line of code is identical to the first two lines above. The right-hand side should be read as if it were parenthesized as follows:

```
(reader.getInput()) . trim()
```

Which version you prefer is mainly a matter of taste. The decision should be made mainly on the basis of readability: use the version that you find easier to read and understand. Often, novice programmers will prefer the two-line version, whereas more experienced programmers get used to the one-line style.

Exercise 5.8 Implement this improvement in your version of the *tech-support1* project. Test it to confirm that it is tolerant of extra space around the word 'bye.'

Now we have solved the problem caused by spaces surrounding the input, but we have not yet solved the problem with capital letters. However, further investigation of the String class's documentation suggests a possible solution because it describes a method named toLowerCase.

> **Exercise 5.9** Improve the code of the SupportSystem class in the *tech-support1* project so that case in the input is ignored. Use the String class's toLowerCase method to do this. Remember that this method will not actually change the string it is called on, but result in the creation of a new one with slightly different contents.

5.3.3 Checking string equality

An alternative solution would have been to check whether the input string *is* the string 'bye' instead of whether it *starts with* the string 'bye.' An (incorrect!) attempt to write this code could look as follows:

```
if(input == "bye") {    // does not always work!
    ...
}
```

The problem here is that it is possible for several independent String objects to exist that all represent the same string. Two String objects, for example, could both contain the characters 'bye.' The equality operator (==) checks whether each side of the operator refers to *the same object*, not whether they have the same value! That is an important difference.

In our example, we are interested in the question whether the input variable and the string constant 'bye' represent the same value, not whether they refer to the same object. Thus using the == operator is wrong. It could return false, even if the value of the input variable is 'bye.'

The solution is to use the equals method, defined in the String class. This method correctly tests whether the value of two String objects is the same. The correct code reads:

```
if(input.equals("bye")) {
    ...
}
```

This can, of course, also be combined with the trim and toLowerCase methods.

> **Pitfall** Comparing strings with the == operator can lead to unintended results. As a general rule, strings should almost always be compared with equals, rather than with the == operator.

> **Exercise 5.10** Find the equals method in the documentation for class String. What is the return type of this method?
>
> **Exercise 5.11** Change your implementation to use the equals method instead of startsWith.

5.4 Adding random behavior

So far, we have made a small improvement to the *TechSupport* project, but overall it remains very basic. One of the main problems is that it always gives the same response, independent of the user's input. We shall now improve this by defining a set of plausible phrases with which to respond. We will then have the program randomly choose one of them each time it is expected to reply. This will be an extension of the `Responder` class in our project.

To do this, we will use an `ArrayList` to store some response strings, generate a random integer number, and use the random number as an index into the response list to pick one of our phrases. In this version, the response will still not depend on the user's input (we'll do that later), but at least it will vary the response and look a lot better.

First, we have to find out how to generate a random integer number.

Random and pseudo-random Generating random numbers on a computer is actually not as easy to do as one might initially think. Since computers operate in a very well-defined, deterministic way that relies on the fact that all computation is predictable and repeatable, there is little space for real random behavior in computers.

Researchers have, over time, proposed many algorithms to produce seemingly random sequences of numbers. These numbers are typically not really random, but follow complicated rules. They are therefore referred to as *pseudo-random* numbers.

In a language like Java, the pseudo-random number generation has fortunately been implemented in a library class, so that all we have to do to receive a pseudo-random number is to make some calls to the library.

If you want to read more about this, do a web search for 'pseudo random numbers'.

5.4.1 The `Random` class

The Java class library contains a class named `Random` that will be helpful for our project.

Exercise 5.12 Find the class `Random` in the Java library documentation. Which package is it in? What does it do? How do you construct an instance? How do you generate a random number? Note that you will probably not understand everything that is stated in the documentation. Just try to find out what you need to know.

Exercise 5.13 Try to write a small code fragment (on paper) that generates a random integer number using this class.

To generate a random number, we have to:

■ create an instance of class `Random`; and
■ make a call to a method of that instance to get a number.

Looking at the documentation, we see that there are various methods called next*Something* to generate random values of various different types. The one that generates a random integer number is called nextInt.

The following illustrates the code needed to generate and print a random integer number:

```
Random randomGenerator;

randomGenerator = new Random();
int index = randomGenerator.nextInt();
System.out.println(index);
```

This code fragment creates a new instance of the Random class and stores it in the randomGenerator variable. It then calls the nextInt method to receive a random number, stores it in the index variable, and eventually prints it out.

Exercise 5.14 Write some code (in BlueJ) to test the generation of random numbers. To do this, create a new class called **RandomTester**. You can create this class in the *tech-support1* project, or you can create a new project for it – it doesn't matter. In class **RandomTester**, implement two methods: **printOneRandom** (which prints out one random number) and **printMultiRandom(int howMany)** (which has a parameter to specify how many numbers you want, and then prints out the appropriate number of random numbers).

Note that your class should create only one single instance of class **Random** (in its constructor) and store it in a field. Do not create a new **Random** instance every time you want a new number. The number might not be very random otherwise.

Pitfall It is a very common error to generate a new **Random** object every time you need a new random number. Since numbers are not really random but *pseudo-random* (see note on random numbers, p. 124), and part of the algorithm to compute the random number is the current time of the system, **Random** objects that are created at almost the same time can produce identical sequences of numbers. Make sure you use only one single random-number generator object and repeatedly call its methods to get multiple random numbers.

5.4.2 Random numbers with limited range

The random numbers we have seen so far were generated from the whole range of Java integers (−2147483648 to 2147483647). That is okay as an experiment, but seldom useful. More often, we want random numbers within a given limited range.

The Random class also offers a method to support this. It is also called nextInt, but it has a parameter to specify the range of numbers that we would like to use.

Exercise 5.15 Find the nextInt method in class **Random** that allows the target range of random numbers to be specified. What are the possible random numbers that are generated when you call this method with 100 as its parameter?

Exercise 5.16 Write a method in your `RandomTester` class called `throwDice` that returns a random number between 1 and 6 (inclusive).

Exercise 5.17 Write a method called `getResponse` that randomly returns one of the strings 'yes,' 'no' or 'maybe.'

Exercise 5.18 Extend your `getResponse` method so that it uses an `ArrayList` to store an arbitrary number of responses, and randomly returns one of them.

When using a method that generates random numbers from a specified range, care must be taken to check whether the boundaries are *inclusive* or *exclusive*. The `nextInt (int n)` method in the Java library `Random` class, for example, specifies that it generates a number from `0` (inclusive) to n (exclusive). That means that the value `0` is included in the possible results, whereas the specified value for n is not. The highest number possibly returned by this call is n−1.

5.4.3 Generating random responses

Now we can look at extending the `Responder` class to select a random response from a list of predefined phrases. Code 5.2 shows the source code of class `Responder` as it is in our first version.

We shall now add code to this first version to:

■ declare a field of type `Random` to hold the random number generator;
■ declare a field of type `ArrayList` to hold our possible responses;
■ create the `Random` and `ArrayList` objects in the `Responder` constructor;
■ fill the responses list with some phrases;
■ select and return a random phrase when `generateResponse` is called.

Code 5.3 shows a version of the `Responder` source code with these additions.

Code 5.3
The `Responder` source code with random responses

```java
import java.util.ArrayList;
import java.util.Random;

/**
 * The responder class represents a response generator object.
 * It is used to generate an automatic response by randomly
 * selecting a phrase from a predefined list of responses.
 *
 * @author     Michael Kölling and David J. Barnes
 * @version    0.2  (2.Feb.2001)
 */
public class Responder
{
    private Random randomGenerator;
    private ArrayList responses;
```

**Code 5.3
continued**

The **Responder**
source code with
random responses

```java
/**
 * Create a responder.
 */
public Responder()
{
    randomGenerator = new Random();
    responses = new ArrayList();
    fillResponses();
}

/**
 * Generate a response.
 * @return  A string that should be displayed as the
 * response
 */
public String generateResponse()
{
    // Pick a random number for the index in the default
    // response list.
    // The number will be between O (inclusive) and the size
    // of the list (exclusive).
    int index = randomGenerator.nextInt(responses.size());
    return (String) responses.get(index);
}

/**
 * Build up a list of default responses from which we can
 * pick one if we don't know what else to say.
 */
private void fillResponses()
{
    responses.add("That sounds odd. Could you describe \n" +
                  "that problem in more detail?");
    responses.add("No other customer has ever \n" +
                  "complained about this before. \n" +
                  "What is your system configuration?");
    responses.add("That sounds interesting. Tell me " +
                  "more...");
    responses.add("I need a bit more information on that.");
    responses.add("Have you checked that you do not \n" +
                  "have a dll conflict?");
    responses.add("That is explained in the manual. \n" +
                  "Have you read the manual?");
    responses.add("Your description is a bit \n" +
                  "wishy-washy. Have you got an expert \n" +
                  "there with you who could describe \n" +
                  "this more precisely?");
    responses.add("That's not a bug, it's a feature!");
    responses.add("Could you elaborate on that?");
}
}
```

In this version we have put the code that fills the response list into its own method, named `fillResponses`, which is called from the constructor. This ensures that the responses list will be filled as soon as a `Responder` object is created, but the source code for filling the list is kept separate to make the class easier to read and understand.

The most interesting code segment in this class is in the `generateResponse` method. Leaving out the comments, it reads

```
public String generateResponse()
{
    int index = randomGenerator.nextInt(responses.size());
    return (String) responses.get(index);
}
```

The first line of code in this method does three things:

- It gets the size of the response list by calling its `size` method.
- It generates a random number between 0 (inclusive) and the size (exclusive).
- It stores that random number in the local variable `index`.

If this seems a lot of code for one line, you could also write

```
int listSize = responses.size();
int index = randomGenerator.nextInt(listSize);
```

This code is equivalent to the first line above. Which version you prefer again depends on which one you find easier to read.

It is important to note that this code segment will generate a random number in the range 0 to `listSize`−1 (inclusive). This fits perfectly with the legal indices for an `ArrayList`. Remember that the range of indices for an `ArrayList` of size `listSize` is 0 to `listSize`−1. Thus the computed random number gives us a perfect index to randomly access one from the complete set of the list's elements.

The last line in the method reads

```
return (String) responses.get(index);
```

Again, this line does three things:

- It retrieves the response at position `index` using the `get` method.

- It uses a cast to state that the type of the result is a `String`. (See section 4.9.3 for details if you are unsure about this.)

- It returns the selected string as a method result, using the `return` statement.

If you are not careful, your code may generate a random number that is outside the valid indices of the `ArrayList`. When you then try to use it as an index to access a list element, you will get an *IndexOutOfBoundsException*.

5.5 Packages and import

There are still two lines at the top of the source file that we need to discuss:

```
import java.util.ArrayList;
import java.util.Random;
```

We encountered the `import` statement for the first time in Chapter 4. Now is the time to look at it a little more closely.

Java classes that are stored in the class library are not automatically available for use, like the other classes in the current project. Rather, we must state in our source code that we would like to use a class from the library. This is called *importing* the class, and is done using the `import` statement. The `import` statement has the form

```
import qualified-class-name;
```

Since the Java library contains several thousand classes, some structure is needed in the organization of the library to make it easier to deal with this large number of classes. Java uses *packages* to arrange library classes into groups that belong together. Packages can be nested (that is, packages can contain other packages).

The classes `ArrayList` and `Random` are both in the package `java.util`. This information can be found in the class documentation. The *full name* or *qualified name* of a class is the name of its package, followed by a dot followed by the class name. Thus the qualified names of the two classes we used here are `java.util.ArrayList` and `java.util.Random`.

Java also allows us to import complete packages with statements of the form

```
import package-name.*;
```

Thus the following statement would import all class names from the `java.util` package:

```
import java.util.*;
```

Listing all used classes separately, as in our first version, is a little more work in terms of typing, but serves well as a piece of documentation. It clearly indicates which classes are actually used by our class. Therefore, in this book, we shall tend to use the style of the first example, listing all imported classes separately.

There is one exception to these rules: some classes are used so frequently that almost every class would import them. These classes have been placed in the package `java.lang`, and this package is automatically imported into every class. The class `String` is an example of a class in `java.lang`.

Exercise 5.19 Implement the random-response solution discussed here in your version of the *tech-support* system.

Exercise 5.20 What happens when you add more (or fewer) possible responses to the responses list? Will the selection of a random response still work properly? Why or why not?

The solution discussed here is also on the CD and web site under the name *tech-support2*. We recommend, however, that you implement it yourself as an extension of the base version.

5.6 Using maps for associations

We now have a solution to our technical support system that generates random responses. This is better than our first version, but still not very convincing. In particular, the input of the user does not influence the response in any way. It is this area that we now want to improve.

The plan is that we shall have a set of words that are likely to occur in typical questions and we will associate these words with particular responses. If the input from the user contains one of our known words we can generate a related response. This is still a very crude method, since it does not pick up any of the meaning of the user's input, nor does it recognize a context, but it can be surprisingly effective. And it is a good next step.

To do this, we will use a `HashMap`. You will find the documentation for the class `HashMap` in the Java library documentation. `HashMap` is a specialization of a `Map`, which you will also find documented. You will see that you need to read the documentation of both to understand what a `HashMap` is and how it works.

> **Exercise 5.21** What is a `HashMap`? What is its purpose and how do you use it? Answer these questions in writing. Use the Java library documentation of `Map` and `HashMap` to answer this question. Note that you will find it hard to understand everything, as the documentation for these classes is not very good. We will discuss the details later in this chapter, but see what you can find out on your own before reading on.

5.6.1 The concept of a map

Concept:

A **map** is a collection that stores key/value pairs as entries. Values can be looked up by providing the key.

A map is a collection of key/value pairs of objects. As with the `ArrayList`, a map can store a flexible number of entries. One difference between the `ArrayList` and a `Map` is that with a `Map` each entry is not an object, but a *pair* of objects. This pair consists of a *key* object and a *value* object.

Instead of looking up entries in this collection using an integer index (as we did with the `ArrayList`) we use the key object to look up the value object.

An everyday example of a map is a telephone directory. A telephone directory contains entries, and each entry is a pair: a name and a phone number. You use a phone book by looking up a name, and getting a phone number. We do not use an index – the position of the entry in the phone book – to find it.

A map can be organized in such a way that looking up a value for a key is easy. In the case of a phone book this is done using alphabetical sorting. By storing the entries in alphabetical order of their keys, finding the key and looking up the value is easy. Reverse lookup (finding the key for a value, i.e. finding the name for a given phone number) is not so easy with a map. Thus maps are ideal for a one-way lookup, where we know the lookup key and need to know a value associated with this key.

5.6.2 Using a `HashMap`

`HashMap` is a particular implementation of `Map`. The most important methods of the `HashMap` class are `put` and `get`.

The `put` method inserts an entry into the map, and `get` retrieves the value for a given key. The following code fragment creates a `HashMap` and inserts three entries into it. Each entry is a key/value pair consisting of a name and a telephone number.

```
HashMap phoneBook = new HashMap();

phoneBook.put("Charles Nguyen", "(531) 9392 4587");
phoneBook.put("Lisa Jones", "(402) 4536 4674");
phoneBook.put("William H. Smith", "(998) 5488 0123");
```

The following code will find the phone number for Lisa Jones and print it out.

```
String number = (String)phoneBook.get("Lisa Jones");
System.out.println(number);
```

Note that you pass the key (the name "Lisa Jones") to the `get` method in order to receive the value (the phone number). You must cast the result back to a string, the same way we did when we accessed a value from an `ArrayList`. This is because any type of object may be stored as a value in a map.

Read the documentation of the `get` and `put` methods of class `HashMap` again and see whether the explanation matches your current understanding.

Exercise 5.22 Create a class `MapTester` (either in your current project or in a new project). In it, use a `HashMap` to implement a phone book similar to the example above. (Remember that you must import `java.util.HashMap`.) In this class implement two methods:

```
public void enterNumber(String name, String number)
```

and

```
public String lookupNumber(String name)
```

The methods should use the `put` and `get` methods of the `HashMap` class to implement their functionality.

Exercise 5.23 What happens when you add an entry to a map with a key that already exists in the map?

Exercise 5.24 What happens when you add an entry to a map with a value that already exists in the map?

Exercise 5.25 How do you check whether a given key is contained in a map? (Give a Java code example.)

Exercise 5.26 What happens when you try to look up a value, and the key does not exist in the map?

Exercise 5.27 How do you check how many entries are contained in a map?

5.6.3 Using a map for the TechSupport system

In the TechSupport system, we can make good use of a map by using known words as keys and associated responses as values. Code 5.4 shows an example in which a HashMap named responseMap is created and three entries are made. For example, the word 'slow' is associated with the text

"I think this has to do with your hardware. Upgrading your processor should solve all performance problems. Have you got a problem with our software?"

Now, whenever somebody enters a question containing the word *slow*, we can look up and print out this response. Note that the response string in the source code spans several lines, but is concatenated with the + operator, so that a single string is entered as a value into the HashMap.

Code 5.4

Associating selected words with possible responses

```java
private HashMap responseMap;

...

public Responder()
{
    responseMap = new HashMap();
    fillResponseMap();
}

/**
 * Enter all the known key words and their associated
 * responses into our response map.
 */
private void fillResponseMap()
{
    responseMap.put("slow",
        "I think this has to do with your hardware. \n" +
        "Upgrading your processor should solve all " +
        "performance problems. \n" +
        "Have you got a problem with our software?");
    responseMap.put("bug",
        "Well, you know, all software has some bugs. \n" +
        "But our software engineers are working very " +
        "hard to fix them. \n" +
        "Can you describe the problem a bit further?");
    responseMap.put("expensive",
        "The cost of our product is quite competitive. \n" +
        "Have you looked around and " +
        "really compared our features?");
}
```

A first attempt at writing a method to generate the responses could now look like the generateResponse method below. Here, to simplify things for the moment, we assume that only a single word (for example 'slow') is entered by the user.

```java
public String generateResponse(String word)
{
    String response = (String) responseMap.get(word);
    if(response != null) {
        return response;
    }
    else {
        // if we get here, the word was not recognized. In
        // this case we pick one of our default responses.

        return pickDefaultResponse();
    }
}
```

In this code fragment, we look up the word entered by the user in our response map. If we find an entry, we use this entry as the response. If we don't find an entry for that word, we call a method called `pickDefaultResponse`. This method can now contain the code of our previous version of `generateResponse`, which randomly picks one of the default responses (as shown in Code 5.3). The new logic then is that we pick an appropriate response if we recognize a word, or a random response out of our list of default responses if we don't.

Exercise 5.28 Implement the changes discussed here in your own version of the TechSupport system. Test it to get a feel for how well it works.

This approach of associating key words with responses works quite well as long as the user does not enter complete questions, but only single words. The final improvement to complete the application is to let the user enter complete questions again, and then pick matching responses if we recognize any of the words in the question.

This poses the problem of recognizing the key words in the sentence that was entered by the user. In the current version, the user input is returned by the `InputReader` as a single string. We shall now change this to a new version in which the `InputReader` returns the input as a set of words. Technically, this will be a set of strings, where each string in the set represents a single word that was entered by the user.

If we can do that, then we can pass the whole set to the `Responder`, which can then check every word in the set to see whether it is known and has an associated response.

To achieve this in Java, we need to know about two things: how to cut a single string containing a whole sentence into words, and how to use sets. These two issues are discussed in the next two sections.

5.7 Using sets

The Java standard library includes different variations of sets, implemented in different classes. The class we shall use is called `HashSet`.

The two types of functionality that we need from a set are to enter elements into it, and to retrieve the elements later. Fortunately, these tasks contain hardly anything new for us. Consider the following code fragment:

```
import java.util.HashSet;
import java.util.Iterator;

...
HashSet mySet = new HashSet();

mySet.add("one");
mySet.add("two");
mySet.add("three");
```

Compare this code with the statements needed to enter elements into an `ArrayList`. There is almost no difference, except that we create a `HashSet` this time instead of an `ArrayList`. Now let us look at iterating over all elements:

```
Iterator it = mySet.iterator();
while(it.hasNext()) {
    call it.next() to get the next object
    do something with that object
}
```

Again, these statements are the same as the ones we used to iterate over an `ArrayList` in Chapter 4.

In short: using collections in Java is quite similar for different types of collection. Once you understand how to use one of them, you can use them all. The differences really lie in the behavior of each collection. A list, for example, will keep all elements entered in the desired order, provides access to elements by index, and can contain the same element multiple times. A set, on the other hand, does not maintain any specific order (the elements may be returned by the iterator in a different order from that in which they were entered), and ensures that each element is in the set at most once. Entering an element a second time simply has no effect.

5.8 Dividing strings

Now that we have seen how to use a set, we can investigate how we can cut the input string into separate words to be stored in a set of words. The solution is shown in a new version of the `InputReader`'s `getInput` method (Code 5.5).

Code 5.5

The `getInput` method returning a set of words

```java
/**
 * Read a line of text from standard input (the text
 * terminal), and return it as a set of words.
 *
 * @return  A set of Strings, where each String is one of the
 *          words typed by the user
 */
public HashSet getInput()
{
    System.out.print("> ");                     // print prompt
    String inputLine = readInputLine().trim().toLowerCase();

    String[] wordArray = inputLine.split(" ");

    // add words from array into hashset
    HashSet words = new HashSet();
    for(int i=0; i < wordArray.length; i++) {
        words.add(wordArray[i]);
    }

    return words;
}
```

Here, in addition to using a `HashSet`, we also use the `split` method of class `String`, which is also defined in the Java standard library.

The `split` method can divide a string into separate substrings, and return those in an array of strings. The parameter to the `split` method defines at what kind of characters the original string should be split. We have defined that we want to cut our string at every space character.

The next few lines of code create a `HashSet` and copy the words from the array into the set, before returning the set.[2]

Exercise 5.30 The `split` method is more powerful than it first seems from our example. How can you define exactly how a string should be split? Give some examples.

Exercise 5.31 How would you call the `split` method if you wanted to split a string at either space or tab characters? How might you break up a string in which the words are separated by colon characters (':')?

Exercise 5.32 What is the difference in result of returning the words in a `HashSet` compared with returning them in an `ArrayList`?

---

[2] There is a shorter, more elegant way of doing this. One could write

```java
HashSet words = new HashSet(Arrays.asList(wordArray));
```

to replace all four lines of code. This uses the `Arrays` class from the standard library and a *static method* (also known as *class method*) that we do not really want to discuss just yet. If you are curious, read about *class methods* in section 7.14.1, and try to use this version.

Exercise 5.33 What happens if there is more than one space between two words (e.g. two or three spaces)? Is there a problem?

Exercise 5.34 *Challenge exercises* Read the footnote about the `Arrays.asList` method. Find and read the sections in this book about class variables and class methods. Explain in your own words how this works.

What are examples of other methods that the `Arrays` class provides?

Create a class called `SortingTest`. In it, create a method that accepts an array of `int` values as a parameter, and prints out the elements sorted (smallest element first) to the terminal.

5.9 Finishing the TechSupport system

To put everything together, we also have to adjust the `SupportSystem` and `Responder` classes to deal correctly with a set of words rather than a single string. Code 5.6 shows the new version of the `start` method from the `SupportSystem` class. It has not changed a great deal. The changes are:

- The `input` variable receiving the result from `reader.getInput()` is now of type `HashSet`.

- The check for ending the application is done using the `contains` method of the `HashSet` class, rather than a string method. (Look this method up in the documentation.)

- The `HashSet` class has to be imported using an `import` statement (not shown here).

Code 5.6

Final version of the `start` method

```java
public void start()
{
    boolean finished = false;

    printWelcome();

    while(!finished) {
        HashSet input = reader.getInput();

        if(input.contains("bye")) {
            finished = true;
        }
        else {
            String response = responder.generateResponse(input);
            System.out.println(response);
        }
    }
    printGoodbye();
}
```

Finally, we have to extend the `generateResponse` method in the `Responder` class to accept a set of words as a parameter. It then has to iterate over these words and check each of them with our map of known words. If any of the words is recognized, we immediately return the associated response. If we do not recognize any of the words, as before, we pick one of our default responses. Code 5.7 shows the solution.

Code 5.7

Final version of the `generateResponse` method

```java
public String generateResponse(HashSet words)
{
    Iterator it = words.iterator();
    while(it.hasNext()) {
        String word = (String) it.next();
        String response = (String) responseMap.get(word);
        if(response != null) {
            return response;
        }
    }
    // If we get here, none of the words from the input line was
    // recognized. In this case we pick one of our default
    // responses.

    return pickDefaultResponse();
}
```

This is the last change to this application discussed here in this chapter. The solution in the project *tech-support-complete* contains all these changes. It also contains more associations of words to responses than are shown in this chapter.

Many more improvements to this application are possible. We shall not discuss them here. Instead, we suggest some in the form of exercises left to the reader. Some of them are quite challenging programming exercises.

Exercise 5.35 Implement the final changes discussed above in your own version of the program.

Exercise 5.36 Add more word/response mappings into your application. You could copy some out of the solution provided and add some yourself.

Exercise 5.37 Sometimes two words (or variations of a word) are mapped to the same response. Deal with this by mapping synonyms or related expressions to the same string, so that you do not need multiple entries in the response map for the same response.

Exercise 5.38 Identify multiple matching words in the user's input, and respond with a more appropriate answer in that case.

Exercise 5.39 When no word is recognized, use other words from the user's input to pick a well-fitting default response: for example, words like 'why,' 'how,' 'who.'

5.10 Writing class documentation

When working on your projects, it is important to write documentation for your classes as you develop the source code. It is quite common for programmers not to take documentation seriously enough, and very frequently this creates serious problems later.

If you do not supply sufficient documentation, it may be very hard for another programmer (or yourself some time later!) to understand your classes. Typically, what you have to do in that case is to read the class's implementation and figure out what it does. This may work with a small student project, but it creates serious problems in real-world projects.

It is not uncommon for commercial applications to consist of hundreds of thousands of lines of code in several thousand classes. Imagine you had to read all that in order to understand how an application works! You would never succeed.

When we used the Java library classes, such as `HashSet` or `Random`, we relied exclusively on the documentation to find out how to use them. We never looked at the implementation of those classes. This worked, because these classes were sufficiently well documented (although even this documentation could be improved). Our task would have been much harder had we been required to read the classes' implementation before using them.

In a software development team, the implementation of classes is typically shared between multiple programmers. While you might be responsible for implementing the `SupportSystem` class from our last example, someone else might implement the `InputReader`. Thus you might write one class while making calls to methods of other classes.

The same argument discussed for library classes holds true for classes that you write: if we can use the classes without having to read and understand the complete implementation, our task becomes a lot easier. As with library classes, we want to see just the public interface of the class, instead of the implementation. Thus it is important to write good class documentation for our own classes as well.

Java systems include a tool called `javadoc` that can be used to generate such an interface description from source files. The standard library documentation that we have used, for example, was created from the classes' source files by `javadoc`.

5.10.1 Using `javadoc` in BlueJ

The BlueJ environment uses `javadoc` to let you create documentation for your class. The *Generate Documentation* function from the main menu generates documentation for all classes in the project, while the *Interface View* option in the editor shows a preview of the documentation for a single class. You can read the BlueJ tutorial for more details if you are interested. You can find the BlueJ tutorial in BlueJ's Help menu.

5.10.2 Elements of class documentation

The documentation of a class should at least include:

- the class name;
- a comment describing the overall purpose and characteristics of the class;

- a version number;
- the author's name (or authors' names);
- documentation for each constructor and each method.

The documentation for each constructor and method should include:

- the name of the method;
- the return type;
- the parameter names and types;
- a description of the purpose and function of the method;
- a description of each parameter;
- a description of the value returned.

In addition, each complete project should have an overall project comment, often contained in a 'ReadMe' file. In BlueJ this project comment is accessible through the text note displayed in the top-left corner of the class diagram.

> **Exercise 5.40** Use BlueJ's *Generate Documentation* function to generate documentation for your TechSupport project. Examine it. Is it accurate? Is it complete? Which parts are useful, which are not? Do you find any errors in the documentation?

Some elements of the documentation, such as names and parameters of methods, can always be extracted from the source code. Other parts, such as comments describing the class, methods, and parameters, need more attention as they can easily be forgotten, be incomplete or be incorrect.

In Java, javadoc comments are written with a special comment symbol at the beginning:

```
/**
    This is a javadoc comment.
 */
```

The comment start symbol must have two asterisks to be recognized as a javadoc comment. Such a comment immediately preceding the class declaration is read as a class comment. If the comment is directly above a method signature, it is considered a method comment.

The exact details of how documentation is produced and formatted are different in different programming languages and environments. The content, however, should be more or less the same.

In Java, using javadoc, several special key symbols are available for formatting the documentation. These key symbols start with the @ symbol and include

```
@version
@author
@param
@return
```

> **Exercise 5.41** Find examples of javadoc key symbols in the source code of the *TechSupport* project. How do they influence the formatting of the documentation?

> **Exercise 5.42** Find out about and describe other `javadoc` key symbols. One place where you can look is the online documentation of Sun Microsystems' Java distribution. It contains a document called *javadoc – The Java API Documentation Generator* (for example, at `http://java.sun.com/j2se/1.4.2/docs/tooldocs/windows/javadoc.html`). In this document the key symbols are called *javadoc tags*.
>
> **Exercise 5.43** Properly document all classes in your version of the *TechSupport* project.

5.11 Public versus private

It is time to discuss in more detail one aspect of classes that we have encountered several times already without saying much about it: *access modifiers*.

Access modifiers are the key words `public` or `private` at the beginning of field declarations and method signatures. For example:

```
// field declaration
private int numberOfSeats;

// methods
public void setAge(int replacementAge)
{ ...
}

private int computeAverage()
{ ...
}
```

Fields, constructors, and methods can all be either public or private, although so far we have seen mostly private fields and public constructors and methods. We shall come back to this below.

Concept:

Access modifiers define the visibility of a field, constructor, or method. Public elements are accessible from inside the same class and from other classes; private elements are accessible only from within the same class.

Access modifiers define the visibility of a field, constructor, or method. If a method, for example, is public, it can be invoked from within the same class or from any other class. Private methods, on the other hand, can be invoked only from within the class in which they are declared. They are not visible to other classes.

Now that we have discussed the difference between the interface and the implementation of a class (section 5.3.1), we can more easily understand the purpose of these key words.

Remember: The interface of a class is the set of details that another programmer using the class needs to see. It provides information about how to use the class. The interface includes constructor and method signatures and comments. It is also referred to as the *public* part of a class. Its purpose is to define *what* the class does.

The implementation is the section of a class that defines precisely *how* the class works. The method bodies, containing the Java statements, and most fields are part of the implementation. The implementation is also referred to as the *private* part of a class. The user of a class does not need to know about the implementation. In fact, there are good reasons why a user *should be prevented from knowing* about the implementation (or at least from making use of this knowledge). This principle is called *information hiding*.

The `public` key word declares an element of a class (a field or method) to be part of the interface (i.e. publicly visible); the `private` key word declares it to be part of the implementation (i.e. hidden from outside access).

5.11.1 Information hiding

In many object-oriented programming languages the internals of a class – its implementation – are hidden from other classes. There are two aspects to this. First, a programmer making use of a class should *not need to know* the internals; second, a user should *not be allowed to know* the internals.

The first principle – *need to know* – has to do with abstraction and modularization as discussed in Chapter 3. If it were necessary to know all internals of all classes we need to use, we would never finish implementing large systems.

The second principle – *not being allowed to know* – is different. It also has to do with modularization, but in a different context. The programming language does not allow access to the private section of one class by statements in another class. This ensures that one class does not depend on exactly how another class is implemented.

This is very important for maintenance work. It is a very common task for a maintenance programmer to later change or extend the implementation of a class to make improvements or fix bugs. Ideally, changing the implementation of one class should not make it necessary to change other classes as well. This issue is known as *coupling*: if changes in one part of a program do not make it necessary to also make changes in another part of the program, this is known as weak coupling or loose coupling. Loose coupling is good, because it makes a maintenance programmer's job much easier. Instead of understanding and changing many classes, she may have to understand and change only one class. For example, if a Java systems programmer makes an improvement to the implementation of the `ArrayList` class, you would hope that you do not need to change your code using this class. This will work, because you have not made any references to the implementation of `ArrayList` in your own code.

So, to be more precise, the rule that a user 'should not be allowed to know the internals of a class' does not refer to the programmer of another class, but to the class itself. It is not usually a problem if a programmer knows the implementation details, but a class should not 'know' (depend on) the internal details of another class. The programmer of both classes might even be the same person, but the classes should still be loosely coupled.

The issues of coupling and information hiding are very important, and we shall have more to say about them in later chapters.

For now, it is important to understand that the `private` key word enforces information hiding by not allowing other classes access to this part of the class. This ensures loose coupling and makes an application more modular and easier to maintain.

5.11.2 Private methods and public fields

Most methods we have seen so far were public. This ensures that other classes can call these methods. Sometimes, though, we have made use of private methods. In the `SupportSystem` class of the *TechSupport* system, for instance, we saw the methods `printWelcome` and `printGoodbye` declared as private methods.

The reason for having both options is that methods are actually used for different purposes. They are used to provide operations to users of a class (public methods), and they are used to break up a larger task into several smaller ones to make the large task easier to handle. In the second case, the sub-tasks are not intended to be invoked directly from outside the class, but are placed in separate methods purely to make the implementation of a class easier to read. In this case, such methods should be private. The `printWelcome` and `printGoodbye` methods are examples of this.

Another good reason for having a private method is for a task that is needed (as a sub-task) in several of a class's methods. Instead of writing the code multiple times, we can write it once in a single private method and then call this method from several different places. We shall see an example of this later.

In Java, fields can also be declared private or public. So far we have not seen examples of public fields, and there is a good reason for this. Declaring fields public breaks the information-hiding principle. It makes a class that is dependent upon that information vulnerable to incorrect operation if the implementation changes. Even though the Java language allows us to declare public fields, we consider this bad style and will not make use of this option. Some other object-oriented languages do not allow public fields at all.

A further reason for keeping fields private is that it allows an object to maintain greater control over its state. If access to a private field is channeled through accessor and mutator methods, then an object has the ability to ensure that the field is never set to a value that would be inconsistent with its overall state. This level of integrity is not possible if fields are made public.

In short: fields should always be private.

Java has two more access levels. One is declared by using the `protected` key word as access modifier; the other one is used if no access modifier is declared at all. We shall discuss these in later chapters.

5.12 Learning about classes from their interfaces

The *balls* project (provided on the CD and the web site) is another good project to use to study the concepts discussed in this chapter. We shall not use it to introduce any new concepts, but rather to revisit the topics discussed above in a different context. Consequently, this section is mainly a sequence of exercises with some comments sprinkled in.

The *balls* project provides three classes: `BallDemo`, `BouncingBall`, and `Canvas` (Figure 5.4).

The `Canvas` class provides a window on screen that can be used to draw on. It has operations to draw lines, shapes, and text. A canvas can be used by creating an instance and making it visible using the `setVisible` method. The `Canvas` class should not need any modification. It is probably best to treat it as a library class: open the editor, and switch to the interface view. This displays the class's interface with the `javadoc` documentation.

The `BallDemo` class provides two short demonstrations showing how to produce graphical output using the canvas. The method `drawDemo` provides an example of various drawing operations, and the `bounce` method demonstrates a small animation of two bouncing balls.

Figure 5.4
The *balls* project

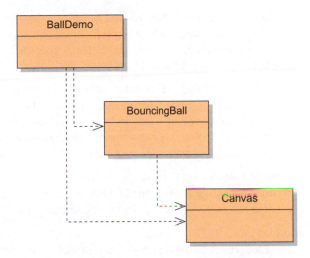

The BouncingBall class is used for the bounce demo. It implements the behavior of a bouncing ball.

The best starting point to understand and experiment with this project is probably the BallDemo class.

> **Exercise 5.44** Create a BallDemo object and execute the drawDemo and bounce methods. Then read the BallDemo source code. Describe, in detail, how these methods work.
>
> **Exercise 5.45** Read the documentation of the Canvas class. Then answer the following questions in writing, including fragments of Java code.
>
> How do you create a Canvas? How do you make it visible? How do you draw a line? How can you erase something? What is the difference between draw and fill? What does wait do?
>
> **Exercise 5.46** Experiment with canvas operations by making changes to the drawDemo method of BallDemo. Draw some more lines, shapes, and text.
>
> **Exercise 5.47** Draw a frame around the canvas by drawing a rectangle 20 pixels inside the window borders. Put this functionality into a method called drawFrame in the BallDemo class.

The last exercise, drawing a frame inside the window borders, presents a few options. First, we can do this by drawing four lines. Alternatively, we can do it by drawing a rectangle using the draw method. The signature of draw is

```
public void draw(Shape shape)
```

The parameter, specified to be of type Shape, can be a Rectangle. It can, in fact, be any special case of a shape that is available in the Java library. This example makes use of specialization through inheritance – a technique that we shall discuss in Chapter 8. The drawDemo method includes an example of how to create and draw a rectangle. You can also study the Rectangle interface in the Java library documentation.

The second issue is how to find out about the size of the rectangle to draw. On the one hand, you can find out how big the canvas object is when it is created. It is, in fact, 600 by 500 pixels. (Find the place where this is specified in the source code!) So we can calculate that we need a rectangle of height 460, width 560, drawn at position 20, 20.

On the other hand, this is not elegant because it is not robust to change. If a maintenance programmer later decides to make the canvas bigger, the frame will be incorrect. The `drawFrame` code also has to be changed then to work as expected. It would be more elegant to use a `drawFrame` method that automatically adapts its frame size to the canvas size. When the canvas size gets changed later, the frame will still be drawn correctly.

We can do this by first asking the canvas for its size. Looking at the `Canvas` interface, we can see that it provides a `getSize` method (good!) that returns an object of type `Dimension` (what is that?). We need to find out by studying the library class documentation.

Exercise 5.48 Improve your `drawFrame` method to adapt automatically to the current canvas's size (that is, do not hard-code the size of the canvas into this method). To do this, you need to find out how to make use of an object of class `Dimension`.

Once you have implemented this exercise, you can test it by manually resizing the canvas and calling `drawFrame` again.

Next, we shall do some more with the bouncing balls.

Exercise 5.49 Change the method `bounce` to let the user choose how many balls should be bouncing.

For this last exercise, you should use a collection to store the balls. This way, the method can deal with one, three, or 75 balls – any number you want. The balls should initially be placed in a row along the top of the canvas.

Which type of collection should you choose? So far, we have seen an `ArrayList`, a `HashMap`, and a `HashSet`. Try the next exercises first, before you write your implementation.

Exercise 5.50 Which type of collection (`ArrayList`, `HashMap`, or `HashSet`) is most suitable for storing the balls for the new bounce method? Discuss in writing, and justify your choice.

Exercise 5.51 Change the `bounce` method to place the balls randomly anywhere in the top half of the screen.

Exercise 5.52 Write a new method named `boxBounce`. This method draws a rectangle (the 'box') on screen, and one or more balls inside the box. For the balls, do not use `BouncingBall`, but create a new class `BoxBall` that moves around inside the box, bouncing off the walls of the box so that it always stays inside. The initial position and speed of the ball should be random. The `boxBounce` method should have a parameter that specifies how many balls are in the box.

Exercise 5.53 Give the balls in **boxBounce** random colors.

5.13 Class variables and constants

So far we have not looked at the `BouncingBall` class. If you are interested in really understanding how this animation works, you may want to study this class as well. It is reasonably simple – the only method that takes some effort to understand is `move`, where the ball changes its position to the next position in its path.

We shall leave it largely to the reader to study this method, except for one detail that we want to discuss here. We start with an exercise.

Exercise 5.54 In class `BouncingBall`, you will find a definition of gravity (a simple integer). Increase or decrease the gravity value, compile and run the bouncing ball demo again. Do you observe a change?

The most interesting detail in this class is the line

```
private static final int GRAVITY = 3;
```

This is a construct we have not seen yet. This one line, in fact, introduces two new key words, which are used together: `static` and `final`.

5.13.1 The `static` key word

Concept:

Classes can have fields. These are known as **class variables** or static variables. Exactly one copy exists of a class variable at all times, independent of the number of created instances.

The key word `static` is Java's syntax to define class variables. Class variables are fields that are stored in a class itself, not in an object. This makes them fundamentally different from instance variables (the fields we have dealt with so far). Consider this segment of code (a part of the `BouncingBall` class):

```
public class BouncingBall
{
    // Effect of gravity.
    private static final int GRAVITY = 3;

    private int xPosition;
    private int yPosition;

    Other fields and method omitted.
}
```

Now imagine we create three `BouncingBall` instances. The resulting situation is shown in Figure 5.5.

As we can see from the diagram, the instance variables (`xPosition` and `yPosition`) are stored in each object. Since we have created three objects, we have three independent copies of these variables.

Figure 5.5
Instance variables
and a class variable

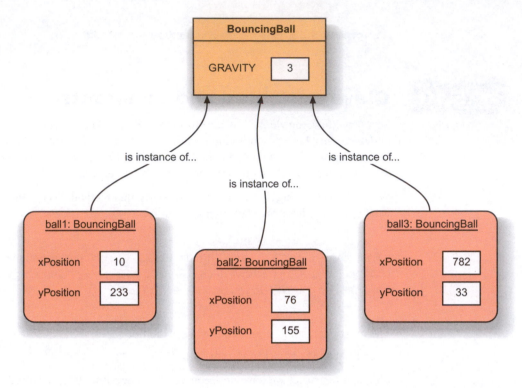

Figure 5.5
Instance variables
and a class variable

The class variable GRAVITY, on the other hand, is stored in the class itself. As a result, there is always only exactly one copy of this variable, independent of the number of created instances.

Source code in the class can access (read and set) this kind of variable just like an instance variable. The class variable can be accessed from any of the class's instances. As a result, the objects share this variable.

Class variables are frequently used if a value should always be the same for all instances of a class. Instead of storing one copy of the same value in each object, which would be a waste of space and might be hard to coordinate, a single value can be shared among all instances.

Java also supports *class methods* (also known as *static methods*), which are methods that belong to a class. We shall discuss those later.

5.13.2   Constants

One frequent use for the `static` key word is to define *constants*. Constants are similar to variables, but they cannot change their value during the execution of an application. In Java, constants are defined with the key word `final`. For example:

```
private final int SIZE = 10;
```

Here, we define a constant named SIZE with the value 10. We notice that constant declarations look similar to field declarations, with two differences:

- they include the key word `final` before the type name; and
- they must be initialized with a value at the point of declaration.

If a value is intended not to change, it is a good idea to declare it final. This ensures that it cannot accidentally be changed later. Any attempt to change a constant field will result in a compile time error message. Constants are, by convention, often written in capital letters. We will follow this convention in this book.

In practice, it is frequently the case that constants apply to all instances of a class. In this situation, we declare *class constants*. Class constants are constant class fields. They are declared by using a combination of the `static` and `final` key words. For example:

```
private static final int SIZE = 10;
```

The definition of GRAVITY from our bouncing ball project is another example of such a constant. This is the style in which constants are defined most of the time. Instance-specific constants are much less frequently used.

5.14 Summary

Dealing with class libraries and class interfaces is essential for a competent programmer. There are two aspects to this topic: reading class library descriptions (especially class interfaces) and writing them.

It is important to know about some essential classes from the standard Java class library, and to be able to find out more when needed. In this chapter we have presented some of the most important classes, and have discussed how to browse the library documentation.

It is also important to be able to document any class that is written in the same style as the library classes, so that other programmers can easily use the class without the need to understand the implementation. This documentation should include good comments for every project, class, and method. Using `javadoc` with Java programs will help you to do this.

Terms introduced in this chapter

interface, implementation, map, set, javadoc, access modifier, information hiding, coupling, class variable, static, constant, final

Concept summary

- **Java library** The Java standard class library contains many classes that are very useful. It is important to know how to use the library.

- **library documentation** The Java standard library documentation shows details about all classes in the library. Using this documentation is essential in order to make good use of library classes.

- **interface** The interface of a class describes what a class does and how it can be used without showing the implementation.

- **implementation** The complete source code that defines a class is called the implementation of that class.

- **immutable** An object is said to be immutable if its contents or state cannot be changed once it has been created. Strings are an example of immutable objects.

- **map** A map is a collection that stores key/value pairs as entries. Values can be looked up by providing the key.

- **set** A set is a collection that stores each individual element at most once. It does not maintain any specific order.

- **documentation** The documentation of a class should be detailed enough for other programmers to use the class without the need to read the implementation.

- **access modifiers** Access modifiers define the visibility of a field, constructor, or method. Public elements are accessible from inside the same class and from other classes; private elements are accessible only from within the same class.

- **information hiding** Information hiding is a principle that states that internal details of a class's implementation should be hidden from other classes. It ensures better modularization of an application.

- **class variables, static variables** Classes can have fields. These are known as class variables or static variables. Exactly one copy exists of a class variable at all times, independent of the number of created instances.

Exercise 5.55 There is a rumor circulating on the internet that George Lucas (the creator of the *Star Wars* movies) uses a formula to create the names for the characters in his stories (Jar Jar Binks, ObiWan Kenobi, etc.). The formula – allegedly – is this:

Your Star Wars first name:
1 Take the first three letters of your last name.
2 Add to that the first two letters of your first name.

Your Star Wars last name:
1 Take the first two letters of your mother's maiden name.
2 Add to this the first three letters of the name of the town or city you were born in.

And now your task: create a new BlueJ project named *star-wars*. In it create a class named **NameGenerator**. This class should have a method named **generateStarWarsName** that generates a Star Wars name following the method described above. You will need to find out about a method of the **String** class that generates a substring.

Exercise 5.56 The following code fragment attempts to print out a string in upper-case letters:

```
public void printUpper(String s)
{
    s.toUpperCase();
    System.out.println(s);
}
```

This code, however, does not work. Find out why, and explain. How should it be written properly?

Exercise 5.57 Assume we want to swap the values of two integer variables, **a** and **b**. To do this, we write a method

```
public void swap(int i1, int i2)
{
    int tmp = i1;
    i1 = i2;
    i2 = tmp;
}
```

Then we call this method with our **a** and **b** variables:

```
swap(a, b);
```

Are **a** and **b** swapped after this call? If you test it you will notice that they are not! Why does this not work? Explain in detail.

Main concepts discussed in this chapter:

- testing
- debugging
- unit testing
- test automation

Java constructs introduced in this chapter:

(No new Java constructs are introduced in this chapter.)

6.1 Introduction

If you have followed the previous chapters in this book and if you have implemented the exercises we have suggested, then you have written a good number of classes by now. One observation that you will likely have made is that a class you write is rarely perfect after the first attempt to write its source code. Usually, it does not work correctly at first, and some more work is needed to complete it.

The problems you are dealing with will shift over time. Beginners typically struggle with Java *syntax errors*. Syntax errors are errors in the structure of the source code itself. They are easy to spot, because the compiler will highlight them and display some sort of error message.

More experienced programmers who tackle more complicated problems usually have less difficulty with the language syntax. They are more concerned with *logical errors* instead.

A logical error is a problem where the program compiles and executes without an obvious error, but delivers the wrong result. Logical problems are much more severe and harder to find than syntax errors. In fact, it is sometimes not easy to detect that there is an error at all in the first place.

Writing syntactically correct programs is relatively easy to learn, and good tools (such as compilers) exist to detect syntax errors and point them out. Writing logically correct programs, on the other hand, is very difficult for any non-trivial problem, and the proof that a program is correct cannot, in general, be automated. It is so hard, in fact, that most software that is sold commercially is known to contain a significant number of bugs.

Thus it is essential for a competent software engineer to learn how to deal with correctness and how to reduce the number of errors in a class.

In this chapter, we shall discuss a variety of activities that are related to improving correctness of a program. These include testing, debugging, and writing for maintainability.

Testing is an activity that is concerned with finding out whether a segment of code contains any errors. Testing well is not easy, and there is much to think about when testing a program.

Debugging comes after testing. If tests have shown that an error is present, we use debugging techniques to find out exactly where the error is and how to fix it. There can be a significant amount of work between knowing that an error exists and finding the cause and fixing it.

Writing for maintainability is maybe the most fundamental topic. It is about trying to write code in such a way that errors are avoided in the first place and, if they still slip in, that they can be found as easily as possible. This is closely related to code style and commenting. Ideally, code should be easy to understand so that the original programmer avoids introducing errors and a maintenance programmer can easily find possible errors.

In practice, this is not always simple. But there are big differences between the number of errors and the effort it takes to debug well-written code and not-so-well-written code.

> **Concept:**
>
> **Testing** is the activity of finding out whether a piece of code (a method, class or program) produces the intended behavior.

> **Concept:**
>
> **Debugging** is the attempt to pinpoint and fix the source of an error.

6.2 Testing and debugging

Testing and debugging are crucial skills in software development. You will often need to check your programs for errors, and then locate the source of those errors when they occur. In addition, you might also be responsible for testing other people's programs, or modifying them. In the latter case, the debugging task is closely related to the process of understanding someone else's code, and there is a lot of overlap in the techniques you might use to do both. In the sections that follow, we shall investigate the following testing and debugging techniques:

- unit testing within BlueJ;
- test automation;
- manual walkthroughs;
- print statements;
- debuggers.

We shall look at the first two testing techniques in the context of some classes that you might have written for yourself, and the remaining debugging techniques in the context of understanding someone else's source code.

6.3 Unit testing within BlueJ

The term *unit testing* refers to a test of individual parts of an application, as opposed to *application testing*, which is testing of the complete application. The units being tested can be of various sizes. They may be a group of classes, a single class, or even a single method. It is worth observing that unit testing can be done long before an application is complete. Any single method, once written and compiled, can be tested.

Because BlueJ allows us to interact directly with individual objects, it offers unique ways to conduct testing on classes and methods. One of the points we want to stress in this section is that it is never too early to start testing. There are several benefits in early experimentation and testing. First, they give us valuable experience with a system that can make it possible to spot problems early enough to fix them at a much lower cost than if they had not been uncovered until much later in the development. Second, we can start to build up a series of test cases and results that can be used over and over again as the system grows. Each time we make a change to the system, these test cases allow us to check that we have not inadvertently introduced errors in the rest of the system as a result of the changes. In order to illustrate this form of testing within BlueJ, we shall use the *diary-prototype* project, which represents an early stage in the development of software to support an electronic desk diary. Once this software has been completed, this system is intended to allow an individual to schedule their daily appointments over the course of a whole year.

Open the *diary-prototype* project. Just three classes have been developed: `Appointment`, `Day`, and `Week`. As these classes will be fundamental within the overall system, we wish both to test that they work as they should, and to see whether we are happy with some of the decisions we have made in their design and implementation. The `Appointment` class describes passive objects whose purpose is to record the reason for an appointment and its duration as a whole number of hours. For our discussion of testing we shall concentrate on the `Day` class, shown in Code 6.1. An object of this class keeps track of the set of appointments that have been made on a single day. Each day records its unique position within the year – a value in the range 1–366. Two simplifications in this version are that appointments always start on an hour boundary, and that they always last a whole number of hours, so appointments can be made at 9 a.m., 10 a.m., and so on through to 5 p.m. (or 17:00 hours in the 24-hour clock).

As part of its testing, there are several aspects of the `Day` class that we should like to check:

■ Does the `appointments` field have sufficient space to maintain the required number of bookings?

■ Does the `showAppointments` method correctly print the list of appointments that have been made?

■ Does the `makeAppointment` method update the `appointments` field correctly when an appointment is made?

■ Does the `findSpace` method return the correct result when asked to find room for a new appointment?

We shall find that all of these can be tested conveniently using the object bench within BlueJ. In addition, we shall see that the interactive nature of BlueJ makes it possible to simplify some of the testing by making controlled alterations to a class under test.

Code 6.1
The `Day` class

```
/**
 * Maintain the appointments for one day in a diary.
 *
 * @author David J. Barnes and Michael Kölling
 * @version 2003.10.08
 */
```

Code 6.1
continued
The **Day** class

```java
public class Day
{
    // The first and final bookable hours in a day.
    public static final int START_OF_DAY = 9;
    public static final int FINAL_APPOINTMENT_TIME = 17;
    // The number of bookable hours in a day.
    public static final int MAX_APPOINTMENTS_PER_DAY =
                        FINAL_APPOINTMENT_TIME -
                        START_OF_DAY + 1;

    // A day number within a particular year. (1-366)
    private int dayNumber;
    // The current list of appointments for this day.
    private Appointment[] appointments;

    /**
     * Constructor for objects of class Day.
     * @param dayNumber The number of this day in the year
     *                  (1-366).
     */
    public Day(int dayNumber)
    {
        this.dayNumber = dayNumber;
        appointments =
                new Appointment[MAX_APPOINTMENTS_PER_DAY];
    }

    /**
     * Try to find space for an appointment.
     * @param appointment The appointment to be accommodated.
     * @return The earliest time today that can accommodate
     *         the appointment. Return -1 if there is
     *         insufficient space.
     */
    public int findSpace(Appointment appointment)
    {
        int duration = appointment.getDuration();
        for(int slot = 0;
                slot < MAX_APPOINTMENTS_PER_DAY; slot++) {
            if(appointments[slot] == null) {
                final int time = START_OF_DAY + slot;
                // Potential start point.
                if(duration == 1) {
                    // Only a single slot needed.
                    return time;
                }
                else {
                    // How many more slots are needed?
                    int further_slots_required = duration - 1;
                    for(int nextSlot = slot + 1;
```

Code 6.1
continued

The Day class

```java
                                further_slots_required > 0 &&
                                appointments[nextSlot] == null;
                                nextSlot++) {
                        further_slots_required—;
                    }
                    if(further_slots_required == 0) {
                        // A big enough space has been found.
                        return time;
                    }
                }
            }
        }
        // Not enough space available.
        return -1;
    }

    /**
     * Make an appointment.
     * @param time The hour at which the appointment starts.
     * @param appointment The appointment to be made.
     * @return true if the appointment was successful,
     *         false otherwise.
     */
    public boolean makeAppointment(int time,
                                   Appointment appointment)
    {
        if(validTime(time)) {
            int startTime = time - START_OF_DAY;
            if(appointments[startTime] == null) {
                int duration = appointment.getDuration();
                // Fill in all the slots for the full duration
                // of the appointment.
                for(int i = 0; i < duration; i++) {
                    appointments[startTime + i] = appointment;
                }
                return true;
            }
            else {
                return false;
            }
        }
        else {
            return false;
        }
    }

    /**
     * @param time Which time of day. This must be between the
     *        START_OF_DAY time and the FINAL_APPOINTMENT_TIME.
     * @return The Appointment at the given time.
```

Code 6.1
continued
The **Day** class

```java
 *          null is returned if either the time is invalid
 *          or there is no Appointment at the given time.
 */
public Appointment getAppointment(int time)
{
    if(validTime(time)) {
        return appointments[time - START_OF_DAY];
    }
    else {
        return null;
    }
}

/**
 * Print a list of the day's appointments.
 */
public void showAppointments()
{
    System.out.println("=== Day " + dayNumber + " ===");
    for(int i = 0; i < MAX_APPOINTMENTS_PER_DAY; i++) {
        System.out.print((START_OF_DAY + i) + ": ");
        if(appointments[i] != null) {
            System.out.println(
                    appointments[i].getDescription());
        }
        else {
            System.out.println();
        }
    }
}

/**
 * @return The number of this day within the year (1-366).
 */
public int getDayNumber()
{
    return dayNumber;
}

/**
 * @return true if the time is between START_OF_DAY and
 *          FINAL_APPOINTMENT_TIME, false otherwise.
 */
public boolean validTime(int time)
{
    return time >= START_OF_DAY &&
            time <= FINAL_APPOINTMENT_TIME;
}
}
```

6.3.1 Using inspectors

In preparation for testing, create a Day object on the object bench and open its inspector by selecting the *Inspect* function from the object's menu. Select the appointments field and open the array's inspector (Figure 6.1). Check that the array contains enough space to contain a full day's appointments. Leave the array inspector open to assist with subsequent tests.

Figure 6.1

Inspector for the
appointments
array

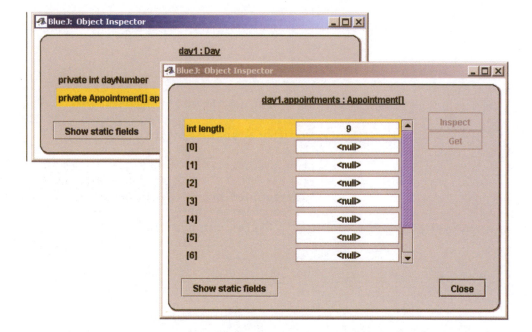

An essential component of testing classes that use data structures is to check that they behave properly both when the data structures are empty and when they are full. So a first test that can be performed on Day is to call its showAppointments method before any appointments have been made. This should list each bookable time period within the day. Later, we shall check that this method also works when the appointments list is full.

A key feature of good testing is to ensure that *boundaries* are checked, because these are often the places at which things go wrong. The boundaries associated with Day class are the start and end of a day. So, as well as checking that we can make appointments in the middle of the day, it will be important to check that we can correctly fill both the first and the last positions in the appointments array. In order to conduct tests along these lines, create three Appointment objects on the object bench, each of one hour's duration. Now try the following exercises as initial tests of the makeAppointment method.

Exercise 6.1 Use the three Appointment objects to make appointments at 9 a.m., 1 p.m., and 5 p.m., respectively. When a successful appointment is made, a result of true will be returned from makeAppointment. Use the array inspector to confirm that each appointment occupies the correct location after it is made.

Exercise 6.2 Call `showAppointments` to confirm that it correctly prints what you see displayed in the array inspector.

Exercise 6.3 Now check that an hour cannot be double-booked. Try to make a new appointment at the same time as one of those already made. The value `false` should be returned, but also use the array inspector to confirm that the new one has not replaced the original appointment.

Exercise 6.4 Good boundary-check testing also involves checking values that lie just beyond the valid range of data. Check that the correct behavior occurs when trying to make an appointment at 8 a.m. or 6 p.m.

Exercise 6.5 Create some further one-hour appointments and fill all of the times in a single **Day** object in order to be sure that this is possible. Check that `show-Appointments` gives the correct output when the array is full.

Exercise 6.6 Check that it is not possible to make another appointment within a day that is full. Do you need to try to double-book every single time period, or is it likely to be safe just to check a few of the possibilities? If you think a few are sufficient, which times would you check? *Hint:* Is the principle of paying particular attention to boundaries relevant here? Would it be enough just to check the boundaries?

Exercise 6.7 Is it possible to reuse a single `Appointment` object at different times within a single day? If you do this, do those tests have the same legitimacy as if you used different objects? Can you envisage circumstances in which you might wish to use a single `Appointment` object in multiple places within the diary as a whole?

Exercise 6.8 *Challenge exercise* Try repeating some of the above tests on a new **Day** object using some two-hour appointments. You should find that these modified tests trigger one or more errors. Try to correct these errors so that two-hour appointments can be made correctly. Having made changes to the **Day** class, is it safe to assume that all of the one-hour tests will still work as before? Section 6.4 will discuss some of the testing issues that arise when software is corrected or enhanced.

From these exercises it is easy to see how valuable inspectors are in giving immediate feedback on the state of an object, often avoiding the need to add print statements to a class when testing or debugging it.

6.3.2 Positive versus negative testing

Concept:

Positive testing is the testing of cases that are expected to succeed.

When deciding about what to test, we generally distinguish *positive* and *negative* test cases. Positive testing is the testing of functionality that we expect to work. For example, entering a one-hour appointment in the middle of an empty day is a positive test. When testing positive test cases, we have to convince ourselves that the code did indeed work as expected.

Negative testing is the test of cases that we expect to fail. Double-booking a time slot, or entering an appointment outside the valid day boundaries, are both examples of negative tests. When testing negative cases, we expect the program to handle this error in some specified, controlled way.

> **Pitfall** It is a very common error for inexperienced testers to conduct only positive tests. Negative tests – testing that what should go wrong, indeed does go wrong, and does so in a well-defined manner – is crucial for a good test procedure.

> **Exercise 6.9** Which of the test cases mentioned in the previous exercises are positive tests and which are negative? Make a table of each category. Can you think of further positive tests? Can you think of further negative ones?

6.4 Test automation

One reason why thorough testing is often neglected is that it is both a time-consuming and a relatively boring activity if done manually. This particularly becomes an issue when tests have to be run not just once but possibly many hundreds or thousands of times. Fortunately, there are techniques available that allow us to automate repetitive testing, and so remove much of the drudgery associated with it. The next section looks at test automation in the context of *regression testing*.

6.4.1 Regression testing

It would be nice if we could assume that correcting errors only ever improves the quality of a program. Sadly, experience shows that it is all too easy to introduce further errors when modifying software. Thus fixing an error at one spot may introduce another error at the same time.

As a consequence, it is desirable to run *regression tests* whenever a change is made to software. Regression testing involves re-running tests that have previously been passed, to ensure that the new version still passes them. It is much more likely to be performed if it can be automated in some way. One of the easiest ways to automate regression tests is to write a program that acts as a *test rig*, or *test harness*. The *diary-testing* project provides an illustration of how we might start to build a test rig for the tests we have been running on the diary prototype. Code 6.2 shows the `OneHourTests` class from that project.

Code 6.2

A basic test rig for one-hour tests

```
/**
 * Perform tests of the Day class that involve
 * making single-hour appointments.
 *
 * @author David J. Barnes and Michael Kölling.
 * @version 2001.09.14
 */
```

**Code 6.2
continued**

A basic test rig for
one-hour tests

```java
public class OneHourTests
{
    // The Day object being tested.
    private Day day;

    /**
     * Constructor for objects of class OneHourTests
     */
    public OneHourTests()
    {
    }

    /**
     * Test basic functionality by booking at either end
     * of a day, and in the middle.
     */
    public void makeThreeAppointments()
    {
        // Start with a fresh Day object.
        day = new Day(1);
        // Create three one-hour appointments.
        Appointment first = new Appointment("Java lecture", 1);
        Appointment second = new Appointment("Java class", 1);
        Appointment third = new Appointment("Meet John", 1);

        // Make each appointment at a different time.
        day.makeAppointment(9, first);
        day.makeAppointment(13, second);
        day.makeAppointment(17, third);

        day.showAppointments();
    }

    /**
     * Check that double-booking is not permitted.
     */
    public void testDoubleBooking()
    {
        // Set up the day with three legitimate appointments.
        makeThreeAppointments();
        Appointment badAppointment =
                        new Appointment("Error", 1);
        day.makeAppointment(9, badAppointment);

        // Show that the badAppointment has not been made.
        day.showAppointments();
    }
```

**Code 6.2
continued**

A basic test rig for
one-hour tests

```java
/**
 * Test basic functionality by filling a complete
 * day with appointments.
 */
public void fillTheDay()
{
    // Start with a fresh Day object.
    day = new Day(1);
    for(int time = Day.START_OF_DAY;
                time <= Day.FINAL_APPOINTMENT_TIME;
                    time++) {
        day.makeAppointment(
                time, new Appointment("Test " + time, 1));
    }

    day.showAppointments();
}
}
```

Each method within the test-rig class has been written to represent a single test, capturing the steps we took when running the tests manually in section 6.3.1. So the makeThree-Appointments method is designed to test that three legitimate appointments can be made in a new Day object, and fillTheDay tests that every hour can be filled. Both of these methods create a new Day object in order to ensure that they are testing it in its starting state. In contrast, testDoubleBooking makes use of the Day object created by makeThreeAppointments because it needs an object with some existing appointments.

A class such as OneHourTests makes it much easier to perform regression testing on the Day class. We simply have to create a single instance, run each of its methods, and check the results.

Exercise 6.10 Add any further methods to the OneHourTests class that you feel are appropriate for testing one-hour appointments. Then run regression tests on your corrected version of the Day class.

Exercise 6.11 Create a TwoHourTests class to capture a set of two-hour appointment tests.

Exercise 6.12 Create further classes to test any remaining functionality of the Day class that you feel is required.

Exercise 6.13 In a complex project, many hundreds or thousands of regression tests might need to be run following maintenance or enhancement activities. How easy do you think it would be to check the results of those tests using the techniques we have outlined in this section? Is there still a manual element to the regression testing process?

6.4.2 Automated checking of test results

The technique described in section 6.4.1 goes some way toward automating the process of testing, but it still requires a significant amount of human involvement in the process. For instance, the printed list of appointments has to be checked by eye, and this also requires the checker to know what the results should be. Automated regression testing would be even more effective if we could make the tests self-checking, requiring human intervention only if the result of one or more of them indicates a possible problem. The project *diary-testing-junit-v1* represents a significant step in this direction. Figure 6.2 shows the class diagram from this project.

Figure 6.2

A project with a test class

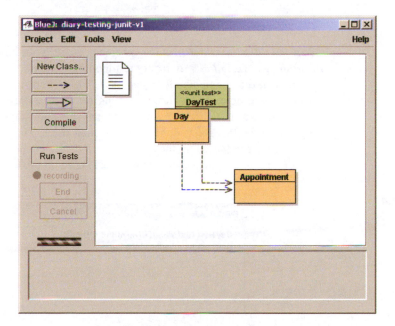

The first thing to note is that the diagram includes a different style of class, `DayTest`, immediately behind the `Day` class. `DayTest` is a *test class* and is annotated by BlueJ as a `<<unit test>>`. Its color is different from that of the ordinary classes in the diagram. A second thing to note is the additional items below the Compile button. See below for how to ensure that these appear in your project window. A further difference is apparent in the menu that appears if we right-click the test class (Figure 6.3). There are three new sections in the menu instead of a list of constructors.

Test classes are a feature of BlueJ designed to support regression testing. They are based on the JUnit testing framework devised by Erich Gamma and Kent Beck. A test class is usually associated with an ordinary project class. In this case `DayTest` is associated with the `Day` class, and we say that `Day` is the *reference class* for `DayTest`.

> **JUnit, www.junit.org** JUnit is a popular testing framework to support organized unit testing and regression testing in Java. It is available independent of specific development environments, as well as integrated in many environments. JUnit was developed by Erich Gamma and Kent Beck. You can find the software and a lot of information about it at `http://www.junit.org`.

Figure 6.3

The popup menu
for a test class

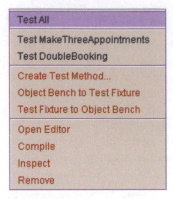

Open the *diary-testing-junit-v1* project. Once you have opened it, select *Tools/ Preferences/Miscellaneous* from the menu and ensure that the *Show unit testing tools* option is ticked. Immediately under the *Compile* button in the main BlueJ window you should see some extra entries, including a *Run Tests* button. Press the button and the window shown in Figure 6.4 should appear. This shows the results of automatically running two of the three tests described in section 6.4.1. The ticks immediately to the left of the test names indicate that the tests succeeded. You can achieve the same by selecting the *Test All* option from the popup menu associated with the test class.

Figure 6.4

The test results
window

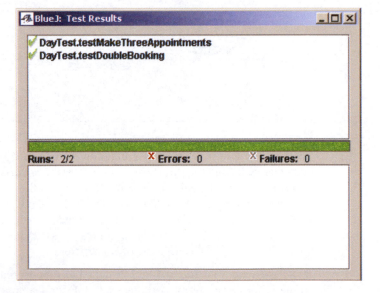

Test classes are clearly different in some way from ordinary classes, and if you open the source code of DayTest you will notice that it has some new features. At this stage of the book we are not going to discuss in detail how test classes work, but it is worth noting that, although the source code of DayTest could have been written by a person, it was, in fact, *automatically generated* by BlueJ. Some of the comments were then added afterwards to make the class more readable. A test class is created first of all by using the right mouse button over a potential reference class and selecting *Create Test Class* from the popup menu. Note that Day already has a test class, so this additional menu item does not appear in its class menu, but the one for Appointment does have it, as it currently has no associated test class.

The key point about a test class is that it contains source code both to run tests on a reference class, and to check whether the tests were successful or not. For instance, here is one of the statements from testDoubleBooking that checks that it is not possible to make a second appointment at 9 a.m.:

```
assertEquals(false, day1.makeAppointment(9, appointm2));
```

When such tests are run, BlueJ is able to display the results in the window shown in Figure 6.4.

In the next section we shall discuss how BlueJ supports automation of regression testing so that you can create your own automated tests.

Exercise 6.14 Create a test class for the Appointment class in the *diary-testing-junit-v1* project.

Exercise 6.15 What methods are created automatically when a new test class is created?

6.4.3 Recording a test

As we discussed at the beginning of section 6.4, test automation is desirable because manually creating and re-creating tests is a time-consuming process. BlueJ makes it possible to combine the effectiveness of manual unit testing with the power of test automation by enabling us to record manual tests, and then replay them later for the purposes of regression testing. The DayTest class from the *diary-testing-junit-v1* project was created via this process. We shall use the *diary-testing-junit-v2* project to illustrate BlueJ's test-recording facilities.

Suppose that we wanted to thoroughly test the findSpace method of the Day class. This method tries to find space for an appointment. There are several tests we would like to make, such as:

- finding space in an empty day (positive);
- finding space when there is at least one appointment already made but the day is not full (positive);
- trying to find space in a day that is fully booked (negative);
- trying to find space for a two-hour appointment when there are no consecutive two-hour spaces (negative).

We shall describe how to create the first of these, and leave the rest as exercises.

Open the *diary-testing-junit-v2* project. A test is recorded by telling BlueJ to start recording, performing the test manually, and then signaling the end of the test.

The first step is done via the menu attached to a test class. This tells BlueJ which class you wish the new test to be stored in. Select *Create Test Method ...* from the DayTest class's popup menu. You will be prompted for a name for the test method. If the name does not start with 'test' then this will be added as a prefix anyway.

For this test we are going to check that calling findSpace on a completely free day will return 9.00 a.m. as the first free time, so a name such as findSpace9 would be appropriate. Once you have entered a name and clicked *Ok*, a red circle appears to the left of the class diagram, and the *End* and *Cancel* buttons become available. *End* is used to indicate the end of the test-creation process and *Cancel* to abandon it.

Once recording is started, we just carry out the actions that we would with a normal manual test:

- Create a Day object.
- Create an Appointment object, with a one-hour duration.
- Call the findSpace method on Day object.

Until the final step, there will be no difference from normal object interaction. However, once findSpace has been called, a new dialog window will appear (Figure 6.5). This is an extended version of the normal method result window, and it is a crucial part of the automated testing process. Its purpose is to allow you to specify what the result of the method call *should be*. This is called an *assertion*.

In this case, we expect the method return value to be 9, and we want to include a check in our test to make sure that this is really the case. We can now make sure that the *Assert that* checkbox is checked, enter 9 in the dialog, and select the *Close* button.

Figure 6.5

The method result dialog with assertion facility

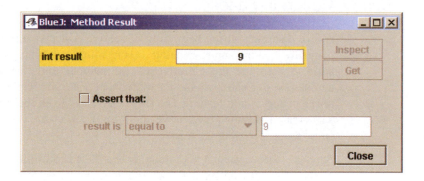

As that is the final stage of the test we then press the *End* button to stop the recording. At that point, BlueJ adds source code to the DayTest class for our new method, testFindSpace9, then compiles the class and clears the object bench. The resulting generated method is shown in Code 6.3.

Code 6.3

An automatically generated test method

```java
public void testFindSpace9()
{
    Day day1 = new Day(1);
    Appointment appointm1 = new Appointment("Java lecture", 1);
    assertEquals(9, day1.findSpace(appointm1));
}
```

As can be seen, the method contains statements that reproduce the actions made when recording it: Day and Appointment objects are created, and the findSpace method is called. The call to assertEquals is what checks that the result returned by findSpace matches the expected value of 9. The exercises below are provided so that you can try this process out for yourself. They include an example to show what happens if the actual value does not match the expected value.

> **Exercise 6.16** Using the *diary-testing-junit-v2* project, create a method in DayTest to check that findSpace returns the value of 10 for a one-hour appointment if a day already has a single one-hour appointment at nine a.m. In essence, you need to perform similar steps to those used to create testFindSpace9 but use makeAppointment for the first appointment and findSpace for the second appointment. You will need to specify assertions for the results of both calls.
>
> **Exercise 6.17** Create a test to check that findSpace returns a value of −1 if an attempt is made to find an appointment in a day that is already full.
>
> **Exercise 6.18** Create a test class that has Appointment as its reference class. Record separate test methods within it that check that the description and duration fields of an Appointment object are initialized correctly following its creation.
>
> **Exercise 6.19** Create the following negative test in the DayTest class. Create a Day object, a one-hour Appointment object, and a two-hour Appointment object. Make the one-hour appointment at 10 a.m., and then try to make the two-hour appointment at 9 a.m. Since this call to makeAppointment should fail, the value to put into the assertion is **false**. Now run the test. What is shown in the test results window?

6.4.4 Fixtures

Concept:

A **fixture** is a set of objects in a defined state that serves as a basis for unit tests.

As a set of test methods is built up, it is common to find yourself creating similar objects for each one. For instance, every test of the Day class will involve creating at least one Day object and one or more Appointment objects. A group of objects that are used in more than one test is known as a *fixture*. Two menu items associated with a test class enable us to work with fixtures in BlueJ: *Object Bench to Test Fixture* and *Test Fixture to Object Bench*. Using the *diary-testing-junit-v2* project, create a Day object and an Appointment object on the object bench. Now select *Object Bench to Test Fixture* from DayTest. The objects will disappear from the object bench, and if you examine the source code of DayTest you will see that its setUp method looks something like Code 6.4, where day1 and appointm1 have been defined as fields.

The significance of the setUp method is that it is automatically called immediately before every test method is called. This means that the individual test methods no longer need to create their own versions of the fixture objects. As a result, we can edit methods such as testDoubleBooking and remove the first two statements:

```
Day day1 = new Day(1);
Appointment appointm1 = new Appointment("Java lecture", 1);
```

because the remaining statements in that method will use the objects of the fixture.

```java
/**
 * Sets up the test fixture.
 *
 * Called before every test case method.
 */
protected void setUp()
{
    day1 = new Day(1);
    appointm1 = new Appointment("Java lecture", 1);
}
```

Once we have a fixture associated with a test class this will also simplify the recording of further tests, because whenever we create a new test method, the objects from the fixture will automatically appear on the object bench.

Should we wish to add further objects to the fixture at any time, one of the easiest ways is to select *Test Fixture to Object Bench*, add further objects to the object bench in the usual way, and then select *Object Bench to Test Fixture*. Of course, we could also simply edit the setUp method and add further fields directly to the test class.

Test automation is a powerful concept because it makes it more likely that tests will be written in the first place, and more likely that they will be run and re-run as a program develops. You should try to get into the habit of starting to write unit tests early in the development of a project, and of keeping them up to date as the project progresses. In Chapter 12 we shall return to the subject of assertions in the context of error handling.

> **Exercise 6.20** Add further automated tests to the **DayTest** class in the *diary-testing-junit-v2* project until you reach a point where you are reasonably confident of the correct operation of the classes. Use both positive and negative tests. If you discover any errors, be sure to record tests that guard against recurrence of these errors in later versions.

In the next section, we look at writing programs from the wider perspective of a multi-person project.

6.5 Modularization and interfaces

In Chapter 3 we introduced the concept of modularization, within the context of a project to implement a digital clock. We pointed out that modularization is crucial in any project in which different people implement the various components. However, simply breaking a task up into multiple classes is not enough in itself. In addition, there must be clear guidelines for the various implementers about who is doing what, and how the various components will fit together in the final application. Without such guidelines, the end result is likely to be the software equivalent of trying to fit a square peg into a round hole.

When software components collaborate to fulfill a task we say that the *interface* between them must be clear and well defined. By 'interface' we mean those parts of a class that are known about and relied upon by other classes. This was the meaning we gave to interfaces in Chapter 5.

Consider, for example, a project to develop software to operate an arithmetic calculator. One way to break down this project is into two major pieces: one part responsible for allowing users to enter calculations, and the other for implementing the arithmetic logic of the calculations. Figure 6.6 seeks to illustrate that for either module to use the other, something must be done to define the interface between them.

Figure 6.6
Separate modules
of a calculator

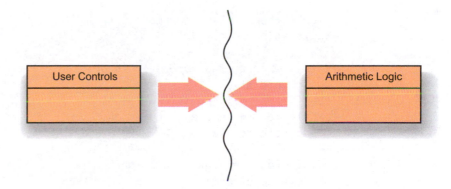

Where two modules are to be developed simultaneously, it will often be necessary to define the interface before work starts on the implementation of either. This can usually be done in the form of method signatures, because they provide sufficient information for one class to know how to interact with another, without needing to know how those methods will be implemented. This is an important concept. We try as much as possible to separate the interface between classes from the exact implementation details. (We have already discussed some advantages of this in Chapter 5.) Within the calculator project there are different ways in which we might choose to implement the user controls: purely as a piece of software with a push-button graphical view (Figure 6.7); or as a piece of hardware in the form of a hand-held device. The implementation of the arithmetic logic component should not be affected by such differences.

Figure 6.7
The user interface of
a software calculator

In the next few sections, we shall explore the implementation of a simple software calculator, based around two separate classes: `CalcEngine` and `UserInterface`. The interface we shall define between them is shown in Code 6.5.

Code 6.5

The interface of the
arithmetic logic unit

```java
// Return the value to be displayed.
public int getDisplayValue();

// Call when a digit button is pressed.
public void numberPressed(int number);

// Call when a plus operator is pressed.
public void plus();

// Call when a minus operator is pressed.
public void minus();

// Call to complete a calculation.
public void equals();

// Call to reset the calculator.
public void clear();
```

The `CalcEngine` class will provide the implementation of this interface. The interface represents a simple form of contract between the `CalcEngine` class and other parts of the program that wish to use it. The interface describes a minimum set of methods that will be implemented in the logic component, and for each method the return type and parameters are fully defined. Note that the interface gives no details of exactly what its implementing class will do internally when notified that a plus operator has pressed, for instance; that is left to its implementers. In addition, the implementing class might well have additional methods not listed here.

In the sections that follow, we shall look at an attempt to implement this interface as an illustration of various code-reading and debugging techniques.

6.6   A debugging scenario

Imagine you have been asked to join an existing project team that is working on an implementation of the calculator described in the previous sections. You have been drafted in because a key member of the programming team – Hacker T. Largebrain – has just been promoted to a management position on another project. Before leaving, Hacker assured the team you are joining that his implementation of the logic interface was finished and fully tested. He had even written some test software to verify that this was the case. You have been asked to take over the class and simply ensure that it is properly commented prior to integration with the classes being written by other members of the team.

You decide that the best way to understand Hacker's software prior to documenting it is to explore its source and the behavior of its objects.

6.7 Commenting and style

Open the *calculator-engine* project to view the classes. The `CalcEngineTester` class takes the place of the user interface at this stage of development. This illustrates another positive feature of defining interfaces between modules: it becomes easier to develop mock-ups of the other modules for the purpose of testing.

If you take a look at the `CalcEngine` class, you will find that its author has paid attention to some important areas of good style:

- The class has been given a multi-line comment at the top indicating the purpose of the class. Also included are annotations indicating author and version number.
- Each method of the interface has a comment indicating its purpose, parameters, and return type. This will certainly make it easier to generate project documentation for the interface, as discussed in Chapter 5.
- The layout of the class is consistent, with appropriate amounts of white-space indentation used to indicate the distinct levels of nested blocks and control structures.
- Expressive variable names and method names have been chosen.

Although these conventions may seem time consuming during implementation, they can be of enormous benefit in helping someone else to understand your code (as we have to in this scenario) or in helping you to remember what a class does if you have taken a break from working on it.

We also note another detail that looks less promising: Hacker has not used a specialized unit test class to capture his tests, but has written his own test class. As we know about unit test support in BlueJ, we wonder why.

This does not necessarily have to be bad. Hand-written test classes may be just as good, but it makes us a little suspicious. Did Hacker really know what he was doing? We shall come back to this point a bit later.

So, maybe Hacker's abilities are as great as he thinks they are, and you will not have much to do to make the class ready for integration with the others?! Try the following exercises to see if this is the case.

Exercise 6.21 Make sure the classes in the project are compiled, and then create a `CalcEngineTester` object within BlueJ. Call the `testAll` method. What is printed in the terminal window? Do you believe the final line of what it says?

Exercise 6.22 Using the object you created in the previous exercise, call the `testPlus` method. What result does it give? Is that the same result as was printed by the call to `testAll`? Call `testPlus` one more time. What result does it give now? Should it always give the same answer? If so, what should that answer be? Take a look at the source of the `testPlus` method to check.

Exercise 6.23 Repeat the previous exercise with the `testMinus` method. Does it always give the same result?

The experiments above should have alerted you to the fact that not all seems to be right with the `CalcEngine` class. It looks like it contains some errors. But what are they, and how can we find them? In the sections that follow, we shall consider a number of different ways in which we can try to locate where errors are occurring in a class.

6.8 Manual walkthroughs

Manual walkthroughs are a relatively underused technique, perhaps because they are a particularly 'low-tech' debugging and testing technique. However, do not let this fool you into thinking that they are not useful. A manual walkthrough involves printing copies of the classes you are trying to understand or debug and then getting right away from your computer! It is all too easy to spend a lot of time sitting in front of a computer screen not making much progress in trying to deal with a programming problem. Relocating and refocusing your efforts can often free your mind to attack a problem from a completely different direction. We have often found that going off to lunch, or driving home from the office, brings enlightenment that has otherwise eluded us through hours of slogging away at the keyboard!

A walkthrough involves both reading classes and tracing the flow of control between classes and objects. This aids understanding both the ways in which objects interact with one another, and how they behave internally. In effect, a walkthrough is a pencil and paper simulation of what happens inside the computer when you run a program. In practice, it is best to focus on a narrow portion of an application, such as a single logical grouping of actions or even a single method call.

6.8.1 A high-level walkthrough

We shall illustrate the walkthrough technique with the *calculator-engine* project. You might find it useful to print out copies of the `CalcEngine` and `CalcEngineTester` classes in order to follow through the steps of this technique.

We shall start by examining the `testPlus` method of the `CalcEngineTester` class, as it contains a single logical grouping of actions that should help us to gain an understanding of how several methods of the `CalcEngine` class work together to fulfill the computation role of a calculator. As we work our way through it, we shall often make penciled notes of questions that arise in our minds.

1 For this first stage we do not want to delve into too much detail. We simply want to look at how the `testPlus` method uses an engine object, without exploring the internal details of the engine. From earlier experimentation it would appear that there are some errors to be found, but we do not know whether the errors are in the tester or the engine. So the first step is to check that the tester appears to be using the engine appropriately.

2 We note that the first statement of `testPlus` assumes that the `engine` field already refers to a valid object:

```
engine.clear();
```

We can verify that this is the case by checking the tester's constructor. It is a common error for an object's fields not to have been initialized properly, either in their declarations or in a constructor. If we attempt to use a field with no associated object, then a `NullPointerException` is a likely runtime error.

3 The first statement's call to `clear` appears to be an attempt to put the calculator engine into a valid starting state, ready to receive instructions to perform a calculation. This looks like a reasonable thing to do – equivalent to pressing a 'reset' or 'clear' key on a real calculator. At this stage, we do not look at the engine class to check exactly what the `clear` method does. That can wait until we have achieved a level of confidence that the tester's actions are reasonable. Instead, we simply make a penciled note to check that `clear` puts the engine into a valid starting state as expected.

4 The next statement in `testPlus` is the entry of a digit via the `numberPressed` method:

```
engine.numberPressed(3);
```

This, too, is reasonable, as the first step in making a calculation is to enter the first operand. Once again, we do not look to see what the engine does with the number. We simply assume that it stores it somewhere for later use in the calculation.

5 The next statement calls `plus`, so we now know that the full value of the left operand is 3. We could make a penciled note of this fact on the printout, or make a tick against this assertion in one of the comments of `testPlus`. Similarly we should note or confirm that the operation being executed is addition. This seems like a trivial thing to do, but it is all too easy for a class's comments to get out of step with the code they are supposed to document. So checking the comments at the same time as we read the code can help us to avoid being misled by them later.

6 Next, another single digit is entered as the right operand by a further call to `number-Pressed`.

7 Completion of the addition is requested by a call to the `equals` method. We might make a penciled note that, from the way it has been used in `testPlus`, the `equals` method appears not to return the result of the calculation, as we might have expected otherwise. This is something else that we can check when we look at `CalcEngine`.

8 The final statement of `testPlus` obtains the value that should appear in the calculator's display:

```
return engine.getDisplayValue();
```

Presumably, this is the result of the addition, but we cannot know that for sure without looking in detail at `CalcEngine`. Once again, we shall make a note to check that this is indeed the case.

With our examination of `testPlus` completed, we have gained a reasonable degree of confidence that it uses the engine appropriately: that is, simulating a recognizable sequence of key presses to complete a simple calculation. We might remark that the method is not particularly ambitious – both operands are single-digit numbers, and only a single operator is used. However, that is not unusual in test methods, because it is important to test for the most basic functionality before testing more complex combinations. Nevertheless, it is useful to observe that some more complex tests could be added to the tester at some stage.

Exercise 6.24 Perform a similar walkthrough of your own with the `testMinus` method. Does that raise any further questions in your mind about things you might like to check when looking at `CalcEngine` in detail?

Before looking at the `CalcEngine` class, it is worth walking through the `testAll` method, to see how it uses the `testPlus` and `testMinus` methods we have been looking at.

1 The `testAll` method is a straight-line sequence of print statements.

2 It contains one call to each of `testPlus` and `testMinus`, and the values they return are printed out for the user to see. We might note that there is nothing to tell the user what the results should be. This makes it hard for the user to confirm that the results are correct.

3 We note that the final statement boldly states:

```
All tests passed.
```

but the method contains no tests to establish the truth of this assertion! There really should be a proper means of establishing both what the result values should be, and whether they have been calculated correctly or not. This is something we should remedy as soon as we have the chance to get back to the source of this class.

At this stage, we should not be distracted by the final point into making changes that do not directly address the errors we are looking for. If we make those sorts of changes, we could easily end up masking the errors. One of the crucial requirements for successful debugging is to be able to trigger the error you are looking for easily and reproducibly. When that is the case, it is much easier to assess the effect of an attempted correction.

Having checked over the test class, we are in a position to examine the source of the `CalcEngine` class. We can do so armed with a reasonable sequence of method calls to explore from the walkthrough of the `testPlus` method, and a set of questions thrown up by it.

6.8.2 Checking state with a walkthrough

A `CalcEngine` object is quite different in style from its tester. This is because the engine is a completely passive object. It initiates no activity of its own, but simply responds to external method calls. This is typical of the server style of behavior. Server objects often rely heavily on their state to determine how they should respond to method calls. This is particularly true of the calculator engine. So, an important part of conducting the walk-through is to be sure that we always have an accurate representation of its state. One way to do this on paper is by making up a table of an object's fields and their values (Figure 6.8). A new line can be entered to keep a running log of the values following each method call.

Figure 6.8
Informal tabulation of an object's state

Method called	displayValue	leftOperand	previousOperator
initial state	0	0	' '
clear	0	0	' '
numberPressed(3)	3	0	' '

This technique makes it quite easy to check back if something appears to go wrong. It is also possible to compare the states after two calls to the same method.

1. As we start the walkthrough of `CalcEngine`, we document the initial state of the engine as in the first row of values in Figure 6.8. All of its fields are initialized in the constructor. As we observed when walking through the tester, object initialization is important, and we might make a note here to check that the default initialization is sufficient – particularly as the default value of `previousOperator` would appear not to represent a meaningful operator. Furthermore, this might make us think about whether it really is meaningful to have a *previous* operator before the first real operator in a calculation. In noting down these questions, we do not necessarily have to try to discover the answers straight away, but they provide prompts as we discover more about the class.

2. The next step is to see how a call to `clear` changes the engine's state. As shown in the second data row of Figure 6.8, the state remains unchanged at this point, because `displayValue` is already set to zero. But we might note another question here: Why is the value of only one of the fields set by this method? If this method is supposed to implement a form of reset, why not clear all of the fields?

3. Next a call to `numberPressed` with an actual parameter of 3 is investigated. The method multiplies an existing value of `displayValue` by 10, and then adds in the new digit. This correctly models the effect of appending a new digit onto the right-hand end of an existing number. It relies on `displayValue` having a sensible initial value of zero when the first digit of a new number is entered, and our investigation of the `clear` method gives us confidence that this will be the case. So this method looks all right.

4. Continuing to follow the order of calls in the `testPlus` method, we next look at `plus`. Its first statement calls the `applyPreviousOperator` method. Here we have to decide whether to continue ignoring nested method calls, or whether to break off and see what it does. Taking a quick look at the `applyPreviousOperator` method we can see that it is fairly short. Furthermore, it is clearly going to alter the state of the engine, and we shall not be able to continue documenting the state changes unless we follow it up. So we would certainly decide to follow the nested call. It is important to remember where we came from, so we would mark the listing just inside the `plus` method before following the `applyPreviousOperator` method through. If following a nested method call is likely to lead to further nested calls, we should need to use something more than a simple mark to help us find our way back to the caller. In that case, it is better to mark the call points with ascending numerical values – reusing previous values as calls return.

5. The `applyPreviousOperator` method gives us some insights into how the `previousOperator` field is used. It also appears to answer one of our earlier questions: whether having a space as the initial value for the previous operator was all right. The method explicitly checks to see that `previousOperator` contains either a `'+'` or a `'-'` before applying it. So another value will not result in an incorrect operation being applied. By the end of this method, the value of `leftOperand` will have been changed, so we would note its new value in the state table.

6. Returning to the `plus` method, the remaining two fields have their values set, so that the next row of the state table will contain the following values:

plus	0	3	`'+'`

The walkthrough of the engine can be continued in a similar fashion, documenting the state changes, gaining insights into its behavior, and raising questions along the way. The following exercises should help you to complete the walkthrough.

Exercise 6.25 Complete the state table based on the following subsequent calls, found in the `testPlus` method:

```
numberPressed(4);
equals();
```

Exercise 6.26 When walking through the `equals` method, did you feel the same reassurances that we felt in `applyPreviousOperator` about the default value of `previousOperator`?

Exercise 6.27 Walk through a call to `clear` immediately following the call to `equals` at the end of your state table, and record the new state. Is the engine in the same state as it was at the previous call to `clear`? If not, what impact do you think this could have on any subsequent calculations?

Exercise 6.28 In the light of your walkthrough, what changes do you think should be made to the `CalcEngine` class? Make those changes to a paper version of the class, and then try the walkthrough all over again. You should not need to walkthrough the `CalcEngineTester` class, just repeat the actions of its `testAll` method.

Exercise 6.29 Try a walkthrough of the following sequence of calls on your corrected version of the engine:

```
clear();
numberPressed(9);
plus();
numberPressed(1);
minus();
numberPressed(4);
equals();
```

What should the result be? Does the engine appear to behave correctly and leave the correct answer in `displayValue`?

6.8.3 Verbal walkthroughs

Another way in which the walkthrough technique can be used to find errors in a program is to try explaining to another person what a class or method does. This works in two completely different ways:

■ The person you explain the code to might spot the error for you.

■ You will often find that the simple act of trying to put into words what a piece of code should do is enough to trigger in your own mind an understanding of why it does not.

This latter effect is so common that it can often be worth explaining a piece of code to someone who is completely unfamiliar with it – not in anticipation that *they* will find the error, but that *you* will!

6.9 Print statements

Probably the most common technique used to understand and debug programs – even amongst experienced programmers – is to annotate methods temporarily with print statements. Print statements are popular because they exist in most languages, they are available to everyone, and they are very easy to add with any editor. No additional software or language features are required to make use of them. As a program runs, these additional print statements will typically provide a user with information such as:

- which methods have been called;
- the values of parameters;
- the order in which methods have been called;
- the values of local variables and fields at strategic points.

Code 6.6 shows an example of how the `numberPressed` method might look with print statements added. Such information is particularly helpful in providing a picture of the way in which the state of an object changes as mutators are called. To help support this, it is often worth including a debugging method that prints out the current values of all the fields of an object. Code 6.7 shows such a `reportState` method for the `CalcEngine` class.

Code 6.6

A method with debugging print statements added

```java
/**
 * A number button was pressed.
 */
public void numberPressed(int number)
{
    System.out.println("numberPressed called with: " +
                        number);

    displayValue = displayValue * 10 + number;

    System.out.println("displayValue is: " + displayValue +
                       " at end of numberPressed.");
}
```

Code 6.7

A state-reporting method

```java
/**
 * Print the values of this object's fields.
 * @param where Where this state occurs.
 */
public void reportState(String where)
{
    System.out.println("displayValue: " + displayValue +
                       " leftOperand: " + leftOperand +
                       " previousOperator: " +
                       previousOperator + " at " + where);
}
```

If each method of `CalcEngine` contained a print statement at its entry point, and a call to `reportState` at its end, Figure 6.9 shows the output that might result from a call to the tester's `testPlus` method. (This was generated from a version of the calculator engine that can be found in the *calculator-engine-print-statements* project.) Such output allows us to build up a picture of how control flows between different methods. For instance, we can see from the order in which the state values are reported that a call to `plus` contains a nested call to `applyPreviousOperator`.

Figure 6.9

Debugging output from a call to `testPlus`

```
clear called
displayValue: 0 leftOperand: 0 previousOperator:  at end of clear
numberPressed called with: 3
displayValue: 3 leftOperand: 0 previousOperator:  at end of number...
plus called
applyPreviousOperator called
displayValue: 3 leftOperand: 3 previousOperator:  at end of apply...
displayValue: 0 leftOperand: 3 previousOperator: + at end of plus
numberPressed called with: 4
displayValue: 4 leftOperand: 3 previousOperator: + at end of number...
equals called
displayValue: 7 leftOperand: 0 previousOperator: + at end of  equals
```

Print statements can be very effective in helping to understand programs or to locate errors, but there are a number of disadvantages:

- It is not usually practical to add print statements to every method in a class. So they are only fully effective if the right methods have been annotated.
- Adding too many print statements can lead to information overload. A large amount of output can make it difficult to identify what you need to see. Print statements inside loops are a particular source of this problem.
- Once their purpose has been served, it can be tedious to remove them again.
- There is also the chance that, having removed them, they will be needed again later. It can be very frustrating to have to put them back in again!

Exercise 6.30 Open the *calculator-engine-print* project and complete the addition of print statements to each method and the constructor.

Exercise 6.31 Create a `CalcEngineTester` in the project and run the `testAll` method. Does the output that results help you to identify where the problem lies?

Exercise 6.32 Do you feel that the amount of output produced by the fully annotated `CalcEngine` class is too little, too much, or about right? If you feel that it is too little or too much, either add further print statements or remove some until you feel that you have the right level of detail.

Exercise 6.33 What are the respective advantages and disadvantages of using manual walkthroughs or print statements for debugging? Discuss.

6.9.1 Turning debugging information on or off

If a class is still under development when print statements are added, we often do not want to see the output every time the class is used. It is best if we can find a way to turn the printing on or off as required. The most common way to achieve this is to add an extra `boolean` debugging field to the class, and then make printing dependent upon the value of the field. Code 6.8 illustrates this idea.

Code 6.8

Controlling whether debugging information is printed or not

```java
/**
 * A number button was pressed.
 */
public void numberPressed(int number)
{
    if(debugging) {
        System.out.println("numberPressed called with: " +
                                number);
    }

    displayValue = displayValue * 10 + number;

    if(debugging) {
        reportState();
    }
}
```

A more economical variation on this theme is to replace the direct calls to print statements with calls to a specialized printing method added to the class.[1] The printing method would print only if the `debugging` field is `true`. Therefore calls to the printing method would not need to be guarded by an if statement. Code 6.9 illustrates this approach. Note that this version assumes that `reportState` either tests the debugging field itself, or also calls the new `printDebugging` method.

Code 6.9

A method for selectively printing debugging information

```java
/**
 * A number button was pressed.
 */
public void numberPressed(int number)
{
    printDebugging("numberPressed called with: " +
                    number);

    displayValue = displayValue * 10 + number;
```

---

[1] In fact, we could move this method to a specialized debugging class, but we shall keep things simple in this discussion.

**Code 6.9
continued**

A method for
selectively printing
debugging
information

```java
        reportState();
}

/**
 * Only print the debugging information if debugging
 * is true.
 * @param info The debugging information.
 */
public void printDebugging(String info)
{
    if(debugging) {
        System.out.println(info);
    }
}
```

6.10 Choosing a test strategy

We have seen that several different test strategies exist: written and verbal walkthroughs, use of print statements (either temporary, or permanent with enabling switches), interactive testing using the object bench, writing your own test class, or using a dedicated unit test class.

In practice, we would use different strategies at different times. Walkthroughs, print statements, and interactive testing are useful for initial testing of newly written code, or to investigate how a program segment works. Their advantage is that these techniques are quick and easy to use, they work in any programming language and are (except for the interactive testing) independent of the environment. The main disadvantage is that these tests cannot easily be repeated later to perform regression testing.

Using unit test classes has the advantage – once they have been set up – that tests can be replayed any number of times.

So Hacker's way of testing – writing his own test class – was one step in the right direction, but was, of course, flawed. We know now that his problem was that, although his class contained reasonable method calls for testing, it did not include any assertions on the method results, and thus did not detect test failure.

We also know, of course, that this could have been done better and easier by using a dedicated unit test class.

Exercise 6.34 Open the first *calculator-engine* project and add better testing by replacing Hacker's test class with a unit test class attached to the `CalcEngine`. Add similar tests to those Hacker used (and any others you find useful) and include correct assertions.

6.11 Debuggers

In Chapter 3 we introduced the use of a debugger to understand how an existing application operates, and how its objects interact. In a very similar manner, we can use the debugger to track down errors.

The debugger is essentially a software tool that provides support for performing a walk-through on a segment of code. We typically set a breakpoint at the statement where we want to start our walkthrough, and then use the *Step* or *Step Into* functions to do the actual walking.

One advantage is that the debugger automatically takes care of keeping track of every object's state, and thus doing this is quicker and less error prone than doing the same manually. A disadvantage is that debuggers typically do not keep a permanent record of state changes, so it is harder to go back and check the state as it was a few statements earlier.

A debugger typically also gives you information about the *call sequence* (or *stack*) at each point in time. The call sequence shows the name of the method containing the current statement, and the name of the method that the current method was called from, and the name of the method that *that* method was called from, and so on. Thus, the call sequence contains a record of all currently active, unfinished methods – similar to what we have done manually during our walkthrough by writing marks next to method call statements.

In BlueJ, the call sequence is displayed on the left-hand side of the debugger window. Every method name in that sequence can be selected to inspect the current values of that method's local variables.

> **Exercise 6.35** *Challenge exercise* In practice you will probably find that Hacker T. Largebrain's attempt to program the `CalcEngine` class is too full of errors to be worth trying to fix. Instead, write your own version of the class from scratch. The *calculator-gui* project contains classes that provide the GUI shown in Figure 6.7. Be sure to document your class thoroughly, and to create a thorough set of tests for your implementation so that your experience with Hacker's code will not have to be repeated by your successor!

6.12 Putting the techniques into practice

This chapter has described several techniques that can be used either to understand a new program or to test for errors in one. The *bricks* project provides a chance for you to try out those techniques with a new scenario. The project contains part of an application for a company producing bricks. Bricks are delivered to customers on palettes (stacks of bricks). The `Palette` class provides methods telling the height and weight of an individual palette, according to the number of bricks on it.

> **Exercise 6.36** Open the *bricks* project. Test it. There are at least four errors in this project. See if you can find them and fix them. What techniques did you use to find the errors? Which technique was most useful?

6.13   Summary

When writing software, we should anticipate that it will contain logical errors. Therefore, it is essential to consider both testing and debugging to be normal activities within the overall development process. BlueJ is particularly good at supporting interactive unit testing of both methods and classes. We have also looked at some basic techniques for automating the testing process, and performing simple debugging. Although we can never eliminate errors entirely, in Chapter 7 we shall look at some of the ways in which we can reduce the opportunities for introducing errors when writing object-oriented programs.

Terms introduced in this chapter

syntax error, logical error, testing, debugging, unit testing, positive testing, negative testing, regression testing, manual walkthrough, call sequence

Concept summary

- **testing** Testing is the activity of finding out whether a piece of code (a method, class or program) produces the intended behavior.

- **debugging** Debugging is the attempt to pinpoint and fix the source of an error.

- **positive testing** Positive testing is the testing of cases that are expected to succeed.

- **negative testing** Negative testing is the testing of cases that are expected to fail.

- **assertion** An assertion is an expression that states a condition that we expect to be true. If the condition is false, we say that the assertion fails. This indicates an error in our program.

- **fixture** A fixture is a set of objects in a defined state that serves as a basis for unit tests.

- **walkthrough** A walkthrough is an activity of working through a segment of code line by line, while observing changes of state and other behavior of the application.

Designing classes

Main concepts discussed in this chapter:

- responsibility-driven design
- coupling
- cohesion
- refactoring

Java constructs discussed in this chapter:

`static` (for methods), `Math`

In this chapter we look at some of the factors that influence the design of a class. What makes a class design either good or bad? Writing good classes can take more effort in the short term than writing bad classes, but in the long term that extra effort will often be justified. To help us write good classes there are some principles that we can follow. In particular, we introduce the view that class design should be responsibility-driven, and that classes should encapsulate their data.

This chapter is, like many of the chapters before, structured around a project. It can be studied by just reading it and following our line of argument, or it can be studied in much more depth by doing the project exercises in parallel with working through the chapter.

The project work is divided into three parts. In the first part, we discuss the necessary changes to the source code and develop and show complete solutions to the exercises. The solution for this part is also available in a project accompanying this book. The second part suggests more changes and extensions, and we discuss possible solutions at a high level (the class design level) but leave it to readers to do the lower-level work and to complete the implementation.

The third part suggests even more improvements in the form of exercises. We do not give solutions – the exercises apply the material discussed throughout the chapter.

Implementing all parts makes a good programming project over several weeks. It can also be done very well as a group project.

7.1 Introduction

It is possible to implement an application and to get it to perform its task with badly designed classes. Just executing a finished application does not usually indicate whether it is structured well internally or not.

The problems typically surface when a maintenance programmer wants to make some changes to an existing application. If, for example, a programmer attempts to fix a bug, or wants to add new functionality to an existing program, a task that might be easy and obvious with well-designed classes may well be very hard and involve a great deal of work if the classes are badly designed.

In larger applications, this effect already occurs during the original implementation. If the implementation starts with a bad structure, then finishing it might later become overly complex, and the complete program may either not be finished, or contain bugs, or take a lot longer to build than necessary. In reality, companies often maintain, extend, and sell an application over many years. It is not uncommon that an implementation for software that we can buy in a software store today was started more than 10 years ago. In this situation, a software company cannot afford to have badly structured code.

Since many of the effects of bad class design become most obvious when trying to adapt or extend an application, we shall do exactly that. In this chapter we will use an example called *world-of-zuul*, which is a simple, rudimentary implementation of a text-based adventure game. In its original state the game is not actually very ambitious: for one thing, it is incomplete. By the end of this chapter, however, you will be in a position to exercise your imagination and design and implement your own game and make it really fun and interesting.

> **world-of-zuul** Our *world-of-zuul* game is modeled on the original Adventure game that was developed in the early 1970s by Will Crowther, and expanded by Don Woods. The original game is also sometimes known as the *Colossal Cave Adventure*. This was a wonderfully imaginative and sophisticated game for its time, involving finding your way through a complex cave system, locating hidden treasure, using secret words, and other mysteries, all in an effort to score the maximum number of points. You can read more about it at places such as `http://jerz.setonhill.edu/if/canon/Adventure.htm` and `http://www.rickadams.org/adventure/`, or try doing a web search for 'Colossal Cave Adventure.'

While we work on extending the original application, we will take the opportunity to discuss aspects of its existing class design. We will see that the implementation we start with has examples of bad design decisions in it, and we will see how this impacts on our tasks and how we can fix them.

In the project examples for this book you will find two versions of the zuul project: *zuul-bad* and *zuul-better*. Both implement exactly the same functionality, but some of the class structure is different, representing bad design in one project and better design in the other. The fact that we can implement the same functionality in either a good way or a bad way illustrates the fact that bad design is not usually a consequence of having a difficult problem to solve. Bad design has more to do with the decisions that we make when solving a particular problem. We cannot use the argument that there was no other way to solve the problem as an excuse for bad design.

So, we will use the project with the bad design so that we can explore why it is bad, and then improve it. The better version is an implementation of the changes we discuss here.

Exercise 7.1 Open the project *zuul-bad*. (This project is called 'bad' because its implementation contains some bad design decisions, and we want to leave no doubt that this should not be used as an example of good programming practice!) Execute and explore the application. The project comment gives you some information about how to run it.

While exploring the application, answer the following questions:

- What does this application do?
- What commands does the game accept?
- What does each command do?
- How many rooms are in the scenario?
- Draw a map of the existing rooms.

Exercise 7.2 After you know what the whole application does, try to find out what each individual class does. Write down for each class the purpose of the class. You need to look at the source code to do this. Note that you might not (and need not) understand all of the source code. Often, reading through comments and looking at method headers is enough.

7.2 The world-of-zuul game example

From exercise 7.1, you have seen that the zuul game is not yet very adventurous. It is, in fact, quite boring in its current state. But it provides a good basis for us to design and implement our own game, which will hopefully be more interesting.

We start by analyzing the classes that are already there in our first version, and trying to find out what they do. The class diagram is shown in Figure 7.1.

Figure 7.1
Zuul class diagram

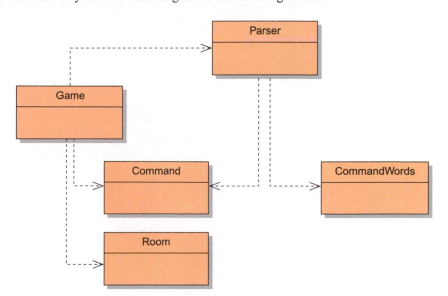

The project shows five classes. They are `Parser`, `CommandWords`, `Command`, `Room`, and `Game`. An investigation of the source code shows, fortunately, that these classes are quite well documented, and we can get an initial overview of what they do by just reading the class comment at the top of each class. (This fact also serves to illustrate that bad design involves something deeper than simply the way that a class looks, or how good its documentation is.) Our understanding of the game will be assisted by having a look at the source code to see what methods each class has, and what some of the methods appear to do. Here, we summarize the purpose of each class:

- *CommandWord* The `CommandWord` class defines all valid commands in the game. It does this by holding an array of strings with the command words.

- *Parser* The parser reads lines of input from the terminal and tries to interpret them as commands. It creates objects of class `Command` that represent the command that was entered.

- *Command* A `Command` object represents a command that was entered by the user. It has methods that make it easy for us to check whether this was a valid command, and to get the first and second words of the command as separate strings.

- *Room* A `Room` object represents a location in a game. Rooms can have exits that lead to other rooms.

- *Game* The `Game` class is the main class of the game. It sets the game up, and then enters a loop to read and execute commands. It also contains the code that implements each user command.

Exercise 7.3 Design your own game scenario. Do this away from the computer. Do not think about implementation, classes, or even programming in general. Just think about inventing an interesting game. This could be done with a group of people.

The game can be anything that has as its base structure a player moving through different locations. Here are some examples:

- You are a white blood cell traveling through the body in search of viruses to attack …
- You are lost in a shopping mall and must find the exit …
- You are a mole in its burrow and you cannot remember where you stored your food reserves before winter …
- You are an adventurer who searches through a dungeon full of monsters and other characters …
- You are from the bomb squad and must find and defuse a bomb before it goes off …

Make sure that your game has a goal (so that it has an end and the player can 'win'). Try to think of many things to make the game interesting (trap doors, magic items, characters that help you only if you feed them, time limits, whatever you like). Let your imagination run wild.

At this stage, do not worry about how to implement these things.

7.3 Introduction to coupling and cohesion

If we are to justify our assertion that some designs are better than others, then we need to define some terms that will allow us to discuss the issues that we consider to be important in class design. Two terms are central when talking about the quality of a class design: *coupling* and *cohesion*.

The term *coupling* refers to the interconnectedness of classes. We have already discussed in earlier chapters that we aim to design our applications as a set of cooperating classes that communicate via well-defined interfaces. The degree of coupling indicates how tightly these classes are connected. We strive for a low degree of coupling, or *loose coupling*.

The degree of coupling determines how hard it is to make changes in an application. In a tightly coupled class structure, a change in one class can make it necessary to change several other classes as well. This is what we try to avoid, because the effect of making one small change can quickly ripple through a complete application. In addition, finding all the places where changes are necessary and actually making the changes can be difficult and time consuming.

In a loosely coupled system, on the other hand, we can often change one class without making any changes to other classes, and the application will still work. We shall discuss particular examples of tight and loose coupling in this chapter.

The term *cohesion* relates to the number and diversity of tasks for which a single unit of an application is responsible. Cohesion is relevant for units of a single class and an individual method.[1]

Ideally, one unit of code should be responsible for one cohesive task (that is, one task that can be seen as a logical unit). A method should implement one logical operation, and a class should represent one type of entity. The main reason behind the principle of cohesion is reuse: if a method or a class is responsible for only one well-defined thing, then it is much more likely that it can be used again in a different context. A complementary advantage of following this principle is that, when change *is* required to some aspect of an application, we are likely to find all the relevant pieces located in the same unit.

We shall discuss how cohesion influences quality of class design with examples below.

> **Concept:**
>
> The term **coupling** describes the interconnectedness of classes. We strive for loose coupling in a system – that is, a system where each class is largely independent and communicates with other classes via a small, well-defined interface.

> **Concept:**
>
> The term **cohesion** describes how well a unit of code maps to a logical task or entity. In a highly cohesive system each unit of code (method, class, or module) is responsible for a well-defined task or entity. Good class design exhibits a high degree of cohesion.

> **Exercise 7.4** Draw (on paper) a map for the game you invented in exercise 7.3. Open the *zuul-bad* project, and save it under a different name (e.g. *zuul*). This is the project you will use to make improvements and modifications throughout this chapter. You can leave off the *-bad* suffix, since it will soon (hopefully) not be that bad anymore.
>
> As a first step, change the `createRooms` method in the `Game` class to create the rooms and exits you invented for your game. Test!

---

[1] We sometimes also use the term *module* (or *package* in Java) to refer to a multi-class unit. Cohesion is relevant at this level, too.

7.4 Code duplication

Code duplication is an indicator of bad design. The Game class shown in Code 7.1 contains a case of code duplication. The problem with code duplication is that any change to one version must also be made to the other if we are to avoid inconsistency. This increases the amount of work a maintenance programmer has to do, and it introduces the danger of bugs. It happens very easily that a maintenance programmer finds one copy of the code and, having changed it, assumes that the job is done. There is nothing indicating that a second copy of the code exists, and it might incorrectly remain unchanged.

Code 7.1

Selected sections
of the (badly
designed) Game
class

```java
public class Game
{
    //   .... some code omitted ...

    private void createRooms()
    {
        Room outside, theatre, pub, lab, office;

        // create the rooms
        outside = new Room(
                    "outside the main entrance of the university");
        theatre = new Room("in a lecture theatre");
        pub = new Room("in the campus pub");
        lab = new Room("in a computing lab");
        office = new Room("in the computing admin office");

        // initialise room exits
        outside.setExits(null, theatre, lab, pub);
        theatre.setExits(null, null, null, outside);
        pub.setExits(null, outside, null, null);
        lab.setExits(outside, office, null, null);
        office.setExits(null, null, null, lab);

        currentRoom = outside;   // start game outside
    }

    //   ... some code omitted ...

    /**
     * Print out the opening message for the player.
     */
    private void printWelcome()
    {
        System.out.println();
        System.out.println("Welcome to the World of Zuul!");
        System.out.println(
            "Zuul is a new, incredibly boring adventure game.");
        System.out.println("Type 'help' if you need help.");
```

Code 7.1 continued

Selected sections of the (badly designed) **Game** class

```java
        System.out.println();
        System.out.println("You are " +
                            currentRoom.getDescription());
        System.out.print("Exits: ");
        if(currentRoom.northExit != null)
            System.out.print("north ");
        if(currentRoom.eastExit != null)
            System.out.print("east ");
        if(currentRoom.southExit != null)
            System.out.print("south ");
        if(currentRoom.westExit != null)
            System.out.print("west ");
        System.out.println();
    }

    //   ... some code omitted ...

    /**
     * Try to go to one direction. If there is an exit, enter
     * the new room, otherwise print an error message.
     */
    private void goRoom(Command command)
    {
        if(!command.hasSecondWord()) {
            // if there is no second word,
            // we don't know where to go
            System.out.println("Go where?");
            return;
        }

        String direction = command.getSecondWord();

        // Try to leave current room.
        Room nextRoom = null;
        if(direction.equals("north"))
            nextRoom = currentRoom.northExit;
        if(direction.equals("east"))
            nextRoom = currentRoom.eastExit;
        if(direction.equals("south"))
            nextRoom = currentRoom.southExit;
        if(direction.equals("west"))
            nextRoom = currentRoom.westExit;

        if (nextRoom == null)
            System.out.println("There is no door!");
        else {
            currentRoom = nextRoom;
            System.out.println("You are " +
                                currentRoom.getDescription());
            System.out.print("Exits: ");
            if(currentRoom.northExit != null)
```

Code 7.1
continued
Selected sections
of the (badly
designed) **Game**
class

```
                    System.out.print("north ");
            if(currentRoom.eastExit != null)
                    System.out.print("east ");
            if(currentRoom.southExit != null)
                    System.out.print("south ");
            if(currentRoom.westExit != null)
                    System.out.print("west ");
            System.out.println();
        }
    }

    //   ... some code omitted ...
}
```

Both the printWelcome and goRoom methods contain the following lines of code:

```
System.out.println("You are " + currentRoom.getDescription());
System.out.print("Exits: ");
if(currentRoom.northExit != null)
    System.out.print("north ");
if(currentRoom.eastExit != null)
    System.out.print("east ");
if(currentRoom.southExit != null)
    System.out.print("south ");
if(currentRoom.westExit != null)
    System.out.print("west ");
System.out.println();
```

Code duplication is usually a symptom of bad cohesion. The problem here has its roots in the fact that both methods in question do two things: printWelcome prints the welcome message and prints the information about the current location, while goRoom changes the current location and then prints information about the (new) current location.

Both methods print information about the current location, but neither can call the other, because they also do other things. This is bad design.

A better design would use a separate, more cohesive method whose sole task is to print the current location information (Code 7.2). Both the printWelcome and goRoom methods can then make calls to this method when they need to print this information. This way, writing the code twice is avoided, and when we need to change it, we need to change it only once.

Code 7.2
printLocationInfo
as a separate
method

```
private void printLocationInfo()
{
    System.out.println("You are " +
        currentRoom.getDescription());
    System.out.print("Exits: ");
    if(currentRoom.northExit != null)
        System.out.print("north ");
    if(currentRoom.eastExit != null)
        System.out.print("east ");
    if(currentRoom.southExit != null)
```

Code 7.2 continued

printLocationInfo
as a separate
method

```
              System.out.print("south ");
      if(currentRoom.westExit != null)
          System.out.print("west ");
      System.out.println();
}
```

Exercise 7.5 Implement and use a separate `printLocationInfo` method in your project, as discussed in this section. Test your changes.

7.5 Making extensions

The *zuul-bad* project does work. We can execute it, and it correctly does everything that it was intended to do. However, it is in some respects quite badly designed. A well-designed alternative would perform in the same way. Just by executing the program we would not notice any difference.

Once we try to make modifications to the project, however, we will notice significant differences in the amount of work involved in changing badly designed code, compared with changing a well-designed application. We will investigate this by making some changes to the project. While we are doing this, we will discuss examples of bad design when we see them in the existing source, and we will improve the class design before we implement our extensions.

7.5.1 The task

The first task we will attempt is to add a new direction of movement. Currently, a player can move in four directions: *north*, *east*, *south*, and *west*. We want to allow for multilevel buildings (or cellars, or dungeons, or whatever you later want to add to your game) and add *up* and *down* as possible directions. A player can then type `"go down"` to move, say, down into a cellar.

7.5.2 Finding the relevant source code

Inspection of the given classes shows us that at least two classes are involved in this change: Room and Game.

Room is the class that stores (among other things) the exits of each room, and, as we saw in Code 7.1, in the Game class the exit information from the current room is used to print out information about exits and to move from one room to another.

The Room class is fairly short. Its source code is shown in Code 7.3. Reading the source, we can see that the exits are mentioned in two different places: they are listed as fields at the top of the class, and they get assigned in the setExits method. To add two new directions, we would need to add two new exits (upExit and downExit) in these two places.

Code 7.3

Source code of the
(badly designed)
Room class

```java
public class Room
{
    public String description;
    public Room northExit;
    public Room southExit;
    public Room eastExit;
    public Room westExit;

    /**
     * Create a room described "description". Initially, it
     * has no exits. "description" is something like "a
     * kitchen" or "an open court yard".
     */
    public Room(String description)
    {
        this.description = description;
    }

    /**
     * Define the exits of this room.  Every direction either
     * leads to another room or is null (no exit there).
     */
    public void setExits(Room north, Room east, Room south,
                         Room west)
    {
        if(north != null)
            northExit = north;
        if(east != null)
            eastExit = east;
        if(south != null)
            southExit = south;
        if(west != null)
            westExit = west;
    }

    /**
     * Return the description of the room (the one that was
     * defined in the constructor).
     */
    public String getDescription()
    {
        return description;
    }
}
```

It is a bit more work to find all relevant places in the Game class. The source code is somewhat longer (it is not shown fully here), and finding all the relevant places takes some patience and care.

Reading the code shown in Code 7.1, we can see that the Game class makes heavy use of the exit information of a room. The Game object holds a reference to one room in the currentRoom variable, and frequently accesses this room's exit information:

- In the `createRoom` method, the exits are defined.

- In the `printWelcome` method, the current room's exits are printed out so that the player knows where to go when the game starts.

- In the `goRoom` method the exits are used to find the next room. They are then used again to print out the exits of the next room we have just entered.

If we now want to add two new exit directions, we will have to add the *up* and *down* options in all these places. However, read the following section before you do this.

7.6 Coupling

The fact that there are so many places where all exits are enumerated is symptomatic of poor class design. When declaring the exit variables in the `Room` class we need to list one variable per exit; in the `setExits` method there is one if statement per exit; in the `goRoom` method there is one if statement per exit; in the `printLocationInfo` method there is one if statement per exit; and so on. This design decision now creates work for us: when adding new exits, we need to find all these places and add two new cases. Imagine the effect if we decided to use directions such as northwest, southeast, etc.!

To improve the situation, we decide to use a `HashMap` to store the exits, rather than separate variables. Doing this, we should be able to write code that can cope with any number of exits and does not need so many modifications. The `HashMap` will contain a mapping from a named direction (e.g. 'north') to the room that lies in that direction (a `Room` object). Thus each entry has a string as the key and a `Room` object as the value.

This is a change in the way a room stores information internally about neighboring rooms. Theoretically, this is a change that should affect only the *implementation* of the `Room` class (*how* the exit information is stored), not the *interface* (*what* the room stores).

Ideally, when only the implementation of a class changes, other classes should not be affected. This would be a case of loose coupling.

In our example, this does not work. If we remove the exit variables in the `Room` class and replace them with a `HashMap`, the `Game` class will not compile any more. It makes numerous references to the room's exit variables, which all would cause errors.

We see that we have a case here of tight coupling. In order to clean this up, we will decouple these classes before we introduce the `HashMap`.

7.6.1 Using encapsulation to reduce coupling

One of the main problems in this example is the use of public fields. The exit fields in the `Room` class have all been declared public. Clearly, the programmer of this class did not follow the guidelines we have set out earlier in this book ('Never make fields public!'). We shall now see the result! The `Game` class in this example can make direct accesses to these fields (and it makes extensive use of this fact). By making the fields public, the `Room` class has exposed in its interface not only the fact that it has exits, but also exactly how the exit information is stored. This breaks one of the fundamental principles of good class design: *encapsulation*.

The encapsulation guideline (hiding implementation information from view) suggests that only information about *what* a class can do should be visible to the outside, not about *how* it does it. This has a great advantage: if no other class knows how our information is stored, then we can easily change how it is stored without breaking other classes.

We can enforce this separation of *what* and *how* by making the fields private and using an accessor method to access them. The first stage of our modified Room class is shown in Code 7.4.

Code 7.4

Using an accessor method to decrease coupling

```java
public class Room
{
    private String description;
    private Room northExit;
    private Room southExit;
    private Room eastExit;
    private Room westExit;

    // existing methods unchanged

    public Room getExit(String direction)
    {
        if(direction.equals("north"))
            return northExit;
        if(direction.equals("east"))
            return eastExit;
        if(direction.equals("south"))
            return southExit;
        if(direction.equals("west"))
            return westExit;
        return null;
    }
}
```

Having made this change to the Room class, we need to change the Game class as well. Wherever an exit variable was accessed, we now use the accessor method. For example, instead of writing

```java
nextRoom = currentRoom.eastExit;
```

we now write

```java
nextRoom = currentRoom.getExit("east");
```

This makes one section in the Game class much easier as well. In the goRoom method, the replacement suggested here will result in the following code segment:

```java
Room nextRoom = null;
if(direction.equals("north"))
    nextRoom = currentRoom.getExit("north");
if(direction.equals("east"))
    nextRoom = currentRoom.getExit("east");
if(direction.equals("south"))
```

```
    nextRoom = currentRoom.getExit("south");
if(direction.equals("west"))
    nextRoom = currentRoom.getExit("west");
```

Instead, this whole code segment can now be replaced with:

```
Room nextRoom = currentRoom.getExit(direction);
```

> **Exercise 7.6** Make the changes we have described to the **Room** and **Game** classes.
>
> **Exercise 7.7** Make a similar change to the `printLocationInfo` method of **Game** so that details of the exits are now prepared by the **Room** rather than the **Game**. Define a method in **Room** with the following signature:
>
> ```
> /**
>  * Return a string describing the room's exits,
>  * for example, "Exits: north west".
>  */
> public String getExitString()
> ```

So far, we have not changed the representation of the exits in the Room class. We have only cleaned up the interface. The *change* in the Game class is minimal – instead of an access of a public field, we use a method call – but the *gain* is dramatic. We can now make a change to the way exits are stored in the room, without any need to worry about breaking anything in the Game class. The internal representation in Room has been completely decoupled from the interface. Now that the design is the way it should have been in the first place, exchanging the separate exit fields for a HashMap is easy. The changed code is shown in Code 7.5.

Code 7.5

Source code of the **Room** class

```java
import java.util.HashMap;

// class comment omitted

class Room
{
    private String description;
    private HashMap exits;

    /**
     * Create a room described "description". Initially, it
     * has no exits. "description" is something like "a
     * kitchen" or "an open court yard".
     */
    public Room(String description)
    {
        this.description = description;
        exits = new HashMap();
    }
```

Code 7.5
continued

Source code of the
Room class

```java
/**
 * Define the exits of this room.  Every direction either
 * leads to another room or is null (no exit there).
 */
public void setExits(Room north, Room east, Room south,
                         Room west)
{
    if(north != null)
        exits.put("north", north);
    if(east != null)
        exits.put("east", east);
    if(south != null)
        exits.put("south", south);
    if(west != null)
        exits.put("west", west);
}

/**
 * Return the room that is reached if we go from this
 * room in direction "direction". If there is no room in
 * that direction, return null.
 */
public Room getExit(String direction)
{
    return (Room)exits.get(direction);
}

/**
 * Return the description of the room (the one that was
 * defined in the constructor).
 */
public String getDescription()
{
    return description;
}
}
```

It is worth emphasizing again that we can make this change now without even checking whether anything will break elsewhere. Since we have changed only private aspects of the Room class, which, by definition, cannot be used in other classes, this change does not impact on other classes. The interface remains unchanged.

A by-product of this change is that our Room class is now even shorter. Instead of listing four separate variables, we have only one. In addition the getExit method is considerably simplified.

Recall that the original aim that set off this series of changes was to make it easier to add the two new possible exits in the *up* and *down* direction. This has already become a lot easier. Since we now use a HashMap to store exits, storing these two additional directions will work without any change. We can also obtain the exit information via the getExit method without any problem.

The only place where knowledge about the four existing exits (*north*, *east*, *south*, *west*) is still coded into the source is in the `setExits` method. This is the last part that needs improvement. At the moment the method's signature is

```
public void setExits(Room north, Room east, Room south, Room west)
```

This method is part of the interface of the `Room` class, so any change we make to it will inevitably affect some other classes by virtue of coupling. It is worth noting that we can never completely decouple the classes in an application, otherwise objects of different classes would not be able to interact with one another. Rather we try to keep the degree of coupling as low as possible. If we have to make a change to `setExits` anyway, to accommodate additional directions, then our preferred solution is to replace it entirely with this method:

```
/**
 * Define an exit from this room.
 */
public void setExit(String direction, Room neighbor)
{
    exits.put(direction, neighbor);
}
```

Now, the exits of this room can be set one exit at a time, and any direction can be used for an exit. In the `Game` class, the change that results from modifying the interface of `Room` is as follows. Instead of writing

```
lab.setExits(outside, office, null, null);
```

we now write

```
lab.setExit("north", outside);
lab.setExit("east", office);
```

We have now completely removed the restriction from `Room` that it can store only four exits. The `Room` class is now ready to store *up* and *down* exits, as well as any other direction you might think of (northwest, southeast, etc.).

> **Exercise 7.8** Implement the changes described in this section in your own *zuul* project.

7.7 Responsibility-driven design

We have seen in the previous section that making use of proper encapsulation reduces coupling and can significantly reduce the amount of work needed to make changes to an application. Encapsulation, however, is not the only factor that influences the degree of coupling. Another aspect is known by the term *responsibility-driven design*.

Responsibility-driven design expresses the idea that each class should be responsible for handling its own data. Often, when we need to add some new functionality to an application, we need to ask ourselves in which class we should add a method to implement this new function. Which class should be responsible for the task? The answer is that the class that is responsible for storing some data should also be responsible for manipulating it.

How well responsibility-driven design is used influences the degree of coupling, and therefore, again, the ease with which an application can be modified or extended. As usual, we will discuss this in more detail with our example.

7.7.1 Responsibilities and coupling

The changes to the Room class that we discussed in section 7.6.1 make it quite easy now to add the new directions for up and down movement in the Game class. We investigate this with an example. Assume we want to add a new room (the cellar) under the office. All we have to do to achieve this is to make some small changes to the Game's createRooms method to create the room, and make two calls to set the exits:

```java
private void createRooms()
{
    Room outside, theatre, pub, lab, office, cellar;
    ...
    cellar = new Room("in the cellar");
    ...
    office.setExit("down", cellar);
    cellar.setExit("up", office);
}
```

Because of the new interface of the Room class, this will work without problems. This change is now very easy and confirms that the design is getting better.

Further evidence of this can be seen if we compare the original version of the printLocationinfo method shown in Code 7.2 with the getExitString method shown in Code 7.6 that represents a solution to exercise 7.7.

Code 7.6

The getExitString method of Room

```java
/**
 * Return a string describing the room's exits, for example
 * "Exits: north west".
 */
public String getExitString()
{
    String exitString = "Exits: ";
    if(northExit != null)
        exitString += "north ";
    if(eastExit != null)
        exitString += "east ";
    if(southExit != null)
        exitString += "south ";
    if(westExit != null)
        exitString += "west ";
    return exitString;
}
```

Because information about its exits is now stored only in the room itself, it is the room that is responsible for providing that information. The room can do this much better than any other object, since it has all the knowledge about the internal storage structure of the exit data. Now inside the Room class we can make use of the knowledge that exits are stored in a HashMap, and we can iterate over that map to describe the exits.

Consequently, we replace the version of getExitString shown in Code 7.6 with the version shown in Code 7.7. This method finds all the names for exits in the HashMap (the keys in the HashMap are the names of the exits) and concatenates them to a single string, which is then returned. (We need to import the classes Set and Iterator for this to work.)

Code 7.7
A revised version of
`getExitString`

```java
/**
 * Return a string describing the room's exits, for example
 * "Exits: north west".
 */
public String getExitString()
{
    String returnString = "Exits:";
    Set keys = exits.keySet();
    for(Iterator iter = keys.iterator(); iter.hasNext(); )
        returnString += " " + iter.next();
    return returnString;
}
```

Exercise 7.9 Look up the `keySet` method in the documentation of `HashMap`. What does it do?

Exercise 7.10 Explain, in detail and in writing, how the `getExitString` method shown in Code 7.7 works.

Our goal to reduce coupling demands that, as far as possible, changes to the `Room` class do not require changes to the `Game` class. We can still improve this.

Currently, we have still encoded in the `Game` class the knowledge that the information we want from a room consists of a description string and the exit string:

```java
System.out.println("You are " + currentRoom.getDescription());
System.out.println(currentRoom.getExitString());
```

What if we add items to rooms in our game? Or monsters? Or other players?

When we describe what we see, the list of items, monsters, and other players should be included in the description of the room. We would need not only to make changes to the `Room` class to add these things, but also to change the code segment above where the description is printed out.

This is again a breach of the responsibility-driven design rule. Since the `Room` class holds information about a room, it should also produce a description for a room. We can improve this by adding to the `Room` class the following method:

```java
/**
 * Return a long description of this room, on the form:
 *     You are in the kitchen.
 *     Exits: north west
 */
public String getLongDescription()

{
    return "You are " + description + ".\n" + getExitString();
}
```

In the `Game` class we then write

```java
System.out.println(currentRoom.getLongDescription());
```

The 'long description' of a room now includes the description string, information about the exits, and may in the future include anything else there is to say about a room. When we make these future extensions, we will have to make changes to only a single class: the Room class.

Exercise 7.11 Implement the changes described in this section in your own *zuul* project.

Exercise 7.12 Draw an object diagram with all objects in your game, the way they are just after starting the game.

Exercise 7.13 How does the object diagram change when you execute a go command?

7.8 Localizing change

Another aspect of the decoupling and responsibility principles is that of *localizing change*. We aim to create a class design that makes later changes easy by localizing the effects of a change.

Concept:

One of the main goals of a good class design is that of **localizing change**: making changes to one class should have minimal effects on other classes.

Ideally, only a single class needs to be changed to make a modification. Sometimes several classes need change, but then we aim at this being as few classes as possible. In addition, the changes needed in other classes should be obvious, easy to detect, and easy to carry out.

To a large extent we can achieve this by following good design rules such as using responsibility-driven design and aiming for loose coupling and high cohesion. In addition, however, we should have modification and extension in mind when we create our applications. It is important to anticipate that an aspect of our program might change, in order to make this change easy.

7.9 Implicit coupling

We have seen that the use of public fields is one practice that is likely to create an unnecessarily tight form of coupling between classes. With this tight coupling, it may be necessary to make changes to more than one class for what should have been a simple modification. Therefore public fields should be avoided. However, there is an even worse form of coupling: *implicit coupling*.

Implicit coupling is a situation where one class depends on internal information of another, but this dependence is not immediately obvious. The tight coupling in the case of the public fields was not good, but at least it was obvious. If we change the public fields in one class, and forget about the other, the application will not compile any more and the compiler will point out the problem. In cases of implicit coupling, omitting a necessary change can go undetected.

We can see the problem arising if we try to add further command words to the game.

Suppose that we want to add the command *look* to the set of legal commands. The purpose of *look* is merely to print out the description of the room and the exits again (we 'look around the room') – this could be helpful if we have entered a sequence of commands in a room so that the description has scrolled out of view, and we cannot remember where the exits of the current room are.

We can introduce a new command word by simply adding it to the array of known words in the `validCommands` array in the `CommandWords` class:

```
// a constant array that holds all valid command words
private static final String validCommands[] = {
    "go", "quit", "help", "look"
};
```

This, by the way, shows an example of good cohesion: instead of defining the command words in the parser, which would have been one obvious possibility, the author created a separate class just to define the command words. This makes it now very easy for us to find the place where command words are defined, and it is easy to add one. The author was obviously thinking ahead, assuming that more commands might be added later, and created a structure that makes this very easy.

We can test this already. However, after making this change, when we execute the game and type the command `look`, nothing happens. This contrasts with the behavior of an unknown command word: if we type any unknown word, we see the reply

```
I don't know what you mean...
```

Thus the fact that we do not see this reply indicates that the word was recognized, but nothing happens because we have not yet implemented an action for this command.

We can fix this by adding a method for the *look* command to the `Game` class:

```
private void look()
{
    System.out.println(currentRoom.getLongDescription());
}
```

After this, we only need to add a case for the *look* command in the `processCommand` method, which will invoke the `look` method when the *look* command is recognized:

```
if (commandWord.equals("help"))
    printHelp();
else if (commandWord.equals("go"))
    goRoom(command);
else if (commandWord.equals("look"))
    look();
else if (commandWord.equals("quit"))
    wantToQuit = quit(command);
```

Try this out, and you will see that it works.

Exercise 7.14 Add the *look* command to your version of the zuul game.

Exercise 7.15 Add another command to your game. For a start, you could choose something simple, such as a command *eat* that, when executed, just prints out '*You have eaten now and you are not hungry any more.*' Later, we can improve this so that you really get hungry over time and you need to find food.

Coupling between the `Game`, `Parser`, and `CommandWord` classes so far seems to have been very good – it was easy to make this extension, and we got it to work quickly.

The problem that was mentioned before – implicit coupling – becomes apparent when we now issue a `help` command. The output is

```
You are lost. You are alone. You wander
around at the university.

Your command words are:
   go quit help
```

Now we notice a small problem. The help text is incomplete: the new command, *look*, is not listed.

This seems easy to fix: we can just edit the help text string in the `Game`'s `printHelp` method. This is quickly done, and does not seem a great problem. But suppose we had not noticed this error now. Did you think of this problem before you just read about it here?

This is a fundamental problem, because every time a command is added the help text needs to be changed, and it is very easy to forget to make this change. The program compiles and runs, and everything seems fine. A maintenance programmer may well believe that the job is finished, and release a program that now contains a bug.

This is an example of implicit coupling. When commands change, the help text must be modified (coupling), but nothing in the program source clearly points out this dependence (thus implicit).

A well-designed class will avoid this form of coupling by following the rule of responsibility-driven design: since the `CommandWord` class is responsible for command words, it should also be responsible for printing command words. Thus we add the following method to the `CommandWord` class:

```
/**
 * Print all valid commands to System.out.
 */
public void showAll()
{
    for(int i = 0; i < validCommands.length; i++) {
        System.out.print(validCommands[i] + "  ");
    }
    System.out.println();
}
```

The idea here is that the `printHelp` method in `Game`, instead of printing a fixed text with the command words, invokes a method that asks the `CommandWords` class to print all its command words. Doing this ensures that the correct command words will always be printed, and adding a new command will also add it to the help text without further change.

The only remaining problem is that the `Game` object does not have a reference to the `CommandWords` object. You can see in the class diagram (Figure 7.1) that there is no arrow from `Game` to `CommandWords`. This indicates that the `Game` class does not even know of the existence of the `CommandWords` class. Instead, the game just has a parser, and the parser has command words.

We could now add a method to the parser that hands the `CommandWords` object to the `Game` object, so that they could communicate. This would, however, increase the degree of coupling in our application: Game would then depend on CommandWords, which it currently does not. We would see this effect in the class diagram: Game would then have an arrow to CommandWords.

The arrows in the diagram are, in fact, a good first indication of how tightly coupled a program is: the more arrows, the more coupling. As an approximation of good class design, we can aim at creating diagrams with few arrows.

Thus the fact that Game did not have a reference to CommandWords is a good thing! We should not change this. From Game's viewpoint, the fact that the CommandWords class exists is an implementation detail of the parser. The parser returns commands, and whether it uses a CommandWords object to achieve this or something else is entirely up to the parser's implementation.

It follows that a better design just lets the Game talk to the Parser, which in turn may talk to CommandWords. We can implement this by adding the following code to the printHelp method in Game:

```
System.out.println("Your command words are:");
parser.showCommands();
```

All that is missing then is the showCommands method in the Parser, which delegates this task to the CommandWords class. Here is the complete method (in class Parser):

```
/**
 * Print out a list of valid command words.
 */
public void showCommands()
{
    commands.showAll();
}
```

Exercise 7.16 Implement the improved version of printing out the command words, as described in this section.

Exercise 7.17 If you now add another new command, do you still need to change the Game class? Why?

The full implementation of all changes discussed in this chapter so far is available in your code examples in a project named *zuul-better*. If you have done the exercises so far, you can ignore this project and continue to use your own. If you have not done the exercises, but want to do the following exercises in this chapter as a programming project, you can use the *zuul-better* project as your starting point.

7.10 Thinking ahead

The design we have implemented now is an important improvement to the original version. It is, however, possible to improve it even more.

One characteristic of a good software designer is the ability to think ahead. What might change? What can we safely assume will stay unchanged for the life of the program?

One assumption that we have hard-coded in most of our classes is that this game will run as a text-based game with terminal input and output. But will it always be like this?

It might be an interesting extension later to add a graphical user interface with menus, buttons, and images. In that case, we would not want to print the information to the text terminal any more. We might still have command words, and we might still want to show them when a player enters a help command. But we might then show them in a text field in a window, rather than using `System.out.println`.

It is good design to try to encapsulate all information about the user interface in a single class or a clearly defined set of classes. Our solution from section 7.9 for example, the `showAll` method in the `CommandWords` class, does not follow this design rule. It would be nicer to define that `CommandWords` is responsible for *producing* (but not *printing*!) the list of command words, but that the `Game` class should decide how it is presented to the user.

We can easily achieve this by changing the `showAll` method so that it returns a string containing all command words instead of printing them out directly. (We should probably rename it `getCommandList` when we make this change.) This string can then be printed in the `printHelp` method in `Game`.

Note that this does not gain us anything right now, but we might profit from this improved design in the future.

Exercise 7.18 Implement the suggested change. Make sure that your program still works as before.

Exercise 7.19 Find out what the *model-view-controller* pattern is. You can do a web search to get information, or you can use any other sources you find. How is it related to the topic discussed here? What does it suggest? How could it be applied to this project? (Only discuss its application to this project, as an actual implementation would be an advanced challenge exercise.)

7.11 Cohesion

We introduced the idea of cohesion in section 7.3: a unit of code should always be responsible for one and only one task. We shall now investigate the cohesion principle in more depth and analyze some examples.

The principle of cohesion can be applied to classes and methods: classes should display a high degree of cohesion, and so should methods.

7.11.1 Cohesion of methods

Concept:

Method cohesion. A cohesive method is responsible for one and only one well-defined task.

When we talk about cohesion of methods, we seek to express the ideal that any one method should be responsible for one and only one well-defined task.

We can see an example of a cohesive method in the `Game` class. This class has a private method named `printWelcome` to show the opening text, and this method is called when the game starts in the `play` method (Code 7.8).

Code 7.8

Two methods with a
good degree of
cohesion

```java
/**
 *  Main play routine.  Loops until end of play.
 */
public void play()
{
    printWelcome();

    // Enter the main command loop.  Here we repeatedly read
    // commands and execute them until the game is over.

    boolean finished = false;
    while (! finished) {
        Command command = parser.getCommand();
        finished = processCommand(command);
    }
    System.out.println("Thank you for playing.  Good bye.");
}

/**
 * Print out the opening message for the player.
 */
private void printWelcome()
{
    System.out.println();
    System.out.println("Welcome to The World of Zuul!");
    System.out.println(
            "Zuul is a new, incredibly boring adventure game.");
    System.out.println("Type 'help' if you need help.");
    System.out.println();
    System.out.println(currentRoom.getLongDescription());
}
```

From a functional point of view we could have just entered the statements from the
`printWelcome` method directly in the `play` method, and achieved the same result without defining an extra method and making a method call. The same can, by the way, be
said for the `processCommand` method that is also invoked in the `play` method: this
code, too, could have been written directly into the `play` method.

It is, however, much easier to understand what a segment of code does, and to make
modifications, if short, cohesive methods are used. In the chosen method structure, all
methods are reasonably short and easy to understand, and their names indicate their purposes
quite clearly. These characteristics represent valuable help for a maintenance programmer.

7.11.2 Cohesion of classes

Concept:

Class cohesion.
A cohesive class
represents one
well-defined entity.

The rule of cohesion of classes states that each class should represent one single, well-
defined entity in the problem domain.

As an example of class cohesion, we now discuss another extension to the *zuul* project.
We now want to add items to the game. Each room may hold an item, and each item has a

description and a weight. An item's weight can be used later to determine whether it can be picked up or not.

A naïve approach would be to add two fields to the `Room` class: `itemDescription` and `itemWeight`. This could work. We could now specify the item details for each room, and we could print out the details whenever we enter a room.

This approach, however, does not display a good degree of cohesion: the `Room` class now describes both a room and an item. It also suggests that an item is bound to a particular room, which we might not wish to be the case.

A better design would create a separate class for items, probably called `Item`. This class would have fields for a description and weight, and a room would simply hold a reference to an item object.

Exercise 7.20 Extend either your adventure project, or the *zuul-better* project, so that a room can contain a single item. Items have a description and a weight. When creating rooms and setting their exits, items for this game should also be created. When a player enters a room, information about an item present in this room should be displayed.

Exercise 7.21 How should the information about an item present in a room be produced? Which class should produce the string describing the item? Which class should print it? Why? Explain in writing. If answering this exercise makes you feel you should change your implementation, go ahead and make the changes.

The real benefits of separating rooms and items in the design can be seen if we change the specification a little: in a further variation of our game, we want to allow not only a single item in each room, but an unlimited number of items. In the design using a separate `Item` class this is easy: we can create multiple `Item` objects and store them in a collection of items in the room.

With the first, naïve approach, this change would be almost impossible to implement.

Exercise 7.22 Modify the project so that a room can hold any number of items. Use a collection to do this. Make sure the room has an **addItem** method that places an item into the room. Make sure all items get shown when a player enters a room.

7.11.3 Cohesion for readability

There are several ways in which high cohesion benefits a design. The two most important ones are *readability* and *reuse*.

The example discussed in section 7.11.1, cohesion of the `printWelcome` method, is clearly an example in which increasing cohesion makes a class more readable and thus easier to understand and maintain.

The class cohesion example in section 7.11.2 also has an element of readability. If a separate `Item` class exists, a maintenance programmer will easily recognize where to start reading code if a change to characteristics of an item is needed. Cohesion of classes also increases readability of a program.

7.11.4 Cohesion for reuse

The second great advantage of cohesion is a higher potential for reuse.

The class cohesion example in section 7.11.2 also shows an example of this: by creating a separate `Item` class, we can create multiple items, and thus use the same code for more than a single item.

Reuse is also an important aspect of method cohesion. Consider a method in the `Room` class with the following signature:

```
public Room leaveRoom(String direction)
```

This method could return the room in the given direction (so that it can be used as the new `currentRoom`), and also print out the description of the new room that we just entered.

This seems like a possible design, and it can indeed be made to work. In our version, however, we have separated this task into two methods:

```
public Room getExit(String direction)
public String getLongDescription()
```

The first one is responsible for returning the next room, whereas the second one produces the room's description.

The advantage of this design is that the separate tasks can be reused more easily. The `getLongDescription` method, for example, is now used not only in the `goRoom` method, but also in `printWelcome` and the implementation of the *look* command. This is only possible because it displays a high degree of cohesion. Reusing it would not be possible in the version with the `leaveRoom` method.

Exercise 7.23 Implement a *back* command. This command does not have a second word. Entering the *back* command takes the player into the last room he/she has been in.

Exercise 7.24 Test your new command properly. Do not forget negative testing! What does your program do if a player types a second word after the *back* command? Does it behave sensibly? Are there more cases of negative testing?

Exercise 7.25 What does your program do if you type *back* twice? Is this behavior sensible?

Exercise 7.26 *Challenge exercise* Implement the *back* command so that using it repeatedly takes you back several rooms, all the way to the beginning of the game if used often enough. Use a `Stack` to do this. (You may need to find out about stacks. Look at the Java library documentation.)

Refactoring

When designing applications we should attempt to think ahead, anticipate possible changes in the future, and create highly cohesive, loosely coupled classes and methods that make modifications easy. This is a noble goal, but of course we cannot always anticipate all future adaptations, and it is not feasible to prepare for all possible extensions we can think of.

This is why *refactoring* is important.

Refactoring is the activity of restructuring existing classes and methods to adapt them to changed functionality and requirements. Often, in the lifetime of an application, functionality is gradually added. One common effect is that, as a side-effect of this, methods and classes slowly grow in length.

It is tempting for a maintenance programmer to add some extra code to existing classes or methods. Doing this for some time, however, decreases the degree of cohesion. When more and more code is added to a method or a class, it is likely that at some stage it will represent more than one clearly defined task or entity.

Refactoring is the rethinking and redesigning of class and method structures. Most commonly the effect is that classes are split into two, or that methods are divided into two or more methods. Refactoring can also include the joining of classes or methods into one, but that case is less common.

7.12.1 Refactoring and testing

Before we provide an example of refactoring, we need to reflect on the fact that when we refactor a program we are usually proposing to make some potentially large changes to something that already works. When something is changed there is a likelihood that errors will be introduced. Therefore it is important to proceed cautiously, and prior to refactoring we should establish that a set of tests exists for the current version of the program. If tests do not exist, then the first stage should be to create some tests that will be suitable for conducting regression testing on the refactored version. Only when these tests exist should the refactoring start. Ideally, the refactoring should then follow in two steps:

■ The first step is to refactor in order to provide the same functionality as that of the original version. In other words, we restructure the source code to improve its quality, not to change or increase its functionality. Once this stage is completed, the regression tests should be run to ensure that we have not introduced unintended errors.

■ The second step is taken only once we have re-established the baseline functionality in the refactored version. Then we are in a safe position to enhance the program. Once that has been done, of course, testing will need to be conducted on the new version.

Making several changes at the same time (refactoring and adding new features) makes it harder to locate the source of problems when they occur.

Exercise 7.27 What sort of baseline functionality tests might we wish to establish on the current version of the game?

Exercise 7.28 How might tests be automated in a program that reads interactive input? Is it possible to introduce some form of scripting? For instance, could a user's input be stored in a file rather than read interactively? What classes would need to be changed to make this possible?

7.12.2 An example of refactoring

As an example, we shall continue with the extension of adding items to the game. In section 7.11.2 we started adding items, suggesting a structure in which rooms can contain any number of items. A logical extension to this arrangement is that a player should be able to pick up items and carry them around. Here is an informal specification of our next goal:

- The player can pick up items from the current room.

- The player can carry any number of items, but only up to a maximum weight.

- Some items cannot be picked up.

- The player can drop items in the current room.

To achieve these goals, we can do the following:

- If not already done, we add a class `Item` to the project. An item has, as discussed above, a description (a string) and a weight (an integer).

- We should also add a field `name` to the item class. This will allow us to refer to the item with a shorter name than the description. If, for instance, there is a book in the current room, the field values of this item might be:

  name: `book`
  description: `an old, dusty book bound in grey leather`
  weight: `1200`

  If we enter a room, we can print out the item's description to tell the player what is there. But, for commands, the name will be easier to use. For instance, the player might then type *take book* to pick up the book.

- We can ensure that some items cannot be picked up, by just making them very heavy (more than a player can carry). Or should we have another boolean field `canBePickedUp`? Which do you think is the better design? Does it matter? Try answering this by thinking about what future changes might be made to the game.

- We add commands *take* and *drop* to pick up and drop items. Both commands have an item name as a second word.

- Somewhere, we have to add a field (holding some form of collection) to store the items currently carried by the player. We also have to add a field with the maximum weight the player can carry, so that we can check it each time we try to pick up something. Where should these go? Once again, think about future extensions to help you make the decision.

This last task is what we will discuss in more detail now, in order to illustrate the process of refactoring.

The first question to ask ourselves when thinking about how to enable players to carry items is: Where should we add the fields for the currently carried items and the maximum weight? A quick look over the existing classes shows that the `Game` class is really the only place where it can be fitted in. It cannot be stored in Room, Item or Command, since there are many different instances of these classes over time, which are not all always accessible. It does not make sense in Parser or CommandWords either.

Reinforcing the decision to place these changes in the Game class is the fact that it already stores the current room (information about where the player is right now), so adding the current items (information about what the player has) seems to fit with this quite well.

This approach could be made to work. It is, however, not a solution that is well designed. The Game class is fairly big already, and there is a good argument that it contains too much as it is. Adding even more does not make this better.

We should ask ourselves again which class or object this information should belong to. Thinking carefully about the type of information we are adding here (carried items, maximum weight) we realize that this is information about a *player*! The logical thing to do (following responsibility-driven design guidelines) is to create a Player class. We can then add these fields to the Player class and create a player object at the start of the game to store the data.

The existing field currentRoom also stores information about the player: the player's current location. Consequently, we should now also move this field into the Player class.

Analyzing it now, it is obvious that this design better fits the principle of responsibility-driven design. Who should be responsible for storing information about the player? The Player class, of course.

In the original version we had only a single piece of information for the player – the current room. Whether we should have had a Player class even back then is up for discussion. There are arguments both ways. It would have been nice design, so yes, maybe we should. But having a class with only a single field and no methods that do anything of significance might be regarded as overkill.

Sometimes there are gray areas like this where either decision is defensible. But after adding our new fields, the situation is quite clear. There is now a strong argument for a Player class. It would store the fields and have methods such as dropItem and pickUpItem (which can include the weight check and might return false if we cannot carry it).

What we did when we introduced the Player class and moved the currentRoom field from Game into Player was refactoring. We have restructured the way we represent our data to achieve a better design under changed requirements.

Programmers not as well trained as us (or just being lazy) might have left the currentRoom field where it was, seeing that the program worked as it was and there did not seem to be a great need to make this change. They would end up with a messy class design.

The effect of making the change can be seen if we think one step further ahead. Assume we now want to extend the game to allow for multiple players.

With our nice new design, this is suddenly very easy. We already have a Player class (the Game holds a Player object), and it is easy to create several Player objects and store in Game a collection of players instead of a single player. Each player object would hold its own current room, items, and maximum weight. Different players could even have different maximum weights, opening up the even wider concept of having players with quite different capabilities – their carrying capability being just one of possibly many.

The lazy programmer who left currentRoom in the Game class, however, has a serious problem now. Since the whole game has only a single current room, current locations of multiple players cannot be easily stored. Bad design usually bites back later to create more work for us in the end.

Doing good refactoring is as much about thinking in a certain mindset as it is about technical skills. While we make changes and extensions to applications, we should regularly question whether an original class design still represents the best solution. As the functionality changes, arguments for or against certain designs change. What was a good design for a simple application might not be good any more when some extensions are added.

Recognizing these changes and actually making the refactoring modifications to the source code usually saves a lot of time and effort in the end. The earlier we clean up our design, the more work we usually save.

We should be prepared to *factor out* methods (turn a sequence of statements from the body of an existing method into a new, independent method) and classes (take parts of a class and create a new class from it). Considering refactoring regularly keeps our class design clean and saves work in the end.

Exercise 7.29 Refactor your project to introduce a separate `Player` class. A player object should store at least the current room of the player, but you may also like to store the player's name or other information.

Exercise 7.30 Implement an extension that allows a player to pick up one single item. This includes implementing two new commands: *take* and *drop*.

Exercise 7.31 Extend your implementation to allow the player to carry any number of items.

Exercise 7.32 Add a restriction that allows the player to carry items only up to a specified maximum weight. The maximum weight a player can carry is an attribute of the player.

Exercise 7.33 Implement an *items* command that prints out all items currently carried and their total weight.

Exercise 7.34 Add a *magic cookie* item to a room. Add an *eat cookie* command. If a player finds and eats the magic cookie, it increases the weight that the player can carry. (You might like to modify this slightly to better fit into your own game scenario.)

7.13 Design guidelines

An often-heard piece of advice to beginners about writing good object-oriented programs is, '*Don't put too much into a single method*,' or '*Don't put everything into one class.*' Both suggestions have merit, but frequently lead to the counter-questions, '*How long should a method be?*' or '*How long should a class be?*'

After the discussion in this chapter, these questions can now be answered in terms of cohesion and coupling. A method is too long if it does more than one logical task. A class is too complex if it represents more than one logical entity.

You will notice that these answers do not give clear-cut rules that specify what exactly to do. Terms such as *one logical task* are still open to interpretation, and different programmers will decide differently in many situations.

These are *guidelines* (not cast-in-stone rules). Keeping these guidelines in mind, though, will significantly improve your class design and enable you to master more complex problems and write better and more interesting programs.

It is important to understand these exercises as suggestions, not as fixed specifications. This game has many possible ways in which it can be extended, and you are encouraged to invent your own extensions. You do not need to do all the exercises here to create an interesting game, you may want to do more, or you may want to do different ones. Here are some suggestions to get you started.

Exercise 7.35 Add some form of time limit to your game. If a certain task is not completed in a specified time, the player loses. A time limit can easily be implemented by counting the number of moves or the number of entered commands. You do not need to use real time.

Exercise 7.36 Implement a trapdoor somewhere (or some other form of door that you can only cross one way).

Exercise 7.37 Add a *beamer* to the game. A beamer is a device that can be *charged*, and *fired*. When you charge the beamer, it memorizes the current room. When you fire the beamer, it transports you immediately back to the room it was charged in. The beamer could either be standard equipment, or an item that the player can find. Of course, you need commands to charge and fire the beamer.

Exercise 7.38 Add locked doors to your game. The player needs to find (or otherwise obtain) a key to open a door.

Exercise 7.39 Add a transporter room. Whenever the player enters this room, he/she is randomly transported into one of the other rooms. Note: Coming up with a good design for this task is not trivial. It might be interesting to discuss design alternatives for this with other students. (We discuss design alternatives for this task at the end of Chapter 9. The adventurous or advanced reader may want to skip ahead and have a look.)

Exercise 7.40 *Challenge exercise* In the `processCommand` method in `Game` there is a sequence of if statements to dispatch commands when a command word is recognized. This is not a very nice design, since every time we add a command, we have to add a case here in this if statement. Can you improve this design? Design the classes so that handling of commands is more modular, and new commands can be added more easily. Implement it. Test it.

Exercise 7.41 Add characters to the game. Characters are similar to items, but they can talk. They speak some text when you first meet them, and they may give you some help if you give them the right item.

Exercise 7.42 Add moving characters. These are like other characters, but every time the player types a command, these characters may move into an adjoining room.

7.14 Executing without BlueJ

When our game is finished, we may want to pass it on to others to play. To do this, it would be nice if people could play the game without the need to start BlueJ. To be able to do this, we need one more thing: *class methods*, which in Java are also referred to as *static methods*.

7.14.1 Class methods

So far, all methods we have seen have been *instance methods*: they are invoked on an instance of a class. What distinguishes class methods from instance methods is that class methods can be invoked without an instance – having the class is enough.

In section 5.13, we discussed class variables. Class methods are conceptually related and use a related syntax (the key word `static` in Java). Just as class variables belong to the class rather than to an instance, so do class methods.

A class method is defined by adding the key word `static` in front of the type name in the method's signature:

```
public static int getNumberOfDaysThisMonth()
{
    ...
}
```

Such a method can then be called by specifying the name of the class in which it is defined before the dot in the usual dot notation. If, for instance, the above method is defined in a class called `Calendar`, the following call invokes it:

```
int days = Calendar.getNumberOfDaysThisMonth();
```

Note that the name of the class is used before the dot – no object has been created.

Exercise 7.43 Read the class documentation for class `Math` in the package `java.lang`. It contains many static methods. Find the method that computes the maximum of two integer numbers. What is its signature?

Exercise 7.44 Why do you think the methods in the `Math` class are static? Could they be written as instance methods?

Exercise 7.45 Write a test class that has a method to test how long it takes to count from 1 to 100 in a loop. You can use the method `currentTimeMillis` from class `System` to help with the time measurement.

7.14.2 The main method

If we want to start a Java application without BlueJ, we need to use a class method. In BlueJ, we typically create an object and invoke one of its methods, but without BlueJ an application starts without any object in existence. Classes are the only things we have initially, so the first method that can be invoked must be a class method.

The Java definition for starting applications is quite simple: the user specifies the class that should be started, and the Java system will then invoke a method called `main` in that class. This method must have a specific signature. If such a method does not exist in that class, an error is reported. Appendix E describes the details of this method and the commands needed to start the Java system without BlueJ.

Exercise 7.46 Find out the details of the `main` method and add such a method to your `Game` class. The method should create a `Game` object and invoke the `play` method on it. Test the `main` method by invoking it from BlueJ. Class methods can be invoked from the class's popup menu.

Exercise 7.47 Execute your game without BlueJ.

7.14.3 Limitations of class methods

Because class methods are associated with a class rather than an instance, they have two important limitations. The first limitation is that a class method may not access any instance fields defined in the class. This is logical, because instance fields are associated with individual objects. Instead, class methods are restricted to accessing class variables from their class. The second limitation is like the first: a class method may not call an instance method from the class. A class method may only invoke other class methods defined in its class.

You will find that we make very little use of class methods in the examples in this book.

7.15 Summary

In this chapter we have discussed what are often called the *non-functional aspects* of an application. Here, the issue is not so much to get a program to perform a certain task, but to do this with well-designed classes.

Good class design can make a huge difference when an application needs to be corrected, modified, or extended. It also allows us to reuse parts of the application in other contexts (for example, for other projects), and thus creates benefits later.

There are two key concepts under which class design can be evaluated: coupling and cohesion. Coupling refers to the interconnectedness of classes; cohesion to modularization into appropriate units. Good design exhibits loose coupling and high cohesion.

One way to achieve a good structure is to follow a process of responsibility-driven design. Whenever we add a function to the application, we try to identify which class should be responsible for which part of the task.

When extending a program, we use regular refactoring to adapt the design to changing requirements, and to ensure that classes and methods remain cohesive and loosely coupled.

Terms introduced in this chapter

code duplication, coupling, cohesion, encapsulation, responsibility-driven design, implicit coupling, refactoring, class method

Concept summary

- **coupling** The term *coupling* describes the interconnectedness of classes. We strive for *loose coupling* in a system – that is, a system where each class is largely independent and communicates with other classes via a small, well defined interface.

- **cohesion** The expression *cohesion* describes how well a unit of code maps to a logical task or entity. In a *highly cohesive* system each unit of code (method, class, or module) is responsible for a well defined task or entity. Good class design exhibits a high degree of cohesion.

- **code duplication** Code duplication (having the same segment of code in an application more than once) is a sign of bad design. It should be avoided.

- **encapsulation** Proper encapsulation in classes reduces coupling, and thus leads to a better design.

- **responsibility-driven design** Responsibility-driven design is the process of designing classes by assigning well-defined responsibilities to each class. This process can be used to determine which class should implement which part of an application function.

- **localizing change** One of the main goals of a good class design is that of localizing change: making changes to one class should have minimal effects on other classes.

- **method cohesion** A cohesive method is responsible for one and only one well-defined task.

- **class cohesion** A cohesive class represents one well-defined entity.

- **refactoring** Refactoring is the activity of restructuring an existing design to maintain a good class design when the application is modified or extended.

Exercise 7.48 Without using BlueJ, edit your *TechSupport* project from Chapter 5 so that it can execute without BlueJ. Then run it from a command line.

Exercise 7.49 Can you call a static method from an instance method? Can you call an instance method from a static method? Can you call a static method from a static method? Answer these questions, then create a test to check your answers and try it. Explain in detail your answers and observations.

Exercise 7.50 Can a class count how many instances have been created of that class? What is needed to do this? Write some code fragments that illustrate what needs to be done. Assume you want a static method called `numberOfInstances` that returns the number of instances created.

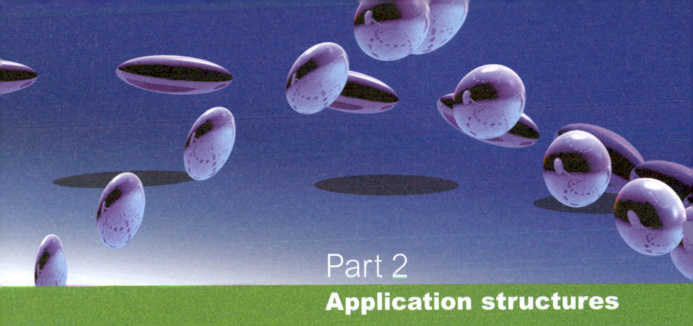

Part 2

Application structures

Improving structure with inheritance

Main concepts discussed in this chapter:

- inheritance
- subtyping
- substitution
- polymorphic variables

Java constructs discussed in this chapter:

`extends`, `super` (in constructor), cast (revisited), `Object`, wrapper classes

In this chapter we introduce some additional object-oriented constructs to improve the general structure of our applications. The main concepts we shall use to design better program structures are *inheritance* and *polymorphism*.

Both of these concepts are central to the idea of object orientation, and you will discover later how they appear in various forms in everything we discuss from now on. However, it is not only the following chapters that rely heavily on these concepts. Many of the constructs and techniques discussed in earlier chapters are influenced by aspects of inheritance and polymorphism, and we shall revisit some issues introduced earlier and gain a fuller understanding of the interconnections between different parts of the Java language.

Inheritance is a powerful construct that can be used to create solutions to a variety of different problems. As always, we will discuss the important aspects using an example. In this example, we will first introduce only some of the problems that are addressed by using inheritance structures, and discuss further uses and advantages of inheritance and polymorphism as we progress through this chapter.

The example we discuss to introduce these new structures is called *DoME*.

8.1 The DoME example

The acronym *DoME* stands for *Database of Multimedia Entertainment*. That is a rather grand name for a rather simple program we are going to develop. (But, hey, marketing is half the game – an impressive name might help make us rich by selling many copies of our program later, right?)

In essence DoME is an application that lets us store information about CDs and videos. The idea is to create a catalogue of all the CDs and videos I own (or all I have ever seen or listened to).

The functionality that we want to provide with DoME should at least include the following:

■ It should allow us to enter information about CDs and videos.

■ It should store this information permanently so that it can be used later.

■ It should provide a search function that allows us to find, for example, all CDs in the database by a certain artist, or all videos by a given director.

■ It should allow us to print lists, such as a list of all videos in the database, or a list of all CDs.

■ It should allow us to remove information.

The details we want to store for each CD are:

■ the title of the album;
■ the artist (name of the band or singer);
■ the number of tracks on the CD;
■ the total playing time;
■ a 'got it' flag that indicates whether I own a copy of this CD; and
■ a comment (some arbitrary text).

The details we want to store for each video are:

■ the title of the video;
■ the name of the director;
■ the total playing time;
■ a 'got it' flag that indicates whether I own a copy of this video; and
■ a comment (some arbitrary text).

8.1.1 DoME classes and objects

To implement this application, we first have to decide what classes to use to model this problem. In this case, some of the classes are easy to identify. It is quite straightforward to decide that we should have a class CD to represent CD objects and a class Video to represent videos.

Objects of these classes should then encapsulate all the data we want to store about these objects (Figure 8.1).

Some of these data items should probably also have accessor and mutator methods (Figure 8.2).[1] For our purpose, it is not important to decide about the exact details of all the methods right now, but just to get a first impression of the design of this application. In this figure, we have defined accessor and mutator methods for those fields that may

---

[1] The notation style for class diagrams that is used in this book and in BlueJ is a subset of a widely used notation called UML. Although we do not use everything from UML (by far), we attempt to use UML notation for those things that we *do* show. The UML style defines how fields and methods are shown in a class diagram. The class is divided into three parts that show (in this order from the top) the class name, the fields, and the methods.

Figure 8.1

Fields in CD and video objects

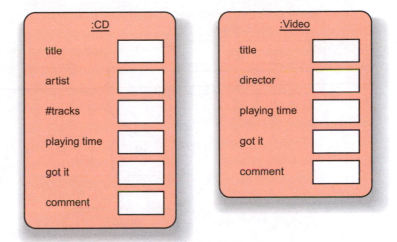

Figure 8.2

Methods of the CD and Video classes

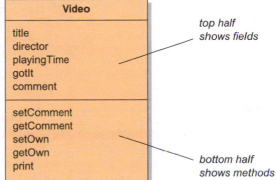

change over time (the flag indicating whether we own it and the comment) and assume for now that the other fields are set in the constructor. We have also added a method called print that will print out details of a CD or video object.

Once we have defined the CD and Video classes, we can create as many CD and video objects as we need – one object per CD or video that we want to store. Apart from this, we then need another object: a database object that can hold a collection of CDs and a collection of videos.

The database object could itself hold two collection objects (for example, of class ArrayList). One of these collections can then hold all CDs, the other all videos. An object diagram for this model is shown in Figure 8.3.

The corresponding class diagram, as BlueJ displays it, is shown in Figure 8.4. Note that BlueJ shows a slightly simplified diagram: classes from the standard Java library (ArrayList in this case) are not shown. Instead, the diagram focuses on user-defined classes. Also, BlueJ does not show field and method names in the diagram.

In practice, to implement a full DoME application, we would have some more classes to handle things such as saving the data to a file and providing a user interface. These are

Figure 8.3
Objects in the DoME
application

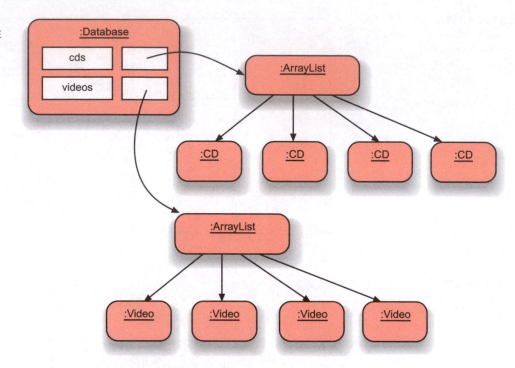

Figure 8.4
BlueJ class diagram
of DoME

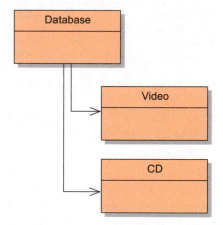

not very relevant to the present discussion, so we shall skip detailing these for now (we shall come back to them later), and concentrate on more detailed discussion of the core classes mentioned here.

8.1.2 DoME source code

So far, the design of these three classes (CD, Video, and Database) has been very straightforward. Translating these ideas into Java code is equally easy. Code 8.1 shows the source code of the CD class. It defines the appropriate fields, sets all the data items that are not expected to change over time in its constructor, and provides accessor and mutator methods for the got-it flag and the comment. It also implements the `print` method to write some details to the text terminal.

Note that we do not intend right now to make this implementation complete in any sense. It serves to provide a feel for what a class such as this might look like. We will use this as the basis for our following discussion of inheritance.

Code 8.1

Source code of the CD class

```java
/**
 * The CD class represents a music CD object. Information about the
 * CD is stored and can be retrieved.
 *
 * @author Michael Kölling and David J. Barnes
 * @version 2002-05-02
 */
public class CD
{
    private String title;
    private String artist;
    private int numberOfTracks;
    private int playingTime;
    private boolean gotIt;
    private String comment;

    /**
     * Initialize the CD.
     */
    public CD(String theTitle, String theArtist, int tracks,
              int time)
    {
        title = theTitle;
        artist = theArtist;
        numberOfTracks = tracks;
        playingTime = time;
        gotIt = false;
        comment = "";
    }

    /**
     * Enter a comment for this CD.
     */
    public void setComment(String comment)
    {
        this.comment = comment;
    }

    /**
     * Return the comment for this CD.
     */
    public String getComment()
    {
        return comment;
    }
```

Code 8.1 continued

Source code of the CD class

```java
    /**
     * Set the flag indicating whether we own this CD.
     */
    public void setOwn(boolean ownIt)
    {
        gotIt = ownIt;
    }


    /**
     * Return information whether we own a copy of this CD.
     */
    public boolean getOwn()
    {
        return gotIt;
    }


    /**
     * Print details about this CD to the text terminal.
     */
    public void print()
    {
        System.out.print("CD: " + title + " (" + playingTime +
                         " mins)");
        if(gotIt) {
            System.out.println("*");
        } else {
            System.out.println();
        }
        System.out.println("    " + artist);
        System.out.println("    tracks: " + numberOfTracks);
        System.out.println("    " + comment);
    }
}
```

Now let us compare the CD source code with the source code of class `Video`, shown in Code 8.2. Looking at both classes, we quickly notice that they are very similar. This is not surprising, since their purpose is similar: both are used to store information about a media item (and the items have some similarities). They differ only in their details, such as some of their fields and the bodies of the `print` method.

Code 8.2

Source code of the Video class

```java
/**
 * The Video class represents a video object. Information about
 * the video is stored and can be retrieved.
 *
 * @author Michael Kölling and David J. Barnes
 * @version 2002-05-02
 */
```

```java
public class Video
{
    private String title;
    private String director;
    private int playingTime;
    private boolean gotIt;
    private String comment;

    /**
     * Constructor for objects of class Video
     */
    public Video(String theTitle, String theDirector, int time)
    {
        title = theTitle;
        director = theDirector;
        playingTime = time;
        gotIt = false;
        comment = "";
    }

    /**
     * Enter a comment for this video.
     */
    public void setComment(String comment)
    {
        this.comment = comment;
    }

    /**
     * Return the comment for this video.
     */
    public String getComment()
    {
        return comment;
    }

    /**
     * Set the flag indicating whether we own this video.
     */
    public void setOwn(boolean ownIt)
    {
        gotIt = ownIt;
    }

    /**
     * Return information whether we own a copy of this video.
     */
    public boolean getOwn()
    {
        return gotIt;
    }
}
```

Code 8.2
continued

Source code of the
Video class

```
    /**
     * Print details about this video to the text terminal.
     */
    public void print()
    {
        System.out.print("video: " + title + " (" + playingTime
                                + " mins)");
        if(gotIt) {
            System.out.println("*");
        } else {
            System.out.println();
        }
        System.out.println("    " + director);
        System.out.println("    " + comment);
    }
}
```

Next, let us examine the source code of the Database class (Code 8.3). It, too, is quite simple. It defines two lists (each of type ArrayList) to hold the collection of CDs and the collection of videos. In the constructor, the empty lists are created. It then provides two methods for adding items – one for adding CDs, one for adding videos. The last method, named list, prints a list of all CDs and videos to the text terminal.

Code 8.3

Source code of the
Database class

```
import java.util.ArrayList;
import java.util.Iterator;

/**
 * The database class provides a facility to store CD and
 * video objects. A list of all CDs and videos can be printed
 * to the terminal.
 *
 * This version does not save the data to disk, and it does
 * not provide any search functions.
 *
 * @author Michael Kölling and David J. Barnes
 * @version 2002-05-02
 */
public class Database
{
    private ArrayList cds;
    private ArrayList videos;

    /**
     * Construct an empty Database.
     */
    public Database()
```

**Code 8.3
continued**

Source code of the
Database class

```java
    {
        cds = new ArrayList();
        videos = new ArrayList();
    }

    /**
     * Add a CD to the database.
     */
    public void addCD(CD theCD)
    {
        cds.add(theCD);
    }

    /**
     * Add a video to the database.
     */
    public void addVideo(Video theVideo)
    {
        videos.add(theVideo);
    }

    /**
     * Print a list of all currently stored CDs and videos to
     * the text terminal.
     */
    public void list()
    {
        // print list of CDs
        for(Iterator iter = cds.iterator(); iter.hasNext(); ) {
            CD cd = (CD)iter.next();
            cd.print();
            System.out.println();    // empty line between items
        }

        // print list of videos
        for(Iterator iter = videos.iterator(); iter.hasNext(); ) {
            Video video = (Video)iter.next();
            video.print();
            System.out.println();    // empty line between items
        }
    }
}
```

Note that this is by no means a complete application. It has no user interface yet (so it will not be usable outside BlueJ), and the data entered is not stored to the file system. This means that all data entered will be lost each time the application ends. Also, the functions for entering and editing data, as well as searching for data and displaying it, are not flexible enough for what we would want from a real program.

However, this does not matter in our context. We can work on improving this application later. The basic structure is there, and it works. This is enough for us to discuss the problems of this design and possible improvements.

Exercise 8.1 Open the project *dome-v1*. It contains the classes exactly as we have discussed them here. Create some CD objects and some video objects. Create a database object. Enter the CDs and videos into the database, and then list the database contents.

Exercise 8.2 Try the following. Create a CD object. Enter it into the database. List the database. You see that the CD has no associated comment. Add a comment to the CD object on the object bench (the one you entered into the database). When you now list the database again, will the CD listed there have a comment attached? Try it. Explain the behavior you observe.

8.1.3 Discussion of the DoME application

Even though our application is not yet complete, we have done the most important part. We have defined the core of the application: the data structure that stores the essential information.

This was fairly straightforward so far, and we could now go ahead and design the rest that is still missing. Before doing that, though, we will discuss the quality of the solution so far.

There are several fundamental problems with our current solution. The most obvious one is *code duplication*.

We have noticed above that the CD and Video classes are very similar. In fact, the majority of the classes' source code is identical, with only a few differences. We have already mentioned the problems associated with code duplication in Chapter 7. Apart from the annoying fact that we have to write everything twice (or copy and paste, then go through and fix all the differences), there are often problems associated with maintaining duplicated code. Many possible changes would have to be done twice. If, for example, the type of the playing time is changed from an int to a float (so that fractions can be handled), this change has to be made once in the CD class and again in the Video class. In addition, associated with maintenance of code duplication is always the danger of introducing errors, since the maintenance programmer might not realize that an identical change is needed at a second (or third) location.

There is another spot where we have code duplication: in the Database class. We can see that everything in that class is done twice – once for CDs and once for videos. The class defines two list variables, then creates two list objects, defines two 'add' methods, and has two almost identical blocks of code in the list method to print out the lists.

The problems with this duplication become clear when we analyze what we would have to do to add another type of media item to this program. Imagine we want to store information not only about CDs and videos, but also about books. Books seem similar enough that it should be easy to modify our application to do this. We would introduce another class, Book, and essentially write a third version of the source code that we already have in the CD and `Video` classes. Then we have to work through the `Database` class and add another list variable, another list object, another `add` method, and another loop in the `list` method.

We would have to do the same for a fourth type of item. The more we do this, the more the code duplication problem increases, and the harder it becomes to make changes later. When we feel uncomfortable about a situation such as this, it is often a good indicator that there may be a better alternative approach. For this particular case, object-oriented languages provide a distinctive feature that has a big impact on programs involving sets of similar classes. In the following sections we will introduce this feature, which is called *inheritance*.

8.2 Using inheritance

Inheritance is a mechanism that provides us with a solution to our problem of duplication. The idea is simple: instead of defining the `CD` and `Video` classes completely independently, we first define a class that contains everything these two have in common. We shall call this class `Item`. Then we can declare that a `CD` is an `Item` and a `Video` is an `Item`. Finally, we add those extra details needed for a CD to the `CD` class, and those for a video to the `Video` class. The essential feature of this technique is that we need to describe the common features only once.

Figure 8.5 shows a class diagram for this new structure. It shows the class `Item` at the top, which defines all fields and methods that are common to all items (CDs and videos). Below the `Item` class, it shows the `CD` and `Video` classes, which hold only those fields and methods that are unique to each particular class. (We have added three methods here, `getArtist` and `getNumberOfTracks` in class `CD`, and `getDirector` in class `Video`, to illustrate that the `CD` and `Video` classes can define their own methods.)

Figure 8.5
CD and Video
inheriting from `Item`

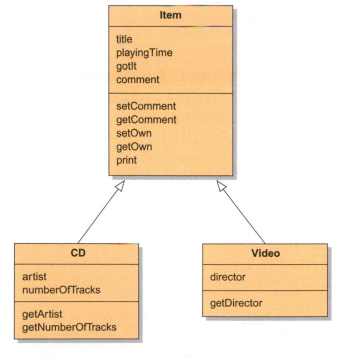

This new feature of object-oriented programming requires some new terminology. In a situation such as this one, we say that the class CD *inherits from* class Item. Class Video also inherits from Item. When talking about Java programs, the expression 'class CD *extends* class Item' is sometimes also used, since Java uses an 'extends' key word to define the inheritance relationship (we shall see this shortly).

The arrows in the class diagram (usually drawn with hollow arrow heads) represent the inheritance relationship.

Concept:

A **superclass** is a class that is extended by another class.

Class Item (the class that the others inherit from) is called the *parent class* or *superclass*. The inheriting classes (CD and Video in this example) are referred to as *child classes* or *subclasses*. In this book we will use the terms 'superclass' and 'subclass' to refer to the classes in an inheritance relationship.

Concept:

A **subclass** is a class that extends (inherits from) another class. It inherits all fields and methods from its superclass.

Inheritance is sometimes also called an *is-a* relationship. The reason is that a subclass is a specialization of a superclass. We can say that 'a CD *is an* item' and 'a video *is an* item.'

The purpose of using inheritance is now fairly obvious. Instances of class CD will have all fields defined in class CD *and* in class Item. (CD inherits the fields from Item.) Instances of Video will have all fields defined in Video and in Item. Thus we achieve the same as before, but we need to define the fields title, playingTime, gotIt, and comment only once (but we can use them in two different places).

The same holds true for methods: instances of subclasses have all methods defined in both the superclass and the subclass. In general we can say: since a CD is an item, a CD object has everything that an item has, and more. And since a video is also an item, it has everything that an item has, and more.

Thus inheritance allows us to create two classes that are quite similar, while avoiding the need to write the identical part twice. Inheritance has a number of other advantages, which we discuss below. First, however, we will take another more general look at inheritance hierarchies.

8.3 Inheritance hierarchies

Inheritance can be used much more generally than shown in the example above. More than two subclasses can inherit from the same superclass, and a subclass can in turn be a superclass to other subclasses. The classes then form an *inheritance hierarchy*.

Concept:

Classes that are linked through inheritance relationships form an **inheritance hierarchy**.

The best-known example of an inheritance hierarchy is probably the classification of species used by biologists. A small part is shown in Figure 8.6. We can see that a poodle is a dog, which is a mammal, which is an animal.

We know some things about poodles, for example that they are alive, they can bark, they eat meat, and they give birth to live young. On closer inspection, we see that we know some of these things not because they are poodles, but because they are dogs, mammals or animals. An instance of class Poodle (an actual poodle) has all the characteristics of a poodle, a dog, a mammal, and an animal, because a poodle is a dog, which is a mammal, and so on.

The principle is simple. Inheritance is an abstraction technique that lets us categorize classes of objects under certain criteria, and helps us specify characteristics of these classes.

Figure 8.6

An example of an
inheritance hierarchy

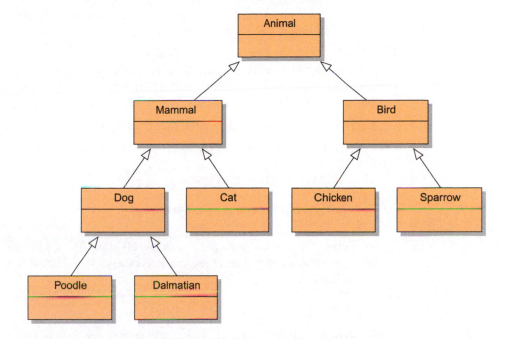

Exercise 8.3 Draw an inheritance hierarchy for the people in your place of study or place of work. For example, if you are a university student, then your university probably has students (first-year students, second-year students, …), professors, tutors, office personnel, etc.

8.4 Inheritance in Java

Before discussing more details of inheritance, we will have a look at how inheritance is expressed in the Java language. Here is a segment of the source code of the `Item` class:

```java
public class Item
{
    private String title;
    private int playingTime;
    private boolean gotIt;
    private String comment;

    //  constructors and methods omitted.

}
```

There is nothing special about this class so far. It starts with a normal class definition, and defines the item's fields in the usual way. Next, we examine the source code of the CD class:

```java
public class CD extends Item
{
    private String artist;
    private int numberOfTracks;

    //  constructors and methods omitted.

}
```

There are two things worth noting here. First, the key word `extends` defines the inheritance relationship. The phrase 'extends Item' specifies that this class is a subclass of the `Item` class.

Second, the `CD` class defines only those fields that are unique to `CD` objects (`artist` and `numberOfTracks`). The fields from `Item` are inherited and do not need to be listed here. Objects of class `CD` will nonetheless have fields for `title`, `playingTime`, and so on.

Next, let us have a look at the source code of class `Video`:

```
public class Video extends Item
{
    private String director;

    // constructors and methods omitted.
}
```

This class follows the same pattern as the `CD` class. It uses the `extends` key word to define itself as a subclass of `Item`, and defines its own additional field.

8.4.1 Inheritance and access rights

To objects of other classes, `Video` or `CD` objects appear just like all other types of object. As a consequence, members defined as `public` in either the superclass or subclass portions will be accessible to objects of other classes, but members defined as `private` will be inaccessible. In fact, the rule on privacy also applies between a subclass and its superclass: a subclass cannot access private members of its superclass. It follows that if a subclass method needed to access or change private fields in its superclass, then the superclass would need to provide appropriate accessor and/or mutator methods. A subclass may call any public methods of its superclass as if they were its own – no variable is needed.

This issue of access rights is one we will discuss further in Chapter 9 when we introduce the `protected` modifier.

> **Exercise 8.4** Open the project *dome-v2*. This project contains a version of the DoME application rewritten to use inheritance, as described above. Note that the class diagram displays the inheritance relationship. Open the source code of the **Video** class and remove the 'extends Item' phrase. Close the editor. What changes do you observe in the class diagram? Add the 'extends Item' phrase again.
>
> **Exercise 8.5** Create a **CD** object. Call some of its methods. Can you call the inherited methods (for example, `setComment`)? What do you observe about the inherited methods?

8.4.2 Inheritance and initialization

When we create an object, the constructor of that object takes care of initializing all object fields to some reasonable state. We have to look more closely at how this is done in classes that inherit from other classes.

When we create a CD object, we pass several parameters to the CD's constructor: the title, the name of the artist, the number of tracks, and the playing time. Some of these contain values for fields defined in class Item and others values for fields defined in class CD. All of these fields must be correctly initialized, and Code 8.4 shows the code segments that are used to achieve this in Java.

Code 8.4

Initialization of subclass and superclass fields

```java
public class Item
{
    private String title;
    private int playingTime;
    private boolean gotIt;
    private String comment;

    /**
     * Initialise the fields of the item.
     */
    public Item(String theTitle, int time)
    {
        title = theTitle;
        playingTime = time;
        gotIt = false;
        comment = "";
    }

    // methods omitted
}

public class CD extends Item
{
    private String artist;
    private int numberOfTracks;

    /**
     * Constructor for objects of class CD
     */
    public CD(String theTitle, String theArtist, int tracks,
            int time)
    {
        super(theTitle, time);
        artist = theArtist;
        numberOfTracks = tracks;
    }

    // methods omitted
}
```

Several observations can be made here. First, the class Item has a constructor, even though we do not intend to create an instance of class Item directly.[2] This constructor receives the parameters needed to initialize the Item fields, and it contains the code to do this initialization.

Second, the CD constructor receives parameters needed to initialize both Item and CD fields. It then contains the following line of code:

```
super(theTitle, time);
```

The key word super is a call to the constructor of the superclass. Its effect is that the Item constructor is executed as part of the CD constructor's execution. When we create a CD, the CD constructor is called, which as its first statement in turn calls the Item constructor. The Item constructor initializes the item fields, and then returns to the CD constructor, which initializes the remaining fields defined in the CD class. For this to work, those parameters needed for the initialization of the item fields are passed on to the superclass constructor as parameters to the super call.

In Java, a subclass constructor must always call the *superclass constructor* as its first statement. If you do not write a call to a superclass constructor, the Java compiler will insert a superclass call automatically, to ensure that the superclass fields get properly initialized. Inserting this call automatically works only if the superclass has a constructor without parameters (since the compiler cannot guess what parameter values should be passed). Otherwise, an error will be reported.

In general, it is a good idea to always include explicit superclass calls in your constructors, even if it is one that the compiler could generate automatically. We consider this good style, since it avoids the possibility of misinterpretation and confusion in case a reader is not aware of the automatic code generation.

> **Concept:**
>
> **Superclass constructor.** The constructor of a subclass must always invoke the constructor of its superclass as its first statement. If the source code does not include such a call, Java will attempt to insert a call automatically.

> **Exercise 8.6** Set a breakpoint in the first line of the **CD** class's constructor. Then create a **CD** object. When the debugger window pops up, use *Step Into* to step through the code. Observe the instance fields and their initialization. Describe your observations.

8.5 DoME: adding other item types

Now that we have our inheritance hierarchy set up for the DoME project, so that the common elements of the items are in the Item class, it becomes a lot easier to add other types of item. If, for instance, we want to add information about video games to our database, we can now define a new subclass of Item named VideoGame (Figure 8.7). Since VideoGame is a subclass of Item, it automatically inherits all fields and methods that we have already defined in Item. Thus VideoGame objects already have a title, a got-it flag, a comment, and a playing time. (The playing time for video games may vary, of course, but we might use this field to store the average time it takes to play one game.) We can then concentrate on adding attributes that are specific to video games, such as the maximum number of players, or the platform they run on.

---

[2] Currently, there is nothing actually preventing us from creating an Item object, although that was not our intention when we designed these classes. In Chapter 10 we shall see some techniques that allow us to make sure that Item objects cannot be created directly, but only CD or Video objects.

Figure 8.7

DoME items with a
`VideoGame` class

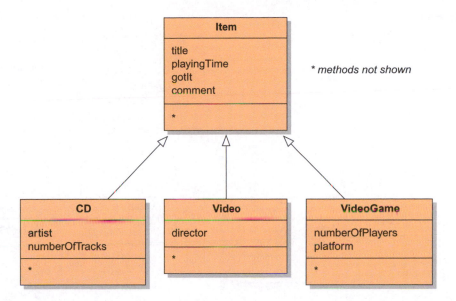

This is an example of how inheritance enables us to *reuse* existing work. We can reuse the code that we have written for videos and CDs (in the `Item` class) so that it also works for the `VideoGame` class. The ability to reuse existing software components is one of the great benefits that we get from the inheritance facility. We will discuss this in more detail later.

This reuse has the effect that a lot less new code is needed when we now introduce additional item types. Since new item types can be defined as subclasses of `Item`, only the code that is actually different from `Item` has to be added.

Now imagine we also want to store our board games in our database. (After all, it is a 'database of multimedia entertainment,' and board games are surely entertainment, just using more low-tech media...)

We could just add a fourth subclass under the `Item` class. Sometimes, however, it is useful to analyze the relationships more carefully. Both video games and board games have an attribute 'maximum number of players.' It would be nice if we did not define this field both in the `VideoGame` and `BoardGame` classes. This would be another example of code duplication (we would duplicate the field and the mutator and accessor methods that go with that field). So the first idea might be that we could make `BoardGame` a subclass of `VideoGame`. This way, we would inherit the `numberOfPlayers` field and the accompanying methods, and we would avoid having to write them twice. But there is a problem: we would also inherit the field that stores information about the platform the game runs on, and this attribute does not make sense for board games.

The solution is to refactor the class hierarchy. We can introduce a new superclass for all games (named `Game`), which still is a subclass of `Item` (Figure 8.8). Now all information relating to games in general (such as the number of players) can be defined in the `Game` class, whereas specific information can be moved to the appropriate subclass. Objects of class `BoardGame` now have all fields and methods of the classes `Item`, `Game`, and `BoardGame`.

Classes that are not intended to be used to create instances, but whose purpose is exclusively to serve as superclasses for other classes (such as `Item` and `Game`), are called *abstract classes*. We shall investigate this in more detail in Chapter 10.

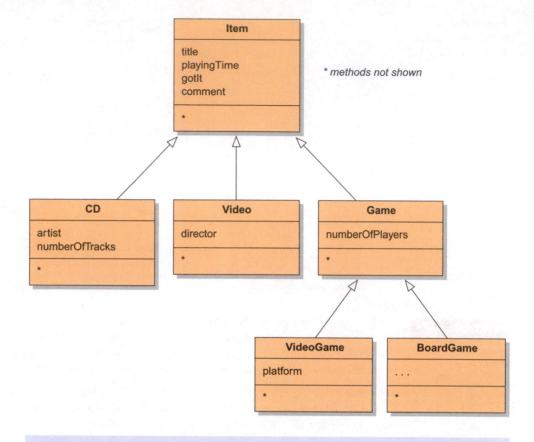

Exercise 8.7 Open the *dome-v2* project. Add a class for video games to the project. Create some video game objects and test that all methods work as expected.

8.6 Advantages of inheritance (so far)

We have seen several advantages of using inheritance for the DoME application. Before we explore other aspects of inheritance, we shall summarize the general advantages we have encountered so far:

- **Avoiding code duplication** The use of inheritance avoids the need to write identical or very similar copies of code twice (or even more often).

- **Code reuse** Existing code can be reused. If a class similar to the one we need already exists, we can sometimes subclass the existing class and reuse some of the existing code, rather than having to implement everything again.

- **Easier maintenance** Maintaining the application becomes easier, since the relationship between the classes is clearly expressed. A change to a field or a method that is shared between different types of subclasses needs to be made only once.

■ **Extendibility** Using inheritance, it becomes much easier to extend an existing application in certain ways.

> **Exercise 8.8** Order these items into an inheritance hierarchy: apple, ice cream, bread, fruit, food-item, cereal, orange, dessert, chocolate mousse, baguette.
>
> **Exercise 8.9** In what inheritance relationship might a *touch pad* and a *mouse* be? (We are talking about computer input devices here, not small furry mammals.)
>
> **Exercise 8.10** Sometimes things are more difficult than they first seem. Consider this: in what kind of inheritance relationship are *Rectangle* and *Square*? What are the arguments? Discuss.

8.7 Subtyping

The one thing we have not yet investigated is how the code in the `Database` class was able to be changed when we modified our project to use inheritance. Code 8.5 shows the full source code of class `Database`. We can compare this with the original source shown in Code 8.3.

Code 8.5

Source code of the
`Database` class
(second version)

```java
import java.util.ArrayList;
import java.util.Iterator;

/**
 * The database class provides a facility to store CD and
 * video objects. A list of all CDs and videos can be printed
 * to the terminal.
 *
 * This version does not save the data to disk, and it does
 * not provide any search functions.
 *
 * @author Michael Kölling and David J. Barnes
 * @version 2002-05-04
 */
public class Database
{
    private ArrayList items;

    /**
     * Construct an empty Database.
     */
    public Database()
    {
        items = new ArrayList();
    }

    /**
     * Add an item to the database.
     */
```

**Code 8.5
continued**

Source code of the
Database class
(second version)

```java
public void addItem(Item theItem)
{
    items.add(theItem);
}


/**
 * Print a list of all currently stored CDs and videos to
 * the text terminal.
 */
public void list()
{
    for(Iterator iter = items.iterator(); iter.hasNext(); ) {
        Item item = (Item)iter.next();
        item.print();
        System.out.println();   // empty line between items
    }
}
}
```

As we can see, the code has become significantly shorter and simpler since our change to use inheritance. Where in the first version (Code 8.3) everything had to be done twice, it now exists only once. We have only one collection, only one method to add items, and one loop in the list method.

The reason why we could shorten the source code is that, in the new version, we can use the type Item where we previously used Video and CD. We investigate this first by examining the addItem method.

In our first version, we had two methods to add items to the database. They had the following signatures:

```java
public void addCD(CD theCD)
public void addVideo(Video theVideo)
```

In our new version, we have a single method to serve the same purpose:

```java
public void addItem(Item theItem)
```

The parameters in the original version are defined with the types Video and CD, ensuring that we pass Video and CD objects to these methods, since actual parameter types must match the formal parameter types. So far, we have interpreted the requirement that parameter types 'must match' as meaning 'must be of the same type': for instance, that the type name of an actual parameter must be the same as the type name of the corresponding formal parameter. This is only part of the truth, in fact, because objects of subclasses can be used wherever their superclass type is required.

Concept:

Subtype. As an analog to the class hierarchy, types form a type hierarchy. The type defined by a subclass definition is a subtype of the type of its superclass.

8.7.1   Subclasses and subtypes

We have discussed earlier that classes define types. The type of an object that was created from class Video is Video. We also just discussed that classes may have subclasses. Thus the types defined by the classes can have subtypes. In our example, the type Video is a subtype of type Item.

8.7.2 Subtyping and assignment

When we want to assign an object to a variable, the type of the object must match the type of the variable. For example,

```
Car myCar = new Car();
```

is a valid assignment because an object of type `Car` is assigned to a variable declared to hold objects of type `Car`. Now that we know about inheritance we must state the typing rule more completely: A variable can hold objects of its declared type or of any subtype of its declared type.

Figure 8.9

An inheritance hierarchy

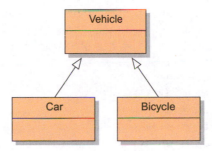

Imagine we have a class `Vehicle` with two subclasses `Car` and `Bicycle` (Figure 8.9). In this case, the typing rule admits that the following assignments are all legal:

```
Vehicle v1 = new Vehicle();
Vehicle v2 = new Car();
Vehicle v3 = new Bicycle();
```

The type of a variable declares what it can store. Declaring a variable of type `Vehicle` states that this variable can hold vehicles. But since a car is a vehicle, it is perfectly legal to store a car in a variable that is intended for vehicles. (Think of the variable as a garage: if someone tells you that you may park a vehicle in a garage, you would think that both parking a car or a bicycle in the garage would be okay.)

This principle is known as *substitution*. In object-oriented languages we can substitute a subclass object where a superclass object is expected, because the subclass object is a special case of the superclass. If, for example, someone asks us to give them a pen, we can fulfill the request perfectly well by giving them a fountain pen or a ballpoint pen. Both fountain pen and ballpoint pen are subclasses of pen, so supplying either where an object of class pen was expected is fine.

However, doing it the other way is not allowed:

```
Car c1 = new Vehicle();    // this is an error!
```

This statement attempts to store a `Vehicle` object in a `Car` variable. Java will not allow this, and an error will be reported if you try to compile this statement. The variable is declared to be able to store cars. A vehicle, on the other hand, may or may not be a car – we do not know. Thus the statement may be wrong and is not allowed.

Similarly:

```
Car c2 = new Bicycle();    // this is an error!
```

This is also an illegal statement. A bicycle is not a car (or, more formally: the type `Bicycle` is not a subtype of `Car`), and thus the assignment is not allowed.

Exercise 8.11 Assume we have four classes: `Person`, `Teacher`, `Student`, and `PhDStudent`. `Teacher` and `Student` are both subclasses of `Person`. `PhDStudent` is a subclass of `Student`.

Which of the following assignments are legal, and why?

```
Person p1 = new Student();
Person p2 = new PhDStudent();
PhDStudent phd1 = new Student();
Teacher t1 = new Person();
Student s1 = new PhDStudent();

s1 = p1;
s1 = p2;
p1 = s1;
t1 = s1;
s1 = phd1;
phd1 = s1;
```

Exercise 8.12 Test your answers to the previous question by creating the classes mentioned in that exercise, and trying it out in BlueJ.

8.7.3 Subtyping and parameter passing

Passing a parameter (that is, assigning an actual parameter to a formal parameter variable) behaves in exactly the same way as an assignment to a variable. This is why we can pass an object of type `Video` to a method that has a parameter of type `Item`. We have the following definition of the `addItem` method in class `Database`:

```
public class Database
{

    public void addItem(Item theItem)
    {
        ...
    }
}
```

We can now use this method to add videos and CDs to the database:

```
Database db = new Database();
Video video = new Video(...);
CD cd = new CD(...);

db.addItem(video);
db.addItem(cd);
```

Because of subtyping rules, we need only one method (with a parameter of type `Item`) to add both `Video` and `CD` objects.

We will discuss subtyping in more detail in the next chapter.

8.7.4 Polymorphic variables

Variables holding object types in Java are *polymorphic* variables. The term 'polymorphic' (literally: *many shapes*) refers to the fact that a variable can hold objects of different types (namely the declared type or any subtype of the declared type). Polymorphism appears in object-oriented languages in several contexts – polymorphic variables are just the first example. We will discuss other incarnations of polymorphism in more detail in the next chapter.

For now, we just observe how the use of a polymorphic variable helps us simplify our `list` method. The body of this method is

```
for(Iterator iter = items.iterator(); iter.hasNext(); ) {
    Item item = (Item)iter.next();
    item.print();
    System.out.println();    // empty line between items
}
```

Here, we iterate through the list of items (held in an `ArrayList` in the `items` variable). We get out each item and then invoke its `print` method. Note that the actual items that we get out of the list are of type `CD` or `Video`, not of type `Item`. We can, however, assign them to the `item` variable (declared to be of type `Item`), because variables are polymorphic. The `item` variable is able to hold `CD` and `Video` objects, because these are subtypes of `Item`.

Thus the use of inheritance in this example has removed the need for two separate loops in the list method. Inheritance avoids code duplication not only in the server classes, but also in clients of those classes.

> **Note** When doing the exercises, you may have noticed that the **print** method has a problem: not all details are printed out. Solving this problem requires some more explanation – we will do this in the next chapter.

> **Exercise 8.13** What has to change in the **Database** class when another item subclass (for example, a class **VideoGame**) is added? Why?

8.8 The `Object` class

Concept:

All classes with no explicit superclass have **Object** as their superclass.

All classes have a superclass. So far, it has appeared as if most classes we have seen do not have a superclass, just classes like `Video` and `CD` that extend another class. In fact, while we can declare an explicit superclass for a class, all classes that have no superclass declaration implicitly inherit from a class called `Object`.

Object is a class from the Java standard library that serves as a superclass for all objects. Writing a class declaration such as

```
public class Person
{
    ...
}
```

is equivalent to writing

```
public class Person extends Object
{
    ...
}
```

The Java compiler automatically inserts the Object superclass for all classes without an explicit extends declaration, so it is never necessary to do this for yourself. Every single class (with the sole exception of the Object class itself) inherits from Object, either directly or indirectly. Figure 8.10 shows some randomly chosen classes to illustrate this.

Figure 8.10
All classes inherit
from Object

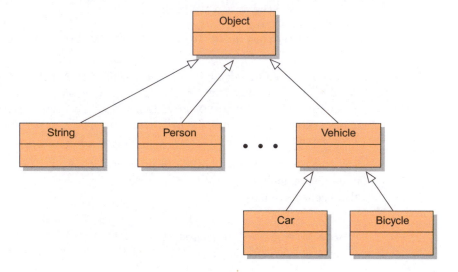

Having a common superclass for all objects serves two purposes: First, the Object class can define some methods that are then automatically available for every existing object. Second, we can declare polymorphic variables of type Object to hold any object. The first point becomes more interesting a bit later, and we shall discuss this in more detail in the next chapter. The second point is used extensively in the Java collection library. We will investigate this further in the next section.

8.9 Polymorphic collections

Throughout this book we have encountered several types of Java collection, including the classes ArrayList, HashSet, and HashMap.

We were able to use them, but so far we have left some details unexplained. Now that we know about inheritance, we can understand more details about these classes.

8.9.1 Element types

The Java collections are *polymorphic collections*. This means that they are able to hold different kinds of element at the same time. We can create a list that stores some `Strings` and some `Items` at the same time (although most of the time that is not very useful). More importantly, we can create an `ArrayList` of `Strings`, or an `ArrayList` of `Items` using the same `ArrayList` class.

We can see how this works by looking at the signature of one of the `add` methods of class `ArrayList`. We can find it in the documentation of the standard Java library. Here is the signature:

```
public void add(Object element)
```

This method can be used to add a new element to the end of the list. We can see that the type of the element parameter is declared to be `Object`. The fact that `Object` is a super-type of all object types, and that subtype objects can be passed to supertype parameters, together enables us to pass objects of any kind into a collection.

8.9.2 Casting revisited

Declaring the element types of collections as `Object` has a great benefit. It allows us to create collections of any kind without the need to have separate classes, such as `PersonList`, `StringList`, `ItemList`, and so on. But it also creates a small problem. When an element is retrieved from a collection, the type system does not know its type.

We retrieve an element with a method such as `get`. Its signature is

```
public Object get(int index)
```

We can see here that the declared type of the return value is `Object`. Assume we have a list called `myList`, which we use to store `String` objects. The following statement generates an error:

```
String s1 = myList.get(1);    // error!
```

We discussed above that assignment of a subtype object to a supertype variable is allowed, but assigning a supertype object to a subtype variable is not. This is exactly the problem here. When we entered the string into the collection using the `add` method, we passed the `String` object to the `Object` parameter – subtype to supertype. When we want to get the string out of the collection again, we try to assign an element of type `Object` to a variable of type `String` – supertype to subtype – and thus an error is generated.

We know that the element really is a `String` (and so the assignment should be okay), but the declared type of the `get` method is just `Object`, so the type system does not know that this is the case, and complains. This is called *type loss*. Note that the element is still of type `String`, but the Java compiler's type system, which tries to check that all assignments are correct, does not know this. We can get around this problem by explicitly telling the type system that the element is a `String`. We do this using the cast operator we have seen earlier:

```
String s1 = (String)myList.get(1);    // okay
```

Doing this will cause the compiler to believe that the object is a `String`, and it will not report an error. At runtime, however, the Java system will check that the element really is a `String`. If we were careful, and it is, everything is fine. If the element at index 1 in this collection is of another type, the runtime system will indicate an error (called a 'ClassCastException') and the program will stop.[3]

In most situations we will use collections in such a way that we enter only elements of a common type into one collection. That way, we can safely cast them back to their real type when we retrieve them, because we know what they are.

Casting can be used not only with collections, but also with all variables. Consider this code fragment, where Car is a subclass of Vehicle:

```
Vehicle v;
Car c;

c = new Car();
v = c;
c = (Car) v;
```

This code segment is legal; it will compile and run. The assignment v = c is allowed, because we are assigning a subtype to a supertype. This is allowed by rule of substitution. The assignment c = (Car)v is legal because we use a cast. Without the cast, it would be an error (attempt to assign a supertype to a subtype – not allowed by substitution rules). Using the cast, however, the assignment is okay, because the object held in the variable v really is a car.

Now consider this code fragment, in which Bicycle is also a subclass of Vehicle:

```
Vehicle v;
Car c;
Bicycle b;

c = new Car();
v = c;              // okay
b = (Bicycle) c;   // compile time error!
b = (Bicycle) v;   // runtime error!
```

The last two assignments will both fail. The attempt to assign c to b (even with the cast) will be compile-time error. The compiler notices that Car and Bicycle do not form a subtype/supertype relationship, and so c can never hold a Bicycle object – the assignment could never work.

The attempt to assign v to b (with the cast) will be accepted at compile time but will fail at runtime. Vehicle is a superclass of Bicycle, and thus v can potentially hold a Bicycle object. At runtime, however, it turns out that the object in v is not a Bicycle but a Car, and the program will terminate prematurely.

8.9.3 Wrapper classes

The fact that the element types of collections are declared to be of type Object enables us to enter any object into a collection, since all classes inherit (directly or indirectly) from Object. There remains one problem, though: Java has some types that are not object types.

---

[3] Exceptions are discussed in detail in Chapter 12.

As we know, the simple types, such as `int`, `boolean`, and `char`, are separate from object types. Their values are not instances of classes, and they do not inherit from the `Object` class. Because of this, they are not subtypes of `Object` and cannot be entered into a collection.

This is a problem. There are situations where we might want to create a list of `ints`, or a set of `chars`. What can we do?

Java's solution to this problem is *wrapper classes*. Every simple type in Java has a corresponding wrapper class that represents the same type, but is a real object type. The wrapper class for `int`, for instance, is called `Integer`. A complete list of simple types and their wrapper classes is given in Appendix B.

When we want to enter an `int` into a collection, we first create an `Integer` object (an instance of the wrapper) to hold the `int` value. `Integer` instances are objects that have only a single `int` field. Thus the `int` is 'wrapped' into an object.

The `Integer` object is a real object, and thus can be passed into the collection. When we retrieve the element from the collection, we get the `Integer` instance back. We can then 'unwrap' the object and get the original `int` value out again. The following code segment illustrates this:

```
int i = 18;                      // the value to be entered
Integer iwrap = new Integer(i);  // the wrapper around i

myCollecton.add(iwrap);          // the wrapper can be stored
...

Integer element = (Integer)myCollection.get(0);  // retrieve the
                                                 // wrapper
int value = element.intValue();  // unwrap the wrapper
```

You can find out more in the library documentation about the individual wrapper classes.

8.10 The collection hierarchy

The Java collection classes use inheritance to allow different types of element to be stored. In addition, inheritance is used extensively in the definition of the collections themselves. Class `ArrayList`, for example, inherits from a class called `AbstractList`, which in turn inherits from `AbstractCollection`. We shall not discuss this hierarchy here, since it is described in detail at various easily accessible places. One good description is at Sun Microsystems' web site at `http://java.sun.com/docs/books/tutorial/collections/index.html`.

Note that some details of this hierarchy require understanding of Java *interfaces*. We discuss those in Chapter 10.

Exercise 8.14 Use the documentation of the Java standard class libraries to find out about the inheritance hierarchy of the collection classes. Draw a diagram showing the hierarchy.

8.11 Summary

This chapter has presented a first view of inheritance. All classes in Java are arranged in an inheritance hierarchy. Each class may have an explicitly declared superclass, or it inherits implicitly from the class `Object`.

Subclasses usually represent specializations of superclasses. Because of this, the inheritance relationship is also referred to as an is-a relationship ('a car *is-a* vehicle').

Subclasses inherit all fields and methods of a superclass. Objects of subclasses have all fields and methods declared in their own class, as well as those from all superclasses. Inheritance relationships can be used to avoid code duplication, to reuse existing code, and to make an application more maintainable and extendable.

Subclasses also form subtypes, which leads to polymorphic variables. Subtype objects may be substituted for supertype objects, and variables are allowed to hold objects that are instances of subtypes of their declared type.

Inheritance allows the design of class structures that are easier to maintain and more flexible. This chapter contained only an introduction to the use of inheritance for the purpose of improving program structures – more uses of inheritance and their benefits will be discussed in the following chapters.

Terms introduced in this chapter

inheritance, superclass (parent), subclass (child), is-a, inheritance hierarchy, abstract class, subtype, substitution, polymorphic variable, polymorphic collection, type loss, wrapper classes

Concept summary

- **inheritance** Inheritance allows us to define one class as an extension of another.

- **superclass** A superclass is a class that is extended by another class.

- **subclass** A subclass is a class that extends (inherits from) another class. It inherits all fields and methods from its superclass.

- **inheritance hierarchy** Classes that are linked through inheritance relationships form an inheritance hierarchy.

- **superclass constructors** The constructor of a subclass must always invoke the constructor of its superclass as its first statement. If the source code does not include such a call, Java will attempt to insert a call automatically.

- **reuse** Inheritance allows us to reuse previously written classes in a new context.

- **subtypes** As an analog to the class hierarchy, types form a type hierarchy. The type defined by a subclass definition is a subtype of the type of its superclass.

- **variables and subtypes** Variables may hold objects of their declared type or of any subtype of their declared type.

- **substitution** Subtype objects may be used wherever objects of a supertype are expected. This is known as substitution.

- **Object** All classes with no explicit superclass have `Object` as their superclass.

Exercise 8.15 Go back to the *lab-class* project from Chapter 1. Add instructors to the project (every lab-class can have many students and a single instructor). Use inheritance to avoid code duplication between students and instructors (both have a name, contact details, etc.).

Exercise 8.16 Draw an inheritance hierarchy representing parts of a computer system (processor, memory, disk drive, CD drive, printer, scanner, keyboard, mouse, etc.)

Exercise 8.17 Look at the code below. You have four classes (O, X, T, and M) and a variable of each of these.

```
O o;
X x;
T t;
M m;
```

The following assignments are all legal (assume that they all compile):

```
m = t;
m = x;
o = t;
```

The following assignments are all illegal (they cause compiler errors):

```
o = m;
o = x;
x = o;
```

What can you say about the relationships of these classes?

Exercise 8.18 Draw an inheritance hierarchy of `AbstractList` and all its (direct and indirect) subclasses, as they are defined in the Java standard library.

More about inheritance

Main concepts discussed in this chapter:

- method polymorphism
- static and dynamic type
- overriding
- dynamic method lookup

Java constructs discussed in this chapter:

super (in method), toString, protected

The last chapter introduced the main concepts of inheritance by discussing the DoME example. While we have seen the foundations of inheritance, there are still numerous important details that we have not yet investigated. Inheritance is central to understanding and using object-oriented languages, and understanding it in detail is necessary to progress from here.

In this chapter we shall continue to use the DoME example to explore the most important of the remaining issues surrounding inheritance and polymorphism.

9.1 The problem: DoME's print method

When you experimented with the DoME examples in Chapter 8, you probably noticed that the second version – the one using inheritance – has a problem: the print method does not show all of an item's data.

Let us look at an example. Assume we create a CD and a Video object with the following data:

```
CD: Frank Sinatra: A Swingin' Affair
    16 tracks
    64 minutes
    got it: yes
    comment: my favorite Sinatra album

Video: O Brother, Where Art Thou?
    directors: Joel & Ethan Coen
```

```
106 minutes
got it: no
comment: The Coen brothers' best movie!
```

If we enter these objects into the database, and then invoke the first version of the database's `list` method (the one without inheritance), it prints

```
CD: A Swingin' Affair (64 mins)*
    Frank Sinatra
    tracks: 16
    my favorite Sinatra album

Video: O Brother, Where Art Thou? (106 mins)
       Joel & Ethan Coen
       The Coen brothers' best movie!
```

All the information is there, and we could change the implementation in the `print` method to print it in any format we like.

Compare this with the second DoME version (with inheritance), which prints only

```
title: A Swingin' Affair (64 mins)*
           my favorite Sinatra album

title: O Brother, Where Art Thou? (106 mins)
           The Coen brothers' best movie!
```

We note that information about the CD's artist and number of tracks, as well as about the video's director, is missing. The reason for this is simple. The `print` method in this version is implemented in the `Item` class, not in `Video` and `CD` (Figure 9.1). In the methods of `Item`, only the fields declared in `Item` are available. If we tried to access the CD's `artist` field from `Item`'s `print` method, an error would be reported. This illustrates the important principle that inheritance is a one-way street: `CD` inherits `Item`'s fields, but `Item` still does not know anything about fields in its subclasses.

Figure 9.1

Printing, version 1: `print` method in superclass

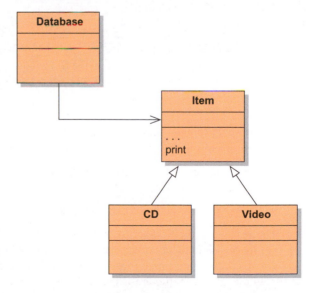

Static type and dynamic type

Trying to solve the problem of developing a complete polymorphic `print` method leads us into a discussion of *static* and *dynamic types* and *method dispatch*. But let us start at the beginning.

A first attempt to solve the print problem might be to move the `print` method to the subclasses (Figure 9.2). That way, since the method would now belong to the `CD` and `Video` classes, it could access the `CD` and `Video` specific fields. It could also access the inherited fields by calling accessor methods defined in the `Item` class. That should enable it to print out a complete set of information again. Try this approach out by completing exercise 9.1.

Figure 9.2

Printing, version 2:
`print` method in
subclasses

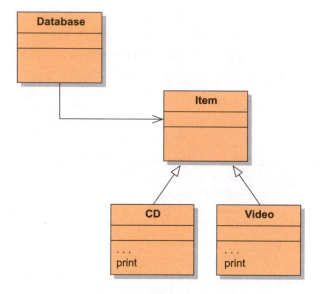

Exercise 9.1 Open your last version of the DoME project. (You can use *dome-v2* if you do not have your own version yet.) Remove the `print` method from class `Item` and move it into the `Video` and `CD` classes. Compile. What do you observe?

When we try to move the `print` method from `Item` to the subclasses, we notice that we have some problems: the project does not compile any more. There are two fundamental issues:

■ We get errors in the `CD` and `Video` classes, because we cannot access the superclass fields.

■ We get an error in the `Database` class, because it cannot find the `print` method.

The reason for the first sort of error is that the fields in `Item` have private access, and so are inaccessible to any other class – including subclasses. Since we do not wish to break encapsulation and make these fields public, the easiest way to solve this is to define public accessor methods for them. However, in section 9.8 we shall introduce a further type of access designed specifically to support the superclass–subclass relationship.

The reason for the second sort of error requires a more detailed explanation, and this is explored in the next section.

9.2.1 Calling `print` from `Database`

First, we investigate the problem of calling the `print` method from `Database`. The relevant lines of code in the `Database` class are

```
Item item = (Item)iter.next();
item.print();
```

The first statement retrieves an item from the collection; the second tries to invoke the `print` method on the item. The compiler informs us that it cannot find a `print` method for the item.

On the one hand, this seems logical; `Item` does not have a `print` method any more (see Figure 9.2). On the other hand, it is annoying. We know that every item object in the collection is in fact a `Video` or a `CD` object, and both have `print` methods. This means that `item.print()` could work. Whatever it is – `CD` or `Video` – we know that it does have a `print` method.

To understand this in detail, we need to look more closely at types. Consider the following statement:

```
Car c1 = new Car();
```

We say that the type of `c1` is `Car`. Before we encountered inheritance, there was no need to distinguish whether by 'type of `c1`' we meant 'the type of the variable `c1`' or 'the type of the object stored in `c1`.' It did not matter, because the type of the variable and the type of the object were always the same.

Now that we know about subtyping, we need to be more precise. Consider the following statement:

```
Vehicle v1 = new Car();
```

What is the type of `v1`? That depends on what precisely we mean by 'type of `v1`.' The type of the variable `v1` is `Vehicle`; the type of the object stored in `v1` is `Car`. Through subtyping and substitution rules, we now have situations where the type of the variable and the type of the object stored in it are not exactly the same.

Let us introduce some terminology to make it easier to talk about this issue:

- We call the declared type of the variable the *static type*, because it is declared in the source code – the static representation of the program.

- We call the type of the object stored in a variable the *dynamic type*, because it depends on assignments at runtime – the dynamic behavior of the program.

Thus, looking at the statement above, we can now state more precisely: the static type of `v1` is `Vehicle`, the dynamic type of `v1` is `Car`.

We can now also rephrase our discussion about the call to the item's `print` method in the `Database` class. At the time of the call

```
item.print();
```

the static type of item is Item, while the dynamic type is either CD or Video (Figure 9.3). We do not know which one of these it is, assuming we have entered both CD and Video objects into the database.

Figure 9.3
Variable of type
Item containing an
object of type Video

Item item

The compiler reports an error because, for type checking, the static type is used. The dynamic type is often only known at runtime, so the compiler has no other choice but to use the static type if it wants to do any checks at compile time. The static type of item is Item, and Item does not have a print method. It makes no difference that all known subtypes of Item do have a print method. The behavior of the compiler is reasonable in this respect because it has no guarantee that *all* subclasses of Item will, indeed, define a print method, and this is impossible to check in practice.

In other words, to make this call work, class Item must have a print method, so we appear to be back to our original problem without having made any progress.

> **Exercise 9.2** In your DoME project, add a **print** method in class **Item** again. For now, write the method body with a single statement that prints out only the title. Then modify the **print** methods in **CD** and **Video** so that the **CD** version prints out only the artist and the **Video** version prints only the director. This removes the other errors encountered above (we shall come back to those below).
>
> You should now have a situation corresponding to Figure 9.4, with **print** methods in three classes. Compile your project. (If there are errors, remove them. This design should work.)
>
> Before executing, predict which of the **print** methods will get called if you execute the **Database list** method.
>
> Try it out. Enter a CD and a video into the database and call the **Database list** method. Which **print** methods were executed? Was your prediction correct? Try to explain your observations.

9.3 Overriding

The next design we shall discuss is one where both the superclass and the subclasses have a print method (Figure 9.4). The signature of all the print methods is exactly the same.

Code 9.1 shows the relevant details of the source code of all three classes. Class Item has a print method that prints out all the fields that are declared in Item (those common to CDs and videos), and the subclasses CD and Video print out the fields specific to CD and Video objects respectively.

Figure 9.4
Printing, version 3:
`print` method in
subclasses and
superclass

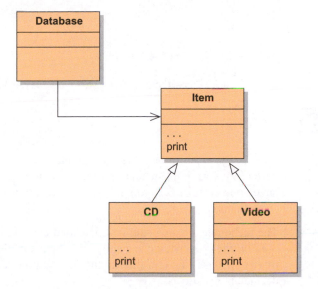

Code 9.1
Source code of the
`print` methods in all
three classes

```java
public class Item
{
    ...

    public void print()
    {
        System.out.print(title + " (" + playingTime + " mins)");
        if(gotIt) {
            System.out.println("*");
        } else {
            System.out.println();
        }
        System.out.println("      " + comment);
    }
}

public class CD extends Item
{
    ...

    public void print()
    {
        System.out.println("      " + artist);
        System.out.println("      tracks: " + numberOfTracks);
    }
}

public class Video extends Item
{
```

Code 9.1 continued

Source code of the print methods in all three classes

```
    ...

    public void print()
    {
        System.out.println("    director: " + director);
    }
}
```

Concept:

Overriding. A subclass can override a method implementation. To do this, the subclass declares a method with the same signature as the superclass, but with a different method body. The overriding method takes precedence for method calls on subclass objects.

This design works a bit better. It compiles, and it can be executed (even though it is not perfect yet). An implementation of this design is provided in the project *dome-v3*. (If you have done exercise 9.2, you already have a similar implementation of this design in your own version.)

The technique we are using here is called *overriding* (sometimes it is also referred to as *redefinition*). Overriding is a situation where a method is defined in a superclass (method print in class Item, in this example) and a method with exactly the same signature is defined in the subclass.

In this situation, objects of the subclass have two methods with the same name and signature: one inherited from the superclass and one from the subclass. Which one will be executed when we call this method?

9.4 Dynamic method lookup

One surprising detail is what exactly is printed once we execute the database's list method. If we again create and enter the objects described in section 9.1, the output of the list method in our new version of the program is

```
Frank Sinatra
tracks: 16

director: Joel & Ethan Coen
```

We can see from this output that the print methods in CD and in Video were executed, but not the one in Item.

This may seem strange at first. Our investigation in section 9.2 has shown that the compiler insisted on a print method in class Item – methods in the subclasses were not enough. This experiment now shows that the method in class Item is then not executed at all, but the subclass methods are. In short:

■ Type checking uses the static type, but at runtime the methods from the dynamic type are executed.

This is a fairly important statement. To understand it better, we look in more detail at how methods are invoked. This procedure is known as *method lookup*, *method binding*, or *method dispatch*. We will use the term 'method lookup' in this book.

We start with a simple method lookup scenario. Assume we have an object of a class Video stored in a variable v1 declared of type Video (Figure 9.5). The Video class has a

Figure 9.5
Method lookup with a simple object

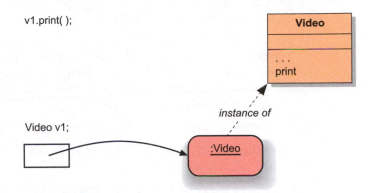

print method and no declared superclass. This is a very simple situation – there is no inheritance or polymorphism involved here. We then execute the statement

```
v1.print();
```

When this statement executes, the print method is invoked in the following steps:

1. The variable v1 is accessed.
2. The object stored in that variable is found (following the reference).
3. The class of the object is found (following the 'instance of' reference).
4. The implementation of the print method is found in the class and executed.

This is all very straightforward and not surprising.

Next, we look at method lookup with inheritance. This scenario is similar, but this time the Video class has a superclass Item, and the print method is defined only in the superclass (Figure 9.6).

We execute the same statement. The method invocation then starts in a similar way: steps 1 to 3 from the previous scenario are executed again, but then it continues differently:

Figure 9.6
Method lookup with inheritance

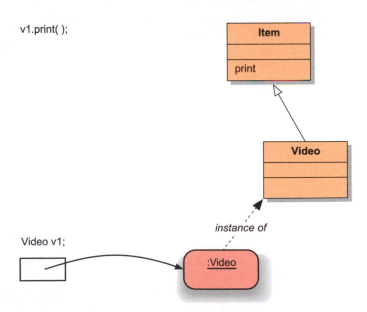

4. No `print` method is found in class `Video`.

5. Because no matching method was found, the superclass is searched for a matching method. If no method is found in the superclass, the next superclass (if it exists) is searched. This continues all the way up the inheritance hierarchy to the `Object` class, until a method is found. Note that at runtime a matching method should definitely be found, or else the class would not have compiled.

6. In our example, the `print` method is found in class `Item`, and will be executed.

This scenario illustrates how objects inherit methods. Any method found in a superclass can be invoked on a subclass object and will correctly be found and executed.

Next, we come to the most interesting scenario: method lookup with a polymorphic variable and method overriding (Figure 9.7). The scenario is again similar to the one before, but there are two changes:

■ The declared type of the variable `v1` is now `Item`, not `Video`.

■ The `print` method is defined in class `Item` and then redefined (overridden) in class `Video`.

This scenario is the most important one for understanding the behavior of our DoME application and in finding a solution to our `print` method problem.

The steps in which method execution takes place are exactly the same as steps 1–4 from scenario 1. Read them again.

Some observations are worth noting:

■ No special lookup rules are used for method lookup in cases where the dynamic type is not equal to the static type. The behavior we observe is a result of the general rules.

■ Which method is found first and executed is determined by the dynamic type, not the static type. In other words, the fact that the declared type of the variable `v1` is now `Item` does not have any effect. The instance we are dealing with is of class `Video` – that is all that counts.

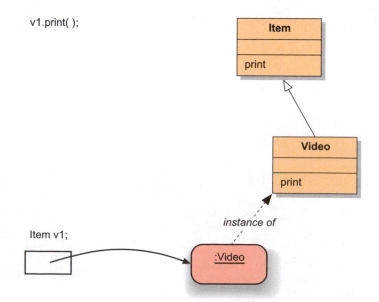

Figure 9.7
Method lookup with polymorphism and overriding

- Overriding methods in subclasses take precedence over superclass methods. Since method lookup starts in the dynamic class of the instance (at the bottom of the inheritance hierarchy), the last redefinition of a method is found first, and this is the one that is executed.

- When a method is overridden, only the last version (the one lowest in the inheritance hierarchy) is executed. Versions of the same method in any superclasses are not also automatically executed.

This explains the behavior that we observe in our DoME project. Only the `print` methods in the subclasses (`CD` and `Video`) are executed when items are printed out, leading to incomplete listings. In the next section, we discuss how to fix this.

9.5 Super call in methods

Now that we know in detail how overridden methods are executed, we can understand the solution to the problem. It is easy to see that what we would want to achieve is for every call to a `print` method of, say, a `CD` object, to result in both the `print` method of the `Item` class and that of the `CD` class to be executed for the same object. Then all the details would be printed out. (A different solution will be discussed later in this chapter.)

This is, in fact, quite easy to achieve. We can simply use the `super` construct, which we have already encountered in the context of constructors in Chapter 8. Code 9.2 illustrates this idea with the `print` method of the `CD` class.

Code 9.2

Redefining method with super call

```java
public void print()
{
    super.print();
    System.out.println("    " + artist);
    System.out.println("    tracks: " + numberOfTracks);
}
```

When `print` is now called on a `CD` object, initially the `print` method in the `CD` class will be invoked. As its first statement, this method will in turn invoke the `print` method of the superclass, which prints out the general item information. When control returns from the superclass method, the remaining statements of the subclass method print the distinctive fields of the `CD` class.

There are three details worth noting:

- Contrary to `super` calls in constructors, the method name of the superclass method is explicitly stated. A super call in a method always has the form

    `super.method-name ( parameters )`

    The parameter list can, of course, be empty.

- Again, contrary to the rule for super calls in constructors, the super call in methods may occur anywhere within that method. It does not have to be the first statement.

■ Contrary to super calls in constructors, no automatic super call is generated and no super call is required; it is entirely optional. So the default behavior gives the effect of a subclass method completely hiding (i.e. overriding) the superclass version of the same method.

Exercise 9.3 Modify your latest version of the DoME project to include the super call in the `print` method. Test it. Does it behave as expected? Do you see any problems with this solution?

Exercise 9.4 Change the format of the output so that it prints the string `"CD: "` or `"Video: "` (depending on the type of the item) in front of the details.

9.6 Method polymorphism

Concept:

Method polymorphism. Method calls in Java are polymorphic. The same method call may at different times invoke different methods, depending on the dynamic type of the variable used to make that call.

What we have just discussed in the previous sections (sections 9.2–9.5) is yet another form of polymorphism. It is what is known as *polymorphic method dispatch* (or *method polymorphism* for short).

Remember that a polymorphic variable is one that can store objects of varying types (every object variable in Java is potentially polymorphic). In a similar manner, Java method calls are polymorphic, since they may invoke different methods at different times. For instance, the statement

```
item.print();
```

could invoke the CD's `print` method at one time and the Video's `print` method at another, depending on the dynamic type of the item variable.

9.7 Object methods: toString

In Chapter 8 we mentioned that the universal superclass, `Object`, implements some methods that are then part of all objects. The most interesting of these methods is `toString`, which we shall introduce here; if you are interested in more detail, you can look up the interface for `Object` in the standard library documentation.

Exercise 9.5 Look up `toString` in the library documentation. What are its parameters? What is its return type?

The purpose of the `toString` method is to create a string representation of an object. This is useful for any objects that are ever to be textually represented in the user interface, but also helps for all other objects – they can then easily be printed out for debugging purposes, for instance.

The default implementation of `toString` in class `Object` cannot supply a great amount of detail. If, for example, we call `toString` on a `Video` object, we receive the string similar to this:

```
Video@6acdd1
```

The return value simply shows the object's class name and a magic number.[1]

Concept:

Every object in Java has a **toString** method that can be used to return a `String` representation of it. Typically, to make it useful, an object should override this method.

> **Exercise 9.6** You can easily try this out. Create an object of class **Video** in your project, and then invoke the **toString** method from the **Object** submenu in the object's popup menu.

To make this method more useful, we would typically override it in our own classes. We can, for example, define the `Item`'s `print` method in terms of a call to its `toString` method. In this case, the `toString` method would not print out the details, but just create a string with the text. Code 9.3 shows the changed source code.

Code 9.3

toString method for **Item** and CD

```java
public class Item
{
    ...

    public String toString()
    {
        String line1 = title + " (" + playingTime + " mins)");
        if(gotIt) {
            return line1 + "*\n" + "      " + comment + "\n";
        }
        else {
            return line1 + "\n" + "      " + comment + "\n";
        }
    }

    public void print()
    {
        System.out.println(toString());
    }
}

public class CD extends Item
{
    ...

    public String toString()
    {
```

---

[1] The number is in fact the memory address where the object is stored. It is not very useful except to establish identity. If this number is the same in two calls, we are looking at the same object. If it is different, we have two distinct objects.

```
            return super.toString() + "      " + artist +
                    "\n     tracks: " + numberOfTracks + "\n";
        }

    public void print()
    {
        System.out.println(toString());
    }
}
```

Ultimately, we would plan on removing the print methods completely from these classes. A great benefit of defining just a toString method is that we do not mandate in the Item classes what exactly is done with the description text. The original version always printed the text to the output terminal. Now, any client (e.g. the Database class) is free to do whatever it chooses with this text. It might show the text in a text area in a graphical user interface, save it to a file, send it over a network, or, as before, print it to the terminal.

The statement used in the client to print the item could now look as follows:

```
System.out.println(item.toString());
```

In fact, the System.out.print and System.out.println methods are special in this respect: if the parameter to one of these methods is not a string object, then the method automatically invokes the object's toString method. Thus we do not need to write the call explicitly, and could instead write

```
System.out.println(item);
```

Now consider the modified version of the list method of class Database shown in Code 9.4. In this version, we have removed not only the toString call, but also the cast of the object to an Item type. Would it compile and run correctly?

```
public class Database
{
    // fields, constructors and other methods omitted

    /**
     * Print a list of all currently stored CDs and videos to
     * the text terminal.
     */
    public void list()
    {
        for(Iterator iter = items.iterator(); iter.hasNext(); ) {
            System.out.println(iter.next());
        }
    }
}
```

In fact, the method *does* work as expected. If you can understand why, then you probably already have a good understanding of most of the concepts that we have introduced in this and the previous chapter! Here is a detailed explanation of the single print statement inside the for loop.

- The call to `iter.next()` returns a value with the static type `Object`. The dynamic type is either `CD` or `Video`.

- Since this object is being printed to `System.out`, and it is not a string, its `toString` method is automatically invoked.

- Invoking this method is valid only because the class `Object` (the static type!) declares a `toString` method. (Remember: Type checking is done with the static type. This call would not be allowed if class `Object` had no `toString` method.)

- The output appears properly with all details, because each possible dynamic type (`CD` and `Video`) overrides the `toString` method, and the dynamic method lookup ensures that the redefined method is executed.

The `toString` method is generally useful for debugging purposes. Often, it is very convenient if objects can easily be printed out in a sensible format. Most of the Java library classes override `toString` (all collections, for instance, can be printed out like this), and often it is a good idea to override this method for our classes as well.

9.8 Protected access

In Chapter 8 we noted that the rules on public and private visibility of class members applied between a subclass and its superclass, as well as between classes in different inheritance hierarchies. This can be somewhat restrictive because the nature of the relationship between a superclass and its subclasses is clearly closer than with other classes. For this reason, object-oriented languages often define a level of access that lies between the complete restriction of private access and the full availability of public access. In Java this is called *protected access*, and is provided by the `protected` key word as an alternative to `public` and `private`. Code 9.5 shows an example of a protected accessor method, which we could add to class `Item`.

Code 9.5

An example of a protected method

```
protected String getTitle()
{
    return title();
}
```

Protected access allows access to the fields or methods within a class itself and from all its subclasses, but not to other classes. The `getTitle` method shown in Code 9.5 can be called from class `Item` or any subclasses, but not from other classes.

Figure 9.8 illustrates this. The oval areas in the diagram show the group of classes that are able to access members in class `SomeClass`.

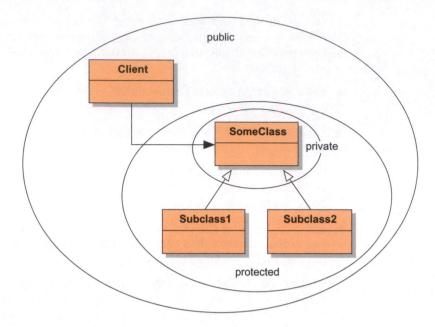

While protected access can be applied to any member of a class, it is usually reserved for methods and constructors. It is not usually applied to fields because that would be a weakening of encapsulation. Wherever possible, mutable fields in superclasses should remain private. There are, however, occasional valid cases where direct access by subclasses is desirable. Inheritance represents a much closer form of coupling than a normal client relationship.

Inheritance binds the classes closer together, and changing the superclass can more easily break the subclass. This should be taken into consideration when designing classes and their relationships.

Exercise 9.7 The version of `print` shown in Code 9.2 produces the output shown in Figure 9.9. Reorder the statements in the method in your version of the DoME project so that it prints the details as shown in Figure 9.10.

Exercise 9.8 Having to use a superclass call in `print` is somewhat restrictive in the ways we can format the output, because it is dependent on the way the superclass formats its fields. Make any necessary changes to the **Item** class and to the `print` method of **CD** so that it produces the output shown in Figure 9.11. Any changes you make to the **Item** class should be visible only to its subclasses. *Hint*: You used to use protected fields to do this.

```
A Swingin' Affair (64 mins)*
    my favorite Sinatra album
    Frank Sinatra
    tracks: 16
```

Figure 9.10

Alternative output from `print` (shaded areas printed by superclass method)

CD: Frank Sinatra: A Swingin' Affair *

64 minutes

my favorite Sinatra album

tracks: 16

Figure 9.11

Output from `print` mixing subclass and superclass details (shaded areas represent superclass details)

CD: Frank Sinatra: A Swingin' Affair *

16 tracks, 64 minutes

my favorite Sinatra album

9.9 Another example of inheritance with overriding

To discuss another example of a similar use of inheritance, we go back to a project from Chapter 7: the *zuul* project. In the *world-of-zuul* game, we used a set of Room objects to create a scene for a simple game. One of the exercises toward the end of the chapter suggested that you implement a transporter room (a room that beams you to a random location in the game if you try to enter or leave it). We revisit this exercise here, since its solution can greatly benefit from inheritance. If you don't remember this project well, have a quick read through Chapter 7 again, or look at your own *zuul* project.

There is no single solution to this task. Many different solutions are possible and can be made to work. Some are better than others, though. They may be more elegant, easier to read, easier to maintain and to extend.

Assume we want to implement this task so that the player is automatically transported to a random room when she tries to leave the magic transporter room. The most straight-forward solution that comes to mind first for many people is to deal with this in the Game class, which implements the player's commands. One of the commands is 'go', which is implemented in the goRoom method. In this method, we used the following statement as the central section of code:

```
nextRoom = currentRoom.getExit(direction);
```

This statement retrieves from the current room the neighboring room in the direction we want to go. To add our magic transportation, we could modify this similar to the following:

```
if(currentRoom.getName().equals("Transporter room")) {
    nextRoom = getRandomRoom();
}
else {
    nextRoom = currentRoom.getExit(direction);
}
```

The idea here is simple: we just check whether we are in the transporter room. If we are, then we find the next room by getting a random room (of course, we have to implement the getRandomRoom method somehow), otherwise we just do the same as before.

While this solution works, it has several drawbacks. The first is that it is a bad idea to use text strings, such as the room's name, to identify the room. Imagine that someone wanted to translate your game into another language – say, to German. They might change the names of the rooms – 'Transporter room' becomes 'Transporterraum' – and suddenly the game does not work any more! This is a clear case of a maintainability problem.

The second solution, which is slightly better, would be to use an instance variable instead of the room's name to identify the transporter room. Similar to this:

```
if(currentRoom == transporterRoom) {
    nextRoom = getRandomRoom();
}
else {
    nextRoom = currentRoom.getExit(direction);
}
```

This time, we assume that we have an instance variable `transporterRoom` of class `Room`, where we store the reference to our transporter room. Now the check is independent of the room's name. That is a bit better.

There is still a case for further improvement, though. We can understand the shortcomings of this solution when we think about another maintenance change. Imagine we want to add two more transporter rooms, so that our game has three different transporter locations.

A very nice aspect of our existing design was that we could set up the floor plan in a single spot, and the rest of the game was completely independent of it. We could easily change the layout of the rooms, and everything would still work – high score for maintainability! With our current solution, though, this is broken. If we add two new transporter rooms, we have to add two more instance variables or an array (to store references to those rooms), and we have to modify our `goRoom` method to add a check for those rooms. In terms of easy changeability, we have gone backwards.

The question, therefore, is: Can we find a solution that does not require a change to the command implementation each time we add a new transporter room? Here is our next idea.

We can add a method `isTransporterRoom` in the `Room` class. This way, the `Game` object does not need to remember all the transporter rooms – the rooms themselves do. When rooms are created, they could get a boolean flag indicating whether this room is a transporter room. The `goRoom` method then could use the following code segment:

```
if(currentRoom.isTransporterRoom()) {
    nextRoom = getRandomRoom();
}
else {
    nextRoom = currentRoom.getExit(direction);
}
```

Now we can add as many transporter rooms as we like – there is no need for any more changes to the `Game` class. However, the `Room` class has an extra field whose value is really needed only because of the nature of one or two of the instances. Special-case code such as this is a typical indicator of a weakness in class design. This approach also does not scale well should we decide to introduce further sorts of special room, each requiring its own flag field and accessor method.

With inheritance we can do better, and implement a solution that is even more flexible than this one.

We can implement a class `TransporterRoom` as a subclass of class `Room`. In this new class we override the `getExit` method and change its implementation so that it returns a random room:

```java
public class TransporterRoom extends Room
{

    /**
     * Return a random room, independent of the direction
     * parameter.
     */
    public Room getExit(String direction)
    {
        return findRandomRoom();
    }

    /*
     * Choose a random room.
     */
    private Room findRandomRoom()
    {
        ...  // implementation omitted

    }
}
```

The elegance of this solution lies in the fact that no change at all is needed in either the original `Game` or `Room` classes! We can simply add this class to the existing game, and the `goRoom` method will continue to work as it is. Simply adding the creation of a `TransporterRoom` to the setup of the floor plan is (almost) enough to make it work. Note, too, that the new class does not need a flag to indicate its special nature – its very type and distinctive behavior supply that information.

Because `TransporterRoom` is a subclass of `Room`, it can be used everywhere a `Room` object is expected. Thus it can be used as a neighboring room for another room, or be held in the `Game` object as the current room.

What we have left out, of course, is the implementation of the `findRandomRoom` method. In reality, this is probably better done in a separate class (say `RoomRandomizer`) than in the `TransporterRoom` class itself. We leave this open as an exercise for the reader.

Exercise 9.9 Implement a transporter room with inheritance in your version of the *zuul* project.

Exercise 9.10 Discuss how inheritance could be used in the *zuul* project to implement a player and a monster class.

Exercise 9.11 Could (or should) inheritance be used to create an inheritance relationship (super-, sub-, or sibling class) between a character in the game and an item?

9.10 Summary

When we deal with classes with subclasses and polymorphic variables, we have to distinguish between the static and dynamic type of a variable. The static type is the declared type, while the dynamic type is the type of the object currently stored in the variable.

Type checking is done by the compiler using the static type, whereas at runtime method lookup uses the dynamic type. This enables us to create very flexible structures by overriding methods. Even when using a supertype variable to make a method call, overriding enables us to ensure that specialized methods are invoked for every particular subtype. This ensures that objects of different classes can react distinctly to the same method call.

When implementing overriding methods, the `super` key word can be used to invoke the superclass version of the method. If fields or methods are declared with the `protected` access modifier, subclasses are allowed to access them, but other classes are not.

Terms introduced in this chapter

static type, dynamic type, overriding, redefinition, method lookup, method dispatch, method polymorphism, protected

Concept summary

- **static type** The static type of a variable **v** is the type as declared in the source code in the variable declaration statement.

- **dynamic type** The dynamic type of a variable **v** is the type of the object that is currently stored in **v**.

- **overriding** A subclass can override a method implementation. To do this, the subclass declares a method with the same signature as the superclass, but with a different method body. The overriding method takes precedence for method calls on subclass objects.

- **method polymorphism** Method calls in Java are polymorphic. The same method call may at different times invoke different methods, depending on the dynamic type of the variable used to make that call.

- **toString** Every object in Java has a `toString` method that can be used to return a `String` representation of it. Typically, to make it useful, a class should override this method.

- **protected** Declaring a field or a method `protected` allows direct access to it from (direct or indirect) subclasses.

Exercise 9.12 Assume you see the following lines of code:

```
Device dev = new Printer();
dev.getName();
```

Printer is a subclass of Device. Which of these classes must have a definition of method getName for this code to compile?

Exercise 9.13 In the same situation as in the previous exercise, if both classes have an implementation of getName, which one will be executed?

Exercise 9.14 Assume you write a class Student, which does not have a declared superclass. You do not write a toString method. Consider the following lines of code:

```
Student st = new Student();
String s = st.toString();
```

Will these lines compile? What exactly will happen when you try to execute?

Exercise 9.15 In the same situation as before (class Student, no toString method), will the following lines compile? Why?

```
Student st = new Student();
System.out.println(st);
```

Exercise 9.16 Assume your class Student overrides toString so that it returns the student's name. You now have a list of students. Will the following code compile? If not, why not? If yes, what will it print? Explain in detail what happens.

```
Iterator it = myList.iterator();
while(it.hasNext()) {
    System.out.println(it.next());
}
```

Exercise 9.17 Write a few lines of code that result in a situation where a variable x has the static type T and the dynamic type D.

Further abstraction techniques

Main concepts discussed in this chapter:

- abstract classes
- interfaces

Java constructs discussed in this chapter:

`abstract`, `implements`, `interface`, `instanceof`

In this chapter we examine further inheritance-related techniques that can be used to enhance class structures and improve maintainability and extendibility. These techniques introduce an improved method of representation of abstractions in object-oriented programs.

The previous two chapters have discussed the most important aspects of inheritance in application design, but several more advanced uses and problems have been ignored so far. We will now complete the picture with a more advanced example.

The next project we use for this chapter is a simulation. We use it to discuss inheritance again, and see that we run into some new problems. *Abstract classes* and *interfaces* are then introduced to deal with these problems.

10.1 Simulations

Computers are frequently used to execute simulations of a real system. These include simulations of traffic in a city, weather forecasting, simulating nuclear explosions, stock market analysis, environmental simulations, and much more. In fact, many of the most powerful computers in the world are used for running some sort of simulation.

When creating a computer simulation, we try to model the behavior of a subset of the real world in a software model. Every simulation is necessarily a simplification of the real thing. Deciding which details to leave out and which to include is often a challenging task. The more detailed a simulation is, the more accurate it may be in forecasting the behavior of the real system. But more detail increases the requirements for both more computing power and more programmer time. A well-known example is weather forecasting: climate models in weather simulations have been improved by adding more and more detail over the last few decades. As a result, weather forecasts have improved significantly in accuracy (but are far from perfect, as we all have experienced at some time). Much of this improvement has been made possible through advances in computer technology.

The benefit of simulations is that we can undertake experiments that we could not do with the real system, either because we have no control over the real thing (for instance, the weather), or because it is too costly, too dangerous, or irreversible in case of disaster. We can use the simulation to investigate the behavior of the system under certain circumstances, or to investigate 'what if' questions.

An example of the use of environmental simulations could be to try to predict the effects of human activity on natural habitats. Consider the case of a national park containing endangered species, and a proposal to build a freeway through the middle of it, completely separating the two halves. The supporters of the freeway proposal claim that splitting the park in half will make no difference to the animals in it, but environmentalists claim otherwise. How can we tell what the effect is likely to be without building the freeway?

The question boils down to whether it is significant for the survival of a species if they have one connected habitat area, or whether two disjoint areas (with the same total size) are just as good. Rather than building the freeway first and then observing what happens, we could try to simulate the effect in order to make a well-informed decision.[1] (In this particular case, by the way, it does matter: the size of a natural park has a significant impact on its usefulness as a habitat for animals.)

For our main example in this chapter we will describe an environmental simulation. This will necessarily be simpler than the scenario we have described because we are using it mainly to illustrate new features of object-oriented design and implementation. Therefore it will not have the potential to simulate accurately many aspects of nature, but some things are nonetheless interesting. In particular, it will demonstrate the structure of typical simulations.

10.2   The foxes-and-rabbits simulation

The simulation scenario we have chosen to work with in this chapter involves tracking populations of foxes and rabbits within an enclosed field. This is just one particular example of what are known as *predator–prey simulations*. Such simulations are often used to model the variation in population sizes that result from a predator species feeding on a prey species. A delicate balance exists between such species. A large population of prey will potentially provide plenty of food for a small population of predators. However, too large a number of predators could kill off all the prey and be left with nothing to eat. Population sizes could also be affected by the size and nature of the environment. For instance, a small, enclosed environment could lead to overcrowding and make it easy for the predators to locate their prey, or a polluted environment could reduce the stock of prey and prevent even a modest population of predators from surviving. Since predators themselves are often prey for other species, loss of one part of the food chain can have dramatic effects on the survival of other parts.

---

[1] A remaining question in all cases of this kind is, of course, how good the simulation is. One can 'prove' just about anything with an over-simplified or ill-designed simulation. Gaining trust in the simulation through controlled experiments is essential.

As we have done in previous chapters, we will start with a version of an application that works perfectly well from a user's point of view, but whose internal view is not so good when judged by the principles of good object-oriented design and implementation. We will use this base version to develop several improved versions that progressively introduce new abstraction techniques.

One particular problem that we wish to address in the base version is that it does not make good use of the inheritance techniques that were introduced in Chapter 8. However, we will start by examining the mechanism of the simulation, without being too critical of its implementation. Once we understand how it works we shall be in a good position to make some improvements.

10.2.1 The foxes-and-rabbits project

Open the *foxes-and-rabbits-v1* project. The class diagram is shown in Figure 10.1.

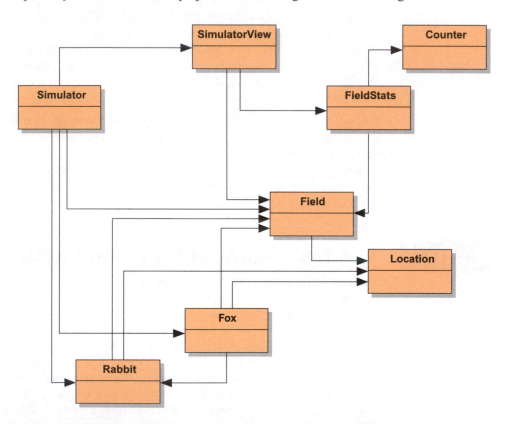

The main classes we will focus on in our discussion are `Simulator`, `Fox`, and `Rabbit`. The `Fox` and `Rabbit` classes provide simple models of the behavior of a predator and prey respectively. In this particular implementation we have not tried to provide an accurate biological model of real foxes and rabbits; rather we are simply trying to illustrate the principles of typical predator–prey simulations. The `Simulator` class is responsible for creating the initial state of the simulation, and then controlling and executing it. The basic idea is simple: the simulator holds a collection of foxes and rabbits, and it performs a sequence of *steps*. In each step, each fox and each rabbit is allowed to move. After each step (when every animal has moved) the current state of the field is displayed on screen.

We can summarize the purpose of the remaining classes as follows:

- `Field` represents a two-dimensional enclosed field. The field is composed of a fixed number of locations, which are arranged in rows and columns. At most one animal may occupy a single location within the field. Each field location can hold a reference to an animal or it can be empty.

- `Location` represents a two-dimensional position within the field. Its position is determined by a row and a column value.

- These classes together (`Simulator`, `Fox`, `Rabbit`, `Field`, and `Location`) provide the model for the simulation. They completely determine the simulation behavior.

- The classes `SimulatorView`, `FieldStats`, and `Counter` together provide a graphical display of the simulation. The display shows an image of the field and counters for each species (the current number of rabbits and foxes).

- `SimulatorView` provides a graphical visualization of the state of the field. An example can be seen in Figure 10.2.

Figure 10.2

The initial state of the foxes-and-rabbits simulation

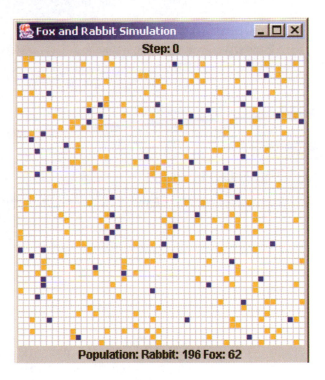

- `FieldStats` provides counts of the numbers of foxes and rabbits in the field to the visualization.

- A `Counter` stores a current count for one type of animal to assist with the counting.

Try the following exercises to gain an understanding of how the simulation operates before reading about its implementation.

Exercise 10.1 Create a `Simulator` object using the constructor without parameters and you should see the initial state of the simulation as shown in Figure 10.2. The more numerous rectangles represent the rabbits. Does the number of foxes change if you call the `simulateOneStep` method just once?

Exercise 10.2 Does the number of foxes change on every step? What natural processes do you think we are modeling that cause the number of foxes to increase or decrease?

Exercise 10.3 Call the `simulate` method to run the simulation continuously for a significant number of steps, such as 50 or 100. Do the numbers of foxes and rabbits increase or decrease at similar rates?

Exercise 10.4 What changes do you notice if you run the simulation for a very long time, say for 500 steps? You can use the `runLongSimulation` method to do this.

Exercise 10.5 Use the `reset` method to restore the starting state of the simulation, and then run it again. Is an identical simulation run this time? If not, do you see broadly similar patterns emerging anyway?

Exercise 10.6 If you run a simulation for long enough, do all of the foxes or all of the rabbits ever die off completely? If so, can you pinpoint any reasons why that might be occurring?

In the following sections we will examine the initial implementation of the `Rabbit`, `Fox`, and `Simulator` classes.

10.2.2 The `Rabbit` class

The source code of the `Rabbit` class is shown in Code 10.1.

Code 10.1

The `Rabbit` class

```java
// import statements and class comment omitted

public class Rabbit
{
    // Characteristics shared by all rabbits (static fields).

    // The age at which a rabbit can start to breed.
    private static final int BREEDING_AGE = 5;
    // The age to which a rabbit can live.
    private static final int MAX_AGE = 50;
    // The likelihood of a rabbit breeding.
    private static final double BREEDING_PROBABILITY = 0.15;
    // The maximum number of births.
    private static final int MAX_LITTER_SIZE = 5;
    // A shared random number generator to control breeding.
```

Code 10.1 continued

The **Rabbit** class

```java
    private static final Random rand = new Random();

    // Individual characteristics (instance fields).

    // The rabbit's age.
    private int age;
    // Whether the rabbit is alive or not.
    private boolean alive;
    // The rabbit's position
    private Location location;

    /**
     * Create a new rabbit. A rabbit may be created with age
     * zero (a new born) or with a random age.
     *
     * @param randomAge If true, the rabbit will have a
     *                  random age.
     */
    public Rabbit(boolean randomAge)
    {
        // body of constructor omitted
    }

    /**
     * This is what the rabbit does most of the time - it
     * runs around. Sometimes it will breed or die of old
     * age.
     * @param updatedField The field to transfer to.
     * @param newRabbits A list to add newly born rabbits to.
     */
    public void run(Field updatedField, List newRabbits)
    {
        incrementAge();
        if(alive) {
            int births = breed();
            for(int b = 0; b < births; b++) {
                Rabbit newRabbit = new Rabbit(false);
                newRabbits.add(newRabbit);
                Location loc =
                    updatedField.randomAdjacentLocation(location);
                newRabbit.setLocation(loc);
                updatedField.place(newRabbit, loc);
            }
            Location newLocation =
                updatedField.freeAdjacentLocation(location);
            // Only transfer to the updated field if there
            // was a free location
            if(newLocation != null) {
                setLocation(newLocation);
                updatedField.place(this, newLocation);
            }
        }
```

```
            else {
                // can neither move nor stay - overcrowding -
                // all locations taken
                alive = false;
            }
        }
    }

    /**
     * Increase the age.
     * This could result in the rabbit's death.
     */
    private void incrementAge()
    {
        age++;
        if(age > MAX_AGE) {
            alive = false;
        }
    }

    /**
     * Generate a number representing the number of births,
     * if it can breed.
     * @return The number of births (may be zero).
     */
    private int breed()
    {
        int births = 0;
        if(canBreed() && rand.nextDouble() <=
                                BREEDING_PROBABILITY) {
            births = rand.nextInt(MAX_LITTER_SIZE) + 1;
        }
        return births;
    }

    // other methods omitted
}
```

The Rabbit class contains a number of static variables that define configuration settings that are common to all rabbits. These include values for the maximum age to which a rabbit can live (defined as a number of simulation steps) and the maximum number of offspring it can produce at any one step. Each individual rabbit has three instance variables that describe its state: its age as a number of steps, whether it is still alive, and its current location in the field.

A rabbit's behavior is defined in its run method, which in turn uses the breed and incrementAge methods, and implements the rabbit's movement. At each simulation step the run method will be called and a rabbit will increase its age, move and, if old enough, it might also breed. Both the movement and the breeding behavior have random components. The direction in which the rabbit moves is randomly chosen, and breeding occurs randomly, controlled by the static field BREEDING_PROBABILITY.

You can already see some of the simplifications that we have made in our model of rabbits: there is no attempt to distinguish males from females, for instance, and a rabbit could potentially give birth to a new litter at every simulation step.

10.2.3 The `Fox` class

There is a lot of similarity between the `Fox` and the `Rabbit` classes, so only the distinctive elements of `Fox` are shown in Code 10.2.

Code 10.2
The Fox class

```
// import statements and class comment omitted

public class Fox
{
    // Characteristics shared by all foxes (static fields).

    // The age at which a fox can start to breed.
    private static final int BREEDING_AGE = 10;

    // other static fields omitted

    // Individual characteristics (instance fields).

    // The fox's age.
    private int age;
    // Whether the fox is alive or not.
    private boolean alive;
    // The fox's position
    private Location location;
    // The fox's food level, which is increased by eating
    // rabbits.
    private int foodLevel;

    /**
     * Create a fox. A fox can be created as a new born (age
     * zero and not hungry) or with random age.
     *
     * @param randomAge If true, the fox will have random age
     *                  and hunger level.
     *
```

**Code 10.2
continued**

The Fox class

```
    */
    public Fox(boolean randomAge)
    {
        // body of constructor omitted
    }

    /**
     * This is what the fox does most of the time: it hunts
     * for rabbits. In the process, it might breed, die of
     * hunger, or die of old age.
     * @param currentField The field currently occupied.
     * @param updatedField The field to transfer to.
     * @param newFoxes A list to add newly born foxes to.
     */
    public void hunt(Field currentField, Field updatedField,
                     List newFoxes)
    {
        incrementAge();
        incrementHunger();
        if(alive) {
            // New foxes are born into adjacent locations.
            int births = breed();
            for(int b = 0; b < births; b++) {
                Fox newFox = new Fox(false);
                newFoxes.add(newFox);
                Location loc =
                  updatedField.randomAdjacentLocation(location);
                newFox.setLocation(loc);
                updatedField.place(newFox, loc);
            }
            // Move towards the source of food if found.
            Location newLocation = findFood(currentField,
                                            location);
            if(newLocation == null) {
                // no food found - move randomly
                newLocation =
                  updatedField.freeAdjacentLocation(location);
            }
            if(newLocation != null) {
                setLocation(newLocation);
                updatedField.place(this, newLocation);
            }
            else {
                // can neither move nor stay - overcrowding -
                // all locations taken
                alive = false;
            }
        }
    }

    /**
     * Tell the fox to look for rabbits adjacent to its
     * current location.
```

Code 10.2
continued

The Fox class

```
     * @param field The field in which it must look.
     * @param location Where in the field it is located.
     * @return Where food was found, or null if it wasn't.
     */
    private Location findFood(Field field, Location location)
    {
        Iterator adjacentLocations =
                        field.adjacentLocations(location);
        while(adjacentLocations.hasNext()) {
            Location where =
                    (Location) adjacentLocations.next();
            Object animal = field.getObjectAt(where);
            if(animal instanceof Rabbit) {
                Rabbit rabbit = (Rabbit) animal;
                if(rabbit.isAlive()) {
                    rabbit.setEaten();
                    foodLevel = RABBIT_FOOD_VALUE;
                    return where;
                }
            }
        }
        return null;
    }

    // other methods omitted
}
```

For foxes, the hunt method is invoked at each step and defines their behavior. In addition to ageing and possibly breeding at each step, a fox searches for food (using the findFood method). If it is able to find a rabbit in an adjacent location then the rabbit is killed and the fox's food level is increased.

Exercise 10.10 As you did for rabbits, assess the degree to which we have simplified the model of foxes and evaluate whether you feel the simplifications are likely to lead to an inaccurate simulation.

Exercise 10.11 Does increasing the maximum age for foxes lead to significantly higher numbers of foxes throughout a simulation, or is the rabbit population more likely to be reduced to zero as a result?

Exercise 10.12 Experiment with different combinations of settings (breeding age, maximum age, breeding probability, litter size, etc.) for foxes and rabbits. Do species always disappear completely in some configurations? Are there configurations that are stable?

Exercise 10.13 Experiment with different sizes of field. (You can do this by using the second Simulator constructor.) Does the size of the field affect the likelihood of species surviving?

Exercise 10.14 Currently a fox will eat at most one rabbit at each step. Modify the `findFood` method so that rabbits in all adjacent locations are eaten at a single step. Assess the impact of this change on the results of the simulation.

Exercise 10.15 When a fox eats a large number of rabbits at a single step, there are several different possibilities as to how we can model its food level. If we add all the rabbit's food values the fox will have a very high food level, making it unlikely to die of hunger for a very long time. Alternatively, we could impose a ceiling on the fox's `foodLevel`. This models the effect of a predator that kills prey regardless of whether it is hungry or not. Assess the impacts of implementing this choice on the resulting simulation.

10.2.4 The `Simulator` class: setup

The `Simulator` class is the central part of the application. Code 10.3 illustrates some of its main features.

Code 10.3

Part of the
`Simulator` class

```
// import statements and class comment omitted

public class Simulator
{
    // static variables omitted

    // The list of animals in the field
    private List animals;
    // The list of animals just born
    private List newAnimals;
    // The current state of the field.
    private Field field;
    // A second field, used to build the next stage of the
    // simulation.
    private Field updatedField;
    // The current step of the simulation.
    private int step;
    // A graphical view of the simulation.
    private SimulatorView view;

    /**
     * Create a simulation field with the given size.
     * @param depth Depth of the field.
     *              Must be greater than zero.
     * @param width Width of the field.
     *              Must be greater than zero.
     */
    public Simulator(int depth, int width)
    {
        if(width <= 0 || depth <= 0) {
            System.out.println(
                "The dimensions must be greater than zero.");
```

**Code 10.3
continued**

Part of the
`Simulator` class

```java
            System.out.println("Using default values.");
            depth = DEFAULT_DEPTH;
            width = DEFAULT_WIDTH;
        }
        animals = new ArrayList();
        newAnimals = new ArrayList();
        field = new Field(depth, width);
        updatedField = new Field(depth, width);

        // Create a view of the state of each location in the
        // field.
        view = new SimulatorView(depth, width);
        view.setColor(Fox.class, Color.blue);
        view.setColor(Rabbit.class, Color.orange);

        // Setup a valid starting point.
        reset();
    }

    /**
     * Run the simulation from its current state for the
     * given number of steps.
     * Stop before the given number of steps if it ceases to
     * be viable.
     */
    public void simulate(int numSteps)
    {
        for(int step = 1; step <= numSteps &&
                            view.isViable(field); step++) {
            simulateOneStep();
        }
    }

    /**
     * Run the simulation from its current state for a single
     * step.
     * Iterate over the whole field updating the state of
     * each fox and rabbit.
     */
    public void simulateOneStep()
    {
        // method body omitted
    }

    /**
     * Reset the simulation to a starting position.
     */
    public void reset()
    {
        step = 0;
        animals.clear();
```

Code 10.3 continued

Part of the
Simulator class

```
        field.clear();
        updatedField.clear();
        populate(field);

        // Show the starting state in the view.
        view.showStatus(step, field);
    }


    /**
     * Populate a field with foxes and rabbits.
     * @param field The field to be populated
     */
    private void populate(Field field)
    {
        Random rand = new Random();
        field.clear();
        for(int row = 0; row < field.getDepth(); row++) {
            for(int col = 0; col < field.getWidth(); col++) {
                if(rand.nextDouble() <=
                            FOX_CREATION_PROBABILITY) {
                    Fox fox = new Fox(true);
                    animals.add(fox);
                    fox.setLocation(row, col);
                    field.place(fox, row, col);
                }
                else if(rand.nextDouble() <=
                            RABBIT_CREATION_PROBABILITY) {
                    Rabbit rabbit = new Rabbit(true);
                    animals.add(rabbit);
                    rabbit.setLocation(row, col);
                    field.place(rabbit, row, col);
                }
                // else leave the location empty.
            }
        }
        Collections.shuffle(animals);
    }

    //  other methods omitted
}
```

The Simulator has three important parts: its constructor, the populate method, and the simulateOneStep method. (The body of simulateOneStep is shown below.)

When a Simulator object is created, all other parts of the simulation are constructed (the field, the lists to hold the animals, and the graphical interface). Once all these have been set up, the simulator's populate method is called (indirectly, via the reset method) to create the initial fox and rabbit populations. Different probabilities are used to decide whether a particular location will contain one of these animals. Note that animals created at the start of the simulation are given a random initial age. This serves two purposes:

- It represents more accurately a mixed-age population that should be the normal state of the simulation.

- If all animals were to start with an age of zero, no new animals would be created until the initial population had reached their respective breeding ages. With foxes eating rabbits regardless of the fox's age, there is a risk that either the rabbit population will be killed off before it has a chance to reproduce, or that the fox population will die of hunger.

Exercise 10.16 Modify the `populate` method of `Simulator` to determine whether not setting an initial random age for foxes and rabbits is catastrophic.

Exercise 10.17 If an initial random age is set for rabbits but not foxes, the rabbit population will tend to grow large while the fox population remains very small. Once the foxes do become old enough to breed, does the simulation tend to behave again like the original version? What does this suggest about the relative sizes of the initial populations and their impact on the outcome of the simulation?

10.2.5 The `Simulator` class: a simulation step

The central part of the `Simulator` class is the `simulateOneStep` method shown in Code 10.4. It uses a loop to let each animal move (and possibly breed, or do whatever it is programmed to do). Running longer simulations is trivial. To do this, the `simulateOneStep` method is called repeatedly in a simple loop.

In order to let each animal act, the simulator holds a list of all animals. Here, we make very limited use of inheritance. The fact that all Java objects inherit from the `Object` class is used to treat both rabbits and foxes as `Object` instances, which are added into the same list. When we retrieve objects from this list, we have to check the actual class of the object (using the `instanceof` operator) and cast the object appropriately. Then we make a call to the animals' respective action method (`run` for rabbits and `hunt` for foxes).

Code 10.4
Inside the `Simulator` class: simulating one step

```java
public void simulateOneStep()
{
    step++;
    newAnimals.clear();

    // let all animals act
    for(Iterator iter = animals.iterator(); iter.hasNext(); ) {
        Object animal = iter.next();
        if(animal instanceof Rabbit) {
            Rabbit rabbit = (Rabbit)animal;
            rabbit.run(updatedField, newAnimals);
        }
        else if(animal instanceof Fox) {
            Fox fox = (Fox)animal;
            fox.hunt(field, updatedField, newAnimals);
        }
        else {
```

**Code 10.4
continued**

Inside the
`Simulator` class:
simulating one step

```
                    System.out.println("found unknown animal");
            }
        }
        // add new born animals to the list of animals
        animals.addAll(newAnimals);

        // Swap the field and updatedField at the end of the step.
        Field temp = field;
        field = updatedField;
        updatedField = temp;
        updatedField.clear();

        // display the new field on screen
        view.showStatus(step, field);
    }
```

The `instanceof` operator tests whether a given object is, directly or indirectly, an instance of a given class. The test

```
    obj instanceof MyClass
```

returns `true` if the dynamic type of `obj` is `MyClass` or any subclass of `MyClass`.

We can already note that this code is a candidate for improvement a bit later on. The fact that each type of animal must be tested and cast separately, and special code exists here for each animal class, is not ideal. It makes the simulator dependent on the exact types of animal in the simulation, and increases the difficulty of adding new animal types. This method creates a degree of coupling between `Simulator` and the animal classes that is much stronger than we would like.

Crucial to the progress of the simulation through a single step is also the use of two `Field` objects, referred to via the `field` and `updatedField` attributes of the simulator. As we process all animals in the current field, each places itself into the `updatedField` after its action. This makes it easy to remove dead animals from the simulation – they simply do not transfer themselves to the updated field.

> **Exercise 10.18** When a rabbit moves to a free location, it is placed in the updated field only if there is not already a fox at that location. What is the effect on the fox population if this constraint is removed? Is the same constraint placed upon newly born rabbits?
>
> **Exercise 10.19** Could two foxes ever try to move to the same location in the updated field? If so, should an attempt be made to avoid this situation?

10.2.6   Taking steps to improve the simulation

Now that we have examined how the simulation operates, we are in a position to make improvements to its internal design and implementation. Making progressive improvements through the introduction of new programming features will be the focus of subsequent sections. There are several points at which we could start, but one of the most obvious weaknesses is that no attempt has been made to exploit the advantages of inheritance in the implementation of the `Fox` and `Rabbit` classes, which share a lot of common elements. In order to do this we shall introduce the concept of an *abstract class*.

10.3 Abstract classes

Chapter 8 introduced concepts such as inheritance and polymorphism, which we ought to be able to exploit in the simulation application. For instance, the `Fox` and `Rabbit` classes share many similar characteristics that suggest they should be subclasses of a common superclass, such as `Animal`. In this section we will start to make such changes in order to improve the design and implementation of the simulation as a whole. As with the DoME example in Chapter 8, using a common superclass should avoid code duplication in the subclasses and simplify the code in the client class (here: `Simulator`). It is important to note that we are undertaking a process of refactoring, and that these changes should not change the essential characteristics of the simulation as seen from a user's viewpoint.

> **Exercise 10.20** Identify the similarities and differences between the `Fox` and `Rabbit` classes. Make separate lists of the fields, methods, and constructors, and distinguish between the class variables (static fields) and instance variables.
>
> **Exercise 10.21** Candidate methods to place in a superclass are those that are identical in all subclasses. Which methods are truly identical in the `Fox` and `Rabbit` classes? In reaching a conclusion, you might like to consider the effect of substituting the values of class variables into the bodies of the methods that use them.
>
> **Exercise 10.22** In the current version of the simulation, the values of all similarly named class variables are different. If the two values of a particular class variable (`BREEDING_AGE`, say) were identical, would it make any difference to your assessment of which methods are identical?

10.3.1 The `Animal` superclass

For the first set of changes we will move the identical elements of `Fox` and `Rabbit` to an `Animal` superclass. The project *foxes-and-rabbits-v1* provides a copy of the base version of the simulation for you to follow through the changes we make.

- Both `Fox` and `Rabbit` define `age`, `alive`, and `location` attributes, and these can be moved to the `Animal` superclass, along with the `isAlive` and `setLocation` methods. Their initial values are set in the constructor of `Animal`.

- Moving these three attributes to `Animal` raises the question of what visibility they should have. The `incrementAge` method, for instance, needs to be able both to get and to set the value of `age`. One possibility is to declare these fields `protected` – this would give subclasses full access to the field. This, however, creates a strong coupling between these classes. We can achieve looser coupling by declaring these fields `private` and providing accessor and mutator methods. The subclasses can then use these to inspect and manipulate the attributes.

■ The Rabbit class defines a setEaten mutator that is used by the Fox class in its findFood method. However, both Fox and Rabbit need to set the alive attribute to false in other places — incrementAge, and incrementHunger. A reasonable change to make, therefore, would be to rename setEaten to the more general setDead and place it in Animal, so that the increment methods can use it.

Exercise 10.23 What sort of regression-testing strategy could you establish before undertaking the process of refactoring on the simulation? Is this something you could conveniently automate?

Exercise 10.24 Create the Animal superclass in your version of the project. Make the changes discussed above. Ensure that the simulation works in a similar manner as before.

Exercise 10.25 How has using inheritance improved the project so far? Discuss.

10.3.2 Abstract methods

So far, use of the Animal superclass has helped to avoid code duplication in the Rabbit and Fox classes, and has made it easier to add new animal types in the future. As we have seen in Chapter 8, intelligent use of inheritance should also simplify the client class. We shall investigate this now.

In the Simulator class we have used explicit type checks (using the instanceof operator) and casts to specific animal types to implement a simulation step. Both these techniques are problematic, since they hard-code the specific animal types in the simulation and make it harder to modify or extend the current types of animals. The relevant code is shown in Code 10.5.

Code 10.5

The original solution to make animals act

```
for(Iterator iter = animals.iterator(); iter.hasNext(); ) {
    Object animal = iter.next();
    if(animal instanceof Rabbit) {
        Rabbit rabbit = (Rabbit)animal;
        rabbit.run(updatedField, newAnimals);
    }
    else if(animal instanceof Fox) {
        Fox fox = (Fox)animal;
        fox.hunt(field, updatedField, newAnimals);
    }
    else {
        System.out.println("found unknown animal");
    }
}
```

Now that we have the Animal class, we can improve this. Since all objects in our animals collection are a subtype of Animal, we can cast each element to Animal instead of casting it to Object. If we then ensure that the superclass (Animal) has a method that lets an animal act, and this method is redefined in each subclass, then we can use a polymorphic method call to let each animal act, without the need to cast to the specific animal types. Let us assume that we create such a method, called `act`, and investigate the resulting source code. Code 10.6 shows the code implementing this solution.

```
// let all animals act
for(Iterator iter = animals.iterator(); iter.hasNext(); ) {
    Animal animal = (Animal)iter.next();
    animal.act(field, updatedField, newAnimals);
}
```

Several observations are important at this point:

- The variable we are using for each collection element (`animal`) is of type `Animal`. This is legal, since all objects in the collection are foxes or rabbits, and thus are all subtypes of `Animal`.

- We assume that the specific action methods (`run` for `Rabbit`, `hunt` for `Fox`) have been renamed `act`. This is more appropriate. Instead of telling each animal exactly what to do, we are just telling it to 'act,' and we leave it up to the animal itself to decide what exactly it wants to do.

- The `run` method for `Rabbit` had only two parameters, `updatedField` and `newRabbits`. We have now added a third parameter, `field`, to make it consistent with the fox's `act` method. Now every animal gets all parameters possibly needed to implement flexible action, and each class can choose to ignore any of the parameters.

- Because the dynamic type of the variable determines which method is actually executed (as discussed in Chapter 9), the fox's action method will be executed for foxes, and the rabbit's method for rabbits.

- Since type checking is done using the static type, this code will compile only if class `Animal` has an act method with the right signature.

The last of these points is the only remaining problem. Since we are using the statement

```
animal.act(field, updatedField, newAnimals);
```

and the variable `animal` is of type `Animal`, we saw in Chapter 9 that this will compile only if `Animal` defines such a method. However, the situation here is rather different from the situation we encountered with the `Item` class's `print` method in Chapter 9. There, the superclass version of `print` had a useful job to do – print the fields defined in the superclass. Here, although each particular animal has a specific set of actions to perform, we cannot describe in any detail the actions for animals in general. The particular actions depend on the specific subtype.

Our problem is to decide how we should define `Animal`'s `act` method.

The problem is a reflection of the fact that no instance of class `Animal` will ever exist. There is no object in our simulation (or in nature) that is just an animal and not also an instance of a more specific subclass. These kinds of class, which are not intended for creating objects but serve only as superclasses, are known as *abstract classes*. For animals, for example, we can say that each animal can act, but we cannot describe exactly how it acts without referring to a more specific subclass. This is typical for abstract classes, and it is reflected in Java constructs.

For the `Animal` class, we wish to state that each animal has an `act` method, but we cannot give a reasonable implementation in class `Animal`. The solution in Java is to declare the method *abstract*. Here is an example of an abstract `act` method:

```
abstract public void act(Field currentField,
                         Field updatedField,
                         List newAnimals);
```

> **Concept:**
>
> An **abstract method** definition consists of a method signature without a method body. It is marked with the key word `abstract`.

An abstract method is characterized by two details:

■ It is prefixed with the key word `abstract`.
■ It does not have a method body. Instead, its header is terminated with a semicolon.

Since the method has no body, it can never be executed. But we have already established that we do not want to execute an `Animal`'s `act` method, so that is not a problem.

Before we investigate in detail the effects of using an abstract method, we shall introduce more formally the concept of an abstract class.

10.3.3 Abstract classes

Not only methods can be declared abstract; classes can be declared abstract as well. Code 10.7 shows an example of class `Animal` as an abstract class. Classes are declared abstract by inserting the key word `abstract` into the class header.

Code 10.7

`Animal` as an abstract class

> **Concept:**
>
> An **abstract class** is a class that is not intended for creating instances. Its purpose is to serve as a superclass for other classes. Abstract classes may contain abstract methods.

```java
public abstract class Animal
{
    // fields omitted

    /**
     * Make this animal act - that is: make it do whatever
     * it wants/needs to do.
     * @param currentField The field currently occupied.
     * @param updatedField The field to transfer to.
     * @param newAnimals A list to add newly born animals to.
     */
    abstract public void act(Field currentField,
                             Field updatedField,
                             List newAnimals);

    // other methods omitted
}
```

Classes that are not abstract (all classes we have seen previously) are called *concrete classes*.

Declaring a class abstract serves several purposes:

- No instances can be created of abstract classes. Trying to use the new key word with an abstract class is an error. This is mirrored in BlueJ: right-clicking on an abstract class in the class diagram will not list any constructors in the popup menu. This serves our intention discussed above: we stated that we did not want instances of class Animal created directly – this class serves only as a superclass. Declaring the class abstract enforces this restriction.

- Only abstract classes can have abstract methods. This ensures that all methods in concrete classes can always be executed. If we allowed an abstract method in a concrete class, we could create an instance of a class that lacked an implementation for a method.

- Abstract classes with abstract methods force subclasses to override and implement those methods declared abstract. If a subclass does not provide an implementation for an inherited abstract method, it is itself abstract, and no instances may be created. For a subclass to be concrete, it must provide implementations for *all* inherited abstract methods.

Now we can start to see the purpose of abstract methods. Although they do not provide an implementation, they nonetheless ensure that all subclasses have an implementation of this method. In other words, even though class Animal does not implement the act method, it ensures that all existing animals have an implemented act method. This is done by ensuring that

- no instance of class Animal can be created directly, and
- all concrete subclasses must implement the act method.

Although we cannot create an instance of an abstract class directly, we can otherwise use an abstract class as a type in the usual ways. For instance, the normal rules of polymorphism allow us to handle foxes and rabbits as instances of the Animal class. So those parts of the simulation that do not need to know whether they are dealing with a specific subclass can use the superclass type instead.

> **Concept:**
>
> **Abstract subclasses.** For a subclass of an abstract class to become concrete, it must provide implementations for all inherited abstract methods. Otherwise it will itself be abstract.

Exercise 10.26 Although the body of the loop in Code 10.6 no longer deals with the Fox and Rabbit types, it still deals with the **Animal** type. Why is it not possible for it to treat each object in the collection simply using the Object type?

Exercise 10.27 Is it necessary for a class with one or more abstract methods to be defined as abstract? If you are not sure, experiment with the source of the Animal class in the *foxes-and-rabbits-v2* project.

Exercise 10.28 Is it possible for a class that has no abstract methods to be defined as abstract? If you are not sure, change act to be a concrete method in the Animal class by giving it a method body with no statements.

Exercise 10.29 Could it ever make sense to define a class as abstract if it has no abstract methods? Discuss this.

Exercise 10.30 Which classes in the `java.util` package are abstract? Some of them have 'Abstract' in the class name, but is there any other way to tell from the documentation? Which concrete classes extend them?

Exercise 10.31 Can you tell from the API documentation for an abstract class which (if any) of its methods are abstract? Do you *need* to know which methods are abstract?

Exercise 10.32 Which of the other simulation classes do not need to be aware of whether they are specifically dealing with foxes or rabbits? Could they be rewritten to use the `Animal` class instead? Would there be any particular benefits in doing this?

Exercise 10.33 Review the overriding rules for methods and fields discussed in Chapter 9. Why are they particularly significant in our attempts to introduce inheritance into this application?

Exercise 10.34 The changes made in this section have removed the dependences (couplings) of the `simulateOneStep` method to the `Fox` and `Rabbit` class. The `Simulator` class, however, is still coupled to `Fox` and `Rabbit`, because these classes are referenced in the `populate` method. There is no way to avoid this; when we create animal instances, we have to specify exactly what kind of animal to create.

This could be improved by splitting the `Simulator` into two classes: one class, `Simulator`, which runs the simulation and is completely decoupled from the concrete animal classes, and another class, `PopulationGenerator` (created and called by the simulator), which creates the population. Only this class is coupled to the concrete animal classes, making it easier for a maintenance programmer to find places where change is necessary when the application is extended. Try implementing this refactoring step. The `PopulationGenerator` class should also define the colors for each type of animal.

Exercise 10.35 *Challenge exercise* The `canBreed` methods of `Fox` and `Rabbit` are textually identical, yet we chose not to move them to the `Animal` class. Why is this? Try moving the methods from `Fox` and `Rabbit` to `Animal` and making them protected. Is there any way to make the resulting classes compile and, even if there is, does the resulting simulation work as it should? How can you tell?

The project *foxes-and-rabbits-v2* provides an implementation of our simulation with the improvements discussed here.

10.4 More abstract methods

When we created the `Animal` superclass in section 10.3, we did this by identifying the common elements of the subclasses. This might be overly conservative. Why not move the `canBreed` method into `Animal`, for instance? The reason for not moving this or other methods is that, although several of the remaining method bodies contain textually identical statements, their use of class variables means that they cannot be moved directly to the super class. In the case of `canBreed`, the problem is the `BREEDING_AGE` variable. If the method is moved to `Animal` then the compiler will need to have access to a value for the breeding age in class `Animal`. It is tempting to define a `BREEDING_AGE` variable in the `Animal` class and assume that its value will be overridden by similarly named variables in the subclasses. However, fields are handled differently from methods in Java: they cannot be overridden by subclass versions.[2]

We can, however, use this idea if we access the breeding age with a method rather than access a field directly. This approach is shown in Code 10.8. Using this method, we can move these remaining methods to the superclass.

Code 10.8

The `canBreed` method of `Animal`

```
/**
 * An animal can breed if it has reached the breeding age.
 * @return true if the animal can breed
 */
public boolean canBreed()
{
    return age >= getBreedingAge();
}
```

The `canBreed` method has been rewritten to use the value returned from a method call rather than the value of a class variable. For this to work, a method `getBreedingAge` must be defined in class `Animal`. Since we cannot specify a breeding age for animals in general, we can again use an abstract method in the `Animal` class, and concrete redefinitions in the subclasses. Both `Fox` and `Rabbit` will define their own versions of `getBreedingAge` to return their particular values of `BREEDING_AGE`:

```
/**
 * @return The age at which a rabbit starts to breed.
 */
public int getBreedingAge()
{
    return BREEDING_AGE;
}
```

This makes it possible for each instance to use the value appropriate to its subclass type.

Exercise 10.36 Using your latest version of the project (or the *foxes-and-rabbits-v2* project in case you have not done all the exercises), move the `canBreed` method from `Fox` and `Rabbit` to `Animal` and rewrite it as shown in Code 10.8. Provide appropriate versions of `getBreedingAge` in `Fox` and `Rabbit`. Are those changes sufficient to recompile the project? If not, what is missing from the `Animal` class?

Exercise 10.37 Move the `incrementAge` method from `Fox` and `Rabbit` to `Animal` by providing an abstract `getMaxAge` method in `Animal` and a concrete version in `Fox` and `Rabbit`.

---

[2] This rule applies regardless of whether a field is static or not.

Exercise 10.38 Can the `breed` method be moved to `Animal`? If so, make this change.

Exercise 10.39 In light of all the changes you have made to these three classes, reconsider the visibility of each method and make any changes you feel are appropriate.

Exercise 10.40 Was it possible to make these changes without having any impact on any other classes in the project? If so, what does this suggest about the degrees of encapsulation and coupling that were present in the original version?

Exercise 10.41 *Challenge exercise* Define a completely new type of animal for the simulation as a subclass of `Animal`. You will need to decide what sort of impact its existence will have on the existing animal types. For instance, your animal might compete with foxes as a predator on the rabbit population, or your animal might prey on foxes but not on rabbits. You will probably find that you need to experiment quite a lot with the configuration settings you use for it. You will need to modify the `populate` method to have some of your animals created at the start of a simulation.

You should also define a new color for your new animal class. You can find a list of predefined color names on the API page documenting the `Color` class in the `java.awt` package.

10.5 Multiple inheritance

10.5.1 An `Actor` class

In this section we discuss some possible future extensions, and some programming constructs to support these extensions.

The first obvious extension for our simulation is the addition of new animals. If you have attempted exercise 10.41, then you have dealt with this already. We should, however, generalize this a bit: maybe not all participants in the simulation will be animals. Our current structure assumes that all acting participants in the simulation are animals and inherit from the `Animal` superclass. One enhancement that we might like to make is the introduction of human predators to the simulation, as either hunters or trappers. They do not neatly fit the existing assumption of purely animal-based actors. We might also extend the simulation to include plants, or even the weather. The growth of plants might influence the population of rabbits, and the plants in turn might be influenced by the weather. All these new components would act in the simulation, but they are clearly not animals.

To deal with this, it seems like a good idea to introduce an `Actor` superclass. The `Actor` class would serve as a superclass to all kinds of simulation participants, independent of what they are. Figure 10.3 shows a class diagram for this part of the simulation. The `Actor` and `Animal` classes are abstract, while `Rabbit`, `Fox`, and `Hunter` are concrete classes.

Figure 10.3
Simulation structure
with `Actor`

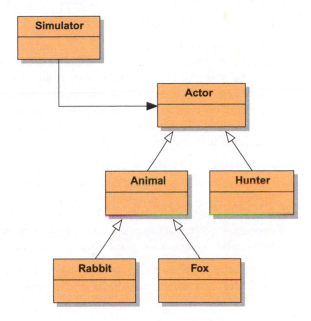

The `Actor` class would include the common part of all actors. One thing all possible actors have in common is that they perform some kind of action. So the only definition in class `Actor` is that of an abstract `act` method:

```
// all comments omitted

public abstract class Actor
{
    abstract public void act(Field currentField,
                             Field updatedField,
                             List newAnimals);
}
```

This should be enough to rewrite the actor loop in the `Simulator` (Code 10.6) using class `Actor` instead of class `Animal`.

Exercise 10.42 Introduce the `Actor` class into your simulation. Rewrite the `simulateOneStep` method in `Simulator` to use `Actor` instead of `Animal`. You can do this even if you have not introduced any new participant types. Does the **Simulator** class compile? Or is there something else that is needed in the **Actor** class?

This new structure is more flexible because it allows easier addition of non-animal actors. In fact, we could even rewrite the statistics-gathering class, `FieldStats`, as an `Actor` – it, too, acts once every step. Its action would be to update its current count of animals.

10.5.2 Flexibility through abstraction

By moving towards the notion of the simulation being responsible for managing actor objects, we have succeeded in abstracting quite a long way away from our original very specific scenario of foxes and rabbits in a rectangular field. This process of abstraction has brought with it an increased flexibility that may allow us to widen the scope of what we might do with a general simulation framework even further. If we think through the requirements of other similar simulation scenarios then we might come up with ideas for additional features that we could introduce.

For instance, it might be useful to simulate other predator–prey scenarios such as a marine simulation involving fish and sharks, or fish and fishing fleets. If the marine simulation were to involve modeling food supplies for the fish then we should probably not want to visualize plankton populations – either because the numbers are too vast, or because their size is too small. Other environmental simulations might involve modeling the weather, which, while it is clearly an actor, also might not require a visualization.

In the next section we shall investigate, as a further extension to our simulation framework, the separation of visualization from acting.

10.5.3 Selective drawing

One way to implement the separation of visualization from acting is to change the way it is performed in the simulation. Instead of iterating over the whole field every time and drawing actors in every position, we could iterate over a separate collection of drawable actors. The code in the simulator class would look similar to this:

```
// let all actors act
for(Iterator iter = actors.iterator(); iter.hasNext(); ) {
    Actor actor = (Actor) iter.next();
    actor.act(...);
}

// draw all drawables
for(Iterator iter = drawables.iterator(); iter.hasNext(); ) {
    Drawable item = (Drawable) iter.next();
    item.draw(...);
}
```

All of the actors would be in the `actors` collection, and those actors we want to show on screen would also be in the `drawables` collection. For this to work, we need another superclass called `Drawable`, which declares an abstract `draw` method. Drawable actors must then inherit from both `Actor` and `Drawable` (Figure 10.4 shows an example where we assume that we have ants, which act but are not visible on screen).

10.5.4 Drawable actors: multiple inheritance

The scenario presented here uses a structure known as *multiple inheritance*. Multiple inheritance exists in cases where one class inherits from more than one superclass. The subclass then has all the features of both superclasses, and those defined in the subclass itself.

Figure 10.4

Actor hierarchy with Drawable class

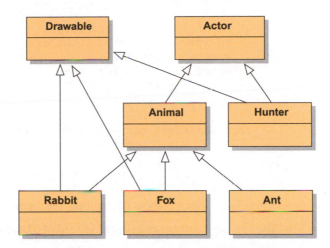

Multiple inheritance is quite easy to understand in principle, but can lead to significant complications in the implementation of a programming language. Different object-oriented languages vary in their treatment of multiple inheritance: some languages allow the inheritance of multiple superclasses, others do not. Java lies somewhere in the middle. It does not allow multiple inheritance of classes, but provides another construct, called 'interfaces,' that allows a limited form of multiple inheritance. Interfaces are discussed in the next section.

10.6 Interfaces

Up to this point in the book we have used the term 'interface' in an informal sense, to represent that part of a class that couples it to other classes. Java captures this concept more formally by allowing *interface types* to be defined.

At first glance, interfaces are similar to classes, with the most obvious difference being that their method definitions do not include method bodies. Thus they are similar to abstract classes in which all methods are abstract.

10.6.1 An Actor interface

Code 10.9 shows Actor defined as an interface type.

Code 10.9

The Actor interface

```
/**
 * The interface to be extended by any class wishing
 * to participate in the simulation.
 */
public interface Actor
{
    /**
     * Perform the actor's daily behavior. Transfer the
```

Code 10.9
continued

The Actor interface

```
         * actor to the updatedField if it is to participate in
         * further steps of the simulation.
         * @param currentField The current state of the field.
         * @param location The actor's location in the current
         *        field.
         * @param updatedField The updated state of the field.
         */
        void act(Field currentField, Location location,
                Field updatedField);
    }
```

Java interfaces have a number of significant features:

- The key word `interface` is used instead of `class` in the header of the declaration.

- All methods in an interface are abstract; no method bodies are permitted. The `abstract` key word is not needed.

- Interfaces do not contain any constructors.

- All method signatures in an interface have public visibility. The visibility does not need to be declared (i.e. the `public` key word is not needed for each method).

- Only constant fields (public, static, and final) are allowed in an interface. The `public`, `static`, and `final` key words may be omitted, but all fields are still treated as public, static, and final.

A class can inherit from an interface in a similar way to the way it inherits from a class. However, Java uses a different key word – `implements` – for inheriting interfaces.

A class is said to *implement* an interface if it includes an *implements clause* in its class header. For instance:

```
public class Fox extends Animal implements Drawable
{
    ...
}
```

As in this case, if a class both extends a class and implements an interface, then the extends clause must be written first in the class header.

Two of our abstract classes in the example above, `Actor` and `Drawable`, are good candidates for being rewritten as interfaces. Both of them contain only the definition of a single method without a method implementation. Thus they already fit the definition of an interface perfectly: they contain no fields, no constructors, and no method bodies.

The class `Animal` is a different case. It is a real abstract class that provides a partial implementation (many methods have method bodies) and only a single abstract method.

Exercise 10.43 Redefine the abstract class `Actor` in your project as an interface. Does the simulation still compile? Does it run?

Exercise 10.44 Are the fields in the following interface static fields or instance fields?

```
public interface Quiz
{
    int CORRECT = 1;
    int INCORRECT = 0;

    ...
}
```

What visibility do they have?

Exercise 10.45 What are the errors in the following interface?

```
public interface Monitor
{
    private static final int THRESHOLD = 50;

    public Monitor (int initial);

    public int getThreshold()
    {
        return THRESHOLD;
    }

    ...
}
```

10.6.2 Multiple inheritance of interfaces

As mentioned above, Java allows any class to extend at most one other class. However, it allows a class to implement any number of interfaces (in addition to possibly extending one class). Thus, if we define both Actor and Drawable as interfaces instead of abstract classes, we can define class Hunter (Figure 10.4) to implement both of them:

```
public class Hunter implements Actor, Drawable
{
    ...
}
```

The class Hunter inherits the method definitions of all interfaces (act and draw, in this case) as abstract methods. It must then provide method definitions for both of them by overriding the methods, or the class itself must be declared abstract.

The Animal class shows an example where a class does not implement an inherited interface method. Animal, in our new structure in Figure 10.4, inherits the abstract method act from Actor. It does not provide a method body for this method, which makes Animal itself abstract (it must include the abstract key word in the class header).

The Animal subclasses then implement the act method and become concrete classes.

Exercise 10.46 *Challenge exercise* Add a non-animal actor to the simulation. For instance, you could introduce a `Hunter` class with the following properties. Hunters have no maximum age and neither feed nor breed. At each step of the simulation, a hunter moves to a random location anywhere in the field and fires a fixed number of shots into random target locations around the field. Any animal in one of the target locations is killed.

Place just a small number of hunters in the field at the start of the simulation. Do the hunters remain in the simulation throughout, or do they ever disappear? If they do disappear, why might that be, and does that represent realistic behavior?

What other classes required changing as a result of introducing hunters? Is there a need to introduce further decoupling to the classes?

10.6.3 Interfaces as types

When a class implements an interface, it does not inherit any implementation from it, since interfaces cannot contain method bodies. The question is then: What do we actually gain by implementing interfaces?

When we introduced inheritance in Chapter 8, we emphasized two great benefits of inheritance:

■ The subclass inherits the code (method implementations and fields) from the superclass. This allows reuse of existing code and avoids code duplication.

■ The subclass becomes a subtype of the superclass. This allows polymorphic variables and method calls. In other words, it allows different special cases of objects (instances of subclasses) to be treated uniformly (as instances of the supertype).

Interfaces do not provide the first benefit (since they do not contain implementations), but they do provide the second. An interface defines a type just as a class does. This means that variables can be declared to be of interface types, even though no objects of that type can exist (only subtypes).

In our example, even though `Actor` is now an interface, we can still declare an `Actor` variable in the `Simulator` class. The simulation loop still works unchanged.

Interfaces can have no direct instances, but they serve as supertypes for instances of other classes.

10.6.4 Interfaces as specifications

In this chapter we have introduced interfaces as a means to implement multiple inheritance in Java. This is one important use of interfaces, but there are others.

The most important characteristic of interfaces is that they completely separate the definition of the functionality (the class's 'interface' in the wider sense of the word) from its implementation. A good example of how this can be used in practice can be found in the Java collection hierarchy.

The collection hierarchy defines (among other types) the interface List and the classes ArrayList and LinkedList (Figure 10.5). The List interface specifies the full functionality of a list, without giving any implementation. The subclasses (LinkedList and ArrayList) provide two different implementations of the same interface. This is interesting, because the two implementations differ greatly in the efficiency of some of their functions. Random access to elements in the middle of the list, for example, is much faster with the ArrayList. Inserting or deleting elements, however, can be much faster in the LinkedList.

Figure 10.5

The List interface and its subclasses

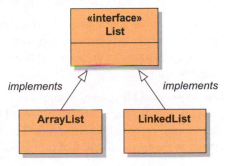

Which implementation is better in any given application can be hard to judge in advance. It depends a lot on the relative frequency with which certain operations are performed, and on some other factors. In practice, the best way to find out is often to try it out: implement the application with both alternatives and measure the performance.

The existence of the List interface makes it very easy to do this. If, instead of using ArrayList or LinkedList as variable and parameter types, we always use List, our application will work independently of the specific type of list we are currently using. Only when we create a new list do we really have to use the name of the specific implementation. We would, for instance, write

```
private List myList = new ArrayList();
```

Note that the field's type is just List. This way, we can change the whole application to use a linked list by just changing ArrayList to LinkedList in a single location, when the list is being created.

Exercise 10.47 Which methods do ArrayList and LinkedList have that are not defined in the List interface? Why do you think that these methods are not included in List?

Exercise 10.48 Read the API description for the sort methods of the Collections class in the java.util package. Which interfaces are mentioned in the descriptions?

Exercise 10.49 *Challenge exercise* Investigate the Comparator interface. Define a simple class that implements Comparator. Create a collection containing objects of this class and sort the collection.

10.6.5   A further example of interfaces

In the previous section we have discussed how interfaces can be used to separate the specification of a component from its implementation, so that different implementations can be 'plugged in,' thus making it easy to replace components of a system.

This is often used to separate parts of a system that are logically only loosely coupled. One example in our simulation is the display. The simulation logic (the field and the actors) is quite separate from the visual display of the simulation. We could imagine completely different ways to present the same application:

- The display could plot a graph representing the population for each species over time. The *x*-axis of the graph could represent time (in simulation steps), while the *y*-axis showed the number of animals. Each species would be shown with its own curve in a different color.

- The output could be purely textual: we could print sequences of text statements to the terminal, one for each simulation step. This would have the advantage that it is very easy to implement and can be saved to a file, for example. As opposed to the animation in the current version, it provides a record of the whole process.

We can support this by making `SimulatorView` an interface. To define this interface, we can search through the `Simulator` class to find all methods that are actually being called from the outside. They are (in this order):

```
view.setColor(class, color);
view.isViable(field);
view.showStatus(step, field);
```

We can now easily define the complete `SimulatorView` interface:

```
import java.awt.Color;

public interface SimulatorView
{
    void setColor(Class cl, Color color);
    boolean isViable(Field field);
    void showStatus(int step, Field field);
}
```

Our current `SimulatorView` class should then be renamed `AnimatedView` (since it provides an animated view of the simulator), and it should implement the `SimulatorView` interface:

```
public class AnimatedView extends JFrame implements SimulatorView
{
    ...
}
```

After making these changes, it becomes fairly easy to implement and 'plug in' other views for the simulation.

Exercise 10.50 Make the changes described above: rename the class `SimulatorView` to `AnimatedView` and implement the `SimulatorView` interface. Make sure that, in class `Simulator`, the name `AnimatedView` is used only one single time (when the view object is created). At all other places, the interface name `SimulatorView` should be used.

Exercise 10.51 Implement a new class `TextView` that implements `SimulatorView`. `TextView` provides a textual view of the simulation. After every simulation step, it prints out one line in the form

    Foxes: 121 Rabbits: 266

Use `TextView` instead of `AnimatedView` for some tests. (Do not delete the `AnimatedView` classes. We want to have the ability to change between both views!)

Exercise 10.52 Can you manage to have both views active at the same time?

10.6.6 Abstract class or interface?

In some situations a choice has to be made between whether to use an abstract class or an interface. Sometimes the choice is easy: when the class is intended to contain implementations for some methods, we need to use an abstract class. In other cases either abstract classes or interfaces can do the job.

If we have a choice, interfaces are usually preferable. If we provide a type as an abstract class, then subclasses cannot extend any other classes. Since interfaces allow multiple inheritance, the use of an interface does not create such a restriction. Therefore using interfaces leads to a more flexible and more extendible structure.

10.7 Summary of inheritance

In the last three chapters we have discussed many different aspects of inheritance techniques. These included code inheritance and subtyping, as well as inheriting from interfaces, abstract classes, and concrete classes.

In general, we can distinguish two main purposes of using inheritance: we can use it to inherit code (code inheritance) and we can use it to inherit the type (subtyping). The first is useful for code reuse, the second for polymorphism and specialization.

When we inherit from ('extend') concrete classes, we do both: we inherit the implementation and the type. When we inherit from ('implement') interfaces, we separate the two: we inherit a type, but no implementation. For cases where parts of both are useful we can inherit from abstract classes; here, we inherit the type and a partial implementation.

When inheriting a complete implementation, we can choose to add or override methods. When no or only partial implementation of a type is inherited, the subclass must provide the implementation before it can be instantiated.

Some other object-oriented languages also provide mechanisms to inherit code without inheriting the type. Java does not provide such a construct.

10.8 Summary

In this chapter we have discussed the fundamental structure of computer simulations.

We have then used this example to introduce abstract classes and interfaces as constructs that allow us to create further abstractions and develop more flexible applications.

Abstract classes are classes that are not intended to have any instances. Their purpose is to serve as superclasses to other classes. Abstract classes may have both abstract methods – methods that have a defined signature, but no implementation – and method implementations. Concrete subclasses of abstract classes must override abstract methods to provide method implementations.

Another construct to define types in Java is the interface. Java interfaces are similar to completely abstract classes – they define method signatures but provide no implementation. Interfaces define types that can be used for variables.

Interfaces can be used to provide a specification for a class (or part of an application) without stating anything about the concrete implementation.

Java allows multiple inheritance of interfaces (which it calls 'implements' relationships), but only single inheritance for classes ('extends' relationships).

Terms introduced in this chapter

abstract method, abstract class, concrete class, multiple inheritance, interface (Java construct), implements

---

Concept summary

- **abstract method** An abstract method definition consists of a method signature without a method body. It is marked with the key word `abstract`.

- **abstract class** An abstract class is a class that is not intended for creating instances. Its purpose is to serve as a superclass for other classes. Abstract classes may contain abstract methods.

- **abstract subclasses** For a subclass of an abstract class to become concrete, it must provide implementations for all inherited abstract methods. Otherwise it will itself be abstract.

- **multiple inheritance** A situation in which a class inherits from more than one superclass is called multiple inheritance.

- **interface** A Java interface is a specification of a type (in the form of a type name and a set of methods) that does not define any implementation for any of the methods.

Exercise 10.53 Can an abstract class have concrete (non-abstract) methods? Can a concrete class have abstract methods? Can you have an abstract class without abstract methods? Justify your answers.

Exercise 10.54 Look at the code below. You have five types (classes or interfaces) (U, G, B, Z and X) and a variable of each of these types.

```
U u;
G g;
B b;
Z z;
X x;
```

The following assignments are all legal (assume that they all compile).

```
u = z;
x = b;
g = u;
x = u;
```

The following assignments are all illegal (they cause compiler errors).

```
u = b;
x = g;
b = u;
z = u;
g = x;
```

What can you say about the types and their relationships? (What relationship are they to each other?)

Exercise 10.55 Assume you want to model people in a university to implement a course management system. There are different people involved: staff members, students, teaching staff, support staff, tutors, technical support staff, and student technicians. Tutors and student technicians are interesting: tutors are students who have been hired to do some teaching, and student technicians are students who have been hired to help with the technical support.

Draw a type hierarchy (classes and interfaces) to represent this situation. Indicate which types are concrete classes, abstract classes, and interfaces.

Exercise 10.56 If you test the *foxes-and-rabbits* project carefully, you may discover that it has a flaw: it runs more and more slowly over time. (To test this, time some executions. For example, run and time it with 500, 1000, 2000, and 3000 steps.) Find the source of this problem and fix it. What debugging techniques did you use?

Exercise 10.57 *Challenge exercise* Sometimes class/interface pairs exist in the Java standard library that define exactly the same methods. Often, the interface name ends with *Listener* and the class name with *Adapter*. An example is **PrintJobListener** and **PrintJobAdapter**. The interface defines some method signatures, and the adapter class defines the same methods, each with an empty method body. What might the reason be for having them both?

Exercise 10.58 The collection library has a class named **TreeSet**, which is an example of a sorted set. Elements in this set are kept in order. Read the description of this class carefully, and then write a class **Person** that can be inserted into a **TreeSet**, which will then sort the **Person** objects by age.

Building graphical user interfaces

Main concepts discussed in this chapter:

- constructing GUIs
- interface components
- GUI layout
- event handling

Java constructs discussed in this chapter:

`JFrame`, `JLabel`, `JButton`, `JMenuBar`, `JMenu`, `JMenuItem`, `ActionEvent`,
`Color`, `FlowLayout`, `BorderLayout`, `GridLayout`, `BoxLayout`,
`Box`, `JOptionPane`, `EtchedBorder`, `EmptyBorder`,
anonymous inner classes

11.1 Introduction

So far we have, in this book, concentrated on writing applications with text-based interfaces. The reason is not that text-based interfaces have any great advantage in principle. They just have the one advantage that they are easier to create.

We did not want to distract too much attention from the important software development issues in the early stages of learning about object-oriented programming. These were issues such as object structure and interaction, class design, and code quality.

Graphical user interfaces (GUIs) are also constructed from interacting objects, but they have a very specialized structure, and we avoided introducing them before learning about object structures in more general terms. Now, however, we are ready to have a look at the construction of GUIs.

GUIs give our applications an interface consisting of windows, menus, buttons, and other graphical components – they make them look much more like a 'typical' application most people are used to nowadays.

Note that we are stumbling about the double meaning of the word *interface* again here. The interfaces we are talking about now are neither interfaces of classes, nor the Java interface construct. We are now talking about *user interfaces* – the part of an application that is visible on screen for the user to interact with.

Once we know how to create GUIs with Java, we can develop much better-looking programs.

11.2 Components, layout, and event handling

The details involved in creating GUIs are extensive. In this book we shall not be able to cover all details of all possible things you can do, but we shall discuss the general principles and a good number of examples.

All GUI programming in Java is done through the use of dedicated standard class libraries. Once we understand the principles, we can find out all the necessary details by working with the standard library documentation.

The principles we need to understand can be divided into three topic areas:

- What kind of elements can we show on screen?
- How do we arrange those elements?
- How do we react to user input?

We shall discuss these questions under the key words *components*, *layout*, and *event handling*.

Components are the individual parts that a GUI is built from. They are things such as buttons, menus, menu items, checkboxes, sliders, text fields, and so on. The Java library contains a good number of ready-made components, and we can also write our own. We shall have to learn what the important components are, how to create them, and how to make them look the way we should like them to look.

Layout deals with the issue of how to arrange the components on screen. Older, more primitive GUI systems handled this with two-dimensional coordinates: the programmer specified x- and y-coordinates (in pixels) for the position and the size of each component. In more modern GUI systems this is too simplistic. We have to take into account different screen resolutions, different fonts, users resizing windows, and many other aspects that make layout more difficult. The solution will be a scheme where we can specify the layout in more general terms. We can, for example, specify that 'this component should be below this other one' or 'this component should be stretched if the window gets resized, but that other component should always have a constant size.' We shall see that this is done using *layout managers*.

Event handling refers to the technique we shall use to deal with user input. Once we have created our components and positioned them on screen, we also have to make sure that something happens when a user clicks a button. The model used by the Java library for this is event-based: if a user activates a component (e.g. clicks a button or selects a menu item) the system will generate an event. Our application can then receive a notification of the event (by having one of its methods invoked), and we can take appropriate action.

We shall discuss each of these areas in much more detail later in this chapter. First, however, we shall briefly introduce a bit more background and terminology.

11.3 AWT and Swing

Java has two GUI libraries. The older one is called *AWT* (Abstract Window Toolkit), and was introduced with the original, first Java system. Later, a much-improved GUI library, called *Swing*, was added to Java.

Figure 11.1
AWT and Swing

Swing makes use of some of the AWT classes, replaces some AWT classes with its own versions, and adds many new classes (Figure 11.1).

In this book, we shall use the Swing libraries. This means that we shall use some AWT classes that are still used with Swing programs, but use the Swing versions of all classes that exist in both libraries.

Wherever there are equivalent classes in AWT and Swing, the Swing versions have been identified by adding the letter 'J' to the start of the class name. You will, for example, see classes named `Button` and `JButton`, `Frame` and `JFrame`, `Menu` and `JMenu`, and so on. The classes starting with a 'J' are the Swing versions – these are the ones we shall use.

That is enough background for a start. Let us look at some code.

11.4 The ImageViewer example

As always, we shall discuss the new concepts by using an example. The application we shall build in this chapter is an image viewer (Figure 11.2). This is a program that can open and display image files in JPEG and PNG formats, perform some image transformations, and save the images back to disk.

Figure 11.2
A simple image
viewer application

Concept:

Image format.
Images can be
stored in different
formats. The
differences
primarily affect
file size and
information content.

As part of this, we shall use our own image class to represent an image while it is in memory, we shall implement various filters to change the image's appearance, and we shall use Swing components to build a user interface. While doing this, we shall concentrate our discussion on the GUI aspects of the program.

If you are curious to see what we shall build, you can open and try out the *imageviewer1-0* project; just create an `ImageViewer` object – that is the version displayed in Figure 11.2. Here, we start slowly, initially with something much simpler, and we shall work our way to the final application step by step.

11.4.1 First experiments: creating a frame

Almost everything you see in a GUI is contained in a top-level window. A top-level window is one that is under the control of the operating system's window management, and which typically can be moved, resized, minimized, and maximized independently.

Java calls these top-level windows *frames*. In Swing, they are represented by a class called `JFrame`.

Code 11.1

A first version of an
`ImageViewer`
class

```java
import java.awt.*;
import java.awt.event.*;
import javax.swing.*;

// comment omitted.

public class ImageViewer
{
    private JFrame frame;

    /**
     * Create an ImageViewer and show it on screen.
     */
    public ImageViewer()
    {
        makeFrame();
    }


    /**
     * Create the Swing frame and its content.
     */
    private void makeFrame()
    {
        frame = new JFrame("ImageViewer");
        Container contentPane = frame.getContentPane();

        JLabel label = new JLabel("I am a label.");
        contentPane.add(label);

        frame.pack();
        frame.setVisible(true);
    }
}
```

To get a GUI on screen, the first thing we have to do is to create and display a frame. Code 11.1 shows a complete class (already named `ImageViewer` in preparation for things to come) that shows a frame on screen. This class is available in the book projects as *imageviewer0-1* (the number stands for version 0.1).

> **Exercise 11.1** Open the *imageviewer0-1* project. (This will become the basis of your own image viewer.) Create an instance of class `ImageViewer`. Resize the resulting frame (make it larger). What do you observe about the placement of the text in the frame?

We shall now discuss the `ImageViewer` class shown in Code 11.1 in some detail.

The first three lines in that class are import statements of all classes in the packages `java.awt`, `java.awt.event`, and `javax.swing`.[1] We need many of the classes in these packages for all Swing applications we create, so we shall always import these three packages completely in all our GUI programs.

Looking at the rest of the class shows very quickly that all the interesting stuff is in the `makeFrame` method. This method takes care of constructing the GUI. The class's constructor contains only a call to this method. We have done this so that all the GUI construction code is at a well-defined place and is easy to find later (cohesion!). We shall do this in all our GUI examples.

The class has one instance variable of type `JFrame`. This is used to hold the frame that the image viewer wants to show on screen.

Let us now take a closer look at the `makeFrame` method.

The first line in this method is

```
frame = new JFrame("ImageViewer");
```

This statement creates a new frame and stores it in our instance variable for later use.

As a general principle you should, in parallel with studying the examples in this book, look at the class documentation for all classes we encounter. This counts for all the classes we use – we shall not point this out every time from now on, but just expect you to do it.

> **Exercise 11.2** Find the documentation for class `JFrame`. What is the purpose of the parameter `"ImageViewer"` that we used in the constructor call above?

Concept:

Components are placed in a frame by adding them to the frame's **menu bar** or **content pane**.

A frame consists of three parts: the *title bar*, an optional *menu bar*, and the *content pane* (Figure 11.3). The exact appearance of the title bar depends on the underlying operating system. It usually contains the window title and a few window controls.

The menu bar and the content pane are under the control of the application. To both, we can add some components to create a GUI. We shall concentrate on the content pane first.

---

[1] The `swing` package really is in a package called `javax` (ending with an 'x'), not `java`. The reason for this is largely historic – there does not seem to be a logical explanation for it.

Figure 11.3
Different parts of
a frame

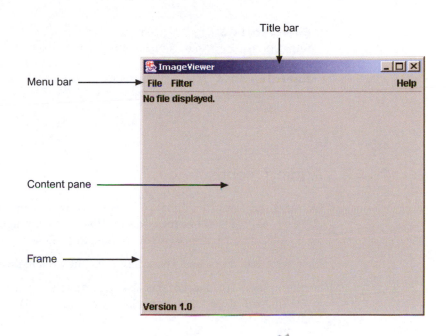

11.4.2 Adding simple components

Immediately following creation of the `JFrame`, the frame will be invisible and its content pane will be empty. We continue by adding a label to the content pane:

```
Container contentPane = frame.getContentPane();

JLabel label = new JLabel("I am a label.");
contentPane.add(label);
```

The first line gets the content pane from the frame. We always have to do this – GUI components are added to a frame by adding them to the frame's content pane.

The content pane itself is of type `Container`. A container is a Swing component that can hold arbitrary groups of other components – rather like an `ArrayList` can hold an arbitrary collection of objects. We shall discuss containers in more detail later.

We then create a label component (type `JLabel`) and add it to the content pane. A label is a component that can display text and/or an image.

Finally, we have the two lines

```
frame.pack();
frame.setVisible(true);
```

The first line causes the frame to arrange the components inside it properly and to size itself appropriately. We always have to call the `pack` method on the frame after we have added or resized components.

The last line finally makes the frame visible on screen. We always start out with the frame being invisible, so that we can arrange all the components inside the frame without the construction process being visible on screen. Then, when the frame is built, we can show it in a completed state.

> **Exercise 11.3** Another often-used Swing component is a button (type `JButton`). Replace the label in the example above with a button.
>
> **Exercise 11.4** What happens when you add two labels (or two buttons) to the content pane? Can you explain what you observe? Experiment with resizing the frame.

11.4.3 Adding menus

Our next step toward building a GUI is to add menus and menu items. This is conceptually easy, but contains one tricky detail: How do we arrange to react to user actions, such as the selection of a menu item? We discuss this below.

First, we create the menus. Three classes are involved in this:

- `JMenuBar` – An object of this class represents a menu bar that can be displayed below the title bar at the top of a window (see Figure 11.3). Every window has at most one `JMenuBar`.[2]
- `JMenu` – Objects of this class represent a single menu (such as the common 'File,' 'Edit,' or 'Help' menus). Menus are often held in a menu bar. They could also appear as popup menus, but we shall not do that now.
- `JMenuItem` – Objects of this class represent a single menu item inside a menu (such as 'Open' or 'Save').

For our image viewer, we shall create one menu bar and several menus and menu items.

The class `JFrame` has a method called `setJMenuBar`. We can create a menu bar and use this method to attach our menu bar to the frame:

```
JMenuBar menubar = new JMenuBar();
frame.setJMenuBar(menubar);
```

Now we are ready to create a menu and add it to the menu bar:

```
JMenu fileMenu = new JMenu("File");
menubar.add(fileMenu);
```

These two lines create a menu labeled 'File' and insert it into our menu bar. Finally, we can add menu items to the menu. The following lines add two items, labeled 'Open' and 'Quit,' to the 'File' menu:

```
JMenuItem openItem = new JMenuItem("Open");
fileMenu.add(openItem);

JMenuItem quitItem = new JMenuItem("Quit");
fileMenu.add(quitItem);
```

---

[2] On MacOS, the native display is different: the menu bar is at the top of the screen, not the top of each window. In Java applications, the default behavior is to attach the menu bar to the window. It can be placed at the top of the screen with Java applications by using a MacOS-specific property.

Exercise 11.5 Add the menu and menu items discussed here to your image viewer project. What happens when you select a menu item?

Exercise 11.6 Add another menu called 'Help' that contains a menu item named 'About ImageViewer.' (Note: To increase readability and cohesion, it may be a good idea to move the creation of the menus into a separate method, perhaps named `makeMenuBar`, which is called from our `makeFrame` method.)

So far, we have achieved half of our task: we can create and display menus. But the second half is missing: nothing happens yet, when a user selects a menu. We now have to add code to react to menu selections. This is discussed in the next section.

11.4.4 Event handling

Swing uses a very flexible model to deal with GUI input: an *event handling* model with *event listeners*.

The Swing framework itself and some of its components raise events when something happens that other objects may be interested in. There are different types of event caused by different types of action. When a button is clicked or a menu item is selected, the component raises an *ActionEvent*. When a mouse is clicked or moved, a *MouseEvent* is raised. When a frame is closed or iconified, a *WindowEvent* is generated. There are many other types of event.

Any of our objects can become an event listener for any of these events. When it is a listener, it will get notified about any of the events it listens to.

An object becomes an event listener by implementing one of several existing listener interfaces. If it implements the right interface, it can register itself with a component it wants to listen to.

Let us look at an example. Menu items (class `JMenuItem`) raise `ActionEvents` when they are activated by a user. Objects that want to listen to these events must implement the `ActionListener` interface from the `java.awt.event` package.

> **Concept:**
>
> An object can listen to component events by implementing an **event listener** interface.

There are two alternative styles for implementing event listeners: either a single object listens for events from many different event sources, or each distinct event source is assigned its own unique listener. We shall discuss both styles in the next two sections.

11.4.5 Centralized receipt of events

In order to make our `ImageViewer` object be the single listener to all events from the menu, we have to do three things:

1 We must declare in the class header that it implements the `ActionListener` interface.
2 We have to implement a method with the signature

```
public void actionPerformed(ActionEvent e)
```

This is the only method defined in the `ActionListener` interface.

3   We must call the `addActionListener` method of the menu item to register the `ImageViewer` object as a listener.

Number 1 and 2 – implementing the interface and defining its method – ensure that our object is a subtype of `ActionListener`. Number 3 then registers our own object as a listener for the menu items. Code 11.2 shows the source code for this in context.

```java
public class ImageViewer
    implements ActionListener
{

    // fields and constructor omitted.

    public void actionPerformed(ActionEvent event)
    {
        System.out.println("Item: " + event.getActionCommand());
    }


    /**
     * Create the Swing frame and its content.
     */
    private void makeFrame()
    {
        frame = new JFrame("ImageViewer");
        makeMenuBar(frame);

        // other GUI building code omitted.
    }


    /**
     * Create the main frame's menu bar.
     */
    private void makeMenuBar(JFrame frame)
    {
        JMenuBar menubar = new JMenuBar();
        frame.setJMenuBar(menubar);

        // create the File menu
        JMenu fileMenu = new JMenu("File");
        menubar.add(fileMenu);

        JMenuItem openItem = new JMenuItem("Open");
        openItem.addActionListener(this);
        fileMenu.add(openItem);

        JMenuItem quitItem = new JMenuItem("Quit");
        quitItem.addActionListener(this);
        fileMenu.add(quitItem);
    }
}
```

Note especially the lines

```
JMenuItem openItem = new JMenuItem("Open");
openItem.addActionListener(this);
```

in the code example. Here, a menu item is created, and the current object (the `ImageViewer` object itself) is registered as an action listener by passing `this` as a parameter to the `addActionListener` method.

The effect of registering our object as a listener with the menu item is that our own `actionPerformed` method will be called by the menu item each time the item is activated. When our method is called, the menu item will pass along a parameter of type `ActionEvent` that provides some details about the event that has occurred. These details include the exact time of the event, the state of the modifier keys (the shift, control, and meta keys), a 'command string,' and more.

The command string is a string that somehow identifies the component that caused the event. For menu items, this is by default the label text of the item.

In our example in Code 11.2 we register the same action object for both menu items. This means that both menu items will invoke the same `actionPerformed` method when they are activated.

In the `actionPerformed` method, we simply print out the command string of the item to demonstrate that this scheme works. Here, we could now add code to properly handle the menu invocation.

This code example, as discussed this far, is available in the book projects as project *imageviewer0-2*.

Exercise 11.7 Implement the menu-handling code discussed above in your own image viewer project. Alternatively, open the *imageviewer0-2* project and carefully examine the source code. Describe in writing and in detail the sequence of events that results from activating the *Quit* menu item.

Exercise 11.8 Add another menu item called *Save*.

Exercise 11.9 Add three private methods to your class, named `openFile`, `saveFile`, and `quit`. Change the `actionPerformed` method so that it calls the corresponding method when a menu item is activated.

Exercise 11.10 If you have done exercise 11.6 (adding a *Help* menu), make sure that its menu item also gets handled appropriately.

We note that this approach works.

We can now implement methods to handle menu items to do our various program tasks. There is, however, one other aspect we should investigate: the current solution is not very nice in terms of maintainability and extendability.

Examine the code that you had to write in the `actionPerformed` method for exercise 11.9. There are several problems. They are:

- You probably used an `if` statement and the `getActionCommand` method to find out which item was activated. For example, you could write:

```
if(event.getActionCommand().equals("Open")) ...
```

Depending on the item label string for performing the function is not a good idea. What if you now translated the interface into another language? Just changing the text on the menu item would have the effect that the program does not work anymore. (Or you would have to find all places in the code where this string was used and change them all – a tedious and error-prone procedure.)

- Having a central dispatch method (such as our `actionPerformed`) is not a nice structure at all. We essentially make every separate item call a single method, only to write tedious code in that method to call separate methods for every item from there. This is annoying in maintenance terms (for every additional menu item we have to add a new `if` statement in `actionPerformed`); it also seems a waste of effort. It would be much nicer if we could make every menu item call a separate method directly.

In the next section we introduce a new language construct that allows us to do this.

11.4.6 Inner classes

To solve the problems with centralized event dispatch mentioned above, we use a new construct that we have not discussed before: *inner classes*. Inner classes are classes that are declared textually inside another class:

```
class EnclosingClass
{
    ...
    class InnerClass
    {
        ....
    }
}
```

Instances of the inner class are attached to instances of the enclosing class – they can only exist together with an enclosing instance. They exist conceptually *inside* the enclosing instance.

One interesting detail is that statements in methods of the inner class can see and access private fields and methods of the enclosing class. The inner class is considered to be a part of the enclosing class just like any of the enclosing class's methods.

We can now use this construct to make a separate action listener class for every menu item we like to listen to. As they are separate classes, they can each have a separate `actionPerformed` method, so that each of these methods handles only a single item's activation. The structure is this:

```
class ImageViewer
{
    ...
    class OpenActionListener implements ActionListener
    {
        public void actionPerformed(ActionEvent event)
        {
```

```
                // perform open action
            }
        }

        class QuitActionListener implements ActionListener
        {
            public void actionPerformed(ActionEvent event)
            {
                // perform quit action
            }
        }
    }
```

As a style guide, we usually write inner classes at the end of the enclosing class (after the methods).

Once we have done this, we can now create instances of these inner classes in exactly the same way as for those of any other class. Note also that ImageViewer does not implement ActionListener any more (we remove its actionPerformed method), but the two inner classes do. This now allows us to use instances of the inner classes as action listeners for the menu items:

```
JMenuItem openItem = new JMenuItem("Open");
openItem.addActionListener(new OpenActionListener());
...
JMenuItem quitItem = new JMenuItem("Quit");
quitItem.addActionListener(new QuitActionListener());
```

In summary, instead of having the image viewer object listen to all action events, we create separate listener objects for each possible event, where each listener object listens to one single event type. As every listener has its own actionPerformed method, we can now write specific handling code in these methods. And as the listener classes are in the scope of the enclosing class (they can access the enclosing class's private fields and methods), we can make full use of the enclosing class in the implementation of the actionPerformed methods.

Exercise 11.11 Implement menu item handling with inner classes as discussed here in your own version of the image viewer.

Inner classes can generally be used in some cases to improve cohesion in larger projects. The *foxes-and-rabbits* project from Chapter 10, for example, has a class SimulatorView that includes an inner class FieldView. You may like to study this example to deepen your understanding.

11.4.7   Anonymous inner classes

The solution to the action dispatch problem using inner classes is fairly good, but we want to take it one step further: we can use *anonymous inner classes*. The project *imageviewer0-3* shows an implementation using this construct.

At the center of the changes in this version is the way the action listeners are set up to listen to menu item action events. The relevant code looks like this:

```
JMenuItem openItem = new JMenuItem("Open");
openItem.addActionListener(new ActionListener() {
                public void actionPerformed(ActionEvent e) {
                    openFile();
                }
            });
```

This code fragment looks quite mysterious when you encounter it for the first time, and you will probably have trouble interpreting it, even if you understood everything we have discussed in this book so far. This construct is probably syntactically the most confusing example that you will ever see in the Java language. But don't worry – we shall investigate this slowly.

What you are seeing here is an anonymous inner class. The idea for this construct is based on the observation from our previous version that we use each inner class only exactly once to create a single instance. For this situation, anonymous inner classes provide a syntactical shortcut: they let us define a class and create a single instance of this class, all in one step. The effect is identical to the inner class version above, with the difference that we do not need to define separate named classes for the listeners, and that the definition of the listener method is closer to the registration of the listener with the menu item.

When using an anonymous inner class, we create an inner class *without naming it* and immediately create a single instance of the class. In the action listener code above, this is done with the code fragment

```
new ActionListener() {
        public void actionPerformed(ActionEvent e) {
            openFile();
        }
    }
```

An anonymous inner class is created by naming a supertype (often an abstract class or an interface, here: **ActionListener**), followed by a block that contains an implementation for its abstract methods.

In this example, we create a new subclass of **ActionListener** that implements the **actionPerformed** method. This new subclass does not receive a name. Instead, we precede it with the **new** key word to create a single instance of this class.

In our example, this single instance is an action listener object (it is of a subtype of `ActionListener`). It can be passed to a menu item's `addActionListener` method, and will invoke the `openFile` method of its enclosing class when activated.

Just like named inner classes, anonymous inner classes are able to access the fields and methods of their enclosing class. In addition, because they are defined inside a method, they are able to access the local variables and parameters of that method. However, an important rule is that local variables accessed in this way must be declared as `final` variables. You will see an example of this in the *imageviewer2-0* project, discussed in section 11.6.

It is worth emphasizing some observations about anonymous inner classes.

First, for our concrete problem, using anonymous inner classes is very useful. It allows us to completely remove the central `actionPerformed` method from our `ImageViewer` class. Instead, we create a separate, custom-made action listener (class and object) for each menu item. This action listener can directly call the method implementing the corresponding function.

This structure is nicely cohesive and extendable. If we need an additional menu item, we just add code to create the item and its listener, and the method that handles its function. No listing in a central method is required.

Second, using anonymous inner classes can make code quite hard to read. It is strongly recommended to use them only for very short classes, and only for well-established code idioms.

Third, we often use anonymous classes where only a single instance of the implementation will be required – the actions associated with each menu item are unique to that particular item. In addition, the instance will always be referred to via its supertype. Both reasons mean there is less need for a name for the new class: hence it can be anonymous.

For us, implementing event listeners is the only example in this book where we use this construct.[3]

For all our following work, we shall avoid the central `actionListener` method and use anonymous inner classes instead. So you should leave the *imageviewer0-2* project behind, and use the structure from *imageviewer0-3* as a basis for your further work.

> **Concept:**
>
> **Anonymous inner classes** are a useful construct to implement event listeners.

11.5 ImageViewer 1.0: the first complete version

Getting to the current state – showing a frame with a label and a few menus – was hard work, and we had to discuss a lot of background concepts. It gets easier from now on – really! Understanding the event handling for menu items was probably the most difficult detail we had to master for our example.

We shall now work on creating the first complete version – one that can really do the main task: display some images.

---

[3] If you'd like to find out more about inner classes, have a look at these two sections of the online Java tutorial: `http://java.sun.com/docs/books/tutorial/java/javaOO/nested.html` and `http://java.sun.com/docs/books/tutorial/java/javaOO/innerclasses.html`

11.5.1 Image-processing classes

On the way to the solution, we shall investigate one more interim version: *imageviewer0-4*. Its class structure is shown in Figure 11.4.

Figure 11.4

The class structure of the image viewer application

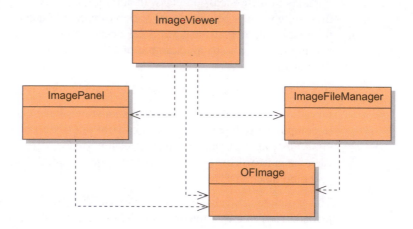

As you can see, we have added three new classes: `OFImage`, `ImagePanel`, and `ImageFileManager`. `OFImage` is a class to represent an image that we want to display and manipulate. `ImageFileManager` is a helper class that provides static methods to read an image file (in JPEG or PNG format) from disk and return it in `OFImage` format, and to save the `OFImage` back to disk. `ImagePanel` is a custom Swing component to show the image in our GUI.

We shall briefly discuss the most important aspects of each of these classes in some more detail. We shall not, however, explain them completely – this is left as an investigation for the curious reader.

The `OFImage` class is our own custom format to represent an image in memory. You can think of an `OFImage` as a two-dimensional array of pixels. Each of the pixels can have a color. We use the standard class `Color` (from package `java.awt`) to represent each pixel's color. (Have a look at the documentation of class `Color` as well – we shall need it later.)

`OFImage` is implemented as a subclass of the Java standard class `BufferedImage` (from package `java.awt.image`). `BufferedImage` gives us most of the functionality we want (it also represents an image as a two-dimensional array), but it does not have methods to set or get a pixel using a `Color` object (it uses different formats for this, which we do not want to use). So we made our own subclass that adds these two methods.

For this project, we can treat `OFImage` like a library class – you will not need to modify this class.

The most important methods from `OFImage` for us are:

- `getPixel` and `setPixel` to read and modify single pixels, and
- `getHeight` and `getWidth` to find out about the image's size.

The `ImageFileManager` class offers three methods: one to read a named image file from disk and return it as an `OFImage`, one to write an `OFImage` file to disk, and one to open a file-chooser dialog to let a user select an image to open. The methods can read files in the standard JPEG and PNG formats, and the `save` method will write files in JPEG format. This is done using the standard Java image I/O methods from the `ImageIO` class (package `javax.imageio`).

The `ImagePanel` class implements a custom-made Swing component to display our image. Custom-made Swing components can easily be created by writing a subclass of an existing component. As such, they can be inserted into a Swing container and displayed in our GUI like any other Swing component. `ImagePanel` is a subclass of `JComponent`.

The other important point to note here is that `ImagePanel` has a `setImage` method that takes an `OFImage` as a parameter to display any given `OFImage`.

11.5.2 Adding the image

Now that we have prepared the classes for dealing with images, adding the image to the user interface is easy. Code 11.3 shows the important differences from previous versions.

Code 11.3

`ImageViewer` class with `ImagePanel`

```java
public class ImageViewer
{
    private JFrame frame;
    private ImagePanel imagePanel;

    // constructor and quit method omitted

    /**
     * Open function: open a file chooser to select a new
     * image file.
     */
    private void openFile()
    {
        OFImage image = ImageFileManager.getImage();
        imagePanel.setImage(image);
        frame.pack();
    }


    /**
     * Create the Swing frame and its content.
     */
    private void makeFrame()
    {
        frame = new JFrame("ImageViewer");
        makeMenuBar(frame);

        Container contentPane = frame.getContentPane();

        imagePanel = new ImagePanel();
        contentPane.add(imagePanel);
```

```
        // building is done – arrange the components and show
        frame.pack();
        frame.setVisible(true);
    }

    //  makeMenuBar method omitted
}
```

When comparing this code with the previous version, we note that there are only two small changes:

■ In method makeFrame, we now create and add an ImagePanel component instead of a JLabel. Doing this is not more complicated than adding the label. The ImagePanel object is stored in an instance field, so that we can access it again later.

■ Our openFile method has now been changed to actually open and display an image file. Using our image processing classes, this also is easy now. The ImageFileManager class has a method to select and open an image, and the ImagePanel object has a method to display that image. One thing to note is that we need to call frame.pack() at the end of the openFile method, as the size of our image component has changed. The pack method will recalculate the frame layout and redraw the frame, so that the size change is properly handled.

Exercise 11.14 Open and test the *imageviewer0-4* project. The folder for this chapter's projects also includes a folder called *images*. Here, you can find some test images you can use. Of course, you can also use your own images.

Exercise 11.15 What happens when you open an image and then resize the frame? What if you first resize the frame and then open an image?

With this version, we have solved the central task: we can now open an image file from disk and display it on screen. Before we call our project 'version 1.0,' however, and thus declare it finished for the first time, we want to add a few more improvements (see Figure 11.2):

■ We want to add two labels: one to display the image file name at the top, and a status text at the bottom.

■ We want to add a *Filter* menu that contains some filters that change the image's appearance.

■ We want to add a *Help* menu that contains an *About ImageViewer* item. Selecting this menu item should display a dialog with the application's name, version number, and author information.

11.5.3 Layout

First, we shall work on the task of adding two text labels to our interface: one at the top that is used to display the file name of the image currently displayed, and one at the bottom that is used for various status messages.

Creating these labels is easy – they are both simple `JLabel` instances. We store them in instance fields, so that we can access them later to change their displayed text. The only question is how to arrange them on screen.

A first – naïve and incorrect – attempt could look like this:

```
Container contentPane = frame.getContentPane();

filenameLabel = new JLabel();
contentPane.add(filenameLabel);

imagePanel = new ImagePanel();
contentPane.add(imagePanel);

statusLabel = new JLabel("Version 1.0");
contentPane.add(statusLabel);
```

The idea here is simple: we get the frame's content pane and add, one after the other, all three components that we wish to display. The only problem is: we did not specify exactly how these three components should be arranged. We might want them to appear next to each other, or one below the other, or any other possible arrangement. As we did not specify any layout, the container (the content pane) uses a default behavior. And this, it turns out, is not what we want.

Exercise 11.16 Continuing from your last version of the project, use the code fragment shown above to add the two labels. Test it. What do you observe?

Swing uses *layout managers* to arrange the layout of components in a GUI. Each container that holds components, such as the content pane, has an associated layout manager that takes care of arranging the components within that container.

Swing provides several different layout managers to support different layout preferences. The most important are: `FlowLayout`, `BorderLayout`, `GridLayout`, and `BoxLayout`. Each of those is represented by a Java class in the Swing library, and each lays out the components under its control in different ways.

Here follows a short description of each layout.

Figure 11.5
`FlowLayout`

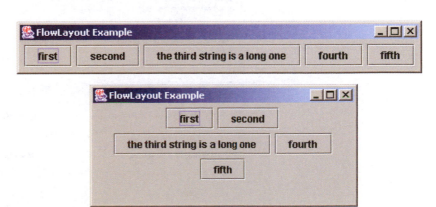

A FlowLayout (Figure 11.5) arranges all components sequentially from left to right. It will leave each component at its preferred size, and center them horizontally. If the horizontal space is not enough to fit all components, they wrap around to a second line. The FlowLayout can also be set to align components left or right.

Figure 11.6
BorderLayout

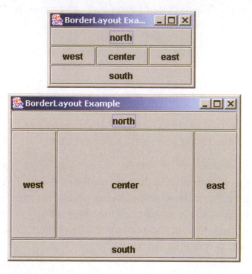

A BorderLayout (Figure 11.6) places up to five components in an arranged pattern: one in the center, and one each at the top, bottom, right and left. Each of these positions may be empty, so it may hold less than five components. The five positions are named CENTER, NORTH, SOUTH, EAST, and WEST.

This layout may seem very specialized at first – one wonders how often this is needed. But in practice this is a surprisingly useful layout, which is used in many applications. In BlueJ, for example, both the main window and the editor use a BorderLayout as the main layout manager.

When a BorderLayout is resized, the middle component is the one that gets stretched in both dimensions. The east and west components change in height, but keep their width. The north and south components keep their height, and only the width changes.

Figure 11.7
GridLayout

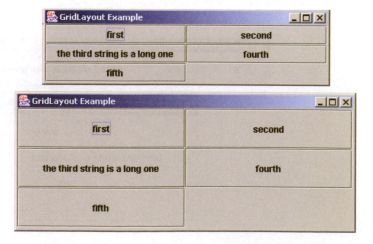

A `GridLayout` is useful (Figure 11.7), as the name suggests, to lay out components in an evenly spaced grid. The numbers of rows and columns can be specified, and the `GridLayout` manager will always keep all components at the same size. This can be useful to force buttons, for example, to have the same width. The width of `JButton` instances is initially determined by the text on the button: each button is made just wide enough to display its text. Inserting buttons into a `GridLayout` will result in all buttons being resized to the width of the widest button.

Figure 11.8
BoxLayout

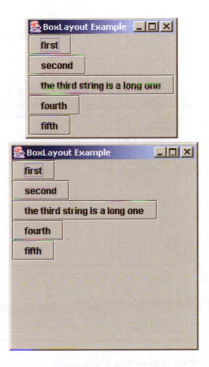

A `BoxLayout` lays out multiple components either vertically or horizontally. It will not wrap when resized (Figure 11.8). By nesting multiple `BoxLayouts` inside each other sophisticated, two-dimensionally aligned layouts may be built.

11.5.4 Nested containers

All the layout strategies discussed above are fairly simple. The key to building good-looking and well-behaved interfaces lies in one last detail: layouts can be nested.

Some of the Swing components are *containers*. Containers appear to the outside as a single component, but they can contain multiple other components. Each container has its own layout manager attached.

The most used container is the class `JPanel`. A `JPanel` can be inserted as a component into the frame's content pane, and then more components can be laid out inside the `JPanel`. Figure 11.9, for example, shows an interface arrangement similar to the BlueJ main window. The content pane of this frame uses a `BorderLayout`, where the EAST position is unused. The NORTH area of this `BorderLayout` contains a `JPanel` with a horizontal `FlowLayout`, which arranges its components (maybe toolbar buttons) in a row. The SOUTH area is similar: another `JPanel` with a `FlowLayout`.

The button group in the WEST area was first placed into a `JPanel` with a one-column `GridLayout` to give all buttons the same width. This `JPanel` was then placed into another `JPanel` with a vertical `FlowLayout`, so that the grid does not extend over the full height of the WEST area. This outer `JPanel` is then inserted into the WEST area of the frame.

Figure 11.9
Building an interface using nested containers

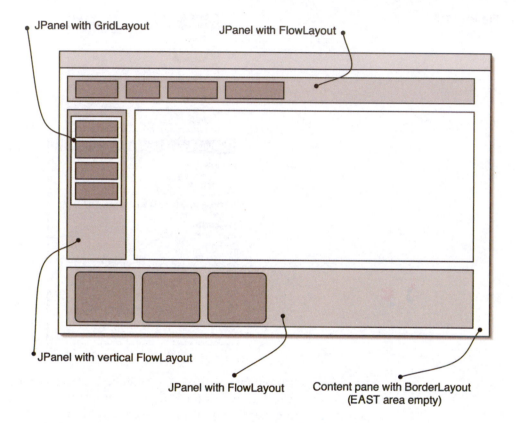

JPanel with GridLayout

JPanel with FlowLayout

JPanel with vertical FlowLayout

JPanel with FlowLayout

Content pane with BorderLayout
(EAST area empty)

Note how the container and the layout manager cooperate in the layout of the components. The container holds the components, but the layout manager decides their exact arrangement on screen. Every container has a layout manager. It will use a default layout manager if we do not explicitly set one. The default is different for different containers: the content pane of a `JFrame`, for example, has by default a `BorderLayout`, whereas `JPanels` use a `FlowLayout` by default.

Exercise 11.17 Look at the GUI of the calculator project used in Chapter 6 (Figure 6.7 on page 167). What kind of containers/layout managers do you think were used to create it? After answering in writing, open the *calculator-gui* project and check your answer by reading the code.

It is time to look at some code for our `ImageViewer` application again. Our goal is quite simple. We want to see three components above each other: a label at the top, the image in the middle, and another label at the bottom. Several layout managers can do this. Which one to choose becomes clearer when we think about resizing behavior. When we enlarge the window, we would like the labels to maintain their height, and the image to receive all the extra space. This suggests a `BorderLayout`: the labels can be in the NORTH and SOUTH areas, and the image in the CENTER. Code 11.4 shows the source code to implement this.

Two details are worth noting. First, the `setLayout` method is used on the content pane to set the intended layout manager.[4] The layout manager itself is an object, so we create an instance of `BorderLayout` and pass it to the `setLayout` method.

Second, when we add a component to a container with a `BorderLayout`, we use a different `add` method that has a second parameter. The value for the second parameter is one of the public constants NORTH, SOUTH, EAST, WEST, or CENTER, which are defined in class `BorderLayout`.

Code 11.4

Using a
`BorderLayout` to
arrange components

```
Container contentPane = frame.getContentPane();

contentPane.setLayout(new BorderLayout());

filenameLabel = new JLabel();
contentPane.add(filenameLabel, BorderLayout.NORTH);

imagePanel = new ImagePanel();
contentPane.add(imagePanel, BorderLayout.CENTER);

statusLabel = new JLabel("Version 1.0");
contentPane.add(statusLabel, BorderLayout.SOUTH);
```

Exercise 11.20 Implement and test the code shown above in your version of the project.

---

[4] Strictly speaking, the `setLayout` call is not needed here as the default layout manager of the content pane is already a `BorderLayout`. We have included the call here for clarity and readability.

Exercise 11.21 Experiment with other layout managers. Try all of the layout managers mentioned above in your project, and test whether they behave as expected.

11.5.5 Image filters

Two things remain to be done until our first image viewer version is finished: adding some image filters and adding a *Help* menu. Next, we shall do the filters.

The image filters are the first step toward image manipulation. Eventually, we do not only want to be able to open and display images, we also want to be able to manipulate them and save them back to disk.

Here, we start by adding three simple filters. A filter is a function that is applied to the whole image. (It could, of course, be modified to be applied to a part of an image, but we are not doing that just yet.)

The three filters are named *darker*, *lighter*, and *threshold*. *Darker* makes the whole image darker, and *lighter* makes it lighter. The threshold filter turns the image into a gray-scale picture with only a few preset shades of gray. We have chosen a three-level threshold. This means, we shall use three colors: black, white, and medium gray. All pixels that are in the upper third value range for brightness will be turned white, all that are in the lower third will be turned black, and the middle third will be gray.

To achieve this, we have to do two things:

- We have to create menu items for each filter with an associated menu listener, and
- we have to implement the actual filter operation.

First the menus. There is nothing really new in this. It is just more of the same menu creation code that we already wrote for our existing menu.

We need to add the following parts:

- We create a new menu (class `JMenu`) named *Filter* and add it to the menu bar.
- We create three menu items (class `JMenuItem`) named *Darker*, *Lighter*, and *Threshold*, and add them to our filter menu.
- To each menu, we add an action listener, using the code idiom for anonymous classes that we discussed for the other menu items. The action listeners should call the methods `makeDarker()`, `makeLighter()`, and `threshold()`, respectively.

Exercise 11.22 Add the new menu and the menu items to your version of the *imageviewer0-4* project, as described here. In order to add the action listeners, you need to create the three methods `makeDarker()`, `makeLighter()`, and `threshold()` as private methods in your **ImageViewer** class. These methods can initially have empty bodies, or they could simply print out that they have been called.

After we have added the menus and created the (initially empty) methods to handle the filter functions, we need to implement each filter.

The simplest kinds of filter involve iterating over the image and making a change of some sort to the color of each pixel. A pattern for this process is shown in Code 11.5. More complicated filters might use the values of neighboring pixels to adjust a pixel's value.

Code 11.5

Pattern for a simple filtering process

```java
int height = getHeight();
int width = getWidth();
for(int y = 0; y < height; y++) {
    for(int x = 0; x < width; x++) {
        Color pixel = getPixel(x, y);
        alter the pixel's color value;
        setPixel(x, y, pixel);
    }
}
```

The filter function itself operates on the image, so following responsibility-driven design guidelines, it should be implemented in the OFImage class. On the other hand, handling the menu invocation also includes some GUI-related code (for instance, we have to check whether an image is open at all when we invoke the filter), and this belongs in the ImageViewer class.

As a result of this reasoning, we create two methods, one in ImageViewer, and one in OFImage, to share the work (Code 11.6 and Code 11.7). We can see that the makeDarker method in ImageViewer contains the part of the task that is related to the GUI (checking that we have an image loaded, displaying a status message, repainting the frame), whereas the darker method in OFImage includes the actual work of making each pixel in the image a bit darker.

Code 11.6

The filter method in the ImageViewer class

```java
public class ImageViewer
{
    //  fields, constructors and all other methods omitted

    /**
     * 'Darker' function: make the picture darker.
     */
    private void makeDarker()
    {
        if(currentImage != null) {
            currentImage.darker();
            frame.repaint();
            showStatus("Applied: darker");
        }
        else {
            showStatus("No image loaded.");
        }
    }
}
```

Code 11.7

Implementation of a
filter in the OFImage
class

```java
public class OFImage extends BufferedImage
{
    // fields, constructors and all other methods omitted

    /**
     * Make this image a bit darker.
     */
    public void darker()
    {
        int height = getHeight();
        int width = getWidth();
        for(int y = 0; y < height; y++) {
            for(int x = 0; x < width; x++) {
                setPixel(x, y, getPixel(x, y).darker());
            }
        }
    }
}
```

Exercise 11.23 What does the method call `frame.repaint()` do, which you can see in the `makeDarker` method?

Exercise 11.24 We can see a call to a method `showStatus`, which is clearly an internal method call. From the name we can guess that this method should display a status message using the status label we created earlier. Implement this method in your version of the *imageviewer0-4* project. (*Hint*: Look at the `setText` method in the `JLabel` class.)

Exercise 11.25 What happens when the *Darker* menu item is selected while no image has been opened?

Exercise 11.26 Explain in detail how the `darker` method in `OFImage` works. (*Hint*: It contains another method call to a method also called `darker` itself. Which class does this method belong to? Look it up.)

Exercise 11.27 Implement the *lighter* filter in `OFImage`.

Exercise 11.28 Implement the *threshold* filter. To get the brightness of a pixel, you can get its red, green and blue values and add them up. The `Color` class defines static references to suitable black, white, and gray objects.

You can find a working implementation of everything described so far in the *imageviewer1-0* project. You should, however, attempt to do the exercises yourself first, before you look at the solution.

11.5.6   A Help menu

Our last task for this version is to add a *Help* menu that holds a menu item labeled *About ImageViewer...* . When this item is selected, a dialog should pop up that displays some short information.

> **Exercise 11.29** Add a menu named *Help* again. In it, add a menu item labeled *About ImageViewer...*.
>
> **Exercise 11.30** Add a method stub (a method with an empty body) named `showAbout()`, and add an action listener to the *About ImageViewer...* menu item that calls this method.

So far, adding the help menu was no different from adding any other menu. There should be one difference, though. By convention, help menus are placed on the far right side of the menu bar on many platforms. (This is not true for all platforms. MacOS, for example, uses by default a top-of-screen menu bar that does not place the help menu to the far right.)

We can achieve this by adding some *glue* to the menu bar.

The menu bar is a container that uses a `BoxLayout`. `BoxLayout`s can contain *struts* and *glue*. Both are invisible components, intended to create some empty space between other components. A strut is an empty space with a fixed size, and glue is a bit of empty space that stretches to fill as much space as possible.

The Swing library contains a helper class called `Box` to create these spacers.

In our menu bar, we can add the first two menus (*File* and *Filter*), then add some glue, and then add the *Help* menu. This will have the effect that the glue takes up all of the empty space in the menu bar, and the help menu will move to the right.

The source code pattern is shown in Code 11.8.

Code 11.8

Adding glue to the menu bar

```
menu = new JMenu("File");
menubar.add(menu);

menu = new JMenu("Filter");
menubar.add(menu);

menubar.add(Box.createHorizontalGlue());

menu = new JMenu("Help");
menubar.add(menu);
```

> **Exercise 11.31** Add glue to the menu bar in your project to place the help menu to the right.

11.5.7 Dialogs

Now we have to implement the showAbout method, so that it displays an 'about' dialog.

One of the main characteristics of a dialog is whether it is *modal* or not. A modal dialog blocks all interaction with other parts of the application until the dialog has been closed. It forces the user to deal with the dialog first. Non-modal dialogs allow interaction in other frames while the dialogs are visible.

Dialogs can be implemented in a similar way to our main JFrame. They often use the class JDialog to display the frame.

For modal dialogs with a standard structure, however, there are some convenience methods in class JOptionPane that make it very easy to show such dialogs. JOptionPane has, among other things, static methods to show three types of standard dialog. They are:

■ *Message dialog*: This is a dialog that displays a message and has an *OK* button to close the dialog.
■ *Confirm dialog*: This dialog usually asks a question and has buttons for the user to make a selection, for example *Yes*, *No*, and *Cancel*.
■ *Input dialog*: This dialog includes a prompt and a text field for the user to enter some text.

Our 'about' box is a simple message dialog. Looking through the JOptionPane documentation, we find that there are static methods named showMessageDialog to do this.

> **Exercise 11.32** Find the documentation for showMessageDialog. How many methods with this name are there? What are the differences between them? Which one should we use? Why?
>
> **Exercise 11.33** Implement the showAbout method in your ImageViewer class, using a call to a showMessageDialog method.
>
> **Exercise 11.34** The showInputDialog methods of JOptionPane allow a user to be prompted via a dialog for input when required. On the other hand, the JTextField component allows a permanent text input area to be displayed within a GUI. Find the documentation for this class. What input causes an ActionListener associated with a JTextField to be notified? Can a user be prevented from editing the text in the field? Is it possible for a listener to be notified of arbitrary changes to the text in the field? (*Hint*: What use does a JTextField make of a Document object?)
>
> You can find an example of a JTextField in the *calculator* project in Chapter 6.

After studying the documentation, we can now implement our 'about' box by making a call to the showMessageDialog method. The code is shown in Code 11.9. Note that we have introduced a string constant named VERSION to hold the current version number.

Code 11.9

Displaying a modal dialog

```
private void showAbout()
{
    JOptionPane.showMessageDialog(frame,
                "ImageViewer\n" + VERSION,
                "About ImageViewer",
                JOptionPane.INFORMATION_MESSAGE);
}
```

This was the last task to be done to complete 'version 1.0' of our image viewer application. If you have done all the exercises, you should now have a version of the project that can open images, apply filters, display status messages, and display a dialog.

The *imageviewer1-0* project, included in the book projects, contains an implementation of all the functionality discussed thus far. You should carefully study this project, and compare it with your own solutions.

In this project, we have also improved the openFile method to include better notification of errors. If the user chooses a file that is not a valid image file, we now show a proper error message. Now that we know about message dialogs, this is easy to do.

11.6 ImageViewer 2.0: improving program structure

Version 1.0 of our application has a useable GUI and can display images. It can also apply three basic filters.

The next obvious idea for an improvement of our application is to add some more interesting filters. Before we rush in and do it, however, let us think about what this involves.

With the current structure of filters, we have to do three things for each filter:

1 add a menu item;
2 add a method to handle the menu activation in ImageViewer; and
3 add an implementation of the filter in OFImage.

Numbers 1 and 3 are unavoidable – we need a menu item and a filter implementation. But number 2 looks suspicious. If we look at these methods in the ImageViewer class (Code 11.10 shows two of them as an example), this looks a lot like code duplication. These methods are essentially the same (except for some small details), and – what is worse – for each new filter we want to add, we have to add another one of these methods that again is almost the same.

Code 11.10

Two of the filter-handling methods from ImageViewer

```
private void makeLighter()
{
    if(currentImage != null) {
        currentImage.lighter();
        frame.repaint();
        showStatus("Applied: lighter");
    }
}
```

**Code 11.10
continued**

Two of the
filter-handling
methods from
`ImageViewer`

```
    else {
        showStatus("No image loaded.");
    }
}

private void threshold()
{
    if(currentImage != null) {
        currentImage.threshold();
        frame.repaint();
        showStatus("Applied: threshold");
    }
    else {
        showStatus("No image loaded.");
    }
}
```

As we know, code duplication is a sign of bad design and should be avoided. We deal with it by refactoring our code.

In this case, we want to find a design that lets us add new filters without having to add a new dispatch method for the filter every time.

To achieve what we want, we need to avoid hard-coding every filter into our `ImageViewer` class. Instead, we shall use a collection of filters, and then write a single filter invocation method that finds and invokes the right filter.

In order to do this, filters must themselves become objects. If we want to store them in a common collection and apply filters directly from that collection, all filters need a common superclass, which we name `Filter` (Figure 11.10).

Figure 11.10

Class structure for
filters as objects

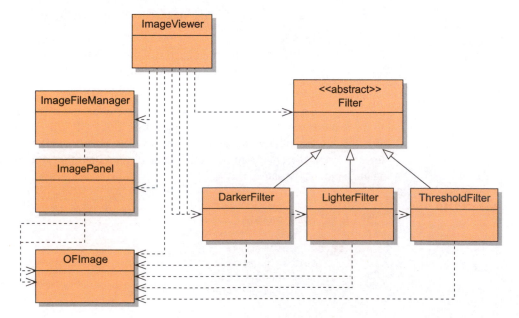

Every filter will have a name and an `apply` method that applies the filter to an image. We can define this in the `Filter` superclass (Code 11.11). Note that this is an abstract class, as the `apply` method has to be abstract at this level, but the `getName` method can be fully implemented.

Code 11.11

Abstract class
`Filter`: superclass
for all filters

```java
public abstract class Filter
{
    private String name;

    /**
     * Create a new filter with a given name.
     */
    public Filter(String name)
    {
        this.name = name;
    }

    /**
     * Return the name of this filter.
     *
     * @return  The name of this filter.
     */
    public String getName()
    {
        return name;
    }

    /**
     * Apply this filter to an image.
     *
     * @param image  The image to be changed by this filter.
     */
    public abstract void apply(OFImage image);
}
```

Once we have the written the superclass, it is not hard to implement specific filters as subclasses. All we need to do is provide an implementation for the `apply` method which manipulates an image (passed in as a parameter) using its `getPixel` and `setPixel` methods. Code 11.12 shows an example.

Code 11.12

Implementation of a
specific filter class

```java
//  All comments omitted.

public class DarkerFilter extends Filter
{
    public DarkerFilter(String name)
    {
        super(name);
    }
```

**Code 11.12
continued**

Implementation of a
specific filter class

```java
public void apply(OFImage image)
{
    int height = image.getHeight();
    int width = image.getWidth();
    for(int y = 0; y < height; y++) {
        for(int x = 0; x < width; x++) {
            image.setPixel(
                x, y, image.getPixel(x, y).darker());
        }
    }
}
```

As a side effect of this, the OFImage class becomes much simpler, as all of the filter methods can be removed from it. It now only defines the setPixel and getPixel methods.

Once we have defined our filters like this, we can create filter objects and store them in a collection (Code 11.13).

Code 11.13

Adding a collection
of filters

```java
public class ImageViewer
{
    // Other fields omitted.

    private List filters;

    public ImageViewer()
    {
        filters = createFilters();
        ...
    }

    private List createFilters()
    {
        List filterList = new ArrayList();
        filterList.add(new DarkerFilter("Darker"));
        filterList.add(new LighterFilter("Lighter"));
        filterList.add(new ThresholdFilter("Threshold"));

        return filterList;
    }

    // Other methods omitted.
}
```

Once we have this structure in place, we can make the last two necessary changes:

■ We change the code that creates the filter menu items, so that it iterates over the filter collection. For every filter, it creates a menu item and uses the filter's getName method to determine the item's label.

■ Having done this, we can write a generic `applyFilter` method that receives a filter as a parameter, and applies this filter to the current image.

The *imageviewer2-0* project includes a complete implementation of these changes.

Exercise 11.35 Open the *imageviewer2-0* project. Study the code for the new method to create and apply filters in class `ImageViewer`. Pay special attention to the `makeMenuBar` and `applyFilter` methods. Explain in detail how the creation of the filter menu items and their activation works. Draw an object diagram. Note, in particular, that the `filter` variable in `makeMenuBar` has been declared as `final`, as discussed in section 11.4.7. Make sure that you understand why this is necessary.

Exercise 11.36 What needs to be changed to add a new filter to your image viewer?

In this section, we have done pure refactoring. We have not changed the functionality of the application at all, but have worked exclusively at improving the implementation structure, so that future changes become easier.

Now, after finishing the refactoring, we should test that all existing functionality still works as expected.

In all development projects, we need phases like this. We do not always make perfect design decisions at the start, and applications grow and requirements change. Even though our main task in this chapter is to work with GUIs, we needed to step back and refactor our code before proceeding. This work will pay off in the long run by making all further changes easier.

Sometimes it is tempting to leave structures as they are, even though we recognize that they are not good. Putting up with a bit of code duplication may be easier in the short term than doing careful refactoring. One can get away with that for a short while, but for projects that are intended to survive for a longer time, this is bound to create problems. As a general rule: Take the time, keep your code clean!

Now that we have done this, we are ready to add some more filters.

Exercise 11.37 Add a *grayscale* filter to your project. The filter turns the image into a black-and-white image in shades of gray. You can make a pixel any shade of gray by giving all three color components (red, green, blue) the same value. The brightness of each pixel should remain unchanged.

Exercise 11.38 Add a *mirror* filter that flips the image horizontally. The pixel at the top left corner will move to the top right, and vice versa, producing the effect of viewing the image in a mirror.

Exercise 11.39 Add an *invert* filter that inverts each color. 'Inverting' a color means replacing each color value x with $255 - x$.

Exercise 11.40 Add a *smooth* filter that 'smoothes' the image. A smooth filter replaces every pixel value with the average of its neighboring pixels and itself (nine pixels in total). You have to be careful at the image's edges, where some neighbors do not exist. You also have to make sure to work with a temporary copy of the image while you process it, because the result is not correct if you work on a single image. (Why is this?) You can easily obtain a copy of the image by creating a new `OFImage` with the original as the parameter to its constructor.

Exercise 11.41 Add a *solarize* filter. Solarization is an effect one can create manually on photo negatives by re-exposing a developed negative. We can simulate this by replacing each color component of each pixel that has a value v of less than 128 with $255 - v$. The brighter components (value of 128 or more) we leave unchanged. (This is a very simple solarization algorithm – you can find more sophisticated ones described in the literature.)

Exercise 11.42 Implement an *edge detection* filter. Do this by analyzing the nine pixels in a three-by-three square around each pixel (similar to the smooth filter), and then set the value of the middle pixel to the difference between the highest and the lowest value found. Do this for each color component (red, green, blue). This also looks good if you invert the image at the same time.

Exercise 11.43 Experiment with your filters on different pictures. Try applying multiple filters after each other.

Once you have implemented some more filters of your own, you should change the version number of your project to 'version 2.1.'

11.7 ImageViewer 3.0: more interface components

Before we leave the image viewer project behind us, we want to add a few last improvements, and in the process, look at two more GUI components: buttons and borders.

11.7.1 Buttons

We now want to add functionality to the image viewer to change the size of the image. We do this by providing two functions: *larger*, which doubles the image size, and *smaller*, which halves the size. (To be exact: we double or halve both the width and the height, not the area.)

One way to do this is to implement filters for these tasks. But we decide against it. So far, filters never change the image size, and we want to leave it at that. Instead, we introduce a toolbar on the left side of our frame with two buttons in it labeled *Larger* and *Smaller* (Figure 11.11). This also gives us a chance to experiment a bit with buttons, containers, and layout managers.

Figure 11.11
Image viewer with
toolbar buttons

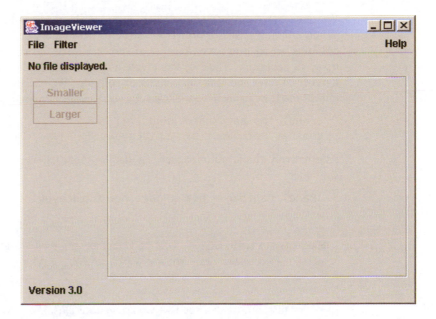

So far, our frame uses a BorderLayout, where the WEST area is empty. We can use this area to add our toolbar buttons. There is one small problem, though. The WEST area of a BorderLayout can hold only one component, but we have two buttons.

The solution is simple. We add a JPanel to the frame's WEST area (as we know, a JPanel is a container), and then stick the two buttons into the JPanel. Code 11.14 shows the code to do this.

Code 11.14
Adding a toolbar
panel with two
buttons

```java
// Create the toolbar with the buttons
JPanel toolbar = new JPanel();

smallerButton = new JButton("Smaller");
toolbar.add(smallerButton);

largerButton = new JButton("Larger");
toolbar.add(largerButton);

contentPane.add(toolbar, BorderLayout.WEST);
```

Exercise 11.44 Add two buttons labeled *Larger* and *Smaller* to your latest version of the project, using code similar to the one above. Test it. What do you observe?

When we try this out, we see that it works partially, but does not look as expected. The reason is that a JPanel uses, by default, a FlowLayout, and a FlowLayout arranges its components horizontally. We would like them arranged vertically.

We can achieve this by using another layout manager. A GridLayout does what we want. When creating a GridLayout, constructor parameters determine how many rows and columns we wish to have. A value of zero has a special meaning here, standing for 'as many as necessary.' Thus we can create a single column GridLayout by using 0 as the number of rows and 1 as the number of columns. We can then use this GridLayout for our JPanel, by using the panel's setLayout method immediately after creating it:

```
JPanel toolbar = new JPanel();
toolbar.setLayout(new GridLayout(0, 1));
```

Alternatively, the layout manager can also be specified as a constructor parameter of the container:

```
JPanel toolbar = new JPanel(new GridLayout(0, 1));
```

> **Exercise 11.45** Change your code so that your toolbar panel uses a GridLayout, as discussed above. Test. What do you observe?

If we try this out, we can see that we are getting closer, but we still do not have what we want. Our buttons now are much larger than we intended.

The reason is that a container in a BorderLayout (our toolbar JPanel in this case) always covers its whole area (the WEST area in our frame). And a GridLayout always resizes its components to fill the whole container.

A FlowLayout does not do this – it is quite happy to leave some empty space around the components. Our solution is therefore to use both: the GridLayout to arrange the buttons in a column, and a FlowLayout around it to allow some space. We end up with a GridLayout panel inside a FlowLayout panel inside a BorderLayout. Code 11.15 shows this solution. Constructions like this are very common. You will often nest various containers inside other containers to create exactly the look you want.

Code 11.15

Using a nested GridLayout container inside a FlowLayout container

```
// Create the toolbar with the buttons
JPanel toolbar = new JPanel();
toolbar.setLayout(new GridLayout(0, 1));

smallerButton = new JButton("Smaller");
toolbar.add(smallerButton);

largerButton = new JButton("Larger");
toolbar.add(largerButton);

// Add toolbar into panel with flow layout for spacing
JPanel flow = new JPanel();
flow.add(toolbar);

contentPane.add(flow, BorderLayout.WEST);
```

Our buttons now look quite close to what we were aiming for. Before adding the finishing polish, we can first work on making the buttons work.

We need to add two methods, named, for instance, `makeLarger` and `makeSmaller`, to do the actual work, and we need to add action listeners to the buttons that invoke these methods.

Exercise 11.46 In your project, add two method stubs named `makeLarger` and `makeSmaller`. Initially, put just a single `println` statement into these method bodies to see when they have been called. The methods can be private.

Exercise 11.47 Add action listeners to the two buttons that invoke the two new methods. Adding action listeners to buttons is identical to adding action listeners to menu items. You can essentially copy the code pattern from there. Test it. Make sure your `makeSmaller` and `makeLarger` methods get called by activating the buttons.

Exercise 11.48 Properly implement the `makeSmaller` and `makeLarger` methods. To do this, you have to create a new `OFImage` with different size, copy the pixels from the current image across (while scaling it up or down), and then set the new image as the current image. At the end of your method, you should call the frame's `pack` method to rearrange the components with the changed size.

Exercise 11.49 All Swing components have a `setEnabled(boolean)` method, that can enable and disable the component. Disabled components are usually displayed in light gray, and do not react to input. Change your image viewer so that the two toolbar buttons are initially disabled. When an image is opened, they are enabled, and when it is closed, they are disabled again.

11.7.2 Borders

The last polish we want to add to our interface is some internal borders. Borders can be used to group components or just to add some space between them. Every Swing component can have a border.

Some layout managers also accept constructor parameters that define their spacing, and the layout manager will then create the requested space between components.

The most used borders are `BevelBorder`, `CompoundBorder`, `EmptyBorder`, `EtchedBorder`, and `TitledBorder`. You should familiarize yourself with these.

We shall do three things to improve the look of our GUI:

- add some empty space around the outside of the frame;
- add spacing between the components of the frame; and
- add a line around the image.

The code to do this is shown in Code 11.16. The `setBorder` call on the content pane with an `EmptyBorder` as a parameter adds empty space around the outside of the frame. Note that we now cast the `contentPane` to a `JPanel`, as the supertype `Container` does not have the `setBorder` method.

Code 11.16

Adding spacing with
gaps and borders

```
JPanel contentPane = (JPanel)frame.getContentPane();
contentPane.setBorder(new EmptyBorder(6, 6, 6, 6));

// Specify the layout manager with nice spacing
contentPane.setLayout(new BorderLayout(6, 6));

imagePanel = new ImagePanel();
imagePanel.setBorder(new EtchedBorder());
contentPane.add(imagePanel, BorderLayout.CENTER);
```

Creating the BorderLayout with two int parameters adds spacing between the components which it lays out. And finally, setting an EtchedBorder for the imagePanel adds a line with an 'etched' look around the image.

Borders are defined in the package javax.swing.border – we have to add an import statement for this package.

All the improvements discussed in the section have been implemented in the last version of this application in the book projects: *imageviewer3-0*. In that version, we have also added a *Save As* function to the file menu so that images can be saved back to disk.

And we have added one more filter, called *Fish Eye*, to give you some more ideas about what you can do. Try it out. It works especially well on portraits.

11.8 Further extensions

Programming GUIs with Swing is a big subject area. Swing has many different types of component, and many different containers and layout managers. And each of these has many attributes and methods.

Becoming familiar with the whole Swing library takes time, and is not something done in a few weeks. Usually, as we work on GUIs, we continue to read about details that we did not know before, and become experts over time.

The example discussed in this chapter, even though it contains a lot of detail, is only a brief introduction to GUI programming. We have discussed most of the important concepts, but there is still a large amount of functionality to be discovered, most of which is beyond the scope of this book.

There are various sources of information available for you to continue. You frequently have to look up the API documentation for the Swing classes. It is not possible to work without it.

There are also many GUI/Swing tutorials available, both in print and on the web.

A very good starting point for this is, as so often, the Java Tutorial that is available publicly on Sun Microsystems' web site. It contains a section titled *Creating a GUI with JFC/Swing* (http://java.sun.com/docs/books/tutorial/uiswing/index.html).

In this section, there are many interesting subsections. One of the most useful may be the section *Using Swing Components*, and in it, the subsection *How To...* . It contains entries titled *How to Use Buttons, Check Boxes, and Radio Buttons*; *How to Use Labels*; *How to Make Dialogs*; *How to Use Panels*; and so on.

Similarly, the top-level section *Laying Out Components Within a Container* also has a *How To...* section that tells you about all available layout managers.

Exercise 11.50 Find the online Java Tutorial section *Creating a GUI with JFC/Swing* (the sections are called *trails* on the web site). Bookmark it.

Exercise 11.51 Write down a list of all available layout managers in Swing.

Exercise 11.52 What is a *slider*? Find a description and summarize. Give a short example in Java code about creating and using a slider.

Exercise 11.53 What is a *tabbed pane*? Find a description and summarize. Give examples of what a tabbed pane might be used for.

Exercise 11.54 What is a *spinner*? Find a description and summarize.

Exercise 11.55 Find the demo application *ProgressBarDemo*. Run it on your computer. Describe what it does.

This is where we shall leave the discussion of the image viewer example. It can, however, be extended in many directions by interested readers. Using the information from the online tutorial, you can add numerous interface components.

The following exercises give you some ideas, and obviously there are many more possibilities.

Exercise 11.56 Implement an *undo* function in your image viewer. This function reverses the last operation.

Exercise 11.57 Disable all menu items that cannot be used when no image is being displayed.

Exercise 11.58 Implement a *reload* function that discards all changes to the current image and reloads it from disk.

Exercise 11.59 The `JMenu` class is actually a subclass of `JMenuItem`. This means that nested menus can be created by placing one `JMenu` inside another. Add an *Adjust* menu to the menu bar. Nest within it a *Rotate* menu that allows the image to be rotated either 90 or 180 degrees, clockwise or anticlockwise. Implement this functionality. The *Adjust* menu could also contain menu items that invoke the existing *Larger* and *Smaller* functionality, for instance.

Exercise 11.60 The application always resizes its frame in order to ensure that the full image is always visible. Having a large frame is not always desirable. Read the documentation on the `JScrollPane` class. Instead of adding the `ImagePanel` directly to the content pane, place the panel in a `JScrollPane` and add the scroll pane to the content pane. Display a large image and experiment with resizing the window. What difference does having a scroll pane make? Does this allow you to display images that would otherwise be too large for the screen?

Exercise 11.61 Change your application so that it can open multiple images at the same time (but only one image is displayed at any time). Then add a popup menu (using class `JComboBox`) to select the image to display.

Exercise 11.62 As an alternative to using a `JComboBox` as in exercise 11.61, use a tabbed pane (class `JTabbedPane`) to hold multiple open images.

Exercise 11.63 Implement a slide show function that lets you choose a directory, and then displays each image in that directory for a specified length of time (say, 5 seconds).

Exercise 11.64 Once you have the slide show, add a slider (class `JSlider`) that lets you select an image in the slide show by moving the slider. While the slide show runs, the slider should move to indicate progress.

11.9 Another example: SoundPlayer

So far, in this chapter, we have discussed one example of a GUI application in detail. We now want to introduce a second application to provide another example to learn from. This program introduces a few additional GUI components.

This second example is a sound player application. We shall not discuss it in any great amount of detail. It is intended as a basis for studying the source code largely on your own, and as a source of code fragments for you to copy and modify.

Here, in this chapter, we shall only point out a few selected aspects of this application that are worth focusing on.

Exercise 11.65 Open the *simplesound* project. Create an instance of `SoundPlayerGUI`, and experiment with the application.

The sound player finds and plays sound clips stored in the *audio* folder inside the project folder. It can play sounds that are stored in AIFF, AU, and some WAV formats. Note that the WAV format uses several different encodings, only some of which can be played by our player. If you have sound files of the right format of your own, you should be able to play them by dropping them in the *simplesound*'s audio folder.

The sound player is implemented in two classes: `SoundPlayerGUI` and `SoundEngine`. Only the first is intended to be studied here. The `SoundEngine` class can be used essentially as a library class. Familiarize yourself with its interface, but you do not need to understand or modify its implementation. (You are welcome, of course, to study this class as well if you like, but it uses some concepts that we shall not discuss in this book.)

Following are some noteworthy observations about this project.

Model/view separation

This application uses a better model/view separation than the previous example. This means that the application functionality (the model) is separated cleanly from the application's user interface (the GUI). Each of those two, the model and the view, may consist of multiple classes, but every class should be clearly in one or the other group to achieve a clear separation. In our example, each half consists of only a single class.

Separating the application's functionality from the interface is good cohesion – it makes the program easier to understand, easier to maintain, and easier to adapt to different requirements (especially different user interfaces). It would, for example, be fairly easy to write a text-based interface for the sound player, effectively replacing the `SoundPlayerGUI` class and leaving the `SoundEngine` class unchanged.

Inheriting from `JFrame`

In this example, we are demonstrating a different popular version of creating frames. Our GUI class does not instantiate a `JFrame` object; instead it extends the `JFrame` class.

As a result, all the `JFrame` methods we need to call (such as `getContentPane`, `setJMenuBar`, `pack`, `setVisible`, and so on) can now be called as internal (inherited) methods.

There is no strong reason for preferring one style (using a `JFrame` instance) over the other (inheriting from `JFrame`). It is largely a matter of personal preference.

Displaying static images

It is very common that we want to display an image in a GUI. The easiest way to do this is to include a `JLabel` in the interface, which has a graphic as its label (`JLabels` can display either text or a graphic or both). The sound player includes an example of doing this.

The relevant source code is

```
JLabel image = new JLabel(new ImageIcon("title.jpg"));
```

This statement will load an image file named 'title.jpg' from the project directory, create an icon with that image, and then create a `JLabel` that displays the icon.

The term 'icon' seems to suggest that we are dealing only with small images here, but the image can in fact be of any size. This method works for JPEG, GIF, and PNG images.

Combo-boxes

The sound player presents an example of using a `JComboBox`. A combo-box is a set of values, one of which is selected at any time. The selected value is displayed, and the selection can be accessed through a popup menu. In the sound player, the combo-box is used to select specific sound formats.

A JComboBox may also be editable, in which case the values are not all predefined, but can be typed by a user.

Lists

The program also includes an example of a list (class JList), for the list of sound clips. A list can hold an arbitrary number of values, and one or more can be selected. The list values in this example are Strings, but other types are possible. A list does not automatically have a scrollbar.

Scrollbars

Another component demonstrated in this example is the use of scrollbars.

Scrollbars can be created by using a special container – an instance of class JScrollPane. GUI objects of any type can be placed into a scroll-pane, and the scroll-pane will, if the held object is too big to be displayed in the available space, provide the necessary scrollbars.

In our example, we have placed our sound clip list into a scroll-pane. The scroll-pane itself is then placed into its parent container.

Other elements demonstrated in this example are the use of a slider, and the use of color for changing the look of an application. Each of the GUI's elements has many methods to modify the component's look or behavior – you should look through the documentation for any component that interests you and experiment with modifying some properties of that component.

Exercise 11.66 Change the sound player so that it displays a different image in its center. Find an image to use on the web, or make your own.

Exercise 11.67 Change the colors of the other components (foreground and background colors) to suit the new main image.

Exercise 11.68 Add a 'Reload' method to the sound player that re-reads the sound files from the *audio* folder. Then you can drop a new sound file into the folder and load it without having to quit the player.

Exercise 11.69 Add an 'Open' function to the file menu. When activated, it presents a file selection dialog that lets the user choose a sound file to open. If the user chooses a directory, the player should open all sound files in that directory (as it does now with the *audio* directory).

Exercise 11.70 Modify the slider, so that the start and end (and possibly other tick marks) are labeled with numbers. The start should be zero, and the end should be the length of the sound clip in seconds.

Exercise 11.71 Modify the sound player so that a double click on a list element in the sound clip list starts playing that sound.

Exercise 11.72 Improve the button look. All buttons that have no function at any point in time should be grayed out at that time, and should be enabled only when they can be reasonably used.

Exercise 11.73 The SoundEngine provides a method for adjusting the volume. Add a slider somewhere in the user interface to adjust the volume.

11.10 Summary

In this chapter we have given an introduction to GUI programming using AWT and Swing. We have discussed the three main conceptual areas: creating GUI components, layout, and event handling.

We have seen that building a GUI usually starts with creating a top-level frame, such as a JFrame. The frame is then filled with various components that provide information and functionality to the user. Among the components we have encountered are menus, menu items, buttons, labels, borders, and others.

Components are arranged on screen with the help of containers and layout managers. Containers hold collections of components, and each container has a layout manager that takes care of arranging the components within the container's screen area.

Interactive components (those that can react to user input) generate events when they are activated by a user. Other objects can become event listeners and be notified of such events by implementing standard interfaces. When the listener object is notified, it can take appropriate action to deal with the user event.

We have introduced the concept of anonymous inner classes as a modular, extendable technique for writing event listeners.

And finally, we have given a pointer to an online reference and tutorial site that may be used to learn about details not covered in the chapter.

Exercise 11.74 Add a GUI to the *world-of-zuul* project from Chapter 7. Every room should have an associated image that is displayed when the player enters the room. There should be a non-editable text area to display text output. To enter commands, you can choose between different possibilities: you can leave the input text based, and use a text field (class JTextField) to type commands, or you can use buttons for command entry.

Exercise 11.75 Add sounds to the *word-of-zuul* game. You can associate individual sounds with rooms, items, or characters.

Exercise 11.76 Design and build a GUI for a text editor. Users should be able to enter text, edit, scroll, etc. Consider functions for formatting (font faces, style, and size), and a character/word count function. You do not need to implement the load and save functions just yet – you may like to wait with that until you have read the next chapter.

Terms introduced in this chapter

GUI, AWT, Swing, component, layout, event, event handling, event listener, frame, menu bar, menu, menu item, content pane, modal dialog, anonymous inner class

Concept summary

- **components** A GUI is built by arranging components on screen. Components are represented by objects.

- **layout** Arranging the layout of components is achieved by using layout managers.

- **event handling** The term event handling refers to the task of reacting to user events, such as mouse button clicks or keyboard input.

- **image formats** Images can be stored in different formats. The differences primarily affect file size and information content.

- **menu bar, content pane** Components are placed in a frame by adding them to the frame's menu bar or content pane.

- **event listener** An object can listen to component events by implementing an event listener interface.

- **anonymous inner classes** Anonymous inner classes are a useful construct to implement event listeners.

Main concepts discussed in this chapter:

- defensive programming
- exception throwing and handling
- error reporting
- simple file processing

Java constructs discussed in this chapter:

`TreeMap`, `TreeSet`, `SortedMap`, `assert`, exception, `throw`, `throws`, `try`, `catch`, `FileReader`, `FileWriter`, stream

In Chapter 6 we noted that logical errors in programs are harder to spot than syntactic errors because a compiler cannot give any help with logical errors. Logical errors arise for several reasons, which may overlap in some situations:

- The solution to a problem has been implemented incorrectly. For instance, a problem involving generating some statistics on data values might have been programmed to find the mean value rather than the median value (the 'middle' value).
- An object might be asked to do something it is unable to. For instance, a collection object's `get` method might be called with an index value outside the valid range.
- An object might be used in ways that have not been anticipated by the class designer, leading to the object being left in an inconsistent or inappropriate state. This often happens when a class is reused in a setting that is different from its original one, perhaps through inheritance.

Although the sort of testing strategies discussed in Chapter 6 can help us to identify and eliminate many logical errors before our programs are put to use, experience suggests that program failures will continue to occur. Furthermore, even the most thoroughly tested program may fail as a result of circumstances beyond the programmer's control. Consider the case of a web-browser asked to display a web page that does not exist; or a program that tries to write data to a disk that has no more space left. These problems are not the result of logical programming errors, but they could easily cause a program to fail if the possibility of their arising has not been anticipated.

In this chapter we look at how to anticipate and respond to error situations as they arise during the execution of a program. In addition, we provide some suggestions on how to report errors when they occur. We also provide a brief introduction to how to perform textual input/output, as one of the situations where errors can easily arise is file processing.

The address-book project

We shall use the *address-book* family of projects to illustrate some of the principles of error reporting and error handling that arise in many applications. The projects represent an application that stores personal contact details – name, address, and phone number – for an arbitrary number of people. The contact details are indexed in the address book by both name and phone number. The main classes we shall be discussing are AddressBook (Code 12.1) and ContactDetails. In addition, the AddressBookDemo class is provided as a convenient means of setting up an initial address book with some sample data.

Code 12.1

The AddressBook class

```java
import java.util.Iterator;
import java.util.LinkedList;
import java.util.SortedMap;
import java.util.TreeMap;
import java.util.TreeSet;

/**
 * A class to maintain an arbitrary number of contact details.
 * Details are indexed by both name and phone number.
 * @author David J. Barnes and Michael Kölling.
 * @version 2002.05.08
 */
public class AddressBook
{
    // Storage for an arbitrary number of details.
    private TreeMap book;
    private int numberOfEntries;

    /**
     * Perform any initialization for the address book.
     */
    public AddressBook()
    {
        book = new TreeMap();
        numberOfEntries = 0;
    }

    /**
     * Look up a name or phone number and return the
     * corresponding contact details.
     * @param key The name or number to be looked up.
     * @return The details corresponding to the key.
     */
    public ContactDetails getDetails(String key)
    {
        return (ContactDetails) book.get(key);
    }

    /**
     * Return whether or not the current key is in use.
```

Code 12.1 continued

The AddressBook class

```java
 * @param key The name or number to be looked up.
 * @return true if the key is in use, false otherwise.
 */
public boolean keyInUse(String key)
{
    return book.containsKey(key);
}


/**
 * Add a new set of details to the notebook.
 * @param details The details to associate with the person.
 */
public void addDetails(ContactDetails details)
{
    book.put(details.getName(), details);
    book.put(details.getPhone(), details);
    numberOfEntries++;
}


/**
 * Change the details previously stored under the given key.
 * @param oldKey One of the keys used to store the details.
 * @param details The replacement details.
 */
public void changeDetails(String oldKey,
                          ContactDetails details)
{
    removeDetails(oldKey);
    addDetails(details);
}


/**
 * Search for all details stored under a key that starts with
 * the given prefix.
 * @param keyPrefix The key prefix to search on.
 * @return An array of those details that have been found.
 */
public ContactDetails[] search(String keyPrefix)
{
    LinkedList matches = new LinkedList();
    // Find keys that are equal-to or greater-than the prefix.
    SortedMap tail = book.tailMap(keyPrefix);
    Iterator it = tail.keySet().iterator();
    boolean endOfSearch = false;
    while(!endOfSearch && it.hasNext()) {
        String key = (String) it.next();
        if(key.startsWith(keyPrefix)) {
            matches.add(book.get(key));
        }
        else {
            endOfSearch = true;
        }
```

Code 12.1 continued

The AddressBook class

```java
        }
        ContactDetails[] results =
                        new ContactDetails[matches.size()];
        matches.toArray(results);
        return results;
    }


    /**
     * @return The number of entries currently in the
     *          address book.
     */
    public int getNumberOfEntries()
    {
        return numberOfEntries;
    }


    /**
     * Remove the entry with the given key from the address book.
     * @param key One of the keys of the entry to be removed.
     */
    public void removeDetails(String key)
    {
        ContactDetails details =
                        (ContactDetails) book.get(key);
        book.remove(details.getName());
        book.remove(details.getPhone());
        numberOfEntries--;
    }


    /**
     * @return A list of all entries in the address.
     * @return A list of all the contact details, sorted according
     *          to the sort order of the ContactDetails class.
     */
    public String listDetails()
    {
        // Because each entry is stored under two keys, it is
        // necessary to build a set of the ContactDetails. This
        // eliminates duplicates.
        StringBuffer allEntries = new StringBuffer();
        TreeSet sortedDetails = new TreeSet(book.values());
        Iterator it = sortedDetails.iterator();
        while(it.hasNext()) {
            ContactDetails details = (ContactDetails) it.next();
            allEntries.append(details);
            allEntries.append('\n');
            allEntries.append('\n');
        }
        return allEntries.toString();
    }
}
```

New details can be stored in the address book via its `addDetails` method. This assumes that the details represent a new contact, and not a change of details for an existing one. To cover the latter case, the `changeDetails` method removes an old entry and replaces it with the revised details. The address book provides two ways to retrieve entries: the `getDetails` method takes a name or phone number as the key and returns the matching details; and the `search` method returns an array of all those details that start with a given search string. For instance, the search string `"08459"` would return all entries with phone numbers having that area prefix.

There are two introductory versions of the *address-book* project for you to explore. Both provide access to the same version of `AddressBook`, as shown in Code 12.1. The *address-book-text-v1t* project provides a text-based user interface, similar in style to the interface of the *zuul* game discussed in Chapter 7. Commands are currently available to list the address book's contents, search it, and add a new entry. Probably more interesting as an interface, however, is the *address-book-v1g* version, which incorporates a simple GUI. Experiment with both versions to gain some experience with what the application can do.

Exercise 12.1 Open the *address-book-v1g* project and create an `Address-BookDemo` object. Call its `showInterface` method to display the GUI and interact with the sample address book.

Exercise 12.2 Repeat your experimentation with the text interface of the *address-book-v1t* project.

Exercise 12.3 Examine the implementation of the `AddressBook` class and assess whether you think it has been well written or not. Do you have any specific criticisms of it?

Exercise 12.4 The `AddressBook` class uses quite a lot of classes from the `java.util` package; if you are not familiar with any of these, check the API documentation to fill in the gaps. Do you think the use of so many different utility classes is justified? Could a `HashMap` have been used in place of the `TreeMap`?

Exercise 12.5 Modify the `CommandWords` and `AddressBookTextInterface` classes of the *address-book-v1t* project to provide interactive access to the `get-Details`, and `removeDetails` methods of `AddressBook`.

Exercise 12.6 The `AddressBook` class defines an attribute to record the number of entries. Do you think it would be more appropriate to calculate this value, as required, from the number of unique entries in the `TreeMap`? For instance, can you think of any circumstances in which the following calculation would not produce the same value?

```
return book.size() / 2;
```

12.2 Defensive programming

12.2.1 Client–server interaction

An `AddressBook` is a typical server object, initiating no actions on its own behalf; all of its activities are driven by client requests. Implementers can adopt at least two possible views when designing and implementing a server:

- They can assume that client objects will know what they are doing, and will request services only in a sensible and well-defined way.
- They can assume that the server will operate in an essentially hostile environment, in which all possible steps must be taken to prevent client objects from using the server incorrectly.

These views clearly represent opposite extremes. In practice, the most likely scenario usually lies somewhere in between. Most client interactions will be reasonable, with the occasional attempt to use the server incorrectly – as the result either of a logical programming error or of misconception on the part of the client programmer. These different views provide a useful base from which to discuss questions such as:

- How much checking should a server's methods perform on client requests?
- How should a server report errors to its clients?
- How can a client anticipate failure of a request to a server?
- How should a client deal with failure of a request?

If we examine the `AddressBook` class with these issues in mind, we shall see that the class has been written to trust completely that its clients will use it appropriately. Exercise 12.7 illustrates one of the ways in which this is the case, and how things can go wrong.

Exercise 12.7 Using the *address-book-v1g* project, create a new **AddressBook** object on the object bench. This will be completely empty of contact details. Now make a call to its **removeDetails** method with any string value for the key. What happens? Can you understand why this happens?

Exercise 12.8 For a programmer, the easiest response to an error situation arising is to allow the program to terminate (i.e. to 'crash'). Can you think of any situations in which just allowing a program to terminate could be very dangerous?

Exercise 12.9 Many commercially sold programs contain errors that are not handled properly in the software and cause the program to crash. Is that unavoidable? Is it acceptable? Discuss.

The problem with the `removeDetails` method is that it assumes that the key passed to it is a valid key for the address book. It uses the supposed key to retrieve the associated contact details:

```
ContactDetails details = (ContactDetails) book.get(key);
```

However, if the key does not have an associated object value, then the `details` variable will now store the `null` value. That, of itself, is not an error; but the error arises from the following statement, where we assume that `details` refers to a valid object:

```
book.remove(details.getName());
```

It is not possible to call a method on the `null` value, and the result is a runtime error. BlueJ reports this as a `NullPointerException`, and highlights the statement from which it resulted. Later in this chapter we shall be discussing exceptions in detail. For now we can simply say that, if an error such as this were to occur in a running application, then the application would terminate prematurely, before it had completed its task.

There is clearly a problem here, but whose fault is it? Is it the fault of the client object for calling the method with a bad argument; or is it the fault of the server object for failing to handle this situation properly? The writer of the client class might argue that there is nothing in the method's documentation to say that the key must be valid. Conversely, the writer of the server class might argue that it is obviously wrong to try to remove details with an invalid key. Our concern in this chapter is not to resolve such disputes, but to try to prevent them from arising in the first place. We shall start by looking at error handling from the point of view of the server class.

Exercise 12.10 Save a copy of one of the *address-book-v1* projects under another name to work on. Make changes to the `removeDetails` method to avoid a `NullPointerException` from arising if the key value does not have a corresponding entry in the address book. If the key is not valid then the method should do nothing.

Exercise 12.11 Is it necessary to report the use of an invalid key in a call to `removeDetails`? If so, how would you report it?

Exercise 12.12 Are there any other methods in the **AddressBook** class that are vulnerable to similar errors? If so, try to correct them in your copy of the project. Is it possible in all cases for the method simply to do nothing if its arguments are inappropriate? Do the errors need reporting in some way? If so, how would you do it, and would it be the same for each error?

12.2.2　Argument checking

A server object is most vulnerable when its constructor and methods receive argument values through their parameters. The values passed to a constructor are used to set up an object's initial state; the values passed to a method will be used to influence the overall effect of the method call, and maybe the result that it produces. Therefore, it is vital that a server knows whether it can trust argument values to be valid, or whether it needs to check their validity for itself. The current situation in both the `ContactDetails` and `Address-Book` classes is that there is no checking at all on argument values. As we have seen with the `removeDetails` method, this can lead to the occurrence of a fatal runtime error.

Preventing a `NullPointerException` from arising in `removeDetails` is relatively easy, and Code 12.2 illustrates how this can be done. Note that, as well as improving the source code in the method, we have updated the method's comment to document the fact that unknown keys are ignored.

Code 12.2

Guarding against an
invalid key in
`removeDetails`

```java
/**
 * Remove the entry with the given key from the address book.
 * If the key does not exist, do nothing.
 * @param key One of the keys of the entry to be removed.
 */
public void removeDetails(String key)
{
    if(keyInUse(key)) {
        ContactDetails details = (ContactDetails) book.get(key);
        book.remove(details.getName());
        book.remove(details.getPhone());
        numberOfEntries--;
    }
}
```

If we examine all the methods of `AddressBook` we find that there are other places where we could make similar improvements:

- The `addDetails` method should check that its argument is not the `null` value.
- The `changeDetails` method should check both that the old key is one that is in use, and that the new details are not `null`.
- The `search` method should check that the key is not `null`.

These changes have all been implemented in the version of the application to be found in the *address-book-v2g* and *address-book-v2t* projects.

Exercise 12.13 Why do you think we have felt it unnecessary to make similar changes to the `getDetails` and `keyInUse` methods?

Exercise 12.14 In dealing with argument errors, we have not printed any error messages. Do you think an **AddressBook** *should* print an error message whenever it receives a bad argument to one of its methods? Are there any situations where a printed error message would be inappropriate?

Exercise 12.15 Are there any further checks you feel we should make on the arguments of other methods, to prevent an **AddressBook** object from functioning incorrectly?

12.3 Server error reporting

Having protected a server from performing an illegal operation through bad parameter values, we could take the view that this is all that the server writer needs to do. However, ideally we should like to avoid such error situations from arising in the first place. Furthermore, it is often the case that incorrect parameter values are the result of some form of programming error in the client that supplied them. Therefore, rather than simply programming around the problem in the server and leaving it at that, it is good practice for the server to make some effort to indicate that a problem has arisen – either to the client itself, or to a human user or programmer. In that way, there is a chance that an incorrectly written client will be fixed. What is the best way for a server to report problems when they occur? There is no single answer to this question, and the most appropriate answer will often depend upon the context in which a particular server object is being used. In the following sections we shall explore a range of options for error reporting by a server.

Exercise 12.16 How many different ways can you think of to indicate that a method has received incorrect parameter values, or is otherwise unable to complete its task? Consider as many different sorts of application as you can. For instance: those with a GUI; those with a textual interface and a human user; those with no sort of interactive user, such as software in an automobile's engine-management system.

12.3.1 Notifying the user

The most obvious way in which an object might try to respond when it detects something wrong is to try to notify the application's user in some way. The main options are either to print an error message, using `System.out`, or to display an error message window.

The two main problems with both approaches are:

- They assume that the application is being used by a human user who will see the error message. There are many applications that run completely independently of a human user. An error message, or an error window, will go completely unnoticed. Indeed, the computer running the application might not have any visual-display device connected to it at all.
- Even where there is a human user to see the error message, it will be rare for that user to be in a position to do something about the problem. Imagine a user at an automatic teller machine being confronted with a `NullPointerException`! Only in those cases where the user's direct action has led to the problem – such as supplying invalid input to the application – are they likely to be able take some appropriate corrective action.

Programs that print inappropriate error messages are more likely to annoy their users rather than achieve a useful outcome. Therefore, except in a very limited set of circumstances, notifying the user is not a general solution to the problem of error reporting.

12.3.2 Notifying the client object

A radically different approach from those we have discussed so far is for the server to feedback an indication to the client object when something has gone wrong. There are two main ways to do this:

- A server can use the return value of the method to return a flag that indicates either success or failure of the method call.
- A server can *throw an exception* from the server method if something goes wrong. This introduces a new feature of Java that is also found in some other programming languages. We shall describe this feature in detail in section 12.4.

Both techniques have the benefit of encouraging the programmer of the client to take into account that a method call on another object could fail. However, only the decision to throw an exception will actively prevent the client's programmer from ignoring the consequences of method failure.

The first approach is easy to introduce to a method that would otherwise have a void return type, such as removeDetails. If the void type is replaced by a boolean type, then the method can return true to indicate that the removal was successful and false to indicate that it failed for some reason (Code 12.3).

Code 12.3 A boolean return type to indicate success or failure

```
/**
 * Remove the entry with the given key from the address book.
 * The key should be one that is currently in use.
 * @param key One of the keys of the entry to be removed.
 * @return true if the entry was successfully removed,
 *          false otherwise.
 */
public boolean removeDetails(String key)
{
    if(keyInUse(key)) {
        ContactDetails details = (ContactDetails) book.get(key);
        book.remove(details.getName());
        book.remove(details.getPhone());
        numberOfEntries--;
        return true;
    }
    else {
        return false;
    }
}
```

This allows a client to use an if statement to guard statements that depend on the successful removal of an entry:

```
if(addresses.removeDetails("...")) {
    // Entry successfully removed. Continue as normal.
    ...
}
else {
    // The removal failed. Attempt a recovery, if possible.
    ...
}
```

Where a server method already has a non-void return type – effectively preventing a boolean diagnostic value from being returned – there may still be a way to indicate that an error has occurred through the return type. This will be the case if a value from the return type's range is available to act as an error diagnostic value. For instance, the getDetails method returns a ContactDetails object corresponding to a given key, and the example below assumes that a particular key will locate a valid set of contact details:

```
// Send David a text message.
ContactDetails details = addresses.getDetails("David");
String phone = details.getPhone();
...
```

One way for the `getDetails` method to indicate that the key is invalid or not in use is to have it return a `null` value instead of a `ContactDetails` object (Code 12.4).

Code 12.4

Returning an out-of-bounds error diagnostic value

```
/**
 * Look up a name or phone number and return the
 * corresponding contact details.
 * @param key The name or number to be looked up.
 * @return The details corresponding to the key, or
 *         null if the key is not in use.
 */
public ContactDetails getDetails(String key)
{
    if(keyInUse(key)) {
        return (ContactDetails) book.get(key);
    }
    else {
        return null;
    }
}
```

This would allow a client to examine the result of the call and then either continue with the normal flow of control, or attempt to recover from the error:

```
ContactDetails details = addresses.getDetails("David");
if(details != null) {
    // Send a text message to David.
    String phone = details.getPhone();
    ...
}
else {
    // Failed to find the entry. Attempt a recovery, if possible.
    ...
}
```

It is common for methods that return object references to use the `null` value as a failure or error indication. With methods that return primitive-type values, there will sometimes be an out-of bounds value that can fulfill a similar rôle: for instance, the `indexOf` method of the `String` class returns a negative value to indicate that it has failed to find the character sought.

Exercise 12.17 Using a copy of the *address-book-v2t* project, make changes to the **AddressBook** class, where appropriate, to provide failure information to a client when a method has received incorrect parameter values, or is otherwise unable to complete its task.

Exercise 12.18 Do you think the different interface styles of the *v2t* and *v2g* projects mean that there should be any difference in the way that errors are reported to users?

Exercise 12.19 Are there any combinations of argument values that you think would be inappropriate to pass to the constructor of the `ContactDetails` class?

Exercise 12.20 Do you think that a call to the `search` method that finds no matches requires an error notification? Justify your answer.

Exercise 12.21 Does a constructor have any means to indicate to a client that it cannot set up the new object's state correctly? What should a constructor do if it receives inappropriate arguments?

Clearly, this approach cannot be used where all values from the return type already have valid meanings to the client. In such cases, it will usually be necessary to resort to the alternative technique of *throwing an exception* (see section 12.4), which does, in fact, offer some significant advantages. To help you appreciate why this might be, it is worth considering two issues associated with the use of return values as failure or error indicators:

- Unfortunately, there is no way to require the client to check the return value for its diagnostic properties. As a consequence, a client could easily carry on as if nothing has happened; it could then end up terminating with a `NullPointerException`; or – worse than that – it could even use the diagnostic return value as if it were a normal return value, creating a difficult-to-diagnose logical error!
- In some cases, we may be using the diagnostic value for two quite different purposes. This is the case in the revised `removeDetails` (Code 12.3) and `getDetails` (Code 12.4). One purpose is to tell the client whether their request was successful or not. The other is to indicate that there was something wrong with their request, such as passing bad argument values.

In many cases, an unsuccessful request will not represent a logical programming error, whereas an incorrect request almost certainly does. We should expect quite different responses from a client in these two cases. There is no general satisfactory way to resolve this conflict simply by using return values.

12.4 Exception-throwing principles

Concept:

An **exception** is an object representing details of a program failure. An exception is thrown to indicate that a failure has occurred.

Throwing an exception is the most effective way that a server object has of indicating that it is unable to fulfill a client request. One of the major advantages this has over using a special return value is that it is (almost) impossible for a client to ignore the fact that an exception has been thrown and carry on regardless. Failure by the client to handle an exception will result in the application terminating immediately. In addition, the exception mechanism is independent from the return value of a method and can be used for all methods, irrespective of what value they return.

12.4.1 Throwing an exception

Code 12.5 shows how an exception is thrown using a *throw statement* within a method. Here, the `getDetails` method is throwing an exception to indicate that passing a `null` value for the key does not make sense.

Code 12.5

Throwing an exception

```java
/**
 * Look up a name or phone number and return the
 * corresponding contact details.
 * @param key The name or number to be looked up.
 * @return The details corresponding to the key,
 *          or null if there are none matching.
 * @throws NullPointerException if the key is null.
 */
public ContactDetails getDetails(String key)
{
    if(key == null){
        throw new NullPointerException(
            "null key in getDetails");
    }
    return (ContactDetails) book.get(key);
}
```

There are two stages to throwing an exception. First an exception object is created (in this case a `NullPointerException` object); then the exception object is thrown using the `throw` key word. These two stages are almost invariably combined in a single statement:

```java
throw new ExceptionType("optional-diagnostic-string");
```

When an exception object is created, a diagnostic string may be passed to its constructor. This string is later available to the receiver of the exception via either the exception object's `getMessage` accessor or its `toString` method.

Code 12.5 also illustrates that the documentation for a method can be expanded to include details of any exceptions it throws, using the javadoc `@throws` tag.

12.4.2 Exception classes

An exception object is always an instance of a class from a special inheritance hierarchy. We can create new exception types by creating subclasses in this hierarchy (Figure 12.1). Strictly speaking, exception classes are always subclasses of the `Throwable` class that is defined in the `java.lang` package. We shall follow the convention of defining and using exception classes that are subclasses of the `Exception` class, also defined in `java.lang`.[1] The `java.lang` package defines a number of commonly seen exception classes that you might already have run across inadvertently in developing programs, such as `Null-PointerException`, `IndexOutOfBoundsException`, and `ClassCastException`.

Java divides exception classes into two categories: *checked exceptions* and *unchecked exceptions*. All subclasses of the Java standard class `RuntimeException` are unchecked exceptions; all other subclasses of `Exception` are checked exceptions.

Figure 12.1 The exception class hierarchy

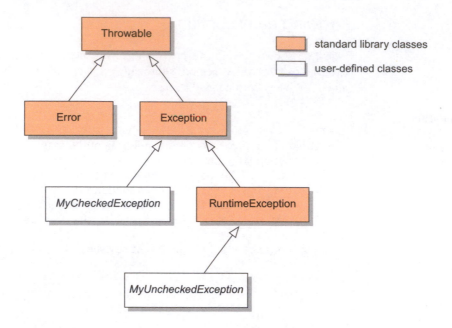

Slightly simplified, the difference is this: checked exceptions are intended for cases where the client should expect that an operation could fail (for example, if we write to a disk, we know that the disk could be full). In these cases, the client should be forced to check whether the operation was successful. Unchecked exceptions are intended for cases that should never fail in normal operation – they usually indicate a program error.

Unfortunately, knowing which category of exception to throw in any particular circumstance is not an exact science, but we can offer the following general advice:

■ One rule of thumb that can be applied is to use unchecked exceptions for situations that should lead to program failure – typically because it is suspected that there is a logical error in the program that will prevent it from continuing any further. It follows that checked exceptions should be used where a problem has arisen but where there may be a possibility of the client effecting a recovery. One problem with this policy is that it assumes that the server is aware enough of the context in which it is being used to be able to determine whether client recovery is likely to be possible or not.

■ Another rule of thumb is to use unchecked exceptions for situations that could reasonably be avoided. For instance, using an invalid index in an array access is the result of a logical programming error that is completely avoidable, and the fact that the `Array-IndexOutOfBoundsException` exception is unchecked fits this model. It follows that checked exceptions should be used for failure situations that are beyond the control of the programmer, such as a disk becoming full when trying to write to a file.

The formal Java rules governing the use of exceptions are significantly different for unchecked and checked exceptions, and we shall outline the differences in detail in

---

[1] `Exception` is one of two direct subclasses of `Throwable`; the other is `Error`. Subclasses of `Error` are usually reserved for runtime-system errors rather than errors over which the programmer has control.

sections 12.4.4 and 12.5.1 respectively. In simplified terms, the rules ensure that a client object calling a method that could throw a checked exception will contain both code that anticipates the possibility of a problem arising and code that attempts to handle the problem whenever it occurs.[2]

Exercise 12.22 List three exception types from the `java.io` package.

Exercise 12.23 Is `SecurityException` from the `java.lang` package a checked or an unchecked exception? What about `NoSuchMethodException`?

12.4.3 The effect of an exception

What happens when an exception is thrown? There are really two effects to consider: the effect in the method where the exception is thrown, and the effect in the caller.

When an exception is thrown, the execution of the throwing method finishes immediately – it does not continue to the end of the method body. A particular consequence of this is that a method with a non-void return type is not required to execute a return statement on a route that throws an exception. This is reasonable, because throwing an exception is an indication of the throwing method's inability to continue normal execution, which includes not being able to return a valid result. We can illustrate this principle with the following alternative version of the method body shown in Code 12.5:

```
if(key == null) {
    throw new NullPointerException("null key in getDetails");
}
else {
    return (ContactDetails) book.get(key);
}
```

The absence of a return statement in the route that throws an exception is acceptable. Indeed, the compiler will indicate an error if any statements are written following a throw statement, because they could never be executed.

The effect of an exception on the point in the program that called the method is a little more complex. In particular, the full effect depends upon whether or not any code has been written to *catch* the exception. Consider the following contrived call to `getDetails`:

```
AddressDetails details = addresses.getDetails(null);
// The following statement will not be reached.
String phone = details.getPhone();
```

We *can* say that in all cases the execution of these statements will be left incomplete – the exception thrown by `getDetails` will interrupt the execution of the first statement, and no assignment will be made to the `details` variable. As a result, the second statement will not be executed, either.

---

[2] In fact, it is still all too easy for the writer of the client to adhere to the rules in principle, but to fail to attempt a proper recovery from the problem.

This neatly illustrates the power of exceptions to prevent a client from carrying on regardless of the fact that a problem has arisen. What actually happens next depends upon whether or not the exception is caught. If it isn't caught, then the program will simply terminate with an indication that an uncaught `NullPointerException` has been thrown. We shall discuss how to catch an exception in section 12.5.2.

12.4.4 Unchecked exceptions

Unchecked exceptions are the easiest to use from a programmer's point of view, because the compiler enforces few rules on their use. This is the meaning of 'unchecked' – the compiler does not apply special checks either on the method in which an unchecked exception is thrown, or on the place from where the method is called. An exception class is unchecked if it is a subclass of the `RuntimeException` class, defined in the `java.lang` package. All of the examples we have used so far to illustrate exception throwing have involved unchecked exceptions. So there is little further to add here about how to throw an unchecked exception: simply use a throw statement.

If we also follow the convention that unchecked exceptions should be used in those situations where we expect the result to be program termination – i.e. the exception is not going to be caught – then there is also nothing further to be discussed about what the method's caller should do, because it will do nothing and let the program fail. However, if there is a need to catch an unchecked exception then an exception handler *can* be written for it, exactly as for a checked exception. How to do this is described in section 12.5.2.

A commonly used unchecked exception is `IllegalArgumentException`. This is thrown by a constructor or method to indicate that its argument values are inappropriate. For instance, the `getDetails` method might throw this if the key string passed to it is blank (Code 12.6).

Code 12.6

Checking for an illegal argument

```java
/**
 * Look up a name or phone number and return the
 * corresponding contact details.
 * @param key The name or number to be looked up.
 * @throws NullPointerException if the key is null.
 * @throws IllegalArgumentException if the key is blank.
 * @return The details corresponding to the key,
 *         or null if there are none matching.
 */
public ContactDetails getDetails(String key)
{
    if(key == null) {
        throw new NullPointerException(
            "null key in getDetails");
    }
    if(key.trim().length() == 0) {
        throw new IllegalArgumentException(
                    "Empty key passed to getDetails");
    }
    return (ContactDetails) book.get(key);
}
```

It is well worth having a method conduct a series of validity checks on its arguments before proceeding with the main purpose of the method. This makes it less likely that a method will get part way through its actions before having to throw an exception because of bad argument values. A particular reason for avoiding this situation is that partial mutation of an object is likely to leave it in an inconsistent state for future use. If an operation fails for any reason, the object should ideally be left in the state it was in before the operation was attempted.

> **Exercise 12.24** Review all of the methods of the **AddressBook** class and decide whether any of them should throw an **IllegalArgumentException**. If so, add the necessary checks and throw statements.
>
> **Exercise 12.25** If you have not already done so, add javadoc documentation to describe any exceptions thrown by methods in the **AddressBook** class.

12.4.5 Preventing object creation

An important use for exceptions is to prevent objects from being created if they cannot be placed in a valid initial state. This will usually be the result of inappropriate arguments being passed to a constructor. We can illustrate this with the `ContactDetails` class. The constructor is currently fairly forgiving of the argument values it receives: it does not reject `null` values but replaces them with empty strings. However, the address book needs at least a name or phone number from each entry to use as a unique index value, so an entry with both `name` and `phone` fields blank would be impossible to index. We can reflect this requirement by preventing construction of a `ContactDetails` object in such a case. The process of throwing an exception from a constructor is exactly the same as throwing one from a method. Code 12.7 shows the revised constructor that will prevent an entry from ever having both blank `name` and `phone` fields.

Code 12.7

The constructor of the `ContactDetails` class

```java
/**
 * Set up the contact details. All details are trimmed to remove
 * trailing white space. Either name or phone must be non-blank.
 * @param name The name.
 * @param phone The phone number.
 * @param address The address.
 * @throws IllegalStateException If both name and phone are blank.
 */
public ContactDetails(String name, String phone, String address)
{
    // Use blank strings if any of the arguments is null.
    if(name == null) {
        name = "";
    }
    if(phone == null) {
        phone = "";
    }
```

Code 12.7 continued

The constructor of the `ContactDetails` class

```
    if(address == null) {
        address = "";
    }

    this.name = name.trim();
    this.phone = phone.trim();
    this.address = address.trim();

    if(this.name.length() == 0 && this.phone.length() == 0) {
        throw new IllegalStateException(
                "Either the name or phone must not be blank.");
    }
}
```

An exception thrown from a constructor has the same effect on the client as an exception thrown from a method. So the following attempt to create an invalid `ContactDetails` object will completely fail; it will not result in a `null` value being stored in the variable:

```
ContactDetails badDetails = new ContactDetails("", "", "");
```

12.5 Exception handling

The principles of exception throwing apply equally to both unchecked and checked exceptions, but the particular rules of Java mean that exception handling becomes a requirement only with checked exceptions. A checked exception class is one that is a subclass of `Exception` but not of `RuntimeException`. There are several more rules to follow when using checked exceptions, because the compiler enforces checks both in a method that throws a checked exception, and in the caller of that method.

12.5.1 Checked exceptions: the throws clause

Concept:

Checked exceptions are a type of exception whose use will require extra checks from the compiler. In particular, checked exceptions in Java require the use of throws clauses and try statements.

The first requirement of the compiler is that a method throwing a checked exception must declare that it does so in a *throws clause* added to the method's header. For instance, a method throwing a checked `IOException` from the `java.io` package might have the following header:[3]

```
public void saveToFile(String destinationFile)
    throws IOException
```

It is permitted to use a throws clause for unchecked exceptions, but the compiler does not require one. We recommend that a throws clause be used only to list the checked exceptions thrown by a method.

It is important to distinguish between a throws clause in the header of a method, and the javadoc comment that precedes the method; the latter is completely optional for both types of exception. Nevertheless, we recommend that javadoc documentation be included for both checked and unchecked exceptions. In that way, as much information as possible will be available to someone wishing to use that particular method.

---

[3] Note that the key word here is `throws` and not `throw`, which is used in a throw statement.

12.5.2   Catching exceptions: the try statement

The second requirement is that a caller of a method that throws a checked exception must make provision for dealing with the exception. This usually means writing an *exception handler* in the form of a *try statement*. Most practical try statements have the general form shown in Code 12.8. This introduces two new Java key words – `try` and `catch` – which mark a *try block* and a *catch block* respectively.

Code 12.8

The try and catch blocks of an exception handler

```
try {
    Protect one or more statements here.
}
catch(Exception e) {
    Report and recover from the exception here.
}
```

Concept:

Program code that protects statements in which an exception might be thrown is called an **exception handler**. It provides reporting and/or recovery code should one arise.

Code 12.9 illustrates a try statement as part of a method that saves the contents of an address book to a file. The user is requested in some way for the name of a file (perhaps via a GUI dialog window), and the address book's `saveToFile` method is then called to write out the list to the file. Because the writing process could fail with an exception, the call to `saveToFile` must be enclosed within a try block. Note that any number of statements can be included in a try block. The catch block will attempt to catch exceptions from any statement within the preceding try block.

Code 12.9

An exception handler

```
String filename = null;
try {
    filename = request-a-file-from-the-user;
    addressbook.saveToFile(filename);
}
catch(IOException e) {
    System.out.println("Unable to save to " + filename);
}
```

In order to understand how an exception handler works it is essential to appreciate that an exception prevents the normal flow of control in the caller from being continued. An exception interrupts the execution of the caller's statement that caused it, and hence any statements immediately following the problem statement will also not be executed. The question then arises, 'Where is execution resumed in the caller?' A try statement provides the answer: If an exception arises from a statement called in the try block, then execution is resumed in the corresponding catch block. So, if we consider the example in Code 12.9, the effect of an `IOException` being thrown from the call to `saveToFile` will be that control will transfer from the try block to the catch block, as shown in Code 12.10.

Statements in a try block are known as *protected statements*. If no exception arises during execution of protected statements then the catch block will be skipped over when the end of the try block is reached. Execution will continue with whatever follows the complete try statement.

1. Exception thrown from here

2. Control transfers to here

```
try {
    addressbook.saveToFile(filename);
    tryAgain = false;
}
catch(IOException e) {
    System.out.println("Unable to save to " + filename);
    tryAgain = true;
}
```

A catch block names the type of exception it is designed to deal with in a pair of parentheses immediately following the `catch` word. As well as the exception type name, this also includes a variable name (traditionally simply 'e') that can be used to refer to the exception object that was thrown. Having a reference to this object can be useful in providing information that will support recovery from the problem. Once the catch block has been completed, control does *not* return to the statement that caused the exception.

Exercise 12.26 The *address-book-v3t* project includes some throwing of unchecked exceptions if argument values are null. The project also includes the checked exception class `NoMatchingDetailsException`, which is currently unused. Modify the `removeDetails` method of `AddressBook` so that it throws this exception if its key argument is not a key that is in use. Add an exception handler to the `remove` method of `AddressBookTextInterface` to catch and report occurrences of this exception.

Exercise 12.27 Make use of `NoMatchingDetailsException` in the `changeDetails` method of `AddressBook`. Enhance the user interface so that the details of an existing entry may be changed. Catch and report exceptions in `AddressBookTextInterface` that arise from use of a key that does not match any existing entry.

Exercise 12.28 Why is the following not a sensible way to use an exception handler?

```
Person p;
try {
    p = database.lookup(details);
}
catch(Exception e) {
}
System.out.println("The details belong to: " + p);
```

12.5.3   Throwing and catching multiple exceptions

Sometimes a method throws more than one type of exception in order to indicate different sorts of problem. Where these are checked exceptions they must all be listed in the throws clause of the method, separated by commas. For instance:

```
public void process()
      throws EOFException, FileNotFoundException
```

An exception handler must cater for all checked exceptions thrown from its protected statements, so a try statement may contain multiple catch blocks, as shown in Code 12.11. Note that the same variable name can be used for the exception object in each case.

```java
try {
    ...
    ref.process();
    ...
}
catch(EOFException e) {
    // Take action appropriate to an end-of-file exception.
    ...
}
catch(FileNotFoundException e) {
    // Take action appropriate to a file-not-found exception.
    ...
}
```

When an exception is thrown by a method call in a try block, the catch blocks are checked in the order in which they are written until a match is found for the exception type. So, if an EOFException is thrown then control will transfer to the first catch block, and if a FileNotFoundException is thrown then control will transfer to the second. Once the end of a single catch block is reached, execution continues below the last catch block.

Polymorphism can be used to avoid writing multiple catch blocks, if desired. However, this could be at the expense of being able to take type-specific recovery actions. In Code 12.12, the single catch block will handle *any* exception thrown by the protected statements. This is because the exception-matching process that looks for an appropriate catch block simply checks that the exception object is an instance of the type named in the block. As all exceptions are subtypes of the Exception class, the single block will catch everything – whether checked or unchecked. From the nature of the matching process, it follows that the order of catch blocks in a single try statement matters, and that a catch block for a particular exception type cannot follow a block for one of its supertypes – because the earlier supertype block will always match before the subtype block is checked.

Code 12.12

Catching all
exceptions in a
single catch block

```java
try {
    ...
    ref.process();
    ...
}
catch(Exception e) {
    // Take action appropriate to all exceptions.
    ...
}
```

Exercise 12.29 Enhance the try statements you wrote as solutions to exercises 12.26 and 12.27, so that they handle checked and unchecked exceptions in different catch blocks.

Exercise 12.30 What is wrong with the following try statement?

```java
try {
    Person p = database.lookup(details);
    System.out.println("The details belong to: " + p);
}
catch(Exception e) {
    // Handle any checked exceptions ...
    ...
}
catch(RuntimeException e) {
    // Handle any unchecked exceptions ...
    ...
}
```

12.5.4 Propagating an exception

So far, we have suggested that an exception must be caught and handled at the earliest possible opportunity. That is, an exception thrown in a method `process` would have to be caught and handled in the method that called `process`. In fact, this is not strictly the case, as Java allows an exception to be *propagated* from a receiving method to its caller, and possibly beyond. A method propagates an exception simply by not including an exception handler to protect the statement that might throw it. However, for a checked exception, the compiler requires that the propagating method include a throws clause, even though it does not, itself, throw the exception. If the exception is unchecked, then the throws clause is optional, and we prefer to omit it.

Propagation is common where the calling method is either unable to, or does not need to, undertake any recovery action itself, but this might be possible or necessary from within higher-level calls.

12.5.5 The finally clause

A try statement can include a third component that is optional. This is the *finally clause* (Code 12.13), and it is often omitted. The finally clause provides for statements that should be executed whether an exception is thrown by the protected statements or not. If control reaches the end of the try block then the catch blocks are skipped and the finally clause is executed. Conversely, if an exception is thrown from the try block, then the appropriate catch block is executed and this is then followed by execution of the finally clause.

Code 12.13

A try statement with a finally clause

```
try {
    Protect one or more statements here.
}
catch(Exception e) {
    Report and recover from the exception here.
}
finally {
    Perform any actions here common to whether or not
    an exception is thrown.
}
```

At first sight, a finally clause would appear to be redundant. Doesn't the following example illustrate the same flow-of-control as Code 12.13?

```
try {
    Protect one or more statements here.
}
catch(Exception e) {
    Report and recover from the exception here.
}
Perform any actions here common to whether or not
an exception is thrown.
```

In fact, there are at least two cases where these two examples would have different effects:

- A finally clause is executed even if a return statement is executed in the try or catch blocks.
- If an exception is thrown in the try block, but not caught, then the finally clause is still executed.

In the latter case, the uncaught exception could be an unchecked exception that does not require a catch block, for instance. However, it could also be a checked exception that is not handled by a catch block but propagated from a method. In such a case, the finally clause would still be executed. As a consequence, it is possible to have zero catch blocks in a try statement that has both a try block and a finally clause:

```
try{
    Protect one or more statements here.
}
finally{
    Perform any actions here common to whether or not
    an exception is thrown.
}
```

12.6 Defining new exception classes

Where the standard exception classes do not satisfactorily describe the nature of the problem, new, more descriptive, exception classes can be defined using inheritance. New checked exception classes can be defined as subclasses of any existing checked exception class (such as `Exception`), and new unchecked exceptions would be subclasses in the `RuntimeException` hierarchy.

All existing exception classes support the inclusion of a diagnostic string passed to a constructor. However, one of the main reasons for defining new exception classes is to include further information within the exception object to support error diagnosis and recovery. For instance, some methods in the address-book application, such as `change-Details`, take a `key` argument that should match an existing entry. If no matching entry can be found then this represents a programming error, as the methods cannot complete their task. In reporting the exception, it is helpful to include details of the key that caused the error. Code 12.14 shows a new checked exception class that is defined in the *address-book-v3t* project. It receives the key in its constructor, and then makes it available through both the diagnostic string and a dedicated accessor method. If this exception were to be caught by an exception handler, the key would be available to the statements that attempt to recover from the error.

Code 12.14

An exception class with extra diagnostic information

```java
/**
 * Capture a key that failed to match an entry
 * in the address book.
 *
 * @author David J. Barnes and Michael Kölling.
 * @version 2002.05.14
 */
public class NoMatchingDetailsException extends Exception
{
    // The key with no match.
    private String key;

    /**
     * Store the details in error.
     * @param key The key with no match.
     */
    public NoMatchingDetailsException(String key)
    {
        this.key = key;
    }

    /**
     * @return The key in error.
     */
    public String getKey()
    {
        return key;
    }
}
```

Code 12.14 continued

An exception class with extra diagnostic information

```java
/**
 * @return A diagnostic string containing the key in error.
 */
public String toString()
{
    return "No details matching '" + key + "' were found.";
}
}
```

The principle of including information that could support error recovery should particularly be kept in mind when defining new checked exception classes. Defining formal parameters in an exception's constructor will help to ensure that diagnostic information is available. In addition, where recovery is either not possible or not attempted, ensuring that the exception's toString method is overridden to include appropriate information will help in diagnosing the reason for the error.

Exercise 12.31 In the *address-book-v3t* project, define a new checked exception class: DuplicateKeyException. This should be thrown by the addDetails method if either of the non-blank key fields of its argument is already currently in use. The exception class should store details of the offending key(s). Make any further changes to the user interface class that are necessary to catch and report the exception.

Exercise 12.32 Do you feel that DuplicateKeyException should be a checked or unchecked exception? Give reasons for your answer.

12.7 Using assertions

12.7.1 Internal consistency checks

When we design or implement a class we often have an intuitive sense of things that should be true at a given point in the execution, but rarely state them formally. For instance, we would expect a ContactDetails object to always contain at least one non-blank field, or, when the removeDetails method is called with a particular key, we would expect that key to be no longer in use at the end of the method. Typically these are conditions we wish to establish while developing a class, before it is released. In one sense, the sort of testing we discussed in Chapter 6 is an attempt to establish whether we have implemented an accurate representation of what a class or method should do. Characteristic of that style of testing is that the tests are *external* to the class being tested. If a class is changed then we should take the time to run regression tests in order to establish that it still works as it should, and it is easy to forget to do that. The practice of checking arguments, which we have introduced in this chapter, slightly shifts the emphasis from wholly external checking to a combination of external and internal checking.

However, argument checking is primarily intended to protect a server object from incorrect usage by a client. That still leaves the question of whether we can include some internal checks to ensure that the server object behaves as it should.

One way we could implement internal checking during development would be through the normal exception-throwing mechanism. In practice we would have to use unchecked exceptions because we could not expect regular clients classes to include exception handlers for what are essentially internal server errors. We would then be faced with the issue of whether to remove these internal checks once the development process has been completed, in order to avoid the potentially high cost of runtime checks that are almost certainly bound to pass.

12.7.2 The assert statement

In order to deal with the need to perform efficient internal consistency checks, which can be turned on in development code but off in released code, an *assertion facility* was introduced into Java from version 1.4 of the SDK. The *address-book-assert* project is a development version of the address book projects that illustrates how assertions are used. Code 12.15 shows the `removeDetails` method, which contains two forms of the *assert statement*.

Code 12.15

Using assertions for internal consistency checks

```java
/**
 * Remove the entry with the given key from the address book.
 * The key should be one that is currently in use.
 * @param key One of the keys of the entry to be removed.
 * @throws IllegalArgumentException If the key is null.
 */
public void removeDetails(String key)
{
    if(key == null){
        throw new IllegalArgumentException(
            "Null key passed to removeDetails.");
    }
    if(keyInUse(key)) {
        ContactDetails details = (ContactDetails) book.get(key);
        book.remove(details.getName());
        book.remove(details.getPhone());
        numberOfEntries--;
    }
    assert !keyInUse(key);
    assert consistentSize() :
            "Inconsistent book size in removeDetails";
}
```

Concept:

An **assertion** is a statement of a fact that should be true in normal program execution. We can use assertions to state our assumptions explicitly, and to detect programming errors more easily.

The `assert` key word is followed by a boolean expression. The purpose of the statement is to assert something that should be true at this point in the method. For instance, the first assert statement in Code 12.15 asserts that `keyInUse` should return false at that point, either because the key wasn't in use in the first place or because it is no longer in use as the associated details have now been removed from the address book. This seemingly obvious assertion is more important than might at first appear; notice that the removal process does not actually involve use of the key with the address book.

Thus an assert statement serves two purposes. It expresses explicitly what we assume to be true at a given point in the execution, and therefore increases readability both for the current developer and for a future maintenance programmer, and it actually performs the check so that we get notified if our assumption turns out to be incorrect. This can greatly help in finding errors early and easily.

If the boolean expression in an assert statement evaluates to `true`, then the assert statement has no further effect. If the statement evaluates to false then an `AssertionError` will be thrown. This is a subclass of `Error` (see Figure 12.1) and is part of the hierarchy regarded as representing unrecoverable errors: hence no handler should be provided in clients.

The second assert statement in Code 12.15 illustrates the alternative form of assert statement. The string following the colon symbol will be passed to the constructor of `AssertionError` to provide a diagnostic string. The second expression does not have to be an explicit string; any value-giving expression is acceptable and will be turned into a `String` before being passed to the constructor.

The first assert statement shows that an assertion will often make use of an existing method within the class (`keyInUse`). The second example illustrates that it might be useful to provide a method specifically for the purpose of performing an assertion test (`consistentSize` in this example). This might be used if the check involves significant computation. Code 12.16 shows the `consistentSize` method whose purpose is to ensure that the `numberOfEntries` field accurately represents the number of unique details in the address book.

Code 12.16

Checking for internal consistency in the address book

```
/**
 * Check that the numberOfEntries field is consistent with
 * the number of entries actually stored in the address book.
 * @return true if the field is consistent, false otherwise.
 */
private boolean consistentSize()
{
    Collection allEntries = book.values();
    // Eliminate duplicates as we are using multiple keys.
    Set uniqueEntries = new HashSet(allEntries);
    int actualCount = uniqueEntries.size();
    return numberOfEntries == actualCount;
}
```

12.7.3 Guidelines for using assertions

Assertions are primarily intended to provide a way to perform consistency checks during the development and testing phases of a project. They are not intended to be used in released code. It is for this reason that a Java compiler will include assert statements in the compiled code only if requested to do so. It follows that assert statements should never be used to perform normal functionality. For instance, it would be wrong to combine assertions with removal of details, as follows, in the address book:

```
// Error: don't use assert with normal processing!
assert book.remove(details.getName()) != null;
assert book.remove(details.getPhone()) != null;
```

Exercise 12.33 Open the *address-book-assert* project. Look through the **AddressBook** class and identify all of the assert statements to be sure that you understand what is being checked and why.

Exercise 12.34 The **AddressBookDemo** class contains several test methods that call methods of **AddressBook** that contain assert statements. Look through the source of **AddressBookDemo** to check that you understand the tests, and then try out each of the test methods. Are any assertion errors generated? If so, do you understand why?

Exercise 12.35 The **changeDetails** method of **AddressBook** currently has no assert statements. One assertion we could make about it is that the address book should contain the same number of entries at the end of the method as it did at the start. Add an assert statement (and any other statements you might need) to check this. Run the **testChange** method of **AddressBookDemo** after doing so. Do you think this method should also include the check for a consistent size?

Exercise 12.36 Suppose that we decide to allow the address book to be indexed by address as well as name and phone number. If we simply add the following statement to the **addDetails** method

```
book.put(details.getAddress(), details);
```

do you anticipate that any assertions will now fail? Try it. Make any further necessary changes to **AddressBook** to ensure that all of the assertions are now successful.

Exercise 12.37 **ContactDetails** are immutable objects – that is, they have no mutator methods. How important is this fact to the internal consistency of an **AddressBook**? Suppose the **ContactDetails** class had a **setPhone** method, for instance? Can you devise some tests to illustrate the problems this could cause?

12.7.4 Assertions and the BlueJ unit testing framework

In Chapter 6 we introduced the support that BlueJ provides for the JUnit unit-testing framework. That support is based on the assertion facility we have been discussing in this section. Methods from the framework, such as `assertEquals`, are built around an assertion statement that contains a boolean expression made up from their arguments. If JUnit test classes are used to test classes containing their own assertion statements, then assertion errors from these statements will be reported in the test-results window along with test-class assertion failures. The *address-book-junit* project contains a test class to illustrate this combination. The `testAddDetailsError` method of `TestAddressBook` will trigger an assertion error because `addDetails` should not be used to change existing details (see exercise 12.31).

12.8 Error recovery and avoidance

So far, the main focus of this chapter has been on the problem of identifying errors in a server object, and ensuring that any problem is reported back to the client if appropriate. There are two complementary issues that go with error reporting: error recovery, and error avoidance.

12.8.1 Error recovery

The first requirement of successful error recovery is that clients take note of any error notification that they receive. This may sound obvious, but it is not uncommon for a programmer to assume that a method call will not fail, and so not bother to check the return value. While ignoring errors is harder to do when exceptions are used, we have often seen the equivalent of the following approach to exception handling:

```java
AddressDetails details = null;
try {
    details = addresses.getDetails(...);
}
catch(Exception e) {
    System.out.println("Error: " + e);
}
String phone = details.getPhone();
```

The exception has been caught and reported, but no account has been taken of the fact that it is probably incorrect just to carry on regardless.

Java's try statement is the key to supplying an error-recovery mechanism when an exception is thrown. Recovery from an error will usually involve taking some form of corrective action within the catch block, and then trying again. Repeated attempts can be made by placing the try statement in a loop. An example of this approach is shown in Code 12.17, which is an expanded version of Code 12.9. The efforts to compose an alternative file name could involve trying a list of possible folders, for instance, or prompting an interactive user for different names.

Code 12.17

An attempt at error recovery

```java
// Try to save the address book.
boolean successful = false;
int attempts = 0;
do {
    try {
        addressbook.saveToFile(filename);
        successful = true;
    }
    catch(IOException e) {
        System.out.println("Unable to save to " + filename);
        attempts++;
        if(attempts < MAX_ATTEMPTS) {
            filename = an alternative file name;
        }
    }
} while(!successful && attempts < MAX_ATTEMPTS);
if(!successful) {
    Report the problem and give up;
}
```

Although this example illustrates recovery for a specific situation, the principles it illustrates are more general:

- Anticipating an error, and recovering from it, will usually require a more complex flow-of control than if an error cannot occur.
- The statements in the catch block are key to setting up the recovery attempt.
- Recovery will often involve having to try again.
- Successful recovery cannot be guaranteed.
- There should be some escape route from endlessly attempting hopeless recovery.

There won't always be a human user around to prompt for alternative input. It might be the client's responsibility to log the error.

12.8.2 Error avoidance

It should be clear that arriving at a situation where an exception is thrown will be, at worst, fatal to the execution of a program, and, at best, messy to recover from in the client. It can be simpler to try to avoid the error in the first place, but this often requires collaboration between server and client.

Many of the cases where an AddressBook object is forced to throw an exception involve null argument values passed to its methods. These represent logical programming errors in the client that could clearly be avoided by simple prior tests in the client. Null arguments are usually the result of making invalid assumptions in the client. For instance, consider the following example:

```
String key = postCodeDatabase.search(postCode);
ContactDetails university = book.getDetails(key);
...
```

If the database search fails, then the key it returns may well be either blank or null. Passing that result directly to the getDetails method will produce a runtime exception. However, using a simple test of the search result, the exception can be avoided, and the real problem of a failed postcode search can be addressed instead:

```
String key = postCodeDatabase.search(postCode);
if(key != null && key.length() > 0) {
    ContactDetails university = book.getDetails(key);
    ...
}
else {
    Deal with the postcode error ...
}
```

In this case the client could establish for itself that it would be inappropriate to call the server's method. This is not always possible, and sometimes the client must enlist the help of the server.

Exercise 12.31 established the principle that the addDetails method should not accept a new set of details if one of the key values is already in use for another set. In order to avoid an inappropriate call, the client could make use of the address book's keyInUse method, as follows:

```
// Add what should be a new set of details to the address book.
if(book.keyInUse(details.getName()) {
    book.changeDetails(details.getName(), details);
}
else if(book.keyInUse(details.getPhone()) {
    book.changeDetails(details.getPhone(), details);
}
else {
    Add the details ...
}
```

Using this approach, it is clearly possible to completely avoid a `Duplicate-KeyException` being thrown from `addDetails`, which suggests that it could be downgraded from a checked to an unchecked exception.

This particular example illustrates some important general principles:

- If a server's validity-check and state-test methods are visible to a client, the client will often be able to avoid causing the server to throw an exception.
- If an exception can be avoided in this way, then the exception being thrown really represents a logical programming error in the client. This suggests use of an unchecked exception for such situations.
- Using unchecked exceptions means that the client does not have to use a try statement when it has already established that the exception will not be thrown. This is a significant gain, because having to write try statements for 'cannot happen' situations is annoying for a programmer, and makes it less likely that providing proper recovery for genuine error situations will be taken seriously.

The effects are not all positive, however. Here are some reasons why this approach is not always practical:

- Making a server's validity-check and state-test methods publicly visible to its clients might represent a significant loss of encapsulation, and result in a higher degree of coupling between server and client than is desirable.
- It will probably not be safe for a server to assume that its clients *will* make the necessary checks that avoid an exception. As a result, those checks will often be duplicated in both client and server. If the checks are computationally 'expensive' to make, then duplication may be undesirable or prohibitive. However, our view would be that it is better to sacrifice supposed efficiency for the sake of safer programming, where the choice is available.

12.9 Case study: text input/output

An important programming area in which error recovery cannot be ignored is input/output. This is because the programmer of an application may have little direct control over the external environment in which that application runs. For instance, a data file required by an application may have been accidentally deleted, or become corrupted in some way, before the application is run; or an attempt to store results to the file system may be thwarted by exceeding a file-system quota. There are many ways in which an input or output operation could fail at any stage.

The Java API includes the java.io package, which contains numerous classes to support input/output operations in a platform-independent manner. The package defines the checked exception class, IOException, as a general indicator that something has gone wrong with an input/output operation. Further exception classes provide more detailed diagnostic information, such as EOFException and FileNotFoundException.

A full description of the many different classes in the java.io package is beyond the scope of this book, but we shall provide a short case study of how some textual input/output operations might be added to the address-book application. This should give you enough background to enable you to experiment with input/output in your own projects. In particular, using the *address-book-io* project, we shall illustrate the following common tasks:

■ writing textual output to a file with the FileWriter class;
■ reading textual input from a file with the FileReader and BufferedReader classes;
■ anticipating IOException exceptions thrown by the input/output classes.

In addition, the project includes methods to read and write binary versions of AddressBook and ContactDetails objects, should you wish to explore Java's *serialization* feature.

For further reading on input/output in Java, we recommend the Sun tutorial, which can be found online at:

    http://java.sun.com/docs/books/tutorial/essential/io/index.html

12.9.1   Readers, writers, and streams

Several of the classes of the java.io package fall into one of two main categories: those dealing with text files, and those dealing with binary files. We can think of text files as containing data in a form similar to Java's char type – typically simple, line-based, human-readable, alphanumeric information. Binary files are more varied: image files are one common example, as are executable programs, such as word processors. Classes concerned with text files are known as *readers* and *writers*, whereas those concerned with binary files are known as *stream* handlers. In this case study, we shall focus exclusively on readers and writers.

12.9.2   The *address-book-io* project

The *address-book-io* project is a version of the address-book application with the user interface removed for the sake of simplicity. It includes the additional class Address-BookFileHandler, part of which is shown in Code 12.18, whose sole purpose is to provide file-handling operations on an AddressBook object. File-handling operations include loading address book contents from a file, saving the contents back, and saving results of an address book search operation.

Code 12.18

The
AddressBookFile-
Handler class

```java
import java.io.*;
import java.net.URL;

/**
 * Provide a range of file-handling operations on an AddressBook.
 * These methods demonstrate a range of basic features of the
 * java.io package.
 *
 * @author David J. Barnes and Michael Kölling.
 * @version 2002.06.13
 */
public class AddressBookFileHandler
{
    // The address book on which i/o operations are performed.
    private AddressBook book;
    // The name of a file used to store search results.
    private static final String RESULTS_FILE = "results.txt";

    /**
     * Constructor for objects of class FileHandler.
     * @param book The address book to use.
     */
    public AddressBookFileHandler(AddressBook book)
    {
        this.book = book;
    }

    /**
     * Save the results of an address-book search to
     * the file "results.txt" in the project folder.
     * @param keyPrefix The key prefix to search on.
     */
    public void saveSearchResults(String keyPrefix)
        throws IOException
    {
        File resultsFile = makeAbsoluteFilename(RESULTS_FILE);
        ContactDetails[] results = book.search(keyPrefix);
        FileWriter writer = new FileWriter(resultsFile);
        for(int i = 0; i < results.length; i++) {
            writer.write(results[i].toString());
            writer.write('\n');
            writer.write('\n');
        }
        writer.close();
    }

    /**
     * Show the results from the most-recent call to
     * saveSearchResults. As output is to the console, any
     * problems are reported directly by this method.
     */
    public void showSearchResults()
```

```java
    {
        File resultsFile = makeAbsoluteFilename(RESULTS_FILE);
        BufferedReader reader = null;
        try {
            reader = new BufferedReader(
                        new FileReader(resultsFile));
            System.out.println("Results ...");
            String line;
            line = reader.readLine();
            while(line != null) {
                System.out.println(line);
                line = reader.readLine();
            }
            System.out.println();
        }
        catch(FileNotFoundException e) {
            System.out.println("Unable to find the file: " +
                                resultsFile);
        }
        catch(IOException e) {
            System.out.println(
                    "Error encountered reading the file: " +
                                resultsFile);
        }
        finally {
            if(reader != null) {
                // Catch any exception, but nothing can be done
                // about it.
                try {
                    reader.close();
                }
                catch(IOException e) {
                    System.out.println("Error on closing: " +
                                        resultsFile);
                }
            }
        }
    }

    // Other methods omitted. ...
}
```

The file-handler class is tightly coupled to the address book class, and you might feel that these two should really be a single class. However, by keeping them as distinct classes, each is thereby made more cohesive. In addition, by not embedding the input/output operations directly within AddressBook, it becomes much easier to create a range of alternative input/output solutions should they be required.

The following sections describe the ways in which classes from the java.io package are used to save and display the results of a search on an address book.

12.9.3 Text output with `FileWriter`

There are three steps involved in storing data in a file:

1. The file is opened.
2. The data is written.
3. The file is closed.

The nature of file output means that any of these steps could fail, for any number of reasons, many completely beyond the application programmer's control. As a consequence, it will be necessary to anticipate exceptions being thrown at every stage.

In order to write a text file, it is usual to create a `FileWriter` object, whose constructor takes the name of the file to be written. The file name can be either in the form of a string, or a `File` object. Creating a `FileWriter` has the effect of opening the external file and preparing it to receive some output. If the attempt to open the file fails for any reason, then the constructor will throw an `IOException`. Reasons for failure might be that file system permissions prevent a user from writing to certain files, or that the given file name does not match a valid location in the file system.

When a file has been opened successfully, then the writer's `write` methods can be used to store characters – often in the form of strings – into the file. Any attempt to write could fail, even if the file has been opened successfully. Such failures are rare, but still possible.

Once all output has been written, it is important to formally close the file. This ensures that all the data really has been written to the external file system, and it often has the effect of freeing some internal or external resources. Once again, on rare occasions, the attempt to close the file could fail.

The basic pattern that emerges from the above discussion might look like this:

```
try {
    FileWriter writer = new FileWriter("... name of file ...");
    while(there is more text to write) {
        ...
        writer.write(next piece of text);
        ...
    }
    writer.close();
}
catch(IOException e) {
    something went wrong with accessing the file
}
```

The main issue that arises is how to deal with any exceptions that are thrown during the three stages. An exception thrown when attempting to open a file is really the only one it is likely to be possible to do anything about, and only then if there is some way to generate an alternative name to try instead. As this will usually require the intervention of a human user of the application, the chances of dealing with it successfully are obviously application- and context-specific. If an attempt to write to the file fails, then it is unlikely that repeating the attempt will succeed. Similarly, failure to close a file is not usually worth a further attempt. The consequence is likely to be an incomplete file.

The difficulty of recovering from an exception thrown during file output is the main reason why the `saveSearchResults` method shown in Code 12.18 simply propagates the exception to its caller, as it may be appropriate to attempt recovery at a higher level of the application.

12.9.4 Text input with `FileReader`

The complement to the output of text with a `FileWriter` is the input with a `FileReader`. As you might expect, a complementary set of three input steps is required: opening the file, reading from it, and closing it. Whereas the natural units for writing text are characters and strings, the natural units for reading text are characters and lines. However, although the `FileReader` class contains a method to read a single character,[4] it does not contain a method to read a line. The problem with reading lines from a file is that there is no predefined limit to the length of a line. This means that any method to return the next complete line from a file must be able to read an arbitrary number of characters. For this reason, a `FileReader` object is usually wrapped in a `BufferedReader` object, because `BufferedReader` defines a `readLine` method. The line-termination character is always removed from the string it returns, and a `null` value is used to indicate the end of file.

This suggests the following basic pattern for reading the contents of a text file:

```
try {
    BufferedReader reader = new BufferedReader(
                            new FileReader("... name of file ..."));
    String line = reader.readLine();
    while(line != null) {
        do something with line
        line = reader.readLine();
    }
    reader.close();
}
catch(FileNotFoundException e) {
    the specified file could not be found
}
catch(IOException e) {
    something went wrong with reading or closing
}
```

As with output, the question arises as to what to do about any exceptions thrown during the whole process. The `File` class does provide methods that make it possible to reduce the likelihood of the file-opening operation failing. For instance, it defines query methods, such as `exists` and `canRead`, that allow a file's status to be checked in advance of its being opened. Such checks are not usually applicable when trying to write a file, because a file does not have to exist in advance to be written.

The `AddressBookFileHandler` class contains two different examples of the use of `FileReader` and `BufferedReader` objects. In particular, the `showSavedResults`

---

[4] In fact, its `read` method returns each character as an `int` value rather than as a `char`, because it uses an extra out-of-bounds value, −1, to indicate the end of file.

method, shown in Code 12.18, includes an example of how an attempt might be made to close a file on failure, but only if the file was successfully opened in the first place. Note that the `reader` variable has been defined *outside* the try block, so that it is available to the finally clause. Note, too, that any exception arising from the attempt to close the file requires a further try statement in the finally clause.

> **Exercise 12.38** Read the API documentation for the `File` class from the `java.io` package. What sort of information is available on files?
>
> **Exercise 12.39** How can you tell whether a file name represents an ordinary file or a directory (folder)?
>
> **Exercise 12.40** Is it possible to determine anything about the contents of a particular file from the information stored in a `File` object?

12.9.5 Object serialization

Concept:

Serialization allows whole objects, and object hierarchies, to be read and written in a single operation. Every object involved must be from a class that implements the `Serializable` interface.

As we noted in the introduction to section 12.9, the `AddressBookFileHandler` includes methods to read and write binary versions of `AddressBook` and `ContactDetails` objects. This utilizes a feature of Java known as *serialization*. In simple terms, serialization allows a whole object to be written to an external file in a single write operation, and read back in at a later stage using a single read operation.[5] This works with both simple objects and multi-component objects, such as collections. This is a significant feature that avoids having to read and write objects field by field, for instance. It is particularly useful in the address book project because it allows all entries created in one session to be saved and then read back in at a later session.

In order to be eligible to participate in serialization, a class must implement the `Serializable` interface that is defined in the `java.io` package. However, it is worth noting that this interface defines no methods. This means that the serialization process is managed automatically by the runtime system, and requires little user-defined code to be written. In our example, both `AddressBook` and `ContactDetails` implement this interface, so that they can be saved to a file.

> **Exercise 12.41** Modify the *tech-support* project from Chapter 5 so that it reads its key words and responses from a text file. That would permit external enhancement and configuration of the system without having to modify the sources.
>
> **Exercise 12.42** Modify the *world-of-zuul* project from Chapter 7 so that it writes a script of user input to a text file as a record of the game. Then make further modifications so that a saved game can be replayed from such a script.

---

[5] This is a simplification, because objects can also be written and read across a network, for instance, and not just within a file system.

12.10 Summary

When two objects interact, there is always the chance that something could go wrong, for a variety of reasons. For instance:

■ The programmer of a client might have misunderstood the state or the capabilities of a particular server object.

■ A server object may be unable to fulfill a client's request because of a particular set of external circumstances.

■ A client might have been programmed incorrectly, causing it to pass inappropriate arguments to a server method.

If something does go wrong, a program is likely either to terminate prematurely (i.e. crash!) or to produce incorrect and undesirable effects. We can go a long way toward avoiding many of these problems by using an exception-throwing mechanism. This provides a clearly defined way for an object to report to a client that something has gone wrong. Exceptions prevent a client from simply ignoring the problem, and encourage programmers to try to find an alternative course of action as a workaround if something does go wrong.

When developing a class, assert statements can be used to provide internal consistency checking. These are typically omitted from production code.

Terms introduced in this chapter

exception, unchecked exception, checked exception, exception handler, assertion, serialization

Concept summary

■ **exception** An exception is an object representing details of a program failure. An exception is thrown to indicate that a failure has occurred.

■ **unchecked exception** Unchecked exceptions are a type of exception whose use will not require checks from the compiler.

■ **checked exception** Checked exceptions are a type of exception whose use will require extra checks from the compiler. In particular, checked exceptions in Java require the use of throws clauses and try statements.

■ **exception handler** Program code that protects statements in which an exception might be thrown is called an exception handler. It provides reporting and/or recovery code should one arise.

■ **assertion** An assertion is a statement of a fact that should be true in normal program execution. We can use assertions to state our assumptions explicitly, and to detect programming errors more easily.

■ **serialization** Serialization allows whole objects, and object hierarchies, to be read and written in a single operation. Every object involved must be from a class that implements the `Serializable` interface.

Main concepts discussed in this chapter:

- discovering classes
- CRC cards
- designing interfaces
- patterns

Java constructs discussed in this chapter:

(No new Java constructs are introduced in this chapter.)

In previous chapters of this book we have described how to write good classes. We have discussed how to design them, how to make them maintainable and robust, and how to make them interact. All of this is important, but we have omitted one aspect of the task: finding the classes.

In all our previous examples we have assumed that we more or less know what the classes are that we should use to solve our problems. In a real software project, deciding what classes to use to implement a solution to a problem can be one of the most difficult tasks. In this chapter we discuss this aspect of the development process.

These initial steps of developing a software system are generally referred to as *analysis and design*. We analyze the problem, and then we design a solution. The first step of design will be at a higher level than the class design discussed in Chapter 7. We will think about what classes we should create to solve our problem, and how exactly they should interact. Once we have a solution to this problem, then we can continue with the design of individual classes and start thinking about their implementation.

13.1 Analysis and design

Analysis and design of software systems is a large and complex problem area. Discussing it in detail is far outside the scope of this book. Many different methodologies have been described in the literature and are used in practice for this task. In this chapter we aim only to give an introduction to the problems encountered in the process.

We will use a fairly simple method to address these tasks, which serves well for relatively small problems. To discover initial classes, we use the *verb/noun method*. Then we will use *CRC cards* to perform the initial application design.

13.1.1 The verb/noun method

This method is all about identifying classes and objects, and the associations and interactions between them. The nouns in a human language describe 'things,' such as people, buildings, and so on. The verbs describe 'actions,' such as writing, eating, and so on. From these natural-language concepts we can see that, in a description of a programming problem, the nouns will often correspond to classes and objects, whereas the verbs will correspond to the things those objects do: that is, to methods. We do not need a very long description to be able to illustrate this technique. The description typically needs to be only a few paragraphs in length.

The example we will use to discuss this process is the design of a cinema booking system.

13.1.2 The cinema booking example

This time, we will not start by extending an existing project. We now assume that we are in a situation where it is our task to create a new application from scratch. The task is to create a system that can be used by a company operating cinemas to handle bookings of seats for movie screenings. People often call in advance to reserve seats. The application should then be able to find empty seats for a requested screening and reserve them for the customer.

We will assume that we have had several meetings with the cinema operators, during which they have described to us the functionality they expect from the system. (Understanding what the expected functionality is, describing it, and agreeing about it with a client, is a significant problem in itself. This, however, is outside the scope of this book, and can be studied in other courses and other books.)

Here is the description we wrote for our cinema booking system:

> *The cinema booking system should store seat bookings for multiple theatres. Each theatre has seats arranged in rows. Customers can reserve seats, and are given a row number and seat number. They may request bookings of several adjoining seats.*

> *Each booking is for a particular show (that is, the screening of a given movie at a certain time). Shows are at an assigned date and time, and scheduled in a theatre where they are screened. The system stores the customer's telephone number.*

Given a reasonably clear description such as this, we can make a first attempt at discovering classes and methods by identifying the nouns and verbs in the text.

13.1.3 Discovering classes

The first step in identifying the classes is to go through the description and mark all the nouns and verbs in the text. Doing this, we find the following nouns and verbs. (The nouns are shown in the order in which they appear in the text; verbs are shown attached to the nouns they refer to.)

Nouns	**Verbs**
cinema booking system	*stores* (seat bookings)
	stores (telephone number)
seat booking	*has* (seats)
theatre	
seat	
row	
customer	*reserves* (seats)
	is given (row number, seat number)
	requests (seat booking)
row number	
seat number	
show	*is scheduled* (in theatre)
movie	
date	
time	
telephone number	

The nouns we identified here give us a first approximation for classes in our system. As a first cut, we can use one class for each noun. This is not an exact method – we might find later that we need a few additional classes, or that some of our nouns are not needed. This, however, we will test a bit later. It is important not to exclude any nouns straight away – we do not yet have enough information to make an informed decision.

You might like to note that all of the nouns have been written in their singular form. It is typical that the names of classes are singular rather than plural. For instance, we would always choose to define a class called Cinema rather than Cinemas. This is because the multiplicity is achieved by creating multiple instances of a class.

> **Exercise 13.1** Review projects from earlier chapters in this book. Are there any cases of a class name being a plural name? If so, are those situations justified for a particular reason?

13.1.4 Using CRC cards

The next step in our design process is to work out interactions between our classes. In order to do this, we shall use a method called *CRC cards*.[1]

CRC stands for Class/Responsibilities/Collaborators. The idea is to take cardboard cards (normal index cards do a good job) and use one card for each class. It is important for this activity to do this using real, physical cards, not just a computer or a single sheet of paper.

---

[1] CRC cards were first described in a paper by Kent Beck and Ward Cunningham, titled *A Laboratory For Teaching Object-Oriented Thinking*. This paper is worth reading as additional information to this chapter. You can find it online at http://c2.com/doc/oopsla89/paper.html, or by doing a web search for its title.

Figure 13.1
A CRC card

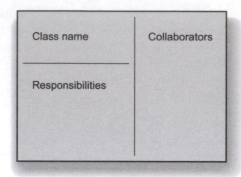

Each card is divided into three areas: one area at the top left, where the name of the class is written; one area below this, to note responsibilities of the class; and one area to the right for writing collaborators of this class (classes which this one uses). Figure 13.1 illustrates the layout of a CRC card.

> **Exercise 13.2** Make CRC cards for the classes in the cinema booking system. At this stage, you need only fill in the class names.

13.1.5 Scenarios

Concept:

Scenarios (also known as 'use cases') can be used to get an understanding of the interactions in a system.

Now we have a first approximation to the classes needed in our system, and a physical representation of them on CRC cards. In order to figure out necessary interactions between the classes in our system, we play through *scenarios*. A scenario is an example of an activity that the system has to carry out or support. Scenarios are also sometimes referred to as *use cases*. We do not use that term here, because it is often used to denote a more formal way of describing scenarios.

Playing through scenarios is best done in a group. Each group member is assigned one class (or a small number of classes), and that person plays their rôle by saying out loud what the class is currently doing. While the scenario is played through, they record on the CRC card everything that is found out about the class in action: what its responsibilities should be, and which other classes it collaborates with.

We start with a simple example scenario. A customer calls the cinema and wants to make a reservation for two seats to watch *The Shawshank Redemption* tonight. The cinema employee starts using the booking system to find and reserve a seat.

Since the human user interacts with the booking system (represented by the `CinemaBookingSystem` class), this is where the scenario starts. Here is what might happen next:

■ The user (the cinema employee) wants to find all showings of *The Shawshank Redemption* that are on tonight. So we can note on the `CinemaBookingSystem` CRC card, as a responsibility: *Can find shows by title and day*. We can also record class `Show` as a collaborator.

■ We have to ask ourselves: How does the system find the show? Who does it ask? One solution might be that the `CinemaBookingSystem` stores a collection of shows. This gives us an additional class: the collection. (This might be implemented later by using an `ArrayList`, a `LinkedList`, a `HashSet`, or some other form of collection. We can make that decision later – for now we just note this as a collection.) This is an example of how we might introduce additional classes during the playing of scenarios. It might happen every now and then that we have to add classes for implementation reasons that we initially overlooked. We add to the responsibilities of the `CinemaBookingSystem` card: *Stores collection of shows*. And we add `Collection` to the collaborators.

> **Exercise 13.3** Make a CRC card for the newly identified collection class, and add it to your system.

- We assume that three shows come up: one at 5:30pm, one at 9:00pm, and one at 11:30pm. The employee informs the customer of the times, and the customer chooses the one at 9:00pm. So the employee wants to check the details of that show (whether it is sold out, which theatre it runs in, etc.). Thus, in our system, the `CinemaBooking-System` must be able to retrieve and display the show's details. Play this through. The person playing the booking system should ask the person playing the show to tell them the required details. Then you note, on the card for `CinemaBookingSystem`: *Retrieves and displays show details*, and on the `Show` card: *Provides details about theatre and number of free seats*.

- Assume there are plenty of free seats. The customer chooses seats 13 and 14 in row 12. The employee makes that reservation. We note on the `CinemaBookingSystem` card: *Accepts seat reservations from user*.

- We now have to play through exactly how the seat reservation works. A seat reservation is clearly attached to a particular show. So the `CinemaBookingSystem` should probably tell the show about the reservation. It delegates the actual task of making the reservation to the `Show` object. We can note for the `Show` class: *Can reserve seats*. (You may have noticed that the notion of objects and classes is blurred when playing through CRC scenarios. In effect, the person representing a class is representing its instances, too. This is intentional, and not usually a problem.)

- Now it is the `Show` class's turn. It has received a request to reserve a seat. What exactly does it do? To be able to store seat reservations, it must have a representation of the seats in the theatre. So we assume that each show has a link to a theatre object. (Note this on the card: *Stores theatre*. This is also a collaborator.) The theatre should probably know about the exact number and arrangement of seats in it. (We can also note in the back of our heads – or on a separate piece of paper – that each show must have its own copy of the theatre object, since several shows can be scheduled for the same theatre, and reserving a seat in one does not reserve the same seat for another show. This is something to look out for when `Show` objects are created. We shall think about that later, when we play through another scenario: scheduling new shows.) So the way a show deals with reserving a seat is probably by passing this reservation request on to the theatre.

- Now the theatre has received a request to make a reservation. (Note this on the card: *Accepts reservation request*.) How does it deal with it? The theatre could have a collection of seats in it. Or it could have a collection of rows (each row being a separate object), and rows in turn hold seats. Which of these alternatives is better? Thinking ahead about other possible scenarios we might decide to go with the idea of storing rows. If, for example, a customer requests four seats together in the same row, it might be easier to find four adjacent seats if we have them all arranged by rows. We note on the Theatre card: *Stores rows*. Row is now a collaborator.

■ We note on the Row class: *Stores collection of seats*. And a new collaborator: Seat.

■ Back to the Theatre class. We have not yet worked out exactly how it should react to the seat reservation request. Let us assume it does two things: find the requested row, and then make a reservation request with the seat number to the Row object.

■ Next, we note on the Row card: *Accepts reservation request for seat*. It must then find the right Seat object (we can note that as a responsibility: *Can find seats by number*) and can make a reservation for that seat. It would do so by telling the Seat object that it is reserved now.

■ We can now add to the Seat card: *Accepts reservations*. The seat itself can remember whether it has been reserved. We note on the Seat card: *Stores reservation status (free/reserved)*.

> **Exercise 13.4** Play this scenario through on your cards (with a group of people, if possible). Add any other information you feel was left out in this description.

Should the seat also store information about who has reserved it? It could store the name of the customer, or the telephone number. Or maybe we should create a customer object as soon as someone makes a reservation, and store the customer object with the seat once the seat has been reserved? These are interesting questions, and we will try to work out the best solution by playing through more scenarios.

This was just the first simple scenario. We need to play through many more scenarios to get a better understanding of how the system should work.

Playing through scenarios works best when a group of people sit around a table and move the cards around on it. Cards that cooperate closely can be placed close together to give an impression of the degree of coupling in the system.

Other scenarios to play through next would include the following:

■ A customer requests five seats together. Work out exactly how five adjoining seats are found.

■ A customer calls and says he forgot the seat numbers he was given for the reservation he made yesterday. Could you please look up the seat numbers again?

■ A customer calls to cancel a reservation. He can give his name and the show, but has forgotten the seat numbers.

■ A customer who has a reservation already calls. She wants to know whether she can reserve another seat next to the ones she already has.

■ A show is cancelled. The cinema wants to call all customers that have reserved a seat for it.

These scenarios should give you a good understanding of the seat lookup and reservation part of the system. Then we need another group of scenarios: those dealing with setting up the theatre and scheduling shows. Here are some possible scenarios:

■ The system has to be set up for a new cinema. The cinema has two theatres with different sizes. Theatre A has 26 rows with 18 seats each. Theatre B has 32 rows. In this theatre, the first six rows have 20 seats, the next 10 rows have 22 seats, and the other rows have 26 seats.

■ A new movie is scheduled for screening. It will be screened for the next two weeks, three times each day (4:40pm, 6:30pm, and 8:30pm). The shows have to be added to the system. All shows run in theatre A.

Exercise 13.5 Play through these scenarios. Note all the questions you have left unanswered on a separate piece of paper. Take a record of all scenarios you have played through.

Exercise 13.6 What other scenarios can you think of? Write them down, and then play them out.

Playing through scenarios takes some patience and some practice. It is important to spend enough time doing this. Playing through the scenarios mentioned here will take several hours.

It is very common for beginners to take shortcuts, and not question and record every detail about the execution of a scenario. This is dangerous! We will soon move on to developing this system in Java, and if details are left unanswered, it is very likely that ad hoc decisions will be made at implementation time, which later turn out to be bad choices.

It is also common for beginners to forget some scenarios. Forgetting to think through a part of the system before starting the class design and implementation can cause a large amount of work later, when an already partially implemented system has to be changed.

Exercise 13.7 Make a class design for an airport control system simulation. Use CRC cards and scenarios. Here is a description of the system:

The program is an airport simulation system. For our new airport we need to know whether we can operate with two runways or whether we need three. The airport works as follows:

The airport has several runways. Planes take off and land on runways. Air traffic controllers coordinate the traffic and give planes permission to take off or land. The controllers sometimes give permission straight away, sometimes they tell planes to wait. Planes must keep a certain distance from one another. The purpose of the program is to simulate the airport in operation.

13.2 Class design

Now it is time for the next big step: moving from CRC cards to Java classes. During the CRC card exercise you should have gained a good understanding of how your application is structured, and how your classes cooperate to solve the program's tasks. You may have come across cases where you had to introduce additional classes (this is often the case with classes that represent internal data structures), and you may have noticed that you have a card for a class that was never used. If that is the case, this card can now be removed.

Recognizing the classes for the implementation is now trivial. The cards show us the complete set of classes we need. Deciding on the interface of each class (that is, the set of public methods that a class should have) is a bit harder, but we have made an important step toward that as well. If the playing of the scenarios was done well, then the responsibilities noted on each class describe the class's public methods (and maybe some of the instance fields). The responsibilities of each class should be evaluated according to the class design principles discussed in Chapter 7: responsibility-driven design, coupling, and cohesion.

13.2.1 Designing class interfaces

Before starting to code our application in Java, we can once more use the cards to make another step toward the final design by translating the informal descriptions into method calls and adding parameters.

To arrive at more formal descriptions, we can now play through the scenarios again, this time talking in terms of method calls, parameters, and return values. The logic and the structure of the application should not change any more, but we try to note down complete information about method signatures and instance fields. We do this on a new set of cards.

> **Exercise 13.8** Make a new set of CRC cards for the classes you have identified. Play through the scenarios again. This time, note exact method names for each method you call from another class, and specify in detail (with type and name) all parameters that are passed and the methods' return values. The method signatures are written on the CRC card instead of the responsibilities. On the back of the card, note the instance fields that each class holds.

Once we have done the exercise described above, writing each class's interface is easy. We can translate directly from the cards into Java. Typically, all classes should be created, and *method stubs* for all public methods should be written. A method stub is a placeholder for the method that has the correct signature and an empty method body.[2]

Many students find doing this in detail tedious. At the end of the project, however, you will hopefully come to appreciate the value of these activities. Many software development teams have realized after the fact that time saved at the design stage had to be spent many times over to fix mistakes or omissions that were not discovered early enough.

Inexperienced programmers often view the writing of the code as the 'real programming.' Doing the initial design is seen as, if not superfluous, then at least annoying, and people cannot wait to get over it so that the real work can start. This is a very misguided picture.

The initial design is one of the most important parts of the project. You should plan to spend at least as much time working on the design as you plan to spend on the implemen-

---

[2] If you wish, you can include trivial return statements in the bodies of methods with non-void return types. Just return a null value for object-returning methods, and a zero or `false` value for primitive types.

tation. Application design is not something that comes before the programming – it *is* (the most important part of) programming!

Mistakes in the code itself can later be fixed fairly easily. Mistakes in the overall design can be, at best, expensive to put right and, at worst, fatal to the whole application. In unlucky cases, they can be almost unfixable (short of starting all over again).

13.2.2 User interface design

One part that we have left out of the discussion so far is the design of the user interface.[3] At some stage, we have to decide in detail what users see on the screen, and how they interact with our system.

In a well-designed application this is quite independent of the underlying logic of the application, so this can be done independently of designing the class structure for the rest of the project. As we saw in Chapter 6, BlueJ gives us the means of interacting with our application before a final user interface is available, so we can choose to work on the internal structure first.

The user interface may be a GUI (graphical user interface) with menus and buttons, it can be text based, or we can decide to run the application using the BlueJ method call mechanism.

For now, we shall ignore the user interface design and use BlueJ method invocation to work with our program.

13.3 Documentation

After identifying the classes and their interfaces, and before starting to implement the methods of a class, the interface should be documented. This involves writing a class comment and method comments for each class in the project. These should be described in sufficient detail to identify the overall purpose of each class and method.

Along with analysis and design, documentation is a further area that is often neglected by beginners. It is not easy for inexperienced programmers to see why documentation is so important. The reason is that inexperienced programmers usually work on projects that have only a handful of classes, and that are written in the span of a few weeks or months. A programmer can get away with bad documentation when working on these mini-projects.

However, even experienced programmers often wonder how it is possible to write the documentation before the implementation. This is because they fail to appreciate that good documentation focuses on high-level issues, such as what a class or method does, rather than low-level issues, such as exactly how it does it. This is usually symptomatic of viewing the implementation as being more important than the design.

---

[3] Note carefully the double meaning of the term 'designing interfaces' here! Above, we were talking about the interfaces of single classes (a set of public methods); now, we talk about the *user interface* – what the user sees on screen to interact with the application. Both are very important issues, and unfortunately the term *interface* is used for both.

If a software developer wants to progress to more interesting problems, and starts to work professionally on real-life applications, it is not unusual to work with dozens of other people on an application over several years. The ad hoc solution of just 'having the documentation in your head' then does not work anymore.

> **Exercise 13.9** Create a BlueJ project for the cinema booking system. Create the necessary classes. Create method stubs for all methods.
>
> **Exercise 13.10** Document all classes and methods. If you have worked in a group, assign responsibilities for classes to different group members. Use the javadoc format for comments, with appropriate javadoc tags to document the details.

13.4 Cooperation

> **Pair programming** Implementation of classes is traditionally done alone. Most programmers work on their own when writing the code, and other people are brought in only after the implementation is finished to test or review the code.
>
> More recently, pair programming has been suggested as an alternative that is intended to produce better-quality code (code with better structure and less bugs). Pair programming is also one of the elements of a technique known as extreme programming. Do a web search for 'pair programming' or 'extreme programming' to find out more.

Software development is usually done in teams. A clean, object-oriented approach provides strong support for teamwork, because it allows the separation of the problem into loosely coupled components (classes) that can be implemented independently.

Although the initial design work was best done in a group, it is now time to split up. If the definition of the class interfaces and the documentation was done well, it should be possible to implement the classes independently. Classes can now be assigned to programmers, who can work on them alone or in pairs.

In the remainder of this chapter we shall not discuss the implementation phase of the cinema booking system in detail. That phase largely involves the sorts of task we have been doing throughout this book in previous chapters, and we hope that, by now, readers can determine for themselves how to continue from here.

13.5 Prototyping

Instead of designing and then building the complete application in one giant leap, *prototyping* can be used to investigate parts of a system.

A prototype is a version of the application where one part is simulated in order to experiment with other parts. You may, for example, implement a prototype to test a graphical user interface. In that case, the logic of the application may not be properly implemented. Instead, we would write simple implementations for those methods that simulate the task. For example, when calling a method to find a free seat in the cinema system, a method

Concept:

Prototyping is the construction of a partially working system, in which some functions of the application are simulated. It serves to provide an understanding of how the system will work early in the development process.

could always return *seat 3, row 15* instead of actually implementing the search. Prototyping allows us to develop an executable (but not fully functional) system quickly, so that we can investigate parts of the application in practice.

Prototypes are also useful for single classes to aid a team development process. Often, when different team members work on different classes, not all classes take the same amount of time to be completed. In some cases a missing class can hold up continuation of development and testing of other classes. In those cases it can be beneficial to write a class prototype. The prototype has implementations of all method stubs, but instead of containing full, final implementations, the prototype only simulates the functionality. Writing a prototype should be possible quickly, and development of client classes can then continue using the prototype until the class is implemented.

As we discuss in section 13.6, one additional benefit of prototyping is that it can give the developers insights into issues and problems that were not considered at an earlier stage.

> **Exercise 13.11** Outline a prototype for your cinema system example. Which of the classes should be implemented first, and which should remain in prototype stage?
>
> **Exercise 13.12** Implement your cinema system prototype.

13.6 Software growth

Several models exist about how software should be built. One of the most commonly known is often referred to as the *waterfall model* (because activity progresses from one level to the next, like water in a cascading waterfall – there is no going back).

13.6.1 Waterfall model

In the waterfall model, several phases of software development are done in a fixed sequence:

- analysis of the problem;
- design of the software;
- implementation of the software components;
- unit testing;
- integration testing;
- delivery of the system to the client.

If any phase fails, we might have to step back to the previous phase to fix it – for example, if testing shows failure, we go back to implementation – but there is no plan to ever revisit earlier phases.

This is probably the most traditional, conservative model of software development, and it has been in widespread use for a long time. However, numerous problems have been discovered with this model over the years. Two of the main flaws are that it assumes that developers understand the full extent of the system's functionality in detail from the start, and that the system does not change after delivery.

In practice, both assumptions are typically not true. It is quite common that the design of a system's functionality is not perfect at the start, often because the client, who knows the problem domain, does not know much about computing, and the software engineers, who know how to program, have only limited knowledge of the problem domain.

13.6.2   Iterative development

One possibility to address the problems of the waterfall model is to use early prototyping and frequent client interaction in the development process. Prototypes of the systems are built, which do not do much but give an impression of what the system would look like and what it would do, and clients comment regularly on the design and functionality. This leads to a more circular process than the waterfall model. Here, the software development iterates several times through an analysis–design–prototype implementation–client feedback cycle.

Another approach is captured in the notion that good software is not designed, it is *grown*. The idea behind this is to design a small and clean system initially, and get it into a working state, where it can be used by end users. Then additional features are gradually added (the software grows) in a controlled manner, and 'finished' states (meaning states in which the software is completely usable and can be delivered to clients) are reached repeatedly and fairly frequently.

In reality, growing software is of course not a contradiction to designing software. Every growth step is carefully designed. What it does not try to do is design the complete software system right from the start. Even more: the notion of a complete software system does not exist at all!

The traditional waterfall model has as its goal the delivery of a complete system. The software growth model assumes that complete systems that are used indefinitely in an unchanged state do not exist. There are only two things that can happen to a software system: either it is continuously improved and adapted, or it will disappear.

This discussion is central to this book, because it influences strongly how we view the tasks and skills required of a programmer or software engineer. You might be able to tell that the authors of this book strongly favor the software growth model over the waterfall model.[4]

As a consequence, certain tasks and skills become much more important than they would be in the waterfall model. Software maintenance, code reading (rather than just writing), designing for extendibility, documentation, coding for understandability, and many other issues we have mentioned in this book take their importance from the fact that we know there will be others coming after us who have to adapt and extend our code.

Viewing a piece of software as a continuously growing, changing, adapting entity, rather than a static piece of text that is written and preserved like a novel, determines our views about how good code should be written. All the techniques we have discussed throughout this book work toward this.

---

[4] An excellent book describing the problems of software development and some possible approaches to solutions is *The Mythical Man-Month* by Frederick P. Brooks Jr, Addison-Wesley. Even though the original edition is over 25 years old, it makes entertaining and very enlightening reading.

Exercise 13.13 In which ways might the cinema booking system be adapted or extended in the future? Which changes are more likely than others? Write down a list of possible future changes.

Exercise 13.14 Are there any other organizations that might use booking systems similar to the one we have discussed? What significant differences exist between the systems?

Exercise 13.15 Do you think it would be possible to design a 'generic' booking system that could be adapted or customized for use in a wide range of different organizations with booking needs? If you were to create such a system, at what point in the development process of the cinema system would you introduce changes? Or would you throw that one away and start again from scratch?

13.7 Using design patterns

In earlier chapters we have discussed in detail some techniques to reuse some of our work, and to make our code more understandable to others. So far, a large part of these discussions has remained on the level of source code in single classes.

As we become more experienced, and move on to design larger software systems, the implementation of single classes is not the most difficult problem any more. The structure of the overall system – the complex relationships between classes – becomes harder to design and to understand than the code of individual classes.

It is a logical step that we should try to achieve the same goals for class structures that we attempted for source code. We want to reuse good bits of work, and we want to enable others to understand what we have done.

At the level of class structures, both these goals can be served by using *design patterns*.

Concept:

A **design pattern** is a description of a common computing problem and a description of a small set of classes and their interaction structure that helps to solve that problem.

A design pattern describes a common problem that occurs regularly in software development, and then describes a general solution to that problem that can be used in many different contexts. For software design patterns the solution is typically a description of a small set of classes and their interactions.

Design patterns help in our task in two ways. First, they document good solutions to problems, so that these solutions can be reused later for similar problems. The reuse in this case is not at the level of source code, but at the level of class structures.

Second, design patterns have names, and thus establish a vocabulary that helps software designers to talk about their designs. When experienced designers discuss the structure of an application, one might say, 'I think we should use a Singleton here.' Singleton is the name of a widely known design pattern, so if both designers are familiar with this pattern, being able to talk about it at this level saves explanation of a lot of detail. Thus the pattern language introduced by commonly known design patterns introduces another level of abstraction, one that allows us to cope with complexity in ever more complex systems.

Software design patterns were made popular by a book published in 1995, which describes a set of patterns, their applications and benefits.[5] This book is still one of the most important works about design patterns today. Here, we do not attempt to give a complete overview of design patterns. Rather, we discuss a small number of patterns to give readers an impression of the benefits of using design patterns, and then we leave it to the reader to continue the study of patterns in other literature.

13.7.1 Structure of a pattern

Descriptions of patterns are usually recorded using a template that contains some minimum information. A pattern description is not only information about a structure of some classes, but also includes a description of the problem(s) this pattern addresses, and competing forces for or against use of the pattern.

A description of a pattern includes at least:

- a *name* that can be used to talk about the pattern conveniently;

- a description of the **problem** that the pattern addresses (often split into sections such as *intent*, *motivation*, *applicability*);

- a description of the **solution** (often listing *structure*, *participants*, and *collaborations*);

- the **consequences** of using the pattern, including results and trade-offs.

In the following section we shall briefly discuss some commonly used patterns.

13.7.2 Decorator

The *Decorator* pattern deals with the problem of adding functionality to an existing object. We assume that we want an object that responds to the same method calls (has the same interface) but has added or altered behavior. We may also want to add to the existing interface.

One way this could be done is by inheritance. A subclass may override the implementation of methods and add additional methods. But using inheritance is a static solution: once created, objects cannot change their behavior.

A more dynamic solution is the use of a Decorator object. The Decorator is an object that encloses an existing object, and can be used instead of the original (it usually implements the same interface). Clients then communicate with the Decorator instead of the original object directly (without a need to know about this substitution). The Decorator passes the method calls on to the enclosed object, but it may perform additional actions. We can find an example in the Java input/output library. There, a BufferedReader is used as a decorator for a Reader (Figure 13.2). The BufferedReader implements the same interface and can be used instead of an unbuffered Reader, but it adds to the basic behavior of a Reader. In contrast to using inheritance, decorators can be added to existing objects.

---

[5] *Design Patterns*: *Elements of Reusable Object-Oriented Software* by Erich Gamma, Richard Helm, Ralph Johnson and John Vlissides, Addison-Wesley, 1995.

Figure 13.2

Structure of the decorator pattern

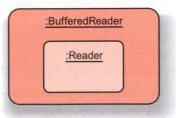

13.7.3 Singleton

A common situation in many programs is to have an object of which there should be only one single instance. In our *World-of-Zuul* game for instance, we want only a single parser. If we write a software development environment, we might want only a single compiler or a single debugger.

The *Singleton* pattern ensures that only one instance will be created from a class, and it provides unified access to it. In Java, a Singleton can be defined by making the constructor private. This ensures that it cannot be called from outside the class, and thus client classes cannot create new instances. We can then write code in the Singleton class itself to create a single instance and provide access to it (Code 13.1 illustrates this for a `Parser` class).

Code 13.1

The Singleton pattern

```java
class Parser
{
    private static Parser instance = new Parser();

    public static Parser getInstance()
    {
        return instance;
    }

    private Parser()
    {
        ...
    }
}
```

In this pattern:

■ The constructor is private, so that instances can be created only by the class itself. This has to be in a static part of the class (initializations of static fields or static methods), since no instance will otherwise exist.

■ A private static field is defined and initialized with the (sole) instance of the parser.

■ A static `getInstance` method is defined, which provides access to the single instance.

Clients of the Singleton can now use that static method to gain access to the parser object:

```java
Parser parser = Parser.getInstance();
```

13.7.4 Factory method

The *Factory method* pattern provides an interface for creating objects, but lets subclasses decide which specific class of object is created. Typically, the client expects a superclass or an interface of the actual object, and the factory method provides specializations.

Iterators of collections are an example of this technique. If we have a variable of type `Collection`, we can ask it for an iterator (using the `iterator` method) and then work with that iterator (Code 13.2). The iterator method in this example is the Factory method.

Code 13.2

A use of a factory method

```java
public void process(Collection coll)
{
    Iterator it = coll.iterator();
    ...
}
```

From the client's point of view (in the code shown in Code 13.2), we are dealing with objects of type `Collection` and `Iterator`. In reality, the (dynamic) type of the collection may be `ArrayList`, in which case the `iterator` method returns an object of type `ArrayListIterator`. Or it may be a `HashSet`, and `iterator` returns a `HashSetIterator`. The Factory method is specialized in subclasses to return specialized instances to the 'official' return type.

We can make good use of this pattern in our *foxes-and-rabbits* simulation to decouple the `Simulator` class from the specific animal classes. (Remember: In our version, `Simulator` was coupled to classes `Fox` and `Rabbit`, because it creates the initial instances.)

Instead, we can introduce an interface `ActorFactory` and classes implementing this interface for each actor (for example `FoxFactory` and `RabbitFactory`). The `Simulator` would simply store a collection of `ActorFactories`, and it would ask each of them to produce a number of actors. Each factory would, of course, produce a different kind of actor, but the `Simulator` talks to them via the `ActorFactory` interface.

13.7.5 Observer

In the discussions of several of the projects in this book we have tried to separate the internal model of the application from the way it is presented on screen (the view). The *Observer* pattern provides one way to achieve this model/view separation.

More generally: the Observer pattern defines a one-to-many relationship, so that, when one object changes its state, many others can be notified. It achieves this with a very low degree of coupling between the observers and the observed object.

We can see from this that the Observer pattern not only supports a decoupled view on the model, it also allows for multiple different views (either as alternatives, or simultaneously). As an example, we can again use our *foxes-and-rabbits* simulation.

In the simulation we presented the animal populations on screen in a two-dimensional animated grid. There are other possibilities. We might have preferred to show the population as a graph of population numbers along a time line, or as an animated bar chart (Figure 13.3). We might even like to see all representations at the same time.

Figure 13.3

Multiple views on one subject

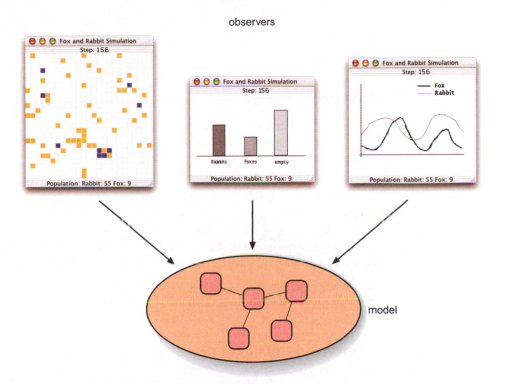

For the Observer pattern, we use two abstract classes: `Observable` and `Observer`.[6] The observable entity (the `Field` in our simulation) extends the `Observable` class, and the observer (`SimulatorView`) extends the `Observer` class (Figure 13.4).

The `Observable` class provides methods for observers to attach themselves to the observed entity. It ensures that the observers' `update` method is called whenever the observed entity (the field) invokes its inherited `notify` method. The actual observers (the viewers) can then get a new, updated state from the field and redisplay.

Figure 13.4

Structure of the Observer pattern

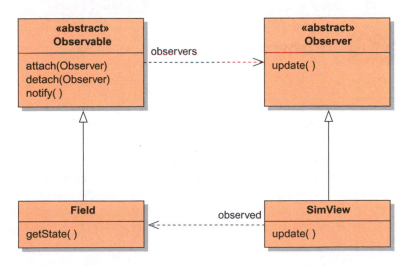

___

[6] In the Java `java.util` package, `Observer` is an interface with a single method, `update`.

The Observer pattern can also be used for problems other than a model/view separation. It can always be applied when the state of one or more objects depends on the state of another object.

13.7.6 Pattern summary

Discussing design patterns and their applications in detail is beyond the scope of this book. Here, we have presented only a brief idea of what design patterns are, and we have given an informal description of some of the more common patterns.

We hope, however, that this discussion serves to show where to go from here. Once we understand how to create good implementations of single classes with well-defined functionality, we can concentrate on deciding what kind of classes we should have in our application, and how they should cooperate. Good solutions are not always obvious, and so design patterns describe structures that have proven useful over and over again to solve recurring classes of problems. They help us in creating good class structures.

The more experienced you get as a software developer, the more time you will spend thinking about higher-level structure rather than about implementation of single methods.

> **Exercise 13.16** Three further, commonly used patterns are the *State* pattern, the *Strategy* pattern, and the *Visitor* pattern. Find descriptions of each of these, and identify at least one example application in which each might be used.
>
> **Exercise 13.17** Late in the development of a project, you find that two teams who have been working independently on two parts of an application have implemented incompatible classes. The interface of several classes implemented by one team is slightly different from the interface the other team is expecting to use. Explain how the *Adapter* pattern might help in this situation, by avoiding having to rewrite any of the existing classes.

13.8 Summary

In this chapter we have moved up one step in terms of abstraction levels, away from thinking about the design of single classes (or cooperation between two classes) to the design of an application as a whole. Central to the design of an object-oriented software system is the decision about the classes to use for its implementation, and the communication structures between these classes.

Some classes are fairly obvious and easy to discover. We have used a method of identifying nouns and verbs in a textual description of the problem as a starting point. After discovering the classes, we can use CRC cards and played-out scenarios to design the dependences and communication details between classes, and to flesh out details about each class's responsibilities. For less experienced designers, it helps to play through scenarios in a group.

CRC cards can be used to refine the design down to the definition of method names and their parameters. Once this has been achieved, classes with method stubs can be coded in Java, and the classes' interfaces can be documented.

Following an organized process like this serves several purposes. It ensures that potential problems with early design ideas are discovered before much time is invested in implementation. It also enables programmers to work on the implementation of several classes independently, without having to wait for the implementation of one class to be finished before implementing another can begin.

Flexible, extendible class structures are not always easy to design. Design patterns are used to document generally good structures that have proven useful in the implementation of different classes of problems. Through the study of design patterns, a software engineer can learn a lot about good application structures and improve application design skills.

The larger a problem, the more important is a good application structure. The more experienced a software engineer becomes, the more time he or she will spend designing application structures rather than just writing code.

Terms introduced in this chapter

analysis and design, noun/verb method, CRC card, scenario, use case, method stub, design pattern

Concept summary

- **noun/verb** Classes in a system roughly correspond to nouns in the system's description. Methods correspond to verbs.

- **scenarios** Scenarios (also known as 'use cases') can be used to get an understanding of the interactions in a system.

- **prototyping** Prototyping is the construction of a partially working system, in which some functions of the application are simulated. It serves to provide an understanding of how the system will work early in the development process.

- **design pattern** A design pattern is a description of a common computing problem and a description of a small set of classes and their interaction structure that helps to solve that problem.

Exercise 13.18 Assume you have a school management system for your school. In it, there is a class called **Database** (a fairly central class) that holds objects of type **Student**. Each student has an address that is held in an **Address** object (i.e. each **Student** object holds a reference to an **Address** object).

Now, from the **Database** class, you need to get access to a student's street, city, and post code. The **Address** class has accessor methods for these. For the design of the **Student** class, you now have two choices:

Either, you implement **getStreet**, **getCity**, and **getPostCode** methods in the **Student** class, which just pass the method call on to the **Address** object and hand the result back; or you implement a **getAddress** method in **Student** that returns the complete **Address** object to the **Database**, and lets the **Database** object call the **Address** object's methods directly.

Which of these alternatives is better? Why? Make a class diagram for each situation, and list arguments either way.

Main concepts discussed in this chapter:

- whole-application development

Java constructs discussed in this chapter:

(No new Java constructs are introduced in this chapter.)

In this chapter we draw together many of the object-oriented principles that we have introduced in this book by presenting an extended case study. We shall take the study from the initial discussion of a problem, through class discovery, design, and an iterative process of implementation and testing. Unlike previous chapters, it is not our intention here to introduce any major new topics. Rather, we are seeking to reinforce those topics that have been covered in the second half of the book, such as inheritance, abstraction techniques, error handling, and application design.

14.1 The case study

The case study we will be using is the development of a model for a taxi company. The company is considering whether to expand its operations into a new part of a city. It operates taxis and shuttles. Taxis drop their passengers at their target locations before taking on new passengers, whereas shuttles may collect several passengers from different locations on the same trip, taking them to similar locations (such as collecting several guests from different hotels and taking them to different terminals at the airport). Based on estimates of the number of potential customers in that area, the company wishes to know whether an expansion would be profitable, and how many cabs it would need there in order to operate effectively.

14.1.1 The problem description

The following paragraph presents an informal description of the taxi company's operating procedures, arrived at following several meetings with them.

The company operates both individual taxis and shuttles. The taxis are used to transport an individual (or small group) from one location to another. The shuttles are used to pick up individuals from different locations and transport them to their several destinations. When the company receives a call from an individual, hotel, entertainment venue, or tourist organization, it tries to schedule a vehicle to pick up the fare. If it has no free vehicles, it does not operate any form of queuing system. When a vehicle arrives at a pickup location, the driver notifies the company. Similarly, when a passenger is dropped off at their destination, the driver notifies the company.

As we suggested in Chapter 10, one of the common purposes of modeling is to help us learn something about the situation being modeled. It is useful to identify at an early stage what we wish to learn, because these goals may well have an influence on the design we produce. For instance, if we are seeking to answer questions about the profitability of running taxis in this area, then we must ensure that we can obtain information from the model that will help us to assess profitability. Two issues we ought to consider, therefore, are: how often potential passengers are lost because no vehicle is available to collect them; and, at the opposite extreme, how much time taxis remain idle for lack of passengers. These influences are not found in the basic description of how the taxi company normally operates, but they do represent scenarios that will have to be played through when we draw up the design.

So we might add the following paragraph to the description:

The system stores details about passenger requests that cannot be satisfied. It also provides details of how much time vehicles spend in each of the following activities: carrying passengers, going to pickup locations, and being idle.

However, as we develop our model, we shall focus on just the original description of the company's operating procedures, and leave the additional features as exercises.

> **Exercise 14.1** Is there any additional data that you feel it would be useful to gather from the model? If so, add these requirements to the descriptions given above, and use them in your own extensions to the project.

14.2   Analysis and design

As suggested in Chapter 13, we will start by seeking to identify the classes and interactions in the system's description, using the verb/noun method.

14.2.1   Discovering classes

The following (singular versions of) nouns are present in the description: company, taxi, shuttle, individual, location, destination, hotel, entertainment venue, tourist organization, vehicle, fare, pickup location, driver, and passenger.

The first point to note is that it would be a mistake to move straight from this list of nouns to a set of classes. Informal descriptions are rarely written in a way that suits that sort of direct mapping.

One refinement that is commonly needed is to identify any *synonyms* in the list of nouns: different words used for the same entity. For instance, 'individual' and 'fare' are both synonyms for 'passenger.'

A further refinement is to eliminate those entities that do not really need to be modeled in the system. For instance, the description identified various ways in which the taxi company might be contacted: by individuals, hotels, entertainment venues, and tourist organizations. Will it really be necessary to maintain these distinctions? The answer will depend upon the information we want from the model. We might wish to arrange discounts for hotels that provide large numbers of customers, or send publicity material to entertainment venues that do not. If this level of detail is not required, then we can simplify the model by just 'injecting' passengers into it according to some statistically reasonable pattern.

Exercise 14.2 Consider simplifying the number of nouns associated with the vehicles. Are 'vehicle' and 'taxi' synonyms in this context? Do we need to distinguish between 'shuttle' and 'taxi'? What about 'driver'? Justify your answers.

Exercise 14.3 Is it possible to eliminate any of the following as synonyms in this context: 'location,' 'destination,' and 'pickup location'?

Exercise 14.4 Identify the nouns from any extensions you have added to the system and make any necessary simplifications.

14.2.2   Using CRC cards

Figure 14.1 contains a summary of the noun and verb associations we are left with once some simplification has been performed on the original description. Each of the nouns should now be assigned to a CRC card, ready to have its responsibilities and collaborators identified.

Figure 14.1

Noun and verb associations in the taxi company

Nouns	Verbs
company	*operates taxis and shuttles*
	receives a call
	schedules a vehicle
taxi	*transports a passenger*
shuttle	*transports one or more passengers*
passenger	
location	
passenger-source	*calls the company*
vehicle	*picks up passenger*
	arrives at pickup location
	notifies company of arrival
	notifies company of drop-off

From that summary, it is clear that taxi and shuttle are distinct specializations of a more general vehicle class. The main distinction between a taxi and a shuttle is that a taxi is only ever concerned with picking up and transporting a single passenger or coherent group, but a shuttle deals with multiple *independent* passengers concurrently. The relationship between these three is suggestive of an inheritance hierarchy, where taxi and shuttle represent subtypes of vehicle.

Exercise 14.5 Create physical CRC cards for the nouns/classes identified in this section, in order to be able to work through the scenarios suggested by the project description.

Exercise 14.6 Do the same for any of your own extensions you wish to follow through in the next stage.

14.2.3 Scenarios

The taxi company does not actually represent a very complex application. We shall find that much of the total interaction in the system is explored by taking the fundamental scenario of trying to satisfy a passenger request to go from one location in the city to another. In practice, this single scenario will be broken down into a number of steps that are followed in sequence, from the initial call to the final drop-off.

■ We have decided that a passenger-source creates all new passenger objects for the system. So a responsibility of `PassengerSource` is *Create a Passenger*, and a collaborator is `Passenger`.

■ The passenger-source calls the taxi company to request a pickup for a passenger. We note `TaxiCompany` as a collaborator of `PassengerSource`, and add *Request a pickup* as a responsibility. Correspondingly, we add to `TaxiCompany` a responsibility to *Receive a pickup request*. Associated with the request will be a passenger and a pickup location. So `TaxiCompany` has `Passenger` and `Location` as collaborators. When it calls the company with the request, the passenger-source could pass the passenger and pickup location as separate objects. However, it is preferable to associate closely the pickup location with the passenger. So a collaborator of `Passenger` is `Location`, and a responsibility will be *Provide pickup location*.

■ From where does the passenger's pickup location originate? The pickup location and destination could be decided when the passenger is created. So add to `PassengerSource` the responsibility *Generate pickup and destination locations for a passenger*, with `Location` as a collaborator; and add to `Passenger` the responsibilities *Receive pickup and destination locations* and *Provide destination location*.

■ On receipt of a request, the `TaxiCompany` has a responsibility to *Schedule a vehicle*. This suggests that a further responsibility is *Store a collection of vehicles*, with a `Collection` and `Vehicle` as collaborators. Since the request might fail – there may be no vehicles free – a success or failure indication should be returned to the passenger-source.

■ There is no indication whether the company seeks to distinguish between taxis and shuttles when scheduling, so we do not need to take that aspect into account here. However, a vehicle can be scheduled only if it is free. This means that a responsibility of `Vehicle` will be *Indicate whether free*.

- When a free vehicle has been identified, it must be directed to the pickup location. `TaxiCompany` has the responsibility *Direct vehicle to pickup*, with the corresponding responsibility in `Vehicle` being *Receive pickup location*. `Location` is added as a collaborator of `Vehicle`.

- On receipt of a pickup location, the behavior of taxis and shuttles may well differ. A taxi will have been free only if it was not already on its way to either a pickup or a destination location. So the responsibility of `Taxi` is *Go to pickup location*. In contrast, a shuttle has to deal with multiple passengers. When it receives a pickup location, it may have to choose between several alternative possible locations to head to next. So we add the responsibility to `Shuttle` to *Choose next target location*, with a `Collection` collaborator to maintain the set of possible target locations to choose from. The fact that a vehicle moves between locations suggests that it has a responsibility to *Maintain a current location*.

- On arrival at a pickup location a `Vehicle` must *Notify the company of pickup arrival*, with `TaxiCompany` as a collaborator; and `TaxiCompany` must *Receive notification of pickup arrival*. In real life, a taxi meets its passenger for the first time when it arrives at the pickup location. So this is the natural point for the vehicle to receive its next passenger. In the model, it does so from the company, which received it originally from the passenger source. `TaxiCompany` responsibility: *Pass passenger to vehicle*; `Vehicle` responsibility: *Receive passenger*, with `Passenger` added as a collaborator to `Vehicle`.

- The vehicle now requests the passenger's intended destination. `Vehicle` responsibility: *Request destination location*, and `Passenger` responsibility: *Provide destination location*. Once again, at this point the behavior of taxis and shuttles will differ. A `Taxi` will simply *Go to passenger destination*. A shuttle will *Add location to collection of target locations*, and choose the next one.

- On arrival at a passenger's destination, a `Vehicle` has responsibilities to *Offload passenger*, and *Notify the company of passenger arrival*. The `TaxiCompany` must *Receive notification of passenger arrival*.

The steps we have outlined represent the fundamental activity of the taxi company, repeated over and over as each new passenger requests the service. An important point to note, however, is that our computer model needs to be able to restart the sequence for each new passenger as soon as each fresh request is received – even if a previous request has not run to completion. In other words, within a single step of the program, one vehicle could be still heading to a pickup location, while another could be arriving at a passenger's destination, and a new passenger might be requesting a pickup.

Exercise 14.7 Review the problem description and the scenario we have worked through. Are there any further scenarios that need to be addressed, before we move on to class design? Have we adequately covered what happens if there is no vehicle available when a request is received, for instance? Complete the scenario analysis if you feel there is more to be done.

Exercise 14.8 Do you feel that we have described the scenario at the correct level of detail? For instance, have we included too little or too much detail in the discussion of the differences between taxis and shuttles?

Exercise 14.9 Do you feel it is necessary to address *how* vehicles move between locations at this stage?

Exercise 14.10 Do you think that a need for further classes will emerge as the application is developed – classes that have no immediate reference in the problem description? If so, why is this the case?

14.3 Class design

In this section, we shall start to make the move from a high-level, abstract design on paper to a concrete, outline design within a BlueJ project.

14.3.1 Designing class interfaces

In Chapter 13, we suggested that the next step was to create a fresh set of CRC cards from the first, turning the responsibilities of each class into a set of method signatures. Without wishing to de-emphasize the importance of that step, we shall leave it for you to do, and move directly to a BlueJ project outline, containing stub classes and methods. This should provide a good feel for the complexity of the project, and whether we have missed anything crucial in the steps taken so far.

It is worth pointing out that, at every stage of the project life cycle, we should expect to find errors or loose ends in what we have done in earlier stages. This does not necessarily imply that there are weaknesses in our techniques or abilities. It is more a reflection of the fact that project development is often a discovery process. It is only by exploring and trying things out that we gain a full understanding of what it is we are trying to achieve. So discovering omissions actually says something positive about the process we are using!

14.3.2 Collaborators

Having identified collaborations between classes, one issue that will often need to be addressed is how a particular object obtains references to its collaborators. There are usually three distinct ways in which this happens, and these often represent three different patterns of object interaction:

- A collaborator is received as an argument to a constructor. Such a collaborator will usually be stored in one of the new object's fields, so that it is available through the new object's life. The collaborator may be shared in this way with several different objects. Example: a `PassengerSource` object receives the `TaxiCompany` object through its constructor.

- A collaborator is received as an argument to a method. Interaction with such a collaborator is usually transitory – just for the period of execution of the method – although the receiving object may choose to store the reference in one of its fields, for longer-term interaction. Example: `TaxiCompany` receives a `Passenger` collaborator through its method to handle a pickup request.

■ The object constructs the collaborator for itself. The collaborator will be for the exclusive use of the constructing object, unless it is passed to another object in one of the previous two ways. If constructed in a method, the collaboration will usually be short term, for the duration of the block in which it is constructed. However, if the collaborator is stored in a field, then the collaboration is likely to last the full lifetime of the creating object. Example: `TaxiCompany` creates a collection to store its vehicles.

Exercise 14.11 As the next section discusses the *taxi-company-outline* project, pay particular attention to where objects are created, and how collaborating objects get to know about each other. Try to identify at least one further example of each of the patterns we have described.

14.3.3 The outline implementation

The project *taxi-company-outline* contains an outline implementation of the classes, responsibilities and collaborations that we have described as part of the design process. You are encouraged to browse through the source code and associate the concrete classes with the corresponding descriptions of section 14.2.3. Code 14.1 shows an outline of the `Vehicle` class from the project.

Code 14.1

An outline of the `Vehicle` class

```java
/**
 * Capture outline details of a vehicle.
 *
 * @author David J. Barnes and Michael Kölling
 * @version 2002.06.20
 */
public abstract class Vehicle
{
    private TaxiCompany company;
    // Where the vehicle is.
    private Location location;
    // Where the vehicle is headed.
    private Location targetLocation;

    /**
     * Constructor of class Vehicle
     * @param company The taxi company. Must not be null.
     * @param location The vehicle's starting point. Must not
     *                       be null.
     * @throws NullPointerException If company or location is
     *                                   null.
     */
    public Vehicle(TaxiCompany company, Location location)
    {
        if(company == null) {
            throw new NullPointerException("company");
        }
        if(location == null) {
```

**Code 14.1
continued**

An outline of the
Vehicle class

```java
            throw new NullPointerException("location");
        }
        this.company = company;
        this.location = location;
        targetLocation = null;
    }

    /**
     * Notify the company of our arrival at a pickup
     * location.
     */
    public void notifyPickupArrival()
    {
        company.arrivedAtPickup(this);
    }

    /**
     * Notify the company of our arrival at a
     * passenger's destination.
     */
    public void notifyPassengerArrival(Passenger passenger)
    {
        company.arrivedAtDestination(this, passenger);
    }

    /**
     * Receive a pickup location.
     * How this is handled depends on the type of vehicle.
     * @param location The pickup location.
     */
    public abstract void setPickupLocation(Location location);

    /**
     * Receive a passenger.
     * How this is handled depends on the type of vehicle.
     * @param passenger The passenger.
     */
    public abstract void pickup(Passenger passenger);

    /**
     * @return Whether or not this vehicle is free.
     */
    public abstract boolean isFree();

    /**
     * Offload any passengers whose destination is the
     * current location.
     */
    public abstract void offloadPassenger();

    /**
     * @return Where this vehicle is currently located.
     */
```

**Code 14.1
continued**

An outline of the
Vehicle class

```java
    public Location getLocation()
    {
        return location;
    }

    /**
     * Set the current location.
     * @param location Where it is. Must not be null.
     * @throws NullPointerException If location is null.
     */
    public void setLocation(Location location)
    {
        if(location != null) {
            this.location = location;
        }
        else {
            throw new NullPointerException();
        }
    }

    /**
     * @return Where this vehicle is currently headed, or
     *         null if it is idle.
     */
    public Location getTargetLocation()
    {
        return targetLocation;
    }

    /**
     * Set the required target location.
     * @param location Where to go. Must not be null.
     * @throws NullPointerException If location is null.
     */
    public void setTargetLocation(Location location)
    {
        if(location != null) {
            targetLocation = location;
        }
        else {
            throw new NullPointerException();
        }
    }

    /**
     * Clear the target location.
     */
    public void clearTargetLocation()
    {
        targetLocation = null;
    }
}
```

The process of creating the outline project raised a number of issues. Here are some of them:

■ You should expect to find some differences between the design and the implementation, owing to the different natures of design and implementation languages. For instance, discussion of the scenarios suggested that `PassengerSource` should have the responsibility *Generate pickup and destination locations for a passenger*, and `Passenger` should have the responsibility *Receive pickup and destination locations*. Rather than mapping these responsibilities to individual method calls, the more natural implementation in Java is to write something like

```
new Passenger(new Location(...), new Location(...))
```

■ We have ensured that our outline project is complete enough to compile successfully. That is not always necessary at this stage, but it does mean that undertaking incremental development at the next stage will be a little easier. However, it does have the corresponding disadvantage of making missing pieces of code potentially harder to spot, because the compiler will not point out the loose ends.

■ The shared and distinct elements of the `Vehicle`, `Taxi`, and `Shuttle` classes only really begin to take shape as we move towards their implementation. For instance, the different ways in which taxis and shuttles respond to a pickup request is reflected in the fact that `Vehicle` defines `setPickupLocation` as an abstract method, which will have separate concrete implementations in the subclasses. On the other hand, even though taxis and shuttles have different ways of deciding where they are heading, they can share the concept of having a single target location. This has been implemented as a `targetLocation` field in the superclass.

■ At two points in the scenario, a vehicle is expected to notify the company of its arrival, at either a pickup point or a destination. There are at least two possible ways to organize this in the implementation. The direct way is for a vehicle to store a reference to its company. This would mean that there would be an explicit association between the two classes on the class diagram.

An alternative is to use the *Observer* pattern introduced in Chapter 13, with `Vehicle` extending the `Observable` class, and `TaxiCompany` implementing the `Observer` interface. Direct coupling between `Vehicle` and `TaxiCompany` is reduced, but implicit coupling is still involved, and the notification process is a little more complex to program.

■ Up to this point there has been no discussion about how many passengers a shuttle can carry. Presumably there could be different-sized shuttles? This aspect of the application has been deferred until a later resolution.

There is no absolute rule about exactly how far to go with the outline implementation in any particular application. The purpose of the outline implementation is not to create a fully working project, but to record the design of the outline structure of the application (which has been developed through the CRC card activities earlier). As you review the classes in the *taxi-company-outline* project, you may feel that we have gone too far in this case, or maybe even not far enough. On the positive side, by attempting to create a version that at least compiles, we certainly found that we were forced to think about the

`Vehicle` inheritance hierarchy in some detail: in particular, which methods could be implemented in full in the superclass, and which were best left as abstract. On the negative side, there is always the risk of making implementation decisions too early: for instance, committing to particular sorts of data structures that might be better left until later, or, as we did here, choosing to reject the *Observer* pattern in favor of the more direct approach.

> **Exercise 14.12** For each of the classes in the project, look at the class interface and write a list of tests that should be used to test the functionality of the class.
>
> **Exercise 14.13** The *taxi-company-outline* project defines a `Demo` class to create a pair of `PassengerSource` and `TaxiCompany` objects. Create a `Demo` object and try its `pickupTest` method. Why is the `TaxiCompany` object unable to grant a pickup request at this stage?
>
> **Exercise 14.14** Do you feel that we should have developed the source code further at this stage to enable at least one pickup request to succeed? If so, how much further would you have taken the development?

14.3.4 Testing

Having made a start on implementation, we should not go too much further before we start to consider how we shall test the application. We do not want to make the mistake of devising tests only once the full implementation is complete. We can already put some tests in place that will gradually evolve as the implementation is evolved. Try the following exercises to get a feel for what is possible at this early stage.

> **Exercise 14.15** The *taxi-company-outline-testing* project introduces an `Outline-Testing` class, containing some initial tests. Add any further tests you feel are appropriate at this stage of the development, to form the basis of a set of tests to be used during future development. Does it matter if the tests we create fail at this stage?
>
> **Exercise 14.16** The `Location` class currently contains no fields or methods. How is further development of this class likely to affect existing methods of the `OutlineTesting` class?

14.3.5 Some remaining issues

One of the major issues that we have not attempted to tackle yet is how to organize the sequencing of the various activities: passenger requests, vehicle movements, and so on. Another is that locations have not been given a detailed concrete form, so movement has no effect. As we develop the application further, resolutions of these issues and others will emerge.

14.4 Iterative development

We obviously still have quite a long way to go from the outline implementation developed in *taxi-company-outline* to the final version. However, rather than being overwhelmed by the magnitude of the overall task, we can make things more manageable by identifying some discrete steps to take toward the ultimate goal, and undertaking a process of iterative development.

14.4.1 Development steps

Planning some development steps helps us to consider how we might break up a single large problem into several smaller problems. Individually, these smaller problems are likely to be both less complex and more manageable than the one big problem, but together they should combine to form the whole. As we seek to solve the smaller problems, we might find that we need to break up some of them even further. In addition, we might find that some of our original assumptions were wrong, or our design inadequate in some way. This process of discovery, when combined with an iterative development approach, means that we obtain valuable feedback on our design, and on the decisions we make, at an early enough stage for us to be able to incorporate it back into a flexible and evolving process.

Considering what steps to break the overall problem into has the added advantage of helping to identify some of the ways in which the various parts of the application are interconnected. In a large project that helps us to identify the interfaces between components. Identifying steps also helps in planning the timing of the development process.

It is important that each step in an iterative development represents a clearly identifiable point in the evolution of the application toward the overall requirements. In particular, we need to be able to determine when each step has been completed. Completion should be marked by the passing of a set of tests, and a review of the step's achievements, so as to be able to incorporate any lessons learned into the steps that follow.

Here is a possible series of development steps for the taxi company application:

- Enable a single passenger to be picked up and taken to their destination by a single taxi.

- Provide sufficient taxis to enable multiple independent passengers to be picked up and taken to their destinations concurrently.

- Enable a single passenger to be picked up and taken to their destination by a single shuttle.

- Ensure that details of passengers for whom there is no free vehicle are recorded.

- Enable a single shuttle to pick up multiple passengers and carry them concurrently to their destinations.

- Provide a GUI to display the activities of all active vehicles and passengers within the simulation.

- Ensure that taxis and shuttles are able to operate concurrently.

- Provide all remaining functionality, including full statistical data.

We will not discuss the implementation of all of these steps in detail, but we will complete the application to a point where you should be able to add the remaining functionality for yourself.

14.4.2   A first stage

For the first stage we want to be able to create a single passenger, have them picked up by a single taxi, and delivered to their destination. This means we shall have to work on a number of different classes: Location, Taxi, and TaxiCompany, for certain, and possibly others. In addition, we shall have to arrange for simulated time to pass as the taxi moves within the city. This suggests that we might be able to reuse some of the ideas involving actors that we saw in Chapter 10.

The *taxi-company-stage-one* project contains an implementation of the requirements of this first stage. The classes have been developed to the point where a taxi picks up and delivers a passenger to their destination. The run method of the Demo class plays out this scenario. However, more important at this stage are really the test classes, DeliveryTests and LocationTests, which we discuss in section 14.4.3.

Rather than discuss this project in detail, we shall simply describe here some of the issues that arose from its development from the previous outline version. You should supplement this discussion with a thorough reading of the source code.

The goals of the first stage were deliberately set to be quite modest, yet still relevant to the fundamental activity of the application – collecting and delivering passengers. There were good reasons for this. By setting a modest goal, the task seemed achievable within a reasonably short time. By setting a relevant goal, the task was clearly taking us closer toward completing the overall project. Such factors help to keep our motivation high.

We borrowed the concept of actors from the *foxes-and-rabbits* project of Chapter 10. For this stage, only taxis needed to be actors, through their Vehicle superclass. At each step a taxi either moves toward a target location, or remains idle (Code 14.2). Although we did not have to record any statistics at this stage, it was simple and convenient to have vehicles record a count of the number of steps for which they are idle. This anticipated part of the work of one of the later stages.

Code 14.2

The Taxi class as an actor

```
/**
 * A taxi is able to carry a single passenger.
 *
 * @author David J. Barnes and Michael Kölling
 * @version 2002.07.02
 */
public class Taxi extends Vehicle
{
    private Passenger passenger;
```

Code 14.2
continued

The Taxi class as an
actor

```java
/**
 * Constructor for objects of class Taxi
 * @param company The taxi company. Must not be null.
 * @param location The vehicle's starting point. Must not be
 *                  null.
 * @throws NullPointerException If company or location is null.
 */
public Taxi(TaxiCompany company, Location location)
{
    super(company, location);
}

/**
 * Carry out a taxi's actions.
 */
public void act()
{
    Location target = getTargetLocation();
    if(target != null) {
        // Find where to move to next.
        Location next = getLocation().nextLocation(target);
        setLocation(next);
        if(next.equals(target)) {
            if(passenger != null) {
                notifyPassengerArrival(passenger);
                offloadPassenger();
            }
            else {
                notifyPickupArrival();
            }
        }
    }
    else {
        incrementIdleCount();
    }
}

/**
 * @return Whether or not this taxi is free.
 */
public boolean isFree()
{
    return getTargetLocation() == null && passenger == null;
}

/**
 * Receive a pickup location. This becomes the
 * target location.
 * @location The pickup location.
 */
```

Code 14.2 continued

The Taxi class as an actor

```java
    public void setPickupLocation(Location location)
    {
        setTargetLocation(location);
    }

    /**
     * Receive a passenger.
     * Set their destination as the target location.
     * @param passenger The passenger.
     */
    public void pickup(Passenger passenger)
    {
        this.passenger = passenger;
        setTargetLocation(passenger.getDestination());
    }

    /**
     * Offload the passenger.
     */
    public void offloadPassenger()
    {
        passenger = null;
        clearTargetLocation();
    }

    public String toString()
    {
        return "Taxi at " + getLocation();
    }
}
```

The need to model movement required the Location class to be implemented more fully than in the outline. On the face of it, this should be a relatively simple container for a two-dimensional position within a rectangular grid. However, in practice, it also needs to provide both a test for coincidence of two locations (equals), and a way for a vehicle to find out where to move to next, based on its current location and its destination (nextLocation). At this stage, no limits were put on the grid area (other than that coordinate values should be positive), but this raises the need in a later stage for something to record the boundaries of the area in which the company operates.

One of the major issues that had to be addressed was how to manage the association between a passenger and a vehicle, between the request for a pickup and the point of the vehicle's arrival. Although we were required only to handle a single taxi and a single passenger, we tried to bear in mind that ultimately there could be multiple pickup requests outstanding at any one time. In section 14.2.3 we had decided that a vehicle should receive its passenger when it notifies the company that it has arrived at the pickup point. So, when a notification is received, the company needs to be able to work out which passenger has been assigned to that vehicle. The solution we chose was to have the company store a *vehicle:passenger* pairing in a map. When the vehicle notifies the company that it has arrived, the company passes the corresponding passenger to it. However, there are various reasons why this solution is not perfect, and we shall explore this issue further in the exercises below.

One error situation we addressed was that there might be no passenger found when a vehicle arrived at a pickup point. This would be the result of a programming error, so we defined the unchecked `MissingPassengerException` class.

As only a single passenger was required for this stage, development of the `PassengerSource` class was deferred to a later stage. Instead, passengers were created directly in the `Demo` and test classes.

Exercise 14.19 If you have not already done so, take a thorough look through the implementation in the *taxi-company-stage-one* project. Ensure that you understand how movement of the taxi is effected through its **act** method.

Exercise 14.20 Do you feel that the **TaxiCompany** object should keep separate lists of those vehicles that are free and those that are not, to improve the efficiency of its scheduling? At what points would a vehicle move between the lists?

Exercise 14.21 The next planned stage of the implementation is to provide multiple taxis to carry multiple passengers concurrently. Review the **TaxiCompany** class with this goal in mind. Do you feel that it already supports this functionality? If not, what changes are required?

Exercise 14.22 Review the way in which *vehicle:passenger* associations are stored in the **assignments** map in **TaxiCompany**. Can you see any weaknesses in this approach? Does it support more than one passenger being picked up from the same location? Could a vehicle ever need to have multiple associations recorded for it?

Exercise 14.23 If you see any problems with the current way in which *vehicle:passenger* associations are stored, would creating a unique identification for each association help – a 'booking number', say? If so, would any of the existing method signatures in the **Vehicle** hierarchy need to be changed? Implement an improved version that supports the requirements of all existing scenarios.

14.4.3 Testing the first stage

As part of the implementation of the first stage, we developed two test classes: `LocationTests` and `DeliveryTests`. The first checks basic functionality of the `Location` class that is crucial to correct movement of vehicles. The second is designed to test that the passenger is picked up and delivered to their destination in the correct number of steps, and that the taxi becomes free again immediately afterwards. In order to develop the second set of tests, the `Location` class was enhanced with the distance method, to provide the number of steps required to move between two locations.[1]

---

[1] We anticipate that this will have an extended use later in the development of the application, as it should enable the company to schedule vehicles on the basis of which one is closest to the pickup point.

In normal operation the application runs silently, and without a GUI there is no visual way to monitor the progress of a taxi. One approach would be to add print statements to the core methods of classes such as Taxi and TaxiCompany. However, BlueJ does offer the alternative of setting a breakpoint within the act method of the Taxi class, say. This would make it possible to 'observe' the movement of a taxi by inspection.

Having reached a reasonable level of confidence in the current state of the implementation, we have simply left print statements in the notification methods of TaxiCompany to provide a minimum of user feedback.

As testimony to the value of developing tests alongside implementation, it is worth recording that the existing test classes enabled us to identify and correct two serious errors in our code.

Exercise 14.24 Review the tests implemented in the **LocationTests** and **DeliveryTests** classes. Should it be possible to use these as regression tests during the next stages, or would they require changing substantially?

Exercise 14.25 Implement further test classes that you feel are necessary to increase your level of confidence in the current implementation. Fix any errors you discover in the process.

14.4.4 A later stage of development

It is not our intention to discuss in full the completion of the development of the taxi company application, as there would be little for you to gain from that. Instead, we shall briefly present the application at a later stage, and encourage you to complete the rest from there.

This more advanced stage can be found in the *taxi-company-later-stage* project. It handles multiple taxis and passengers, and a GUI provides a progressive view of the movements of both (Figure 14.2). Here is an outline of some of the major developments in this version from the previous one.

- A Simulation class now manages the actors, much as it did in the *foxes-and-rabbits* project. The actors are the vehicles, the passenger source, and a GUI provided by the CityGUI class. After each step, the simulation pauses for a brief period so that the GUI does not change too quickly.

- The need for something like the City class was identified during development of stage one. The City object defines the dimensions of the city's grid, and holds a collection of all the items of interest that are in the city: the vehicles and the passengers.

- Items in the city may optionally implement the DrawableItem interface, which allows the GUI to display them. Images of vehicles and people are provided in the images folder within the project folder for this purpose.

- The Taxi class implements the DrawableItem interface. It returns alternative images to the GUI, depending on whether it is occupied or empty. Image files exist in the images folder for a shuttle to do the same.

Figure 14.2
A visualization of the city

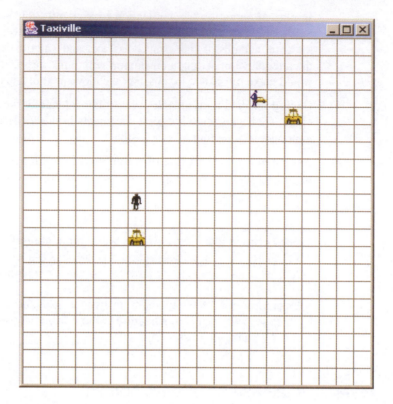

- The `PassengerSource` class has been refactored significantly from the previous version, to better fit its role as an actor. In addition, it maintains a count of missed pickups for statistical analysis.

- The `TaxiCompany` class is responsible for creating the taxis to be used in the simulation.

As you explore the source code of the *taxi-company-later-stage* project, you will find illustrations of many of the topics we have covered in the second half of this book: inheritance, polymorphism, abstraction classes, interfaces, and error handling.

Exercise 14.26 Add assertian exception-throwing consistency checks within each class to guard against inappropriate use. For instance: ensure that a `Passenger` is never created with pickup and destination locations that are the same; ensure that a taxi is never requested to go to a pickup when it already has a target location; etc.

Exercise 14.27 Report on the statistical information that is being gathered by taxis and the passenger source; on taxi idle time and missed pickups. Experiment with different numbers of taxis to see how the balance between these two sets of data varies.

Exercise 14.28 Adapt the vehicle classes so that records are kept of the amount of time spent traveling to pickup locations, and passenger destinations. Can you see a possible conflict here for shuttles?

14.4.5   Further ideas for development

The version of the application provided in the *taxi-company-later-stage* project represents a significant point in the development toward full implementation. However, there is still a lot that can be added. For instance, we have hardly developed the `Shuttle` class at all, so there are plenty of challenges to be found in completing its implementation. The major difference between shuttles and taxis is that a shuttle has to be concerned with multiple passengers, whereas a taxi has to be concerned with only one. The fact that a shuttle is already carrying a passenger should not prevent it from being sent to pick up another. Similarly, if it is already on its way to a pickup, it could still accept a further pickup request. These issues raise questions about how a shuttle organizes its priorities. Could a passenger end up being driven back and forth while the shuttle responds to competing requests, and the passenger never getting delivered? What does it mean for a shuttle to not be free? Does it mean that it is full of passengers, or that it has enough pickup requests to fill it? Suppose at least one of those pickups will reach their destination before the final pickup is reached: does that mean it could accept more pickup requests than its capacity?!

Another area for further development is vehicle scheduling. The taxi company does not operate particularly intelligently at present. How should it decide which vehicle to send when there may be more than one available? No attempt is made to assign vehicles on the basis of their distance from a pickup location. The company could use the `distance` method of the `Location` class to work out which is the nearest free vehicle to a pickup. Would this make a significant difference to the average waiting time of passengers? How might data be gathered on how long passengers wait to be picked up? What about having idle taxis move to a central location ready for their next pickup, in order to reduce potential waiting times? Does the size of the city have an impact on the effectiveness of this approach? For instance, in a large city is it better to have idle taxis space themselves out from one another, rather than all gather at the center?

Could the simulation be used to model competing taxi companies operating in the same area of the city? Multiple `TaxiCompany` objects could be created, and the passenger source allocate passengers to them competitively, on the basis of how quickly they could be picked up. Is this too fundamental a change to graft onto the existing application?

14.4.6   Reuse

Currently, our goal has been to simulate the operation of vehicles in order to assess the commercial viability of operating a business. You may have noticed that substantial parts of the application may actually be useful once the business is in operation.

Assuming that we develop a clever scheduling algorithm for our simulation to decide which vehicle should take which call, or that we have worked out a good scheme for deciding where to send the vehicles to wait while they are idle, we might decide to use the same algorithms when the company actually operates. The visual representation of each vehicle's location could also help.

In other words, there is potential to turn the simulation of the taxi company into a taxi management system used to help the real company in its operations. The structure of the application would change, of course: The program would not control and move the taxis, but rather record their positions, which it might receive from GPS (global positioning system) receivers in each vehicle. However, many of the classes developed for the simulation could be reused with little or no change. This illustrates the power of reuse that we gain from good class structure and class design.

14.5 Another example

There are many other projects that you could undertake along similar lines to the taxi company application. A popular alternative is the issue of how to schedule elevators in a large building. Coordination between elevators becomes particularly significant here. In addition, within an enclosed building, it may be possible to estimate numbers of people on each floor, and hence to anticipate demand. There are also time-related behaviors to take account of – morning arrivals, evening departures, and local peaks of activities around lunch times.

Use the approach we have outlined in this chapter to implement a simulation of a building with one or more elevators.

14.6 Taking things further

We can only take you so far by presenting our own project ideas and showing you how we would develop them. You will find that you can go much further if you develop your own ideas for projects, and implement them in your own way. Pick a topic that interests you, and work through the stages we have outlined: analyze the problem, work out some scenarios, sketch out a design, plan some implementation stages, and then make a start.

Designing and implementing programs is an exciting and creative activity. Like any worthwhile activity it takes time and practice to become proficient at it. So do not become discouraged if your early efforts seem to take for ever, or are full of errors. That is normal, and you will gradually improve with experience. Do not be too ambitious to start with, and expect to have to rework your ideas as you go – that is all part of the natural learning process.

Most of all: have fun!

Working with a BlueJ Project

A.1   Installing BlueJ

To work with BlueJ, you must install a Java 2 Standard Edition (J2SE) Software Development Kit (SDK) and the BlueJ environment.

You can find the J2SE SDK and detailed installation instructions on this book's CD or at `http://java.sun.com/j2se/`

You can find the BlueJ environment and installation instructions on this book's CD or at `http://www.bluej.org/`

A.2   Opening a project

To use any of the example projects included on this book's CD, the projects must be copied to a writable disk. BlueJ projects can be opened but not executed from a CD (to execute, BlueJ needs to write to the project folder). Therefore, it does not usually work to use projects from the CD directly.

The easiest way is to copy the folder containing all of the book's projects (named *projects*) to your hard disk.

After installing and starting BlueJ by double-clicking its icon, select *Open...* from the *Project* menu. Navigate to the *projects* folder and select a project. You can have multiple projects open at the same time.

More information about the use of BlueJ is included in the BlueJ Tutorial. The tutorial is on the book's CD, and it is also accessible via the *BlueJ Tutorial* item in BlueJ's *Help* menu.

A.3   The BlueJ debugger

Information on using the BlueJ debugger may be found in Appendix G and in the BlueJ Tutorial. The tutorial is on the book's CD, and it is also accessible via the *BlueJ Tutorial* item in BlueJ's *Help* menu.

A.4   CD contents

On the CD that is included in this book, you will find the following files and directories:

Folder	Comment
acrobat/	*Acrobat Reader for various operating systems. Acrobat Reader is a program to display and print files in PDF format. It is needed to read/print the BlueJ Tutorial. (Acrobat Reader may already be installed on your system – install this only if you cannot open the tutorial.)*
mac/	*Acrobat Reader for MacOS X.*
linux/	*Acrobat Reader for Linux.*
solaris/	*Acrobat Reader for Solaris.*
windows/	*Acrobat Reader for Microsoft Windows (all versions).*
bluej/	*The BlueJ system and documentation.*
bluejsetup-135.exe	*BlueJ installer for Microsoft Windows (all versions).*
BlueJ-135.sit	*BlueJ for MacOS X (StuffIt file).*
bluej-135.jar	*BlueJ for other systems.*
tutorial.pdf	*The BlueJ Tutorial.*
index.html	*CD documentation. Open this file in a web browser to read it. Contains CD content overview, installation instructions and other useful pointers.*
j2sdk/	*Contains Java 2 systems (Java 2 SDK) for various operating systems.*
linux/	*Java 2 SDK installer for Linux.*
solaris/	*Java 2 SDK installer for Solaris.*
windows/	*Java 2 SDK installer for Microsoft Windows (all versions).*
j2sdk-doc/	*Contains the Java 2 library documentation. This is a single zip-file. Copy this file to your hard disk and uncompress to use the documentation.*
projects/	*Contains all projects discussed in this book. Copy this complete folder to your hard disk before using the projects. Contains subfolders for each chapter.*
runthis.exe	*Support program for Microsoft Windows auto-open feature (no further relevance for this book).*
intro/	*Support files for the CD documentation text. You do not need to use the files in this directory directly. Open* index.html *instead.*

Java data types

Java knows two kinds of types: primitive types and object types. Primitive types are stored in variables directly, and they have value semantics (values are copied when assigned to another variable). Object types are stored by storing references to the object (not the object itself). When assigned to another variable, only the reference is copied, not the object.

B.1 Primitive types

The following table lists all the primitive types of the Java language:

Type name	Description	Example literals
Integer numbers		
byte	byte-sized integer (8 bit)	24 −2
short	short integer (16 bit)	137 −119
int	integer (32 bit)	5409 −2003
long	long integer (64 bit)	423266353L 55L
Real numbers		
float	single-precision floating point	43.889F
double	double-precision floating point	45.63 2.4e5
Other types		
char	a single character (16 bit)	'm' '?' '\u00F6'
boolean	a boolean value (true or false)	true false

Notes:

■ A number without a decimal point is generally interpreted as an int, but automatically converted to byte, short, or long types when assigned (if the value fits). You can declare a literal as long by putting an 'L' after the number. ('l' – lower-case L – works as well but should be avoided because it can easily be mistaken for a one.)

■ A number with a decimal point is of type double. You can specify a float literal by putting an 'F' or 'f' after the number.

■ A character can be written as a single Unicode character in single quotes or as a four-digit Unicode value, preceded by '\u'.

■ The two boolean literals are true and false.

Because variables of the primitive types do not refer to objects, there are no methods associated with the primitive types.

The following table details minimum and maximum values available in the numerical types.

Type	Minimum	Maximum
byte	−128	127
short	−32768	32767
int	−2147483648	2147483647
long	−9223372036854775808	9223372036854775807

	Positive minimum	Positive maximum
float	1.4e−45	3.4028235e38
double	4.9e−324	1.7976931348623157e308

B.2 Object types

All types not listed in the *Primitive types* section are object types. These include class and interface types from the standard Java library (such as String) and user-defined types.

A variable of an object type holds a reference (or 'pointer') to an object. Assignments and parameter passing have reference semantics (i.e. the reference is copied, not the object). After assigning a variable to another one, both variables refer to the same object. The two variables are said to be aliases for the same object.

Classes are the templates for objects, defining the fields and methods that each instance possesses.

Arrays behave like object types – they also have reference semantics.

B.3 Wrapper classes

Every primitive type in Java has a corresponding wrapper class that represents the same type but is a real object type. This makes it possible to use values from the primitive types where object types are required. The following table lists the primitive types and their corresponding wrapper type from the java.lang package. Apart from Integer and Character, the wrapper class names are the same as the primitive type names, but with an upper-case first letter.

Primitive type	Wrapper type
byte	Byte
short	Short
int	Integer
long	Long
float	Float
double	Double
char	Character
boolean	Boolean

APPENDIX C

Java control structures

C.1 Selection statements

if-else

The *if-else* statement has two forms:

```java
if (expression) {
    statements
}
```

```java
if (expression) {
    statements
}
else {
    statements
}
```

Examples:

```java
if(field.size() == 0) {
    System.out.println("The field is empty.");
}
```

```java
if(number < 0) {
    reportError();
}
else {
    processNumber(number);
}
```

```java
if(n < 0) {
    handleNegative();
}
else if(number == 0) {
    handleZero();
}
else {
    handlePositive();
}
```

switch

The *switch* statement switches on a single value to one of an arbitrary number of cases. Two possible use patterns are:

```
switch (expression) {               switch (expression) {
    case value: statements;             case value1:
            break;                      case value2:
    case value: statements;             case value3:
            break;                          statements;
    further cases omitted                   break;
    default: statements;                case value4:
            break;                      case value5:
}                                           statements;
                                            break;
                                        further cases omitted
                                        default:
                                            statements;
                                            break;
                                    }
```

Notes:

- A *switch* statement can have any number of case labels.
- The *break* instruction after every case is needed, otherwise the execution 'falls through' into the next label's statements. The second form above makes use of this. In this case, all three of the first values will execute the first *statements* section, whereas values four and five will execute the second *statements* section.
- The *default* case is optional. If no default is given, it may happen that no case is executed.
- The *break* instruction after the default (or the last case, if there is no default) is not needed, but is considered good style.

Examples:

```
switch(day) {
    case 1:  dayString = "Monday";
            break;
    case 2:  dayString = "Tuesday";
            break;
    case 3:  dayString = "Wednesday";
            break;
    case 4:  dayString = "Thursday";
            break;
    case 5:  dayString = "Friday";
            break;
    case 6:  dayString = "Saturday";
            break;
    case 7:  dayString = "Sunday";
            break;
    default: dayString = "invalid day";
            break;
}
```

```
switch(month) {
    case 1:
    case 3:
    case 5:
    case 7:
    case 8:
    case 10:
    case 12:
        numberOfDays = 31;
        break;
    case 4:
    case 6:
    case 9:
    case 11:
        numberOfDays = 30;
        break;
    case 2:
        if(isLeapYear())
            numberOfDays = 29;
        else
            numberOfDays = 28;
        break;
}
```

C.2 Loops

Java has three loops: *while*, *do-while*, and *for*.

while

The *while* loop executes a block of statements as long as a given expression evaluates to *true*. The expression is tested before execution of the loop body, so the body may be executed zero times (not at all).

```
while (expression) {
    statements
}
```

Examples:

```
int i = 0;
while(i < text.size()) {
    System.out.println(text.get(i));
    i++;
}


while(iter.hasNext()) {
    processObject(iter.next());
}
```

do-while

The *do-while* loop executes a block of statements as long as a given expression evaluates to *true*. The expression is tested after execution of the loop body, so the body always executes at least once.

```
do {
    statements
} while (expression);
```

Example:

```
do {
    input = readInput();
    if(input == null) {
        System.out.println("try again");
    }
} while(input == null);
```

for

The *for* loop executes as long as a *condition* evaluates to *true*. Before the loop starts, an *initialization* statement is executed exactly once. The *condition* is evaluated before every execution of the loop body (so the loop may execute zero times). An *increment* statement is executed after each execution of the loop body.

```
for (initialization; condition; increment) {
    statements
}
```

Example:

```
for(int i = 0; i < text.size(); i++) {
    System.out.println(text.get(i));
}
```

C.3 Exceptions

Throwing and catching exceptions provides another pair of constructs to alter control flow.

```
try {
    statements
}
catch (exception-type name) {
    statements
}
finally {
    statements
}
```

Example:

```java
try {
    FileWriter writer = new FileWriter("foo.txt");
    writer.write(text);
    writer.close();
}
catch(IOException e) {
    Debug.reportError("writing text to file failed");
    Debug.reportError("The exception is: " + e);
}
```

An exception statement may have any number of catch clauses. They are evaluated in order of appearance, and only the first matching clause is executed. (A clause matches if the dynamic type of the exception object being thrown is assignment-compatible with the declared exception type in the catch clause.) The finally clause is optional.

C.4   Assertions

There are two forms of assert statement:

```java
assert boolean-expression ;
assert boolean-expression : expression ;
```

Examples:

```java
assert getDetails(key) != null;

assert expected == actual :
        "Actual value: " + actual +
        " does not match expected value: " + expected;
```

If the assertion expression evaluates to *false* then an `AssertionError` will be thrown.

D.1 Arithmetic expressions

Java has a considerable number of operators available for both arithmetic and logical expressions. Table D.1 shows everything that is classified as an operator, including things such as type casting and parameter passing. The main arithmetic operations are:

+	*addition*
–	*subtraction*
*	*multiplication*
/	*division*
%	*modulus* or *remainder-after-division*

The results of both division and modulus operations depend on whether their operands are integers or floating point values. Between two integer values, division yields an integer result and discards any remainder, but between floating point values a floating point value is the result:

```
5 / 3 gives a result of 1
5.0 / 3 gives a result of 1.6666666666666667
```

(Note that only one of the operands needs to be of a floating point type to produce a floating point result.)

When more than one operator appears in an expression, then *rules of precedence* have to be used to work out the order of application. In Table D.1 those operators having the highest precedence appear at the top, so we can see that multiplication, division, and modulus all take precedence over addition and subtraction, for instance. This means that both of the following examples give the result 100:

```
51 * 3 − 53
154 − 2 * 27
```

Operators with the same precedence level are evaluated from left to right.

When it is necessary to alter the normal order of evaluation, parentheses can be used. So both of the following examples give the result 100:

```
(205 − 5) / 2
2 * (47 + 3)
```

Table D.1

Java operators, highest precedence at the top

[]	.	++	--	(parameters)	
++	--	+	-	!	~
new	(cast)				
*	/	%			
+	-				
<<	>>	>>>			
<	>	>=	<=	instanceof	
==	!=				
&					
^					
&&					
||					
?:					
=	+=	-=	*=	/=	%=	>>=	<<=	>>>=	&=	|=	^=

D.2   Boolean expressions

In boolean expressions, operators are used to combine operands to produce a value of either `true` or `false`. Such expressions are usually found in the test expressions of *if-else statements* and loops.

The relational operators usually combine a pair of arithmetic operands, although the tests for equality and inequality are also used with object references. Java's relational operators are:

==	*equal-to*		!=	*not-equal-to*
<	*less-than*		<=	*less-than-or-equal-to*
>	*greater-than*		>=	*greater-than-or-equal-to*

The binary logical operators combine two boolean expressions to produce another boolean value. The operators are:

&&	*and*
||	*or*
^	*exclusive-or*

In addition,

!	*not*

takes a single boolean expression and changes it from `true` to `false`, and vice versa.

Running Java without BlueJ

Throughout this book we have used BlueJ to develop and execute our Java applications. There is a good reason for this: BlueJ gives us some tools to make some development tasks very easy. In particular, it lets us execute individual methods of classes and objects easily – this is very useful if we want to quickly test a segment of new code.

We separate the discussion of working without BlueJ into two categories: executing an application without BlueJ, and developing without BlueJ.

E.1   Executing without BlueJ

Usually, when applications are delivered to end users, they are executed differently. They then have one single starting point, which defines where execution begins when a user starts an application.

The exact mechanism used to start an application depends on the operating system. Usually, this is done by double-clicking an application icon, or by entering the name of the application on a command line. The operating system then needs to know which method of which class to invoke to execute the complete program.

In Java, this problem is solved using a convention. When a Java program is started, the name of the class is specified as a parameter of the start command, and the name of the method is fixed: it is 'main.' For example, consider the following command, entered at a command line, such as the Windows command prompt or a Unix terminal:

```
java Game
```

The `java` command starts the Java virtual machine. It is part of the Java Software Development Kit (SDK), which must be installed on your system. `Game` is the name of the class that we want to start.

The Java system will then look for a method in class `Game` with exactly the following signature:

```
public static void main(String[] args)
```

The method has to be public, so that it can be invoked from the outside. It has to be static, because no objects exist when we start off. Initially, we have only classes, so static methods are all we can call. This static method then typically creates the first object. The return type is void, as this method does not return a value. The name 'main' is arbitrarily chosen by the Java developers, but it is fixed: the method must have this name. (The choice of 'main' for the name of the initial method actually goes back to the C language, from which Java inherits much of its syntax.)

The parameter is a `String` array. This allows users to pass in additional arguments. In our example, the value of the `args` parameter will be an array of length zero. The command line starting the program can, however, define arguments:

```
java Game 2 Fred
```

Every word after the class name in this command line will be read as a separate `String` and passed into the `main` method as an element in the string array. In this case, the `args` array would contain two elements, which are the strings `"2"` and `"Fred"`. Command line parameters are not very often used with Java.

The body of the main method can theoretically contain any statements you like. Good style, however, dictates that the length of the main method should be kept to a minimum. Specifically, it should not contain anything that is part of the application logic.

Typically, the `main` method should do exactly what you did interactively to start the same application in BlueJ. If, for instance, you created an object of class `Game` and invoked a method named `start` to start an application, you should add the following main method to the `Game` class:

```
public static void main(String[] args)
{
    Game game = new Game();
    game.start();
}
```

Now, executing the `main` method will mimic your interactive invocation of the game.

Java projects are usually stored in a separate directory for each project. All classes for the project are placed inside this directory. When you execute the command to start Java and execute your application, make sure that the project directory is the active directory in your command terminal. This ensures that the classes will be found.

If the specified class cannot be found, the Java virtual machine will generate an error message similar to this:

```
Exception in thread "main" java.lang.NoClassDefFoundError: Game
```

If you see a message like this, make sure that you have typed the class name correctly, and that the current directory actually contains this class. The class is stored in a file with the suffix '.class'. The code for class `Game`, for example, is stored in a file named `Game.class`.

If the class is found, but it does not contain a main method (or the main method does not have the right signature), you will see a message similar to this:

```
Exception in thread "main" java.lang.NoSuchMethodError: main
```

In that case, make sure that the class you want to execute has a correct main method.

E.2   Creating executable .jar files

Java projects are typically stored as a collection of files in a directory (or 'folder'). We shall briefly discuss the different files below.

To distribute applications to others it is often easier if the whole application is stored in a single file. Java's mechanism for doing this is the Java Archive ('.jar') format. All of the files of an application can be bundled into a single file, and they can still be executed. (If you are familiar with the 'zip' compression format, it might be interesting to know that the format is, in fact, the same. Jar files can be opened with zip programs and vice versa.)

To make a .jar file executable, it is necessary to specify the main class somewhere. (Remember: The executed method is always `main`, but we need to specify the class this method is in.) This is done by including a text file in the .jar file (the **manifest file**) with this information. Luckily, BlueJ takes care of this for you.

To create an executable .jar file in BlueJ, use the *Project – Export* function, and specify the class that contains the main method in the following dialog. (You must still write a main method exactly as discussed above.)

For details with this function, read the BlueJ tutorial, which you can get through the BlueJ menu *Help – Tutorial*, or from the BlueJ web site.

Once the executable .jar file has been created, it can be executed by double-clicking it. The computer that executes this .jar file must have the JDK (Java Development Kit) or JRE (Java Runtime Environment) installed and associated with .jar files.

E.3   Developing without BlueJ

If you not only want to execute but also to develop your programs without BlueJ, you will need to edit and compile the classes. The source code of a class is stored in a file ending in '.java'. For example, class `Game` is stored in a file called `Game.java`. Source files can be edited with any text editor. There are many free or inexpensive text editors around. Some, such as *Notepad* or *Wordpad*, are distributed with Windows, but if you really want to use the editor for more than a quick test, you will soon want to get a better one. Be careful with word processors, though. Word processors typically do not save the text in plain text format, and the Java system will not be able to read it.

The source files can then be compiled from a command line with the Java compiler that is included with the JDK. It is called `javac`. To compile a source file named `Game.java`, use the command

```
javac Game.java
```

This command will compile the `Game` class, and any other classes it depends on. It will create a file called `Game.class`. This file contains the code that can be executed by the Java virtual machine. To execute it, use the command

```
java Game
```

Note that this command does not include the '.class' suffix.

Configuring BlueJ

Many of the settings of BlueJ can be configured to better suit your personal situation. Some configuration options are available through the *Preferences* dialog in the BlueJ system, but many more configuration options are accessible by editing the 'BlueJ definitions file.' The location of that file is *<bluej_home>/lib/bluej.defs*, where *<bluej_home>* is the folder where the BlueJ system is installed.

Configuration details are explained in the 'Tips archive' on the BlueJ web site. You can access it at

```
http://www.bluej.org/help/archive.html
```

Following are some of the most common things people like to configure. Many more configuration options can be found by reading the *bluej.defs* file.

F.1 Changing the interface language

You can change the interface language to one of several available languages. To do this, open the *bluej.defs* file, and find the line that reads

```
bluej.language=english
```

Change it to one of the other available languages. For example:

```
bluej.language=spanish
```

Comments in the file list all available languages. They include at least Afrikaans, Chinese, Czech, English, French, German, Italian, Japanese, Korean, Portuguese, Spanish, and Swedish.

F.2 Using local API documentation

You can use a local copy of the Java class library (API) documentation. That way, access to the documentation is faster, and you can use the documentation without being online.

To do this, copy the Java documentation file from the book's CD (a zip file) and unzip it at a location where you want to store the Java documentation. This will create a folder named *docs*.

Then open a web browser, and using the 'Open File...' (or equivalent) function, open the file *api/index.html* inside the *docs* folder.

Once the API view is correctly displayed in the browser, copy the URL (web address) from your browser's address field, open BlueJ, open the *Preferences* dialog, go to the *Miscellaneous* tab, and paste the copied URL into the field labeled *JDK documentation URL*.

Using the *Java Class Libraries* item from the *Help* menu should now open your local copy.

F.3 Changing the new class templates

When you create a new class, the class's source is set to a default source text. This text is taken from a template, and can be changed to suit your preferences.

Templates are stored in the folders

> *<bluej_home>/lib/<language>/templates/* and

> *<bluej_home>/lib/<language>/templates/newclass/*

where *<bluej_home>* is the BlueJ installation folder, and *<language>* is your currently used language setting (for example *english*).

Template files are pure text files and can be edited in any standard text editor.

APPENDIX
G
Using the debugger

The BlueJ debugger provides a set of basic debugging features that are intentionally simplified yet genuinely useful, both for debugging programs and for gaining an understanding of the runtime behavior of programs.

The debugger window can be accessed by selecting the *Show Debugger* item from the *View* menu, or by pressing the right mouse button over the work indicator and selecting *Show Debugger* from the popup menu. Figure G.1 shows the debugger window.

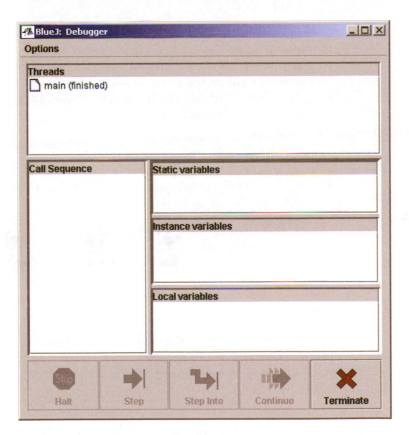

Figure G.1 The BlueJ debugger window

The debugger window contains five display areas and five control buttons. The areas and buttons become active only when a program reaches a breakpoint or halts for some other reason. The following sections describe how to set breakpoints, how to control program execution, and the purpose of each of the display areas.

G.1 Breakpoints

A breakpoint is a flag attached to a line of code (Figure G.2). When a breakpoint is reached during program execution, the debugger's displays and controls become active, allowing you to inspect the state of the program and control further execution.

```
31    /**
32     * Print the next mail item (if any) for this user to the text
33     * terminal.
34     */
35    public void printNextMailItem()
36    {
      MailItem item = server.getNextMailItem(user);
38        if(item == null) {
39            System.out.println("No new mail.");
40        }
41        else {
42            item.print();
43        }
44    }
```

Breakpoints are set via the editor window. Either press the left mouse button in the breakpoint area to the left of the source text, or place the cursor on the line of code where the breakpoint should be and select *Set/Clear Breakpoint* from the editor's *Tools* menu. Breakpoints can be removed by the reverse process. Breakpoints can be set only within classes that have been compiled.

G.2 The control buttons

Figure G.3 shows the control buttons that are active at a breakpoint.

G.2.1 Halt

The *Halt* button is active when the program is running, thus allowing execution to be interrupted should that be necessary. If execution is halted, the debugger will show the state of the program as if a breakpoint had been reached.

G.2.2 Step

The *Step* button resumes execution at the current statement. Execution will pause again when the statement is completed. If the statement involves a method call, the complete method call is completed before the execution pauses again (unless the call leads to another explicit breakpoint).

G.2.3 Step Into

The *Step Into* button resumes execution at the current statement. If this statement is a method call, then execution will step into that method and be paused at the first statement inside it.

G.2.4 Continue

The *Continue* button resumes execution until the next breakpoint is reached, execution is interrupted via the *Halt* button, or the execution completes normally.

G.2.5 Terminate

The *Terminate* button aggressively finishes execution of the current program such that it cannot be resumed again. If it is simply desired to interrupt the execution in order to examine the current program state, then the *Halt* operation is to be preferred.

G.3 The variable displays

Figure G.4 shows all three variable display areas active at a breakpoint, in an example taken from the predator–prey simulation discussed in Chapter 10. Static variables are displayed in the upper area, instance variables in the middle area, and local variables in the lower area.

Figure G.4

Active variable displays

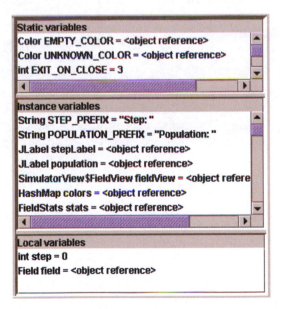

When a breakpoint is reached, execution will be halted at a statement of an arbitrary object within the current program. The *Static variables* area displays the values of the static variables defined in the class of that object. The *Instance variables* area displays the values of that particular object's instance variables. Both areas also include any variables inherited from superclasses.

The *Local variables* area displays the values of local variables and parameters of the currently executing method or constructor. Local variables will appear in this area only once they have been initialized, as it is only at that point that they come into existence within the virtual machine.

A variable in any of these areas that is an object reference may be inspected by double-clicking on it.

G.4 The Call Sequence display

Figure G.5 shows the *Call Sequence* display, containing a sequence four methods deep. Methods appear in the format `Class.method` in the sequence, irrespective of whether they are static methods or instance methods. Constructors appear as `Class.<init>` in the sequence.

Figure G.5

A call sequence

The call sequence operates as a stack, with the method at the top of the sequence being the one where flow of execution currently lies. The variable display areas reflect the details of the method or constructor currently highlighted in the call sequence. Selecting a different line of the sequence will update the contents of the other display areas.

G.5 The Threads display

The *Threads display* area is beyond the scope of this book and will not be discussed further.

JUnit unit-testing tools

In this appendix we give a brief outline of the main features of BlueJ's support for JUnit-style unit testing. More detail can be found in the testing tutorial that is available from the book's CD and the BlueJ web site.

H.1 Enabling unit-testing functionality

In order to enable the unit-testing functionality of BlueJ, it is necessary to ensure that the *Show unit testing tools* box is ticked under the *Tools-Preferences-Miscellaneous* menu. The main BlueJ window will then contain a number of extra buttons that are active when a project is open.

H.2 Creating a test class

A test class is created by right-clicking a class in the class diagram and choosing *Create Test Class*. The name of the test class is determined automatically by adding `Test` as a suffix to the name of the associated class. Alternatively, a test class may be created by selecting the *New Class...* button and choosing *Unit Test* for the class type. In this case you have a free choice over its name.

Test classes are annotated with `<<unit test>>` in the class diagram, and they have a color distinct from ordinary classes.

H.3 Creating a test method

Test methods can be created interactively. A sequence of user interactions with the class diagram and object bench are recorded, and then captured as a sequence of Java statements and declarations in a method of the test class. Start recording by selecting *Create Test Method* from the popup menu associated with a test class. You will be prompted for the name of the new method. If the name does not start with `test` then this will be added as a prefix to the method name. The *recording* symbol to the left of the class diagram will then be colored red, and the *End* and *Cancel* buttons become available.

Once recording has started, any object creations or method calls will form part of the code of the method being created. Select *End* to complete the recording and capture the test, or *Cancel* to discard the recording leaving the test class unchanged.

H.4 Test assertions

While recording a test method, any method calls that return a result will bring up a *Method Result* window. This offers the opportunity to assert something about the result value by ticking the *Assert that* box. A drop-down menu contains a set of possible assertions for the result value. If an assertion is made, this will be encoded as a method call in the test method that is intended to lead to an `AssertionError` if the test fails.

H.5 Running tests

Individual test methods can be run by selecting them from the popup menu associated with the test class. A successful test will be indicated by a message in the main window's status line. An unsuccessful test will cause the *Test Results* window to appear. Selecting *Test All* from the test class's popup menu runs all tests from a single test class. The *Test Results* window will detail the success or failure of each method.

H.6 Fixtures

The contents of the object bench may be captured as a *fixture* by selecting *Object Bench to Test Fixture* from the popup menu associated with the test class. The effect of creating a fixture is that a field definition for each object is added to the test class, and statements are added to its `setUp` method that re-create the exact state of the objects as they were on the bench. The objects are then removed from the bench.

The `setUp` method is automatically executed before the run of any test method, so all objects in a fixture are available for all tests.

The objects of a fixture may be recreated on the object bench by selecting *Test Fixture to Object Bench* from the test class's menu.

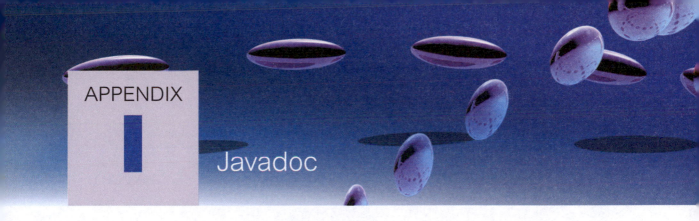

Javadoc

Writing good documentation for class and interface definitions is an important complement to writing good quality source code. Documentation allows you to communicate your intentions to human readers in the form of a natural-language high-level overview, rather than forcing them to read relatively low-level source code. Of particular value is documentation for the public elements of a class or interface, so that programmers can make use of it without having to know details of its implementation.

In all of the project examples in this book we have used a particular commenting style that is recognized by the javadoc documentation tool, which is distributed as part of Sun Microsystems' Java SDK. This tool automates the generation of class documentation in the form of HTML pages in a consistent style. The Java API has been documented using this same tool, and its value is appreciated when using library classes.

In this appendix we give a brief summary of the main elements of the documentation comments that you should get into the habit of using in your own source code.

I.1 Documentation comments

The elements of a class to be documented are the class definition as a whole, its fields, constructors, and methods. Most important from the viewpoint of a user of your class is to have documentation for the class and its public constructors and methods. We have tended not to provide javadoc-style commenting for fields because we regard these as private implementation-level detail and not something to be relied upon by users.

Documentation comments are always opened with the character triplet '/**' and closed by the character pair '*/'. Between these symbols, a comment will have a **main description** followed by a **tag section**, although both are optional.

I.1.1 The main description

The main description for a class should be a general description of the purpose of the class. Code I.1 shows part of a typical main description, taken from the Game class of the *world-of-zuul* project. Note how the description includes details of how to use this class to start the game.

Code I.1

The main description of a class comment

```
/**
 * This class is the main class of the "World of Zuul"
 * application.
 * "World of Zuul" is a very simple, text based adventure game.
 * Users can walk around some scenery. That's all. It should
 * really be extended to make it more interesting!
 * To play this game, create an instance of this class and call
 * the "play" method.
 */
```

The main description for a method should be kept fairly general, without going into a lot of detail about how the method is implemented. Indeed, the main description for a method will often only need to be a single sentence, such as

```
/**
 * Create a new passenger with distinct pickup and destination
 * locations.
 */
```

Particular thought should be given to the first sentence of the main description for a class, interface, or method as it is used in a separate summary at the top of the generated documentation.

Javadoc also supports the use of HTML mark-up within these comments.

I.1.2 The tag section

Following the main description comes the tag section. Javadoc recognizes around 20 tags, of which we discuss only the most important here (Table I.1). Tags can be used in two forms: **block tags** and **in-line tags**. We shall only discuss block tags, as these are the most commonly used. Further details about in-line tags and the remaining available tags can be found in the *javadoc* section of the *Tools and Utilities* documentation that is part of the Java SDK.

Table I.1

Common javadoc tags

Tag	Associated text
@author	author name(s)
@param	parameter name and description
@return	description of the return value
@see	cross reference
@throws	exception-type thrown and the circumstances
@version	version description

The @author and @version tags are regularly found in class and interface comments and cannot be used in constructor, method, or field comments. Both are followed by free-text and there is no required format for either. Examples are

```
@author Hacker T. Largebrain
@version 2004.12.31
```

The `@param` and `@throws` tags are used with methods and constructors, whereas `@return` is just used with methods. Examples are

```
@param limit The maximum value allowed.
@return A random number in the range 1 to limit (inclusive).
@throws IllegalLimitException If limit is less than 1.
```

The `@see` tag has several different forms, and may be used in any documentation comment. It provides a way to cross-reference a comment to another class, method, or other form of documentation. A *See Also* section is added to the item being commented. Here are some typical examples:

```
@see "The Java Language Specification, by Joy et al"
@see <a href=http://www.bluej.org/>The BlueJ web site</a>
@see #isAlive
@see java.util.ArrayList#add
```

The first simply embeds a text string with no hyperlink; the second embeds a hyperlink to the specified document; the third links to the documentation for the `isAlive` method in the same class; the fourth links to the documentation for the `add` method in the `java.util.ArrayList` class.

I.2   BlueJ support for javadoc

If a project has been commented using the `javadoc` style, then BlueJ provides support for generating the complete HTML documentation. In the main window, select the *Tools/Project Documentation* menu item and the documentation will be generated (if necessary) and displayed within a browser window.

Within the BlueJ editor, the source-code view of a class can be switched to the documentation view by changing the *Implementation* option to *Interface* at the right of the window (Figure I.1). This provides a quick preview of the documentation, but will not contain references to documentation of superclasses or used classes.

Figure I.1

The Implementation- and Interface-View option

More detail is available at:

```
http://java.sun.com/j2se/javadoc/writingdoccomments/index.html
```

Program style guide

1 Naming

1.1 Use meaningful names

Use descriptive names for all identifiers (names of classes, variables, and methods). Avoid ambiguity. Avoid abbreviations. Simple mutator methods should be named *setSomething(...)*. Simple accessor methods should be named *getSomething(...)*. Accessor methods with boolean return values are often called *isSomething(...)* – for example, `isEmpty()`.

1.2 Class names start with a capital letter

1.3 Class names are singular nouns

1.4 Method and variable names start with lower-case letters

All three – class, method, and variable names – use capital letters in the middle to increase readability of compound identifiers, e.g. `numberOfItems`.

1.5 Constants are written in UPPER-CASE

Constants occasionally use underscores to indicate compound identifiers: MAXIMUM_SIZE.

2 Layout

2.1 One level of indentation is four spaces

2.2 All statements within a block are indented one level

2.3 Braces for classes and methods are alone on one line

The braces for class and method blocks are on separate lines and are at the same indentation level. For example:

```
public int getAge()
{
    statements
}
```

2.4 For all other blocks, braces open at the end of a line

All other blocks open with braces at the end of the line that contains the key word defining the block. The closing brace is on a separate line, aligned under the key word that defines the block. For example:

```
while(condition) {
    statements
}

if(condition) {
    statements
}
else {
    statements
}
```

2.5 Always use braces in control structures

Braces are used in if-statements and loops even if the body is only a single statement.

2.6 Use a space before the opening brace of a control structure's block

2.7 Use a space around operators

2.8 Use a blank line between methods (and constructors)

Use blank lines to separate logical blocks of code. This means at least between methods, but also between logical parts within a method.

3   Documentation

3.1 Every class has a class comment at the top

The class comment contains at least

- a general description of the class;
- the author's name(s);
- a version number.

Every person who has contributed to the class has to be named as an author or has to be otherwise appropriately credited.

A version number can be a simple number, a date, or other formats. The important thing is that a reader must be able to recognize whether two versions are not the same, and be able to determine which one is newer.

3.2 Every method has a method comment

3.3 Comments are Javadoc-readable

Class and method comments must be recognized by Javadoc. In other words: they should start with the comment symbol /**.

3.4 Code comments (only) where necessary

Comments in the code should be included where the code is not obvious or difficult to understand (and preference should be given to make the code obvious or easy to understand where possible), and where it helps understanding of a method. Do not comment obvious statements – assume your reader understands Java!

4   Language use restrictions

4.1 Order of declarations: fields, constructors, methods

The elements of a class definition appear (if present) in the following order: package statement; import statements; class comment; class header; field definitions; constructors; methods.

4.2 Fields may not be public (except for final fields)

4.3 Always use an access modifier

Specify all fields and methods as either private, public, or protected. Never use default (package private) access.

4.4 Import classes separately

Import statements explicitly naming every class are preferred over importing whole packages. For example:

```
import java.util.ArrayList;
import java.util.HashSet;
```

is better than

```
import java.util.*;
```

4.5 Always include a constructor (even if the body is empty)

4.6 Always include a superclass constructor call

In constructors of subclasses, do not rely on automatic insertion of a superclass call. Include the super(...) call explicitly, even if it would work without it.

4.7 Initialize all fields in the constructor

5 Code idioms

5.1 Use iterators with collections

To iterate over a collection, use iterators, not `int` indices.

Important library classes

The Java 2 Platform includes a rich set of libraries that support a wide variety of programming tasks.

In this appendix we briefly summarize details of some classes and interfaces from the most important packages of the Java 2 Platform API. A competent Java programmer should be familiar with most of these. This appendix is only a summary, and it should be read in conjunction with the full API documentation.

K.1 The `java.lang` package

Classes and interfaces in the `java.lang` package are fundamental to the Java language. As such, this package is automatically imported implicitly into any class definition.

package `java.lang` – Summary of the most important classes	
class `Math`	`Math` is a class containing only static fields and methods. Values for the mathematical constants `e` and π are defined here, along with trigonometric functions, and others such as `abs`, `min`, `max`, and `sqrt`.
class `Object`	All classes have `Object` as a superclass at the root of their class hierarchy. From it all objects inherit default implementations for important methods such as `equals` and `toString`. Other significant methods defined by this class are `clone` and `hashCode`.
class `String`	Strings are an important feature of many applications, and they receive special treatment in Java. Key methods of the `String` class are `charAt`, `equals`, `indexOf`, `length`, `split`, and `substring`. Strings are immutable objects, so methods such as `trim` that appear to be mutators actually return a new `String` object representing the result of the operation.
class `StringBuffer`	The `StringBuffer` class offers an efficient alternative to `String` when it is required to build up a string from a number of components: e.g. via concatenation. Its key methods are `append`, `insert`, and `toString`.

K.2 The `java.util` package

The `java.util` package is a relatively incoherent collection of useful classes and interfaces.

package `java.util` – Summary of the most important classes and interfaces	
interface `Collection`	This interface provides the core set of methods for most of the collection-based classes defined in the `java.util` package, such as `ArrayList`, `HashSet`, and `LinkedList`. It defines signatures for the `add`, `clear`, `iterator`, `remove`, and `size` methods.
interface `Iterator`	`Iterator` defines a simple and consistent interface for iterating over the contents of a collection. Its three methods are `hasNext`, `next`, and `remove`.
interface `List`	`List` is an extension of the `Collection` interface, and provides a means to impose a sequence on the selection. As such, many of its methods take an index parameter: for instance, `add`, `get`, `remove`, and `set`. Classes such as `ArrayList` and `LinkedList` implement `List`.
interface `Map`	The `Map` interface offers an alternative to list-based collections by supporting the idea of associating each object in a collection with a *key* value. Objects are added and retrieved via its `put` and `get` methods. Note that a `Map` does not return an `Iterator`, but its `keySet` method returns a `Set` of the keys, and its `values` method returns a `Collection` of the objects in the map.
interface `Set`	`Set` extends the `Collection` interface with the intention of mandating that a collection contains no duplicate elements. It is worth pointing out that, because it is an interface, `Set` has no actual implication to enforce this restriction. This means that `Set` is actually provided as a marker interface to enable collection implementers to indicate that their classes fulfill this particular restriction.
class `ArrayList`	An implementation of the `List` interface that uses an array to provide efficient direct access via integer indices to the objects it stores. If objects are added or removed from anywhere other than the last position in the list, then following items have to be moved to make space or close the gap. Key methods are `add`, `get`, `iterator`, `remove`, and `size`.
class `Collections`	`Collections` is a collecting point for static methods that are used to manipulate collections. Key methods are `binarySearch`, `fill`, and `sort`.
class `HashMap`	`HashMap` is an implementation of the `Map` interface. Key methods are `get`, `put`, `remove`, and `size`. Iteration over a `HashMap` is usually a two-stage process: obtain the set of keys via its `keySet` method, and then iterate over the keys.
class `HashSet`	`HashSet` is a hash-based implementation of the `Set` interface. It is closer in usage to a `Collection` than to a `HashMap`. Key methods are `add`, `remove`, and `size`.
class `LinkedList`	`LinkedList` is an implementation of the `List` interface that uses an internal linked structure to store objects. Direct access to the ends of the list is efficient, but access to individual objects via an index is less efficient than with an `ArrayList`. On the other hand, adding objects or removing them from within the list requires no shifting of existing objects. Key methods are `add`, `getFirst`, `getLast`, `iterator`, `removeFirst`, `removeLast`, and `size`.

package `java.util` – Summary of the most important classes and interfaces	
class `Random`	The `Random` class supports generation of pseudo-random values – typically random numbers. The sequence of numbers generated is determined by a seed value, which may be passed to a constructor or set via a call to `setSeed`. Two `Random` objects starting from the same seed will return the same sequence of values to identical calls. Key methods are `nextBoolean`, `nextDouble`, `nextInt`, and `setSeed`.
class `StringTokenizer`	The `StringTokenizer` class provides an alternative to the `split` method of `String` for breaking up strings. It uses a set of delimiters to identify the boundaries between tokens. Key methods are `countTokens`, `hasMoreTokens`, and `nextToken`.

K.3 The `java.io` package

The `java.io` package contains classes that support input and output. Many of the input/output classes are distinguished by whether they are stream-based – operating on binary data – or `readers` and `writers` – operating on characters.

package `java.io` – Summary of the most important classes and interfaces	
interface `Serializable`	The `Serializable` interface is an empty interface requiring no code to be written in an implementing class. Classes implement this interface in order to be able to participate in the serialization process. `Serializable` objects may be written and read as a whole to and from sources of output and input. This makes storage and retrieval of persistent data a relatively simple process in Java. See the `ObjectInputStream` and `ObjectOutputStream` classes for further information.
class `BufferedReader`	`BufferedReader` is a class that provides buffered character-based access to a source of input. Buffered input is often more efficient than unbuffered, particularly if the source of input is in the external file system. Because it buffers input, it is able to offer a `readLine` method that is not available in most other input classes. Key methods are `close`, `read`, and `readLine`.
class `BufferedWriter`	`BufferedWriter` is a class that provides buffered character-based output. Buffered output is often more efficient than unbuffered, particularly if the destination of the output is in the external file system. Key methods are `close`, `flush`, and `write`.
class `File`	The `File` class provides an object representation for files and folders (directories) in an external file system. Methods exist to indicate whether a file is readable and/or writeable, and whether it is a file or a folder. A `File` object can be created for a non-existent file, which may be a first step in creating a physical file on the file system. Key methods are `canRead`, `canWrite`, `createNewFile`, `createTempFile`, `getName`, `getParent`, `getPath`, `isDirectory`, `isFile`, and `listFiles`.

package `java.io` – Summary of the most important classes and interfaces	
class `FileReader`	The `FileReader` class is used to open an external file ready for reading its contents as characters. A `FileReader` object is often passed to the constructor of another reader class (such as a `BufferedReader`) rather than being used directly. Key methods are `close` and `read`.
class `FileWriter`	The `FileWriter` class is used to open an external file ready for writing character-based data. Pairs of constructors determine whether an existing file will be appended or its existing contents discarded. A `FileWriter` object is often passed to the constructor of another writer class (such as a `BufferedWriter`) rather than being used directly. Key methods are `close`, `flush`, and `write`.
class `IOException`	`IOException` is a checked exception class that is at the root of the exception hierarchy of most input/output exceptions.

K.4 The `java.net` package

The `java.net` package contains classes and interfaces supporting networked applications. Most of these are outside the scope of this book.

package `java.net` – Summary of the most important classes	
class `URL`	The `URL` class represents a Uniform Resource Locator: in other words, it provides a way to describe the location of something on the Internet. In fact, it can also be used to describe the location of something on a local file system. We have included it here because classes from the `java.io` and `javax.swing` packages often use `URL` objects. Key methods are `getContent`, `getFile`, `getHost`, `getPath`, and `openStream`.

K.5 Other important packages

Other important packages are

```
java.awt
java.awt.event
javax.swing
javax.swing.event
```

These are used extensively when writing graphical user interfaces (GUIs), and they contain many useful classes that a GUI programmer should become familiar with.

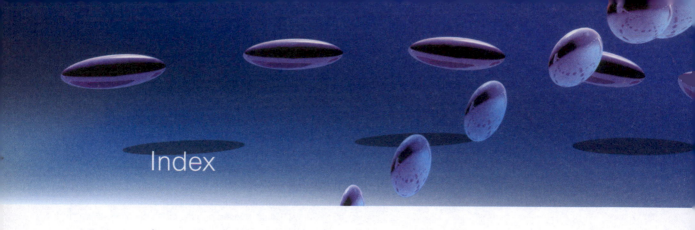

Index

End User License Agreements

Sun Confidential Agreement No. 81464

EXHIBIT C-1

Sun Microsystems, Inc. Binary Code License Agreement

READ THE TERMS OF THIS AGREEMENT AND ANY PROVIDED SUPPLEMENTAL LICENSE TERMS (COLLECTIVELY "AGREEMENT") CAREFULLY BEFORE OPENING THE SOFTWARE MEDIA PACKAGE. BY OPENING THE SOFTWARE MEDIA PACKAGE, YOU AGREE TO THE TERMS OF THIS AGREEMENT. IF YOU ARE ACCESSING THE SOFTWARE ELECTRONICALLY, INDICATE YOUR ACCEPTANCE OF THESE TERMS BY SELECTING THE "ACCEPT" BUTTON AT THE END OF THIS AGREEMENT. IF YOU DO NOT AGREE TO ALL THESE TERMS, PROMPTLY RETURN THE UNUSED SOFTWARE TO YOUR PLACE OF PURCHASE FOR A REFUND OR, IF THE SOFTWARE IS ACCESSED ELECTRONICALLY, SELECT THE "DECLINE" BUTTON AT THE END OF THIS AGREEMENT.

1. LICENSE TO USE. Sun grants you a non-exclusive and non-transferable license for the internal use only of the accompanying software and documentation and any error corrections provided by Sun (collectively "Software"), by the number of users and the class of computer hardware for which the corresponding fee has been paid.

2. RESTRICTIONS Software is confidential and copyrighted. Title to Software and all associated intellectual property rights is retained by Sun and/or its licensors. Except as specifically authorized in any Supplemental License Terms, you may not make copies of Software, other than a single copy of Software for archival purposes. Unless enforcement is prohibited by applicable law, you may not modify, decompile, or reverse engineer Software. You acknowledge that Software is not designed, licensed or intended for use in the design, construction, operation or maintenance of any nuclear facility. Sun disclaims any express or implied warranty of fitness for such uses. No right, title or interest in or to any trademark, service mark, logo or trade name of Sun or its licensors is granted under this Agreement.

3. LIMITED WARRANTY. Sun warrants to you that for a period of ninety (90) days from the date of purchase, as evidenced by a copy of the receipt, the media on which Software is furnished (if any and if provided by Sun) will be free of defects in materials and workmanship under normal use. Except for the foregoing, Software is provided "AS IS". Your exclusive remedy and Sun's entire liability under this limited warranty will be at Sun's option to replace Software media or refund the fee paid for Software, if any.

4. DISCLAIMER OF WARRANTY. **UNLESS SPECIFIED IN THIS AGREEMENT, ALL EXPRESS OR IMPLIED CONDITIONS, REPRESENTATIONS AND WARRANTIES, INCLUDING ANY IMPLIED WARRANTY OF MERCHANTABILITY, FITNESS FOR A PARTICULAR PURPOSE OR NON-INFRINGEMENT ARE DISCLAIMED, EXCEPT TO THE EXTENT THAT THESE DISCLAIMERS ARE HELD TO BE LEGALLY INVALID.**

5. LIMITATION OF LIABILITY. **TO THE EXTENT NOT PROHIBITED BY LAW, IN NO EVENT WILL SUN OR ITS LICENSORS BE LIABLE FOR ANY LOST REVENUE, PROFIT OR DATA, OR FOR SPECIAL, INDIRECT, CONSEQUENTIAL, INCIDENTAL OR PUNITIVE DAMAGES, HOWEVER CAUSED REGARDLESS OF THE THEORY OF LIABILITY, ARISING OUT OF OR RELATED TO THE USE OF OR INABILITY TO USE SOFTWARE, EVEN IF SUN HAS BEEN ADVISED OF THE POSSIBILITY OF SUCH DAMAGES.** In no event will Sun's liability to you, whether in contract, tort (including negligence), or otherwise, exceed the amount paid by you for Software under this Agreement. The foregoing limitations will apply even if the above stated warranty fails of its essential purpose.

6. Termination. This Agreement is effective until terminated. You may terminate this Agreement at any time by destroying all copies of Software. This Agreement will terminate immediately without notice from Sun if you fail to comply with any provision of this Agreement. Upon Termination, you must destroy all copies of Software. Sun Confidential Agreement No. 81464

7. Export Regulations. All Software and technical data delivered under this Agreement are subject to US export control laws and may be subject to export or import regulations in other countries. You agree to comply strictly with all such laws and regulations and acknowledge that you have the responsibility to obtain such licenses to export, re-export, or import as may be required after delivery to you.

8. U.S. Government Restricted Rights. If Software is being acquired by or on behalf of the U.S. Government or by a U.S. Government prime contractor or subcontractor (at any tier), then the Government's rights in Software and accompanying documentation will be only as set forth in this Agreement; this is in accordance with 48 CFR 227.7201 through 227.7202-4 (for Department of Defense (DOD) acquisitions) and with 48 CFR 2.101 and 12.212 (for non-DOD acquisitions).

9. Governing Law. Any action related to this Agreement will be governed by California law and controlling US federal law. No choice of law rules of any jurisdiction will apply.

10. Severability. If any provision of this Agreement is held to be unenforceable, this Agreement will remain in effect with the provision omitted, unless omission would frustrate the intent of the parties, in which case this Agreement will immediately terminate.